Identity Politics and Ethnic Conflicts in Rwanda and Burundi: A Comparative Study

Godfrey Mwakikagile

1

Identity Politics and Ethnic Conflicts in Rwanda and
Burundi: A Comparative Study

First Edition

ISBN 978-9987-16-029-7

New Africa Press
Dar es Salaam, Tanzania

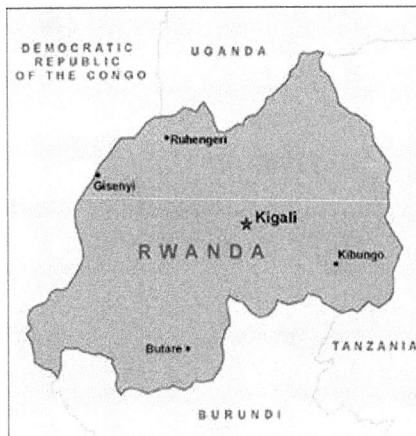

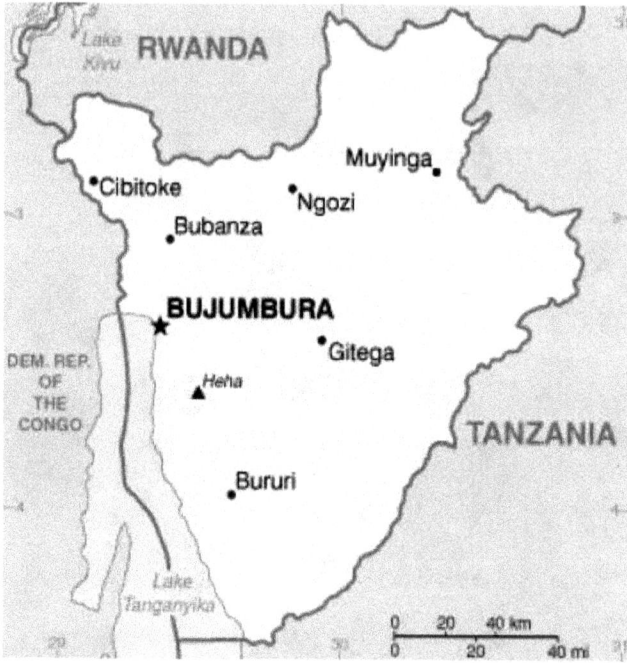

Contents

Special note

I WROTE this book more than ten years ago. It was accepted for publication during that time by my publisher who had already published five of my books between 1999 and 2001.

Although I signed a contract with the publisher, I decided to cancel it for a number of reasons and have my work published elsewhere.

But instead of pursuing the project, I set it aside until now, as I continued to write other books.

The work is essentially the same as it was more than ten years ago when I first wrote it. And I wanted to keep it that way to retain and reflect the times and context in which I wrote it, including the sources I cited during that period to document this study. In that sense, it is a work from the past. But it is also for the present.

There is very little change in terms of content and the

work's central thesis, except for a few things – in fact very few – which I have added here and there in different parts of the book. And you can tell what they are based on the dated material I have cited for further documentation of my work which is "frozen" in time.

Acknowledgements

THE EXECUTION of this project owes its completion to many individuals and institutions especially in Africa, Britain and the United States.

They include journalists and academics, African leaders and ordinary citizens, civic and religious organisations as well as human rights groups and the United Nations, all of whom have been an indispensable source of information I have used in different contexts to document my work.

Among the sources I have cited are the *Daily News*, Dar es Salaam, Tanzania; the *Daily Nation*, Nairobi, Kenya; *The Economist*, *The New York Times*, *The Washington Post*, *The Boston Globe*, *The Christian Science Monitor*, *The Wall Street Journal*, the *International Herald Tribune*, and other newspapers and publications including *Foreign Affairs* and *Current History: A Journal of Contemporary World Affairs*, whose coverage of Africa has been of great help in the completion of this work.

And for that I am deeply grateful to all the reporters – and their newspapers and magazines – who have covered this embattled continent especially during its most turbulent years since independence in the sixties.

The nineties were probably the most violent. It was the decade when almost the entire continent was engulfed in civil wars and countless other smaller conflicts most people never even heard of. Tragically, the wars, big and small, are still going on today.

In addition to all those I have just named, I am equally indebted to specific individuals such as Keith B. Richburg, author of the highly controversial book, *Out of America: A Black Man Confronts Africa*, I have quoted in my study.

Others to whom I am no less indebted include Professor Michael Chege, a Kenyan, whose article, "Africa's Murderous Professors," published in *The National Interest*, is a blunt appraisal of the role the Hutu academic elite played in instigating the 1994 Rwandan genocide, as did some Kenyan professors in inflaming passions against the Kikuyu in Kenya during the 1990s; and Professor George B.N. Ayittey, a Ghanaian, whose works, *Africa Betrayed*, and *Africa in Chaos*, are a devastating critique of Africa's brutal and kleptocratic regimes and an equally searing indictment against the academic elite for their collusion with corrupt government officials and politicians in plundering the continent and suffocating dissent.

My profound gratitude also goes to the following for citing some of their works in this study: René Lemarchand, professor emeritus, Political Science Department at the University of Florida, USA; Alfred Ndahiro, an African lecturer at Liverpool University, England, together with Vincent Gasana, a freelance journalist and fellow African; Jorge G. Castañeda of the Political Science and Latin American Studies Departments at New York University, USA, who later became Mexico's minister of foreign affairs; and Gérard Prunier, senior researcher at *Centre National de la Recherche Scientifique* in Paris, France.

Others are Harvey Glickman, professor of political science and director of African Studies at Haverford College, Pennsylvania, USA; I. William Zartman, director of the African Studies Center and professor of international relations at Johns Hopkins University, Maryland, USA; and Crawford Young, professor of political science at the University of Wisconsin in the United States who also was the dean of the Social Science Faculty, National University of Zaire, Lubumbashi campus, Zaire, from 1973 to 1995.

I am equally grateful to Edward Luttwak, senior fellow at the Center for Strategic and International Studies, Georgetown University, Washington, D.C.; Alan J. Kuperman of MIT's Center for International Studies and Fellow of the Institute for the Study of World Politics; Neil J. Kresssel of William Paterson College, New Jersey, USA; and David Rieff for his illuminating insights into Africa's predicament in his article in *The New Republic*.

And to millions of Rwandans and Burundians goes my deepest gratitude for inspiring this study. Their suffering has touched the hearts of countless people round the globe, even though many of them have not responded to their plight the way they should have, if at all. But their survival against insurmountable odds is an enduring testimony to the resilience of the human spirit capable of enduring the unendurable.

It has not been an easy book to write, given the nature of the subject. There is just too much suffering, too much bloodshed, going on in those two countries, in addition to what has already taken place through the years.

But I have done my best to highlight the plight of the people of Rwanda and Burundi and suggest some solutions to their perennial problems which may be applicable in other African contexts as well; although conflict resolution is contextual, even if its underlying principles and some solutions have universal validity.

Therefore, solutions offered in this book are not meant to take precedence over what the people of Rwanda and Burundi themselves are trying to do to solve their problems. Only they know what is best for them. But I, as an African, also have the right to suggest some solutions to African problems. Even non-Africans have the right to do so as an integral part of the human family.

Many of my fellow Africans are going to disagree with some of the solutions I have suggested here; so will others. Besides what they may consider to be faulty analysis, they may also find other faults in the book. But that is something we all expect in life. And it should not discourage us from taking bold initiatives to try to make this world a better place than we found it.

I therefore welcome criticism and take full responsibility for any mistakes some people may be able to find in my book. Such is the nature of any human undertaking. We strive for excellence. But we don't always excel even if we think we do. Doing one's best is always the best.

Introduction

THIS WORK looks at conflicts between the Hutu and the Tutsi in Rwanda and Burundi.

It is an abridged version of my forthcoming book, *Civil Wars in Rwanda and Burundi: Conflict Resolution in Africa*.

The conflicts between the two groups have sometimes been characterised as ethnic, although neither group has fundamental attributes of ethnicity or ethnic identity which separate one from the other. They share a common identity.

They don't have a common ancestry, which is one of the fundamental attributes of ethnic identity. The two groups have different origins. But they do have the same culture. They also speak the same language. And they have had a common history at least during the past four centuries.

They have intermingled and intermarried for so long –

since the Tutsi arrived in the region more than 400 years ago – that whatever differences existed between them in the past in terms of culture, identity, and biology have been erased.

Yet they do exist as distinct social groups, but not as biological entities each with its own gene pool. They maintain separate group identities, as Hutus and as Tutsis, mainly because of the asymmetrical relationship between them. Inequity of power has solidified those identities which have assumed "characteristics" of ethnicity.

Historically, the Tutsi minority have been the rulers. Their status as the dominant group was enhanced during colonial rule when the Belgians favoured and recognised them as the "natural" rulers, superior to the Hutu, thus legitimising inequalities between the two groups.

The differences between them were even given official sanction. And the subordinate status of the Hutu majority was used by the Belgians to justify discrimination against them in terms of employment and educational opportunities while favouring the Tutsi.

The colonial rulers also reinforced prejudice against the Hutu majority who were considered to be intellectually inferior to the Tutsi. Both the Tutsi and the Belgians considered the Hutu to be inferior, in fact in more than one way. They were even considered ugly.

The conflict between the two groups is rooted in inequity of power, fuelled by stereotypes against the Hutu majority.

Domination of the Hutu majority by the Tutsi minority, which started before the advent of colonial rule, has also solidified ethnic identities of the two groups through the years.

A shared consciousness among the members of each group and their distinctiveness – each seeing themselves as different from the other – have also played a major role in the evolution and consolidation of these separate identities, giving legitimacy to ethnicity as an

14

identification label for the two groups.

The rivalries between the Hutu and the Tutsi can be defined by one thing: the struggle for power. No group wants to be dominated by the other. And no amount of talk and reconciliation is going to end conflicts between them unless this fundamental problem is solved.

Chapter One:

The Killing Fields of Africa:
Background and Aftermath

THE 1994 RWANDAN GENOCIDE in which about one million Tutsis and their Hutu sympathisers were massacred triggered a chain of events which plunged the entire Great Lakes region of East-Central Africa into turmoil on a scale never witnessed before.

This chapter attempts to comprehend the complex web of events and interrelated forces that led to the upheaval and shaped the context in which the future of the region will be determined for many years, as the countries involved remain trapped in a vicious cycle of violence and a chronic state of instability.

Just before the remaining Tutsis in Rwanda were to be

wiped out, their brethren in the Rwandan Patriotic Front (RPF) – an army of Tutsi exiles and some Hutus – invaded the country from their bases in Uganda and seized power from the genocidal Hutu regime which instigated the massacres. The remaining Tutsis were saved. But the violence continued.

The collapse of the Hutu ethnocracy whose army was routed by the RPF triggered a massive exodus of Hutus who feared reprisals at the hands of the new Tutsi rulers. About 2 million Hutus fled to neighbouring Zaire (renamed the Democratic Republic of Congo) and Tanzania.

Most of them sought refuge in Zaire which soon became the scene of more massacres of genocidal proportions; this time, directed against the Hutu refugees who perished at the hands of their Tutsi conquerors exacting retribution for the atrocities perpetrated against their kinsmen in the Rwandan genocide. They went in hot pursuit of the Hutus.

Thus, what started out as a genocidal campaign by the Rwandan Hutu regime and its extremist supporters to exterminate the Tutsi also led to a genocidal rampage against hundreds of thousands of innocent Hutu civilians including the perpetrators of the 1994 genocide and plunged the entire region into chaos.

Regional Imbroglio

The root cause of all this violence and regional instability is exclusion from power of one group by the other, mostly the Hutu by the Tutsi.

Hutus constitute the vast majority of the population (at least 85%) in both Rwanda and Burundi where the two groups have been in conflict at different times during the past 400 years even when some of the conflicts have not escalated into violence or full-scale war.

Yet, in spite of their minority status, it is the Tutsi who have held power in both countries except for 32 years in Rwanda where the Hutu ruled from 1962 – when the country won independence from Belgium – until 1994 when they were ousted by the invading force of the Tutsi-dominated Rwandan Patriotic Front (RPF). And the regional dimension of the conflict can be directly attributed to the security threat posed by the Hutu rebels to the Tutsi-dominated states of Rwanda and Burundi, and by Ugandan insurgents trying to overthrow the government of their country.

The conflict also assumed regional proportions because of the expansionist ambitions of both Rwanda and Uganda, and to a smaller extent Burundi, to annex parts of eastern Congo ostensibly to create a buffer zone and secure their borders. But the creation of such a "security corridor," if successful, would only perpetuate conflict and take the war deeper into Congo.

The conflict in the Great Lakes region assumed a much wider dimension when neighbouring countries – Rwanda, Uganda and Burundi – supported a rebellion launched by a coalition of forces to oust Zaire's long-ruling dictator Mobutu Sese Seko from power.

The insurgency was spearheaded by Tutsi-led forces whose nominal head was Laurent Kabila, a member of the Luba ethnic group from the northern part of Shaba Province which was renamed Katanga.

The rebel army was organised by Rwandan leaders. They are also the ones who chose Kabila to be the leader of the rebel movement, hoping that he would be more friendly to them than Mobutu was, once he became president of Zaire.

Kabila seized power in May 1997 and renamed the country the Democratic Republic of Congo (DRC).

During his first months in office, Kabila worked closely with Rwandan and Ugandan leaders, mostly out of sheer necessity. He owed his rise to power to the leaders of those two countries. And he remained in power because of the protection provided to him by Rwandan Tutsi soldiers who masterminded the military campaign that ousted Mobutu and remained in Kinshasa, Congo's capital, to help him consolidate his rule.

But Kabila did not become the kind of leader Rwanda and Uganda thought they would have. They thought they would be able to control and manipulate him. Like any true nationalist, he resented outside control. And there was strong resentment across Congo against Rwandan Tutsis whose presence in the capital Kinshasa was interpreted by many Congolese as a violation of their sovereignty, with Rwandans being seen as an occupation army on conquered territory. It was the ultimate insult.

Both Rwanda and Uganda, as well as Burundi which was ruled by the Tutsi like Rwanda, also became disillusioned with Kabila even in the early months of his rule because he failed or simply refused to restrain – it was actually a combination of both – the Hutu rebels and Ugandan insurgents based in eastern Congo from attacking them.

It was this security threat which prompted Rwanda and Uganda, with the assistance of Burundi, to organise a rebellion and directly intervene in Congo in an attempt to overthrow Kabila and replace him with a more friendly Congolese government which would take the security interests of the three countries into account.

The rebellion started in August 1998 when President Kabila expelled Rwandan Tutsi soldiers from Kinshasa. Rwanda, Uganda, and Burundi intervened immediately, although they denied such involvement until later when they admitted that.

Kabila got a lot of help from his allies to resist the invasion. Angola, Zimbabwe, Namibia, Chad, and Sudan sent troops and weapons to bolster Congo's fragile army and got directly involved in combat against the rebels who were supported by Rwanda and Uganda. Burundi also supported the insurgents although it was Rwanda which played the biggest role.

None of that would have happened had the Tutsi in Rwanda and Burundi agreed to share power – on meaningful basis – with the Hutu majority in those two countries.

There would have been no Hutu rebels operating from Congo in an attempt to dislodge the Tutsi minority from power, and therefore no need for Rwanda and Burundi to try and neutralise them by invading Congo where the rebels were based; an invasion which drew in other national armies in what came to be Africa's most internationalised conflict which had its origin in the 1994 Rwandan genocide and the Hutu-Tutsi conflict in Burundi. The conflict came to be known as "Africa's World War."

The Rwandan genocide itself – instigated by Hutu leaders and the academic elite who, considering their history of hundreds of years of Hutu domination by the Tutsi, did not want and were afraid to share power with their "historical enemies" – can be traced back to the mass uprising by the Hutu against their Tutsi aristocratic rulers in November 1959; and to the repeated attempts by the Tutsi during most of the next 35 years to regain the power they lost in that peasant uprising which could even be called a peasant revolution since it led to fundamental change in terms of who later ruled Rwanda after the Tutsi were ousted. The Hutu finally seized power.

Compounding the problem is the centuries-old hatred or mistrust between the two groups – whether some people want to admit it or not – which, like the desire to monopolise power on an ethnic basis, contributed to the genocide. As many Hutu leaders publicly stated just before and during the 1994 massacres of the Tutsi, the biggest mistake that the Hutu made during the 1959 mass uprising was that they did not wipe out the Tutsi; a job they urged their followers to finish in 1994.

During the 1959 Hutu uprising, more than 100,000

Tutsis were massacred in what was indeed a genocide but whose magnitude was overshadowed 35 years later by the 1994 holocaust.

Many Hutus, probably the majority, never regretted the massacre of the Tutsi. As Professor Leon Mugesira, a renowned Hutu historian at the Rwandan National University in Butare, told a Hutu extremist gathering in November 1992 almost exactly 33 years after the 1959 mass uprising by the Hutu against the Tutsi:

"The fatal mistake we made in 1959 was to let the Tutsi get out....We have to act. Wipe them all out!"[1]

Calls for Tutsi extermination were also made in newspapers, on the radio and on television – but mostly by word of mouth – to incite Hutus across the country to isolate and kill their Tutsi neighbours, friends and any other Tutsis including their own relatives and children who were half-Tutsi or who had any identifiable Tutsi lineage. For example, *Kangura*, a Hutu newspaper edited by Hassan Ngeze, listed the "Hutu ten commandments" which included isolating the "evil" Tutsis and condemned intermarriage with them as a pollution of "pure Hutu."[2] And the Hutu-edited *La Medaille*, a magazine, stated in its February 1994 edition, not long before the massacres started in April, that "the Tutsi race could be extinguished."[3]

But the most virulent and effective campaign was carried out by Radio/Television Libre des Mille Collines (RTLM) because of its wide coverage across the country and its ability to transmit its message of hate and incitement to every Hutu including illiterates who could not read the newspapers. And educated Hutus played a critical role in this campaign of genocide. As Kenyan Professor Michael Chege stated:

"The radio's intellectual braintrust was made up of

Ferdinand Nahimana, a professor of history at the Rwandan National University at Butare, and Casimir Bizimungu, the articulate multilingual foreign minister of a former government, and the manager of this 'independent' radio station.

Indeed, so strong was the academic input...that, after the massacres, Emmanuel Bugingo, the new and irreproachable rector of the Butare campus, confessed that 'all the killing in Rwanda was carefully planned by intellectuals and those intellectuals passed through this university.'"[4]

Coincidentally, but in a chilling way, the nearly one million Tutsis who were exterminated in 1994 were "replaced" by one million Tutsis who returned from exile in Uganda.

Other returnees came from Burundi and Tanzania. But most of them came from Uganda. They included many who were born in exile, returning with their parents who fled Rwanda in 1959 as adults or as children. One of the exiles was Paul Kagame, Rwanda's vice president and defence minister and the country's *de facto* ruler, who fled to Uganda with his parents when he was two years old.

The Rwandan Patriotic Front (RPF) ousted the murderous Hutu regime in July 1994, only to institute another tyranny; this time, an ethnocracy dominated by the Tutsi who went on to launch their own campaign of terror against the Hutu majority.

It was systematic, yet indiscriminate, in its retaliation against the Hutu for the extermination of one million Tutsis and their Hutu sympathisers.

Countless innocent Hutu civilians were murdered during the following years. They included innocent women, children and the elderly, ostensibly in a search-and-destroy mission directed against the perpetrators of the 1994 genocide.

The retaliatory campaign continues today, cold and

calculated, pursued with malicious vindictiveness. The result of this government-sponsored terror and exclusion of the Hutu majority from power is increased polarisation between the two ethnic groups that are already divided by intense hatred and deep mistrust in Africa's most densely populated country; with the two "historical enemies" living side by side as they have for the past 400 years in a feudal relationship dominated by the Tutsi.

Exclusion of the Hutu majority from power, again by the Tutsi, also explains Burundi's descent into chaos including the 1972 genocide against the Hutu.

Burundi, Africa's second most populous country, is almost an exact mirror image of Rwanda – its neighbouring twin state to the north – both in terms of ethnic composition and troubled history.

Oppression of the Hutu by the Tutsi in Burundi led to a Hutu uprising in 1972 – 1973 which claimed 10,000 Tutsi lives. The Tutsi retaliated and massacred more than 200,000 Hutus within three months.

In an attempt to eliminate the Hutu threat to their hegemonic control of the country, they also killed every Hutu who had secondary school education, a government job, and money. Most of them were killed in 1972, the year of the biggest uprising.

Yet hardly anyone talks about this genocide by the Tutsi against the Hutu in Burundi which took place 22 years before Rwanda's 1994 genocide, and was just one among several massacres of genocidal proportions perpetrated by the Tutsi against the Hutu through the years including the massacre of more than 200,000 Rwandan Hutu refugees in the late 1990s in Zaire whose fate was inextricably linked to what had been going on in both Rwanda and Burundi. As Professor René Lemarchand states in "The Fire in the Great Lakes":

"Today the 1972 Burundi genocide has fallen into virtual oblivion – except among the Hutu masses – yet its

24

significance is crucial to understanding subsequent events in both Burundi and Rwanda.

Although the magnitude of the Rwanda holocaust is without precedent – it is estimated to have caused the deaths of a million people – the killing of tens of thousands of Hutu refugees at the hands of the Rwandan Patriotic Army (RPA, the armed forces of the RPF government) in eastern Congo in 1996 and 1997 can be considered a third holocaust (after Burundi's 1972 and Rwanda's 1994 genocides)....

As many as 200,000 Hutu refugees may have been killed by RPA troops and Kabila's rebel army...(and) as many as 300,000 must have died of starvation and disease...in Zaire....And to this might be added the Kibeho killings, perpetrated inside Rwanda in April 1995, when at least 5,000 Hutu refugees were killed in cold blood by RPA units."[5]

A discussion of Hutu massacres by the Tutsi is not in any way intended to justify or provide an excuse of the extermination of nearly one million Tutsis in Rwanda in 1994. It is, rather, an attempt to understand why that genocide took place by putting it in the broader context of the volatile ethnic politics of the region (in both Rwanda and Burundi whose fates are inextricably linked) and the long history of antagonism between the two groups.

Traditionally, the Hutu and the Tutsi in both countries have had a lord-serf relationship for centuries, with the Hutu tending the farmlands and cattle owned by the Tutsi. The imposition of this overlordship on the Hutu by the Tutsi still rankles the vast majority of the Hutu who have been relegated to an inferior status in their own homeland and have worked for the Tutsi as virtual slaves for 400 years.

Any attempt to ignore or gloss over this unsavoury part of history makes it impossible for anybody to comprehend the enmity and deep mistrust between the two groups which has surfaced in recent years; and why the Hutu revolted against their Tutsi aristocratic rulers in Rwanda in November 1959; also why the Tutsi in Burundi have slaughtered hundreds of thousands – probably one million Hutus since 1972 alone; and why the 1994 Rwandan genocide – in which nearly one million Tutsis were exterminated – took place.

A look at the massacre of the Hutu by the Tutsi in both Rwanda and Burundi, and in what was then Zaire, through the years is also intended to show that the 1994 Rwandan genocide, tragic as it was, did not occur in a vacuum and is not the only large-scale massacre which has taken place in this highly combustible region. It is also intended to show the combustible elements, and the context, which led to that explosion.

It is true that the near-extermination of the entire Tutsi population in the Rwandan genocide is unprecedented in its magnitude although not in its motives. But simply because it is unprecedented in terms of magnitude does not mean that we should lose proportional perspective on reality, out of lopsided sympathy for the victims of that holocaust, while ignoring or overlooking the suffering of others, the Hutu, and the atrocities committed against them by the Tutsi in both Rwanda and Burundi through the years, and why they are fighting.

To ascribe ulterior motives – or of a bestial nature – to their struggle for inclusion in the political process, however excessive some of the means they have employed in pursuit of their goal, does not portray them or their enemies fairly; nor does it facilitate the quest for peace and stability in the region. For example, Philip Gourevitch who is the author of *We Wish to Inform You That Tomorrow We Will Be Killed With Our Families* which is otherwise a well-balanced account, stated in his article, "The Psychology of Slaughter," in *The New York Times*:

"The killers...are usually described as 'Hutu rebels,' a

26

label that suggests they are fighting for something. In fact, these terrorists have no identifiable cause, no idea other than rape, pillage and mass murder....

The prospect of overcoming the Hutu terrorist scourge remains remote. According to United Nations estimates, as many as 30,000 of these terrorists remain active in Central Africa.

The vast majority of them...are based in Congo, under the patronage of President Laurent Kabila...(who) has made these forces into a cornerstone of his defense forces.

Yet there is no great international outcry against him, or his many allies – including South Africa – for being in league with the most horrific political criminals on the continent....

And as Rwanda prepares to commemorate the fifth anniversary of the start of the genocide, on April 6, one can't help wondering whether the end is in sight."[6]

It is interesting to note that although Gourevitch contends that these Hutu fighters have no identifiable cause which they are fighting for, and are no more than outright rapists, pillagers and mass murderers, he contradicts himself – obviously inadvertently – when he goes on to describe them as "political criminals," thus implicitly admitting that their crimes are politically motivated. Nelson Mandela was imprisoned for almost 30 years as a political prisoner. He and his compatriots were a even described by the apartheid regime and its supporters as a terrorists. Yet they had an identifiable and just cause they were fighting for.

If the crimes of the Hutu rebels are indeed politically motivated, as most of them are, in order to bring about fundamental political change contrary to what Gourevitch says, then the label "rebels" is appropriate in this context as a way of describing them since they have rebelled against authority and are fighting for something: to overthrow the Tutsi-dominated governments which are oppressing Hutus in both Rwanda and Burundi.

It is, of course true, as Gourevitch contends, that we can't help wondering whether or not the end to these massacres is in sight; not only in Rwanda but also in Burundi; and not only of the Tutsi by the Hutu but also of the Hutu by the Tutsi – probably even more so.

The brutal excesses committed by the Hutu rebels – and by the Tutsi-dominated armies and security forces against Hutu civilians in both Rwanda and Burundi – can not be excused or condoned; although, depending on the context, one man's terrorist is another man's freedom fighter: from Menachem Begin and Moshe Dayan in Israel to Nelson Mandela, Oliver Tambo, Robert Mangaliso Sobukwe, Walter Sisulu and Govan Mbeki in South Africa; from Dedan Kimathi in Kenya to Josiah Tongogara, Edgar Tekere, Robert Mugabe and Joshua Nkomo in Zimbabwe; from Amilcar Cabral in Guinea-Bissau to Samora Machel in Mozambique. The list goes on and on.

The fundamental question that should be addressed is: Why are tens of thousands of Hutus fighting in both Rwanda and Burundi? Just to rape, loot and kill as Gourevitch and others contend?

Is that why they risk their lives and those of their families?

Is that why they seek international support for their struggle and understanding of their cause?

And is that the reason why hundreds of thousands of Hutus, most of them civilians, have fled their home countries and sought refuge in Congo and Tanzania through the years?

Is there no other motive behind the Hutu rebel attacks? Is the armed struggle by the rebels not being waged in pursuit of political objectives?

Wasn't the assassination of the first democratically elected president of Burundi, Melchior Ndadaye, a Hutu, in October 1993 by Tutsi soldiers who bayoneted him to death, enough reason to provoke many Hutus even some of the most timid ones – "enough is enough" – into violence in retaliation for the murder, given their history of oppression by the Tutsi?

Would the 1994 Rwandan genocide have taken place had the Hutu not been oppressed and exploited, virtually enslaved, by the Tutsi for 400 years in both Rwanda and Burundi?

Would it have occurred if the Tutsi-dominated Rwandan Patriotic Front (RPF) did not invade Rwanda from Uganda for the first time in October 1990, posing a threat to the Hutu?

In the late 1990s, President Benjamin Mkapa of Tanzania once described the attacks by the Hutus rebels as "military expressions of political intent." By saying so, he was not trying to justify the attacks but was trying to explain what motivated the rebels in many – if not in most – cases to launch such attacks against the dominant group, the Tutsi, who were the rulers of both countries.

There probably were some Hutu rebels who had no political agenda and were motivated purely by ethnic hatred in attacking Tutsis, although even such attacks can not in all cases be attributed to sheer hatred of the Tutsi without any political motivation.

To dismiss all Hutu rebels as nothing but a bunch of killers without any political agenda or aspirations is being utterly simplistic.

In many cases, Rwanda is Burundi, and Burundi is Rwanda. It is a tangled web. What happens in one country very often affects the other. The conflicts feed on each other. As Lemarchand states:

"The 1972 genocide (in Burundi) had 'cleansed' the country of all educated Hutu elites – including secondary school and university students – allowing the rise of a solidly entrenched Tutsi ethnocracy.

It is thus easy to see why the assassination of Burundi's

Hutu President Ndadaye in 1993 was viewed by many Tutsi hard-liners as the quickest way to ward off the threat posed to their hegemony; what was not anticipated was the outburst of rage that seized the Hutu population in the face of an event that conjured up memories of 1972.

After killing thousands of Tutsi civilians in October 1993, some 300,000 Hutus fled to Rwanda to escape an extremely brutal repression by the (Tutsi) army. It is reasonable to assume that a great many joined hands with the Interahamwe during the 1994 (Rwandan) genocide, before seeking refuge in Congo or Tanzania, or returning to Burundi."[7]

Many of these tragedies through the years in both Rwanda and Burundi could have been avoided – or at the very least they could have been mitigated – if the ruling Tutsis had agreed to genuine power sharing with the Hutu majority on the basis of proportional representation; taking into account legitimate fears and concerns of the Tutsi minority that they would be exterminated (in retaliation for their oppression and exploitation of the Hutu for centuries, although that is something the Tutsi would not admit but would instead contend that the Hutu would exterminate them simply because they hated them); and accommodating the interests and genuine aspirations of the Hutu majority who have been denied the right to participate in the political process on democratic basis.

And the 1994 Rwandan genocide could have been avoided if the Hutu – who were in power for 32 years from July 1962 to July 1994 – had agreed back in the 1960s, soon after independence, to share power with the Tutsi on meaningful basis instead of excluding them and consigning them to subordinate status.

Democracy on the basis of majority rule is totally out of the question in that context. It will exclude the Tutsi minority from power – they will never win a democratic election against the Hutu majority – and will guarantee hegemonic control of both Rwanda and Burundi by the Hutu forever.

That is what the Hutu attempted to do in Rwanda in the mass uprising of November 1959 (assume full control of the country), with tragic consequences for the entire region during the following decades, which culminated in the 1994 genocide of the Tutsi.

The Rwandan holocaust in turn led to a wider conflict that engulfed the entire Great Lakes region and the heart of Africa, Congo, involving national armies from nine African countries: Congo itself, Rwanda, Uganda, Burundi, Angola, Zimbabwe, Namibia, Chad, and Sudan, and at least 20 rebel and militia groups including the Angola rebels of UNITA, a Portuguese acronym for National Union for the Total Independence of Angola.

But even before the multinational conflict erupted in 1998, with Congo as the battleground, the Great Lakes region had already been the scene of massive bloodshed between the Hutu and the Tutsi since 1962 when both Rwanda and Burundi won independence from Belgium. While the Tutsi in Burundi thwarted attempts by the Hutu majority to become the rulers of the newly independent nation on democratic basis – given their numerical preponderance, victory for the Hutu was a foregone conclusion – and therefore remained in control; their kinsmen in Rwanda had been sidelined since the 1959 Hutu mass uprising and never even had the initiative to position themselves in an advantageous position to assume power at independence.

Therefore, when independence came, the Hutu automatically became the new rulers of Rwanda, with tens of thousands of Tutsis and their aristocratic elite having fled into exile. And every major political event in the region during the next three decades was, in one way or another, linked to the 1959 Hutu uprising:

"Each event of political significance in the region

31

during those 32 years (1962 – 1994) was related to the (1959) Rwandan revolution: the fall of two monarchies – Rwanda in 1962, Burundi in 1966; the assassination of two leading Hutu personalities in Burundi – Prime Minister Pierre Ngendadumwe in 1965, and President Melchior Ndadaye in 1993; several military takeovers – the 1973 coup in Rwanda and the 1965, 1976, 1987, and 1996 coups in Burundi; the 1972 Burundi genocide of Hutus; the rural uprising in North Kivu (Zaire) in 1993; the 1990 invasion of Rwanda by RPF (the Tutsi Rwandan Patriotic Front from its bases in Uganda), and the 1994 genocide of Tutsis and moderate Hutus; and the transformation of North and South Kivu (provinces in eastern Zaire) into a privileged sanctuary for Hutu-sponsored border raids into Rwanda – and ultimately, into a killing ground for fleeing Hutu refugees (by Rwandan Tutsi soldiers and Zairean Tutsi rebels allied with their Rwandan kinsmen)."[8]

Another Hutu prime minister of Burundi, Joseph Bamina who succeeded Ngendadumwe, was assassinated later in 1965 after an uprising by the Hutu against Tutsi domination failed. Bamina was a member of the Tutsi political party, UPRONA (*Union pour le Progrès national* – the Union for National Progress) which dominated the country.

The success of the 1959 mass uprising by the Hutu in Rwanda raised hope among the Hutu in both Rwanda and Burundi that they had the capacity to free themselves from their Tutsi oppressors, and that they would one day become the rulers of the two countries as they indeed succeeded in doing in Rwanda from 1962 to 1994.

The 1959 peasant revolution also inspired a significant number of Hutus to take bold initiatives to achieve their goals and radicalised many of them into a potent political force ready to take up arms to end Tutsi supremacy.

But it also frightened the Tutsi minority who feared

that they were about to be dominated and possibly exterminated by the Hutu majority whom they knew they had been oppressing for centuries, unless they did something to stave off the Hutu onslaught.

To ward off this danger, the Tutsi resorted to brutal repression and large-scale massacres of the Hutu in Burundi where the Tutsi were still in control. The country won independence on 1 July 1962 under an absolute Tutsi monarchy and changed its name from Urundi to Burundi.

The situation was different in Rwanda. There, the rise of the Hutu to power at independence, also on 1 July 1962 – the country was until then called Ruanda, not Rwanda – triggered another exodus of the Tutsi, following the first one in 1959 when the Hutu emerged victorious in a mass uprising which toppled the Tutsi aristocracy.

But there were also similarities. In Burundi, consolidation of power and increased repression by the Tutsi aristocratic rulers and the Tutsi army in the early 1960s led to an exodus – reminiscent of the 1959 Tutsi exodus from Rwanda – of tens of thousands of Hutus to Rwanda which was then under Hutu leadership, and to Tanganyika which was renamed Tanzania on 29 October 1964 after uniting with Zanzibar on 26 April in the same year.

Many Hutu politicians in Burundi dreamt of transforming that aristocratic state into a republican one like neighbouring Rwanda where their kinsmen were firmly entrenched and exercised virtual absolute power over the Tutsi.

But prospects for such fundamental change remained bleak. The Tutsi were in full control in Burundi. And their fear of Hutu majority rule was heightened when their brethren, tens of thousands of them (at least 100,000), fled Rwanda and sought refuge in Burundi in the wake of the 1959 mass uprising which effectively ended about 400 years of Tutsi aristocratic rule and replaced it with a Hutu-dominated republican form of government at independence in 1962. Their fear was also compounded by the exclusion of their kinsmen from power in Rwanda where the Hutu assumed full control of the country soon after the Belgian colonial rulers left.

The fleeing Tutsis recounted horror stories of what happened to them in Rwanda at the hands of the Hutu in the 1959 revolution, inflaming passions among their kinsmen in Burundi. Burundi's Tutsis vowed they would never allow that to happen to them and welcomed their brethren with open arms.

In due course, Burundi was to become a launching pad for military raids into Rwanda by these Tutsi exiles who were determined to overthrow the Hutu and regain power in their homeland which they lost in 1959. Naturally, the incursions provoked a retaliatory response by the Hutu against the Tutsi who remained in Rwanda, forcing more to flee to Burundi, Uganda, Congo, and Tanzania.

But it was a flight – into forced exile – which also had combustible elements. For example, the 20,000 Tutsi refugees from Rwanda who settled in eastern Congo in the early 1960s inflamed passions among the members of the local tribes who were hostile to immigrants from Rwanda – Tutsis as well as Hutus (there even some from Burundi) – who had lived in the region since precolonial times.

Rwandan Tutsis first settled in the area – what came to be known as eastern Congo – in the 1700s. And the 1959 revolution in Rwanda only made things worse for them by forcing them into exile in some places where they were not welcome, especially eastern Congo and Uganda.

Hostility towards them only intensified through the decades. In 1982, Rwanda appealed for international help when Uganda uprooted about 25,000 Rwandan – mostly Tutsi – immigrants, burning their homes and stealing their cattle. Thousands fled back to Rwanda, pleading for help – food and shelter.[9] And through the years, the Tutsi government of Burundi also accused the Hutu government of Rwanda of massacring Tutsis.

In turn, the Rwandan government accused Burundi of harbouring Tutsi guerrillas who were trying to overthrow it and re-institute a Tutsi ethnocracy in Rwanda.

Both were credible charges.

Besides attempting to overthrow the Hutu government in Rwanda from their bases in Burundi, the Tutsi refugees from the 1959 Rwandan Hutu mass uprising also got involved in another major political struggle and military activity. These were the refugees who settled in eastern Congo, and their involvement had to do with a rebellion going on in that country against the central government.

But unlike their kinsmen who settled in Burundi where fellow Tutsis were in control of the country, the Rwandan Tutsis who had sought refuge in eastern Congo found no indigenous ethnic constituency comparable in stature and power to the Tutsi ethnic base in Burundi which could provide them with shelter and help them pursue their objectives, in spite of the fact that many Tutsis – mostly from Rwanda – had been living in Congo since the 1700s.

Although they had lived there for a long time, they still were in a precarious position. They were not powerful. And the local tribes had always been hostile towards them, although they themselves were, historically speaking, native to the region, having lived there for about 200years after they migrated from Rwanda. As Vincent Gasana and Alfred Ndahiro stated in their report, "Zaire Crisis Provokes Tribalism," in *Africa Analysis*:

"Long before the conflict in eastern Zaire developed into a full-blown war, the little-known Banyamurenge (also known as Banyamulenge) had been trying to make their point: they want to go on living quietly as they have done for centuries, away not from the rest of the world, but from the rest of the Zaireans....

Their story starts in the 16th century, when King Kigeri Nyamuheshera of Rwanda sent a group of Rwandan families to occupy the newly-conquered area of

Bunyabungo, present-day Uvira.

There was a second wave and a third followed in the 19th century.

As Batutsi, the Banyamurenge were pastoralists. They moved and settled in the high altitude area of eastern Zaire to protect their cattle from disease and themselves from local Zairean hostility. They evolved a highly organised, inter-linked community. To this very day, their adherence to traditional forms of communication, means that no sooner does a stranger arrive in their area than his presence is communicated throughout the while community.

The modern state of Zaire never acknowledged them as Zaireans. They asked and got nothing from the Zairean government....

There have been periodic attempts by their Zairean neighbours to dislodge them from their lands. These were always repulsed by force of arms. Their martial prowess and skilful use of bows and arrows has long been passed into the region's folkrole.

Every Zairean, Rwandan and Murundi child will tell you how the Banyamurenge can shoot a fly off you with an arrow and leave you unscathed.

Such fairy tales bolstered by frequent victories against their attackers enabled the Banyamurenge to live unmolested until recently.

Following the first ethnic massacres in Rwanda in 1959, large numbers of Batutsi fled to neighbouring countries, including Zaire (then known as Congo). Though sympathetic, the Banyamurenge wanted to keep their distinct identity. But the Zaireans lumped them together and refused to recognise any distinction. The 1990 – 94 Rwandan civil war further complicated the situation."[10]

Although the Tutsi refugees who settled in eastern Congo after they fled Rwanda in the wake of the 1959 Hutu uprising found no large ethnic constituency of fellow

36

Tutsis who could provide them with sanctuary in Congo and forge links with them in pursuit of a common cause, they did find a different ally: the followers of the late Congolese prime minister, Patrice Lumumba, who were fighting a guerrilla war in an attempt to oust the central government installed by the CIA which masterminded Lumumba's assassination.

The rebellion in eastern Congo was known as a Mulelist insurgency which started in 1964. It was named after Pierre Mulele, Lumumba's 35-year-old education minister and heir-apparent, although he did not lead this particular insurrection in the east. He led an insurgency in Kwilu Province in western Congo from 1963 – 1968, while the eastern insurrection was led by Gaston Soumialot who was assisted by Nicolas Olenga and Laurent Kabila.[11]

The Tutsi refugees from the 1959 Rwandan uprising allied themselves with the pro-Lumumbist rebels in eastern Congo out of necessity in order to secure the support which they hoped they would get one day and enable them to regain power in their homeland. But it was a matter of expediency on both sides.

Many of those rebels in the eastern part of Congo were Tutsi. They were led by Joseph Mudandi who was trained in guerrilla warfare in China together with several other Rwandan Tutsis who had fled their homeland.

China had also intervened in Burundi's ethnic conflict by supporting the Tutsi. In 1963, the Chinese trained a number of Tutsis in guerrilla warfare in China. The massacres that followed, mostly of the Hutu by the Tutsi in Burundi, were thus facilitated by China, earning the Chinese a bad reputation in African circles beyond Burundi.

The Chinese committed the same blunder in Rwanda when in the same year, 1963, they supported Tutsi guerrillas who invaded their homeland in an attempt to overthrow the Hutu-dominated government. The Tutsi guerrillas killed more than 20,000 Hutus, mostly civilians, in that invasion which they launched from their bases in Burundi.

In eastern Congo, hundreds of Tutsis fought pitched battles alongside the Congolese insurgents of the People's Liberation Army (APL) against the Congo National Army in South Kivu which was supported by the CIA and anti-Castro Cubans (recruited by the United States government), as well as by Belgium and South African white mercenaries.

The pro-Lumumba nationalist forces were backed by China, the Soviet Union, Cuba which sent Che Guevara and hundreds of troops, and by a number of African countries, especially Tanzania, Ghana, Egypt, Algeria, Guinea and Mali whose leaders – Nyerere, Nkrumah, Nasser, Ben Bella, Sekou Toure and Modibo Keita – constituted what was known within the Organisation of African Unity (OAU) as The Group of Six.

In an interview in Geneva, Switzerland, on 4 November 1995 with Jorge Castañeda, the author of *Compañero: The Life and Death of Che Guevara*, Ben Bella said the six leaders worked secretly among themselves on a number of African issues, excluding other African leaders. One of the most urgent subjects they dealt with during that period was the Congo crisis.

Recalling those days, Ben Bella said in the same interview: "We arrived in the Congo too late."

He was talking about the progressive African countries including his, Algeria, which intervened in Congo to help pro-Lumumbist forces.

One of those countries was Tanzania, Congo's neighbour, which, under Nyerere's leadership, served as a conduit for material assistance to Lumumba's followers fighting the puppet central government. Che Guevara and Cuban troops also went to Congo through Tanzania.

Tutsi guerrillas in eastern Congo were some of the most important players on the Congo scene during that turbulent period. While the Tutsi guerrillas played a significant role in spreading the rebellion to the south and into northern Katanga Province together with the Congolese nationalist rebels, they also launched many cross-border raids into Rwanda in an attempt to destabilise and overthrow the Rwandan Hutu-dominated government.

As expected, those incursions, which failed to dislodge the Hutu from power, triggered a vicious retaliatory response by the Rwandan army and other Hutus against the Tutsi living in Rwanda; the majority of them still lived in Rwanda, their home country. Those who fled into exile constituted a minority of the Rwandan Tutsi population, although a significant one.

Thirty years later, the Hutu genocidal murderers – known as Interahamwe, which means "those who kill together" – employed some of the same strategies and tactics to try and dislodge the Tutsi-dominated government of the Rwandan Patriotic Front (RPF) which ousted the Hutu regime in July 1994 and stopped the genocide. Again, like the Rwandan Tutsi refugees who fled to eastern Congo during the 1960s, the Hutu perpetrators of the 1994 Rwandan genocide also sought refuge in eastern Zaire (renamed Congo in May 1997), together with hundreds of thousands of other Hutus. They also used eastern Congo as their operational base from which they launched raids into Rwanda in an attempt to remove the Tutsi-dominated RPF government.

But there were also some differences between the two. Hundreds of Rwandan Tutsi refugees fought as guerrillas in the 1964 Congolese rebellion against the Congolese national government. In contrast to that, an even much larger force of tens of thousands – no fewer than 30,000 – of Hutu rebels (including the Interahamwe and remnants of the defeated Hutu army who also sought refuge in eastern Zaire after losing to the Rwandan Patriotic Army (RPA) of the RPF in Rwanda) were actively involved in the insurgency against the Tutsi-dominated Rwandan government. The insurgency was launched in 1995 from the Hutu refugee camps in eastern Zaire and went on for years.

The Hutu rebels operating from eastern Zaire during the 1990s and thereafter also had perfect cover, hiding and moving freely among their kinsmen in the refugee camps. The Rwandan Tutsis launching cross-border raids against the Hutu regime in the sixties had no such sanctuary in eastern Congo.

The Hutu insurgents also controlled the refugee camps. And President Mobutu Sese Seko of Zaire, who was hostile to the Tutsi regimes in both Rwanda and Burundi – he was also hostile to the Ugandan government of President Yoweri Museveni – supplied the Hutu rebels with a lot of weapons and ammunition which they used to wage war against the Rwandan government, dominated by Tutsis, making them an even bigger threat to Rwanda's and even to Burundi's security.

And unlike in 1964 when there was a rebellion in eastern Congo which some of the Rwandan Tutsi refugees joined, there was no such uprising in eastern Zaire in 1995 when the Rwandan Hutu rebels launched their first raid into Rwanda. When one started in October – November 1996, it was with the full support of the Tutsi Rwandan army in order to destroy the perpetrators of the 1994 genocide – the Interahamwe and the remnants of the Hutu Rwandan Armed Forces (FAR) – and oust their ally, Mobutu Sese Seko, from power. The rebellion was also under Rwandan control.

The 1996 rebellion was launched and spearheaded by the Tutsi in eastern Zaire against Mobutu's regime which stripped them of their citizenship in 1981 – and in fact insisted that they had never even been citizens before then. But when it gained momentum rolling across the country towards the capital Kinshasa to oust Mobutu, it was Tutsi army officers from the Rwandan national army who provided the leadership; with Laurent Kabila, anointed by

Rwanda's *de facto* ruler Paul Kagame, as the nominal head of the rebellion.

The 1996 – 1997 Congolese (Zairean) insurgency succeeded in ousting the central government, while the 1964 insurrection fail to accomplish the same objective.

After the end of the Cold War, Mobutu became an expendable commodity. He was no longer seen by the United States as an asset; it was the Americans and their allies who installed him in power to use him in their struggle to contain Soviet expansionism in Africa.

By contrast, the pro-Lumumbist forces failed to dislodge him from power during the sixties for exactly the opposite reason. The West saw Mobutu as an indispensable ally against the Soviet Union right in the heart of Africa where the Soviets and their satellites in the Eastern bloc, including the anti-Soviet and anti-West People's Republic of China, were trying to gain a foothold. And both the Congolese nationalist rebels and their Rwandan Tutsi allies in the 1964 uprising were regarded by the United States and other Western powers as the vanguard of communist penetration into the heart of the African continent.

That was one of the reasons why the CIA actively intervened to neutralise the insurgency. And it succeeded in doing so.

But the main reason for the intervention – even if the Soviet Union and China had never existed – was continued domination and exploitation of Africa the United States and other Western countries, especially the former colonial powers, saw as their sphere of influence they had been entitled to since the advent of colonial rule.

Although the two rebellions – in 1964 and 1996 – had little in common in terms of ideology and objectives besides the desire to overthrow the central government even if for different reasons, they had one thing in common: Tutsi involvement. The Tutsi played a major role in both uprisings. They also had one actor on the political scene who provided a historical link between them. And that was Laurent Kabila.

Before he became the leader of the Alliance of Democratic Forces for the Liberation of Congo-Zaire (ADFL) which ousted Mobutu from power, Kabila had been active at different times in the Fizi-Baraka area along Lake Tanganyika in eastern Zaire as the head of a small group – a continuation from the sixties' pro-Lumumbist rebellion – fighting to overthrow the regal autocrat, Mobutu, who rose to power with the help of the CIA. In fact, during his tenure as president of Zaire for 32 years, the largest CIA station in Africa was in Kinshasa.

But the group Kabila led in the Fizi-Baraka area was handicapped by its ethnic base, small membership, diminishing revolutionary stature, and by its inability to wage war even against the decaying Zairean state which had only a rag-tag army incapable of defending the country.

Kabila's group further compromised whatever stature and status it had when its members kidnapped four American students from Stanford University doing research in Kigoma Region in western Tanzania, across Lake Tanganyika from the rebel base on the lake's western shore in Zaire. They took them across the lake to their base in Zaire. As Professor Crawford Young stated in "Zaire: The Unending Crisis," in *Foreign Affairs*:

"One insurgent movement within the country lingers from the 1964 – 65 wave of rebellions.

Localized in the Fizi-Baraka area by Lake Tanganyika, this group – known in recent years as the *Parti de la Révolution Populaire* (PRP) – achieved notoriety in 1975 by kidnapping four Stanford students from a zoological research station in Tanzania.

Its composition is ethnically restricted to Bembe, though its leader, Laurent Kabila, is a Shaba (formerly Katanga) Luba.

The movement now has only a few hundred followers, and has no possibility of enlarging its base of operations."[12]

Kabila himself had lost some credibility because of his frequent long absences from his operational base in eastern Zaire preferring, instead, to live in Dar es Salaam, Tanzania's capital, which became his home for more than 20 years.

Even his revolutionary credentials during the 1960s were questionable. He did not spend as much time in Congo as he should have, leaving his soldiers alone. As Che Guevara, who went to Congo to help the guerrillas, stated about Kabila's leadership: "I always thought that he did not have enough military experience; he was an agitator who had the stuff of a leader, yet lacked seriousness, aplomb, knowledge, in short this innate talent that one senses in Fidel the minute you meet him."[13] And as Che stated in another assessment of Kabila and the other Congolese rebel leaders including Soumialot in his letter from the shores of Lake Tanganyika in eastern Congo to Fidel Castro in October 1965:

"Sumialot and his companions have sold you an enormous bridge. It would take us forever to enumerate the huge number of lies they told you....I know Kabila well enough to have no illusions in his regard....

I have some background on Sumialot, like for example the lies he told you, the fact that he has not set foot on this godforsaken land, his frequent drinking bouts in Dar-es-Salaam, where he stays in the best hotels....

They are given huge amounts of money, all at once, to live splendidly in every African capital, not to mention that they are housed by the main progressive countries who often finance their travel expenses....The scotch and the women are also covered by friendly governments and if one likes good scotch and beautiful women, that costs a lot of money."[14]

When Che Guevara sent the letter to Castro, the Congolese rebel leaders had just been received in Havana, Cuba, like true revolutionaries and were treated with great respect, with Castro and other Cuban leaders who were backing them, unaware of their true characters.

Thirty years later during the the 1996 – 1997 rebellion which finally toppled Mobutu, most people still did not know much about Kabila. He had just been plucked out of obscurity and made the leader of the insurgency, riding on a wave of anti-Mobutu sentiments prevalent across the nation. He also had one major asset in a rebel movement whose driving force was Tutsi, an ethnic group hated not only in eastern Zaire where the rebellion started in 1996, but also in the rest of the country. He was not a Tutsi.

He was a member of the Luba tribe from northern Shaba Province (the former Katanga Province), an ethnic group accepted by the other tribes in Congo as native to the country unlike the Tutsi who were considered to be foreigners in spite of the fact that they have lived in Congo for more than 200 years. The Luba are also one of the largest ethnic groups in Congo.

Kabila's stature among his fellow countrymen, after Rwanda's *de facto* ruler General Paul Kagame chose him to lead the 1996 uprising against Mobutu, was enhanced by his own revolutionary credentials during the 1960s, however dubious those credentials were; by his political base as head of the small but resilient Afro-Marxist People's Revolutionary Party he founded in northern Katanga Province in 1967 which was now based in the Fizi-Baraka area on the western shore of Lake Tanganyika in South Kivu Province; and by his virulently anti-Mobutist stand as well as his credentials as a disciple of Patrice Lumumba.

But all those advantages were not enough to form a solid foundation on which to build a cohesive anti-

Mobutist alliance.

The Anti-Mobutu Coalition

As we learned earlier, the fighting in eastern Zaire started in October – November 1996.

That was when Mobutu's rag-tag army and members of different tribes made a move against the Banyamulenge Tutsis – so named because of the mountainous Mulenge area in which they settled in South Kivu Province – whom they did not consider to be citizens.

The Banyamulenge fought back to protect their rights, especially the land which their enemies wanted to seize and force them to flee to Rwanda and Burundi to live with their fellow Tutsis.

Opposition to Mobutu's brutal kleptocratic rule by different groups in and out of Zaire led to the convening of a national conference in 1991 in the capital Kinshasa to address the nation's problems across the spectrum. After 30 years of chaos, anarchy and dictatorship during which all institutions of civic organisation and democratic tradition collapsed and were pulverised by the vampire state, the conference was willing to discuss any political or social problems facing the nation.

Such frank discussion was undoubtedly democratic. But it also had potential for catastrophe in the context of Zaire's toxic ethno-regional politics, given the intense tribal hostilities in some parts of the country, especially in North and South Kivu provinces.

The delegates from Kivu competed against each other as they articulated conflicting ethnic interests, each tribe promoting its own. But they agreed on one thing: the Tutsi had to go.

It was, however, a broad agenda, calling for the neutralisation of all Kinyarwanda speakers (hence Hutus as well) – Kinyarwanda is the national language of

Rwanda spoken by Hutus and Tutsis – in the two Kivu provinces and, as a final solution, possibly their expulsion from Zaire, forcing them to "go back" where they "came from," Rwanda, a place most of them had never been to, and which they knew about only from historical ties.

But the primary target of the campaign was the Tutsi, citizens of Zaire, yet not "citizens." They were not considered to be citizens even by the national government of Mobutu, let alone by their fellow countrymen.

Although their migration from Rwanda to what came to be known as Congo started in the 16th century when King Kigeri Nyamuheshera sent a number of Tutsi families to settle in the newly conquered area of Bunyabungo in what is Uvira today in South Kivu Province in the eastern part of the country, it was the latter migrations – including the second and third waves in the 1800s – which drew more attention because of their cumulative impact.

Others followed, and a larger part of them, including the previous ones, settled mainly in what is now North Kivu Province across the border from Rwanda. As Gérard Prunier stated in "The Great Lakes Crisis":

"There were many layers of Rwandan immigration in eastern Zaire, especially in North Kivu.

The first group of Rwandans had arrived there probably over 200 years ago. These were both Tutsi and Hutu.

Many – mostly Hutu – were later 'imported' by the Belgians, who were short of manpower in the Congo during the colonial years while their mandate territory of Ruanda-Urundi (now Rwanda and Burundi) was overpopulated....

Rwanda and Burundi were parts of German East Africa (Tanganyika which is now Tanzania); they were conquered by the Belgian army in 1916 and later given to Brussels as mandate territories by the League of Nations....

46

A third and purely Tutsi layer was made up of refugees who had fled the 1959 to 1963 massacres and the imposition of a Hutu ethnic state at the time of Rwanda's independence in 1962. And a fourth and exclusively Hutu group had arrived in August 1994, fleeing the RPF (the Tutsi Rwandan Patriotic Front) takeover in Rwanda."[15]

Delegates to the 1991 national conference in Kinshasa resorted to a legal manoeuvre to strip the Banyarwanda of their citizenship by selective implementation of citizenship laws to enforce the 1981 decree which revoked their status as citizens of Zaire.

President Mobutu himself supported the move by the delegates which helped divert some attention from his rotten dictatorship by mobilising nationalist sentiment against these "foreigners."

It was a tactic typical of Mobutu: divide and rule.

Earlier, he had used the Banyarwanda in Kivu provinces to help contain and neutralise local opposition to his rule from other tribes. It was one of the reasons why these ethnic groups became even more hostile towards the Banyarwanda (mostly Tutsis) and towards Mobutu himself.

Members of these tribes in eastern Zaire proceeded to disenfranchise "outsiders" by launching a campaign of ethnic cleansing.

The campaign had a broad mandate – to expel all non-indigenes including non-Banyarwanda – but was specific in intent, and selective in its application, by targeting the Banyarwanda.

By early 1993, tribal militia groups were ransacking villages and killing the Banyarwanda in North Kivu Province which borders Rwanda. The victims included Hutus but the primary target was Tutsis because of the intense hostility towards them by the local tribes and other Zaireans.

In the past, the Tutsi and the Hutu in Congo had,

collectively as Banyarwanda, formed a united front against their common enemy: the other tribes in eastern Congo who did not want them there. But with the civil war in Rwanda between their kinsmen, Hutu versus Tutsi, they also turned against each other in Congo (Zaire). No longer were they fellow Banyarwanda, with a shared identity based on common national origin, Rwanda; they were simply Hutus and Tutsis. Each to his own.

In 1993, North Kivu became a battleground and witnessed some of the most violent conflicts between different tribes in recent times. Hutus fought Tutsis, and vice versa; and members of the other tribes fought both.

The influx of the Hutu Rwandan refugees into the region in mid-1994, fleeing from Rwanda after the Tutsi-dominated Rwandan Patriotic Front (RPF) took over the country and stopped the genocide of Tutsis, aggravated the situation.

Among the Hutu refugees were tens of thousands of well-armed and virulently anti-Tutsi elements who had participated in the massacre of almost one million Tutsis in Rwanda during the 1994 genocide.

The result was ethnic cleansing in eastern Zaire reminiscent of what had just taken place across the border in Rwanda. Thousands of Tutsis were killed, and the rest fled to Rwanda where the Tutsi-led Rwandan Patriotic Front had just seized power.

The ethnic conflict had overflown national boundaries with dire consequences, adding a new dimension to the genocide against the Tutsi.

The situation in South Kivu Province was somewhat different. Like their counterparts in North Kivu Province, the leaders of South Kivu had also decided to disenfranchise the Banyarwanda. However, the division between the Hutu and the Tutsi was not as pronounced as it was in North Kivu.

The Banyarwanda who had settled in this region (South Kivu) are the ones who were named Banyamulenge by the members of the other tribes in the region. They were mostly Tutsi who settled in the area in the early 1800s after losing in intra-tribal feudal wars with fellow Tutsis in Rwanda. They were accompanied by their Hutu servants who became assimilated into the larger Tutsi community, "losing" their Hutu identity in the process. Like their Tutsi masters, they simply came to be known as Banyamulenge, or just "Tutsis."

In 1993 and 1994, the Banyamulenge witnessed with horror the ethnic cleansing of fellow Tutsis in North Kivu Province and prepared for the worst. By mid-1996, when provincial leaders of South Kivu with the full support of the central government in Kinshasa began to target them, they decided to take decisive action. And they got immediate help from Rwanda where their kinsmen were now in control.

They also sought help from Burundi, which was under under Tutsi leadership like Rwanda, and from Uganda whose president, Kaguta Yoweri Museveni, was himself identified as a Tutsi, although he identified himself as a Munyankole, a member of the Banyankole ethnic group in southwestern Uganda who are related to the Tutsi.

But among all their supporters, it was Rwanda, their original homeland, which was their patron.

By November 1996, eastern Zaire was engulfed in civil war. As the fighting intensified between the Banyamulenge Tutsis and the Zairean army with its anti-Tutsi local supporters, the Tutsi won the support of other Zairean opposition groups which wanted to oust Mobutu from power. It was a marriage of convenience. According to *Africa Analysis*:

"[The opposition groups include] the Popular Revolutionary Party of Shaba Province, the Revolutionary Liberation Movement and the National Democratic Resistance from the Kasai region.

These have now joined the Banyamurenge to form an

umbrella organisation, the Alliance of Democratic Liberation Forces of Zaire and Congo.

It aims to oust the ailing President Mobutu Sese Seko from power. Even more ominously, Rwandan troops have reportedly joined the fighting. Zaire claims some fighters captured in the country belong to Rwanda's 7th infantry battalion and also accuses Ugandan and Burundian forces of aiding the rebels."[16]

Other countries besides Rwanda which joined the anti-Mobutu coalition included Angola, Tanzania, Eritrea, Ethiopia, Zimbabwe, and Zambia.

The Banyamulenge, whose oppression ignited the rebellion, were no longer an isolated group in their campaign against Mobutu.

Ironically, in the late 1960s when Pierre Mulele led Congo's longest uprising, the "Kwilu" rebellion from his operational base in his home Kwilu Province in the western part of the country, it was the Banyamulenge who helped Mobutu fight the pro-Lumumbist rebels.

It was he who first armed them with modern weapons, enthusiastically embracing them as fellow Congolese in his hour of need. Before then, the Banyamulenge had depended on bows and arrows.

Thirty years later, they switched sides and fought to overthrow the very same man they once helped to keep in power. They also formed an alliance with the pro-Lumumbist forces of Laurent Kabila, the same forces they fought thirty years before, helping Mobutu to neutralise them.

The advance by the insurgents across Zaire during the 1996 – 1997 rebellion was directed by the military leaderships of Rwanda, Uganda, and Burundi. And there was evidence from the beginning showing that Rwanda had been arming the Banyamulenge in the same way that Uganda had armed the Rwandan Patriotic Front (RPF) fighters who went on to seize power in Kigali, Rwanda's capital. In fact, Rwanda's ruler Paul Kagame conceded later that the war was planned primarily by Rwanda, and that the plan to topple Mobutu also originated in Kigali.

He disclosed in an interview with *The Washington Post*, 9 July 1997, that "the Rwandan government planned and directed the rebellion that ousted the long-time dictator and that Rwandan troops and officers led the rebel forces."[17]

The prominent role played by the Banyamulenge in overthrowing Mobutu in May 1997 was deeply resented by the members of the other tribes in eastern Zaire where the rebellion started. Those with deep resentment included the Babembe, the Bahunda, the Banande, and the Bashi. The Banyamulenge were also resented by others across the country, including the Baluba, Laurent Kabila's tribe in Shaba (Katanga) Province.

The resentment got even deeper when several Banyamulenge Tutsis assumed key positions in the national government in Kinshasa under President Laurent Kabila who was seen by many of his fellow countrymen as a puppet of Rwanda, and their giant nation a virtual colony of their tiny neighbour: Rwanda. And the contrast is glaring. Congo which is the size of Western Europe or the entire United States of America east of the Mississippi River is about 90 times the size of Rwanda.

And the role played by Rwanda, Uganda, and Burundi in overthrowing Mobutu and in installing a new government in Kinshasa raised speculation of a concerted effort by the leaders of the three countries to create a Tutsi empire in East-Central Africa, from the Great Lakes region to the Atlantic Ocean.

Rwanda and Burundi were clearly Tutsi-dominated states. In the case of Uganda, Tutsi leadership of that country centred on President Kaguta Yoweri Museveni, a member of the Hima branch of the Tutsi from the southwestern part of Uganda bordering Rwanda and Tanzania. Also, there were those who contended that

Museveni was actually a Tutsi from Rwanda. And they have maintained the same position through the years.

Expansionist ambitions of the three countries could not be ruled out. And they were directed at Congo ostensibly for security reasons to secure the borders of those countries against incursions by rebel groups based in Congo who were trying to overthrow the governments of the three countries.

But even if they had territorial ambitions to annex parts of Congo, directly or indirectly, there is no question that security of their borders also figured prominently in their decision to intervene in Congo.

Of the three countries, Rwanda was most vulnerable because of the tens of thousands of armed Hutu extremists – including members of the former Hutu Rwandan national army who were defeated by the Rwandan Patriotic Army (RPA) of the RPF in 1994 – who had fled the country after the Rwandan genocide and found sanctuary just across the border in Congo. But whether or not such concern about security was of paramount importance, eclipsing everything else, in Rwanda's intervention in Congo is a matter for argument.

Rwanda's Strategic Initiatives in Congo

Rwanda intervened in Congo for several reasons and in a vengeful mood: to kill, indiscriminately, hundreds of thousands of Hutu refugees – including innocent men, women and children and the elderly – in retaliation for the 1994 genocide in which one million Tutsis perished at the hands of Hutu extremists and, in fact, succeeded in massacring more than 200,000 of those refugees in only a few months.

Rwandan Tutsi leaders also intervened in Congo to hunt down the perpetrators of the 1994 genocide who were hiding among the refugees in refugee camps, making it almost impossible to identify them when they were mixed with other people in the camps. To kill them, Rwandan Tutsi soldiers also had to kill innocent Hutu refugees, virtually sparing none, to make sure the perpetrators of the genocide hiding among them were dead.

Rwanda also went into Congo to install a puppet regime in Kinshasa it could manipulate at will in pursuit of its national interests; to secure its borders by any means at its disposal; to create a buffer zone, in effect, a *de facto* autonomous state inhabited by Congolese Tutsis, along the Rwandan-Congolese border ostensibly as a security measure but in fact as an expansionist move to create a Tutsi federation or confederation of the two Tutsi political entities: Rwanda and the newly created Tutsi state in the "security corridor."

Rwanda also intervened in Congo for economic reasons: to extract Congo's mineral resources and agricultural products, including gold, diamonds, coffee, and timber; and if possible, to annex parts of eastern Congo in pursuit of its hegemonic ambitions in East-Central Africa as a power broker in the region despite its small size. Rwanda is one of the smallest countries in Africa and in the entire world, yet one of the most influential in the Great Lakes region of East-Central Africa.

But foremost among all those objectives was security for this tiny, highly vulnerable, desperately poor and landlocked nation in the hinterland of Africa. Even its expansionist ambition may be justified by the "imperial" authorities in Kigali in terms of security concerns, although it can not be defended on rational grounds. Rwanda's security can not be guaranteed in Congo but in Rwanda itself, especially by treating all its citizens equally without discrimination across the spectrum.

Yet there were grounds for such intervention in Congo by Rwanda.

The immediate cause of Rwanda's intervention was the

persecution of the Banyamulenge Tutsi in eastern Congo – then known as Zaire – by the other tribes in South Kivu Province; a persecution which led to armed conflict in August 1996 between the Banyamulenge and the other ethnic groups supported by Mobutu's national army.

It was, at first, seen as a local conflict. But it assumed larger dimensions when it became clear that the two Tutsi-dominated states of Rwanda and Burundi intervened to help their kinsmen.

The conflict escalated even further when Uganda intervened in November 1996, forming a tripartite alliance with Rwanda and Burundi which went on to overthrow Mobutu and later plunge Congo into a much bigger war involving armies from nine African countries.

All three – Rwanda, Burundi and Uganda – intervened in eastern Zaire ostensibly to secure their borders because Mobutu's government was harbouring rebel groups fighting to overthrow their governments. Yet the threat to Uganda was not as serious as the Ugandan authorities claimed it was.

It came mainly from northern and northwestern Uganda where the West Nile Bank Liberation Front, linked to the remnants of Idi Amin's regime, and the Lord's Resistance Army (LRA), were operating.

The Lord's Resistance Army was made up of members of the Holy Spirit Movement, a millenarian cult mostly composed of Acholi tribesmen indigenous to northern Uganda.

Both groups were armed by the Sudanese government in retaliation for Uganda's support of the black African rebels of the Sudanese People's Liberation Army (SPLA) in southern Sudan fighting against the Arab-dominated government in Khartoum in pursuit of autonomy and ultimately independence. And both had operational bases in Zaire, in addition to those in Sudan, and within Uganda itself.

But neither posed a serious threat to the Ugandan

government because they operated mainly in northern Uganda far from the capital Kampala which is in the south. Also, both groups were weak. And they were severely compromised by their ethnic appeal in the region – northern Uganda – which is ethnically heterogeneous, a diversity which made it very difficult, if not impossible, for them to broaden their support.

The threat to Burundi from the Hutu rebels operating from Zaire, although very serious, was not enough to oust the government because of the entrenched Tutsi ethnocracy which had consolidated its power since independence in 1962 by systematically destroying the Hutu elite and massacring hundreds of thousands of Hutus through the years.

Its firm grip on power is attested to by the fact that Burundi's capital, Bujumbura, is only 10 miles from the border with the Democratic Republic of Congo, formerly Zaire. Yet, in spite of such proximity making Burundi even more vulnerable to attack, Burundian Hutu rebels operating from their bases in Congo and within Burundi itself have not been able to threaten the capital seriously, let alone oust the Tutsi from power.

The situation was different in Rwanda by mid-1996 when the regime in Kigali intervened in Zaire.

Devastated by the 1994 holocaust, the country was still in a daze. The economy was in ruins, and institutions of governance and civic organisation had also been destroyed.

The victorious Rwandan Patriotic Front (RPF) – which ousted and replaced the genocidal Hutu regime and assumed power as Rwanda's "legitimate" government although without electoral mandate – was mostly Tutsi and therefore not trusted by the Hutu majority who were excluded from the government in terms of meaningful representation besides token leadership.

And the new Tutsi rulers knew that they could not trust most Hutus – who also constitute the vast majority of the population – because there was no guarantee that they disassociated themselves from or turned their backs on the perpetrators of the 1994 genocide.

Distrust of the new Tutsi rulers among the Hutu deepened when Prime Minister Faustin Twagiramungu and Interior Minister Seth Sendashonga, both Hutus, were forced to resign in August 1995. The remaining Hutu government ministers were also forced out shortly thereafter, leaving the RPF regime, already Tutsi-dominated, ethnically isolated, despite its earlier promises to form an inclusive government.

Such politics of exclusion could guarantee only one thing: perpetual conflict between the two groups. And that is exactly what happened during the following years.

Compounding the problem for the Tutsi-dominated government was the fact that more than 2 million Rwandan Hutu refugees, many of whom – if not the majority – were hostile to the new rulers and other Tutsis in Rwanda, had found refuge just across the border in eastern Zaire and western Tanzania.

Among them were 50,000 soldiers of the former Hutu-dominated Rwandan Armed Forces (FAR), routed by the predominantly Tutsi Rwandan Patriotic Front (RPF) in July 1994. They were Hutu and most of them were camped in Zaire together with civilian Hutu refugees. And they were in the process of rearming themselves in the refugee camps and getting ready to invade Rwanda.

It was in this context that Rwanda decided to act. Its intervention to protect the Banyamulenge in eastern Zaire was indeed a prime motive. But it was linked to the greater security concerns of Rwanda, important as ethnic solidarity was.

Therefore even if there had been no Tutsis – the Banyamuluenge – who were being persecuted in Zaire, the Tutsi-dominated government of Rwanda would have intervened, anyway, to go after the perpetrators of the 1994 genocide who were hiding among the rest of the

Hutu refugees in the refugee camps in eastern Zaire and who were preparing to invade Rwanda and oust the Tutsi from power.

The Rwandan government also intervened in Zaire out of malicious vindictiveness to exact retribution for the extermination of about one million Tutsis during the Rwandan genocide by massacring hundreds of thousands of Hutus, including women and children, who had sought refuge in Zaire.

The distrust and hatred between the two sides was mutual.

Hutu rebels were already launching raids into Rwanda from their bases in Zaire, killing and planting mines and trying to destabilise the Tutsi-dominated government before the Rwandan authorities intervened in Zaire. President Mobutu supplied them with weapons. He also gave them a lot of money. He hated the Tutsi regime in Rwanda which he also derisively dismissed as a puppet of Ugandan President Yoweri Museveni, his nemesis.

But even if Mobutu had wanted to restrain the rebels, he probably would not have been able to do so. The best he could have done would have been to deny them assistance, money and weapons, thus limiting their capability to attack Rwanda.

The Zairean state over which he presided was no more than an empty shell, crumbling and falling apart, pulverised from within due to neglect during his 30 years in office. Yet Zaire was potentially one of the richest countries in the world, in fact richer than South Africa in terms of mineral wealth. And the national army itself, the Zairian Armed Forces (FAZ), was in disarray and in tatters. It was no more than a rag-tag army of thugs, undisciplined, poorly trained, and underpaid solders who survived on robbery and looting, to pay themselves.

The Hutu rebels in Zaire were a formidable force, not only impossible to dislodge, but constantly replenished with weapons. They were also well-funded by other patrons besides Mobutu.

In addition to the weapons and ammunition they took when they fled Rwanda in 1994 and the supplies they got from President Mobutu, these former members of the Hutu Rwandan national army and the country's political leaders who were also among the refugees in Zaire or lived elsewhere while supporting the rebels had also looted Rwanda's national treasury when they fled their homeland.

They used the money to buy more weapons on the international black market, especially from the People's Republic of China, a country which also had a history of meddling in the Hutu-Tutsi ethnic conflicts since the early 1960s when it first intervened in both Rwanda and Burundi.

Towards the end of 1995 and in early 1996, Hutu incursions into Rwanda had escalated to the point where they posed a serious threat to the nation's security. But the attacks also triggered a brutal retaliatory response from the Tutsi Rwandan national army directed against Hutu civilians in Rwanda, most of whom were poor peasants living in villages across the country.

Such indiscriminate violence and brutal tactics, which amounted to state-sponsored terror, against the Hutu peasants probably the majority of whom were innocent, only aggravated the situation in a country where relations between the two ethnic groups were already bad. It also helped the Hutu rebels recruit even more fighters, driven into the rebels' arms by the terror campaign conducted by the Tutsi army against Hutu civilians.

The decision by many Hutus to join the rebels was understandable. It is only when you are in another man's condition that you may be able to understand his predicament. As Ehud Barak confessed in 1999 before being elected prime minister of Israel, had he been born a Palestinian, he would have joined the Palestine Liberation Organisation (PLO).[18]

Had the Tutsi been Hutus, they probably would be

doing the same thing Hutu rebels are doing today.

However, that does not mean Rwanda under Tutsi leadership never had legitimate security concerns, as Hutu insurgents continued to launch cross-border raids into the country. For several months, Rwanda's ruler Paul Kagame had warned against such attacks from Zaire and complained that the refugee camps in Kivu provided cover for these rebels, enabling them to attack Rwanda with impunity.

He asked the international community to intervene and stop such subversive activities in the camps which had been set up with UN assistance and were under UN supervision. But his plea went unheeded.

Yet he also knew that an invasion of the refugee camps by his army to neutralise the rebels would tarnish Rwanda's image – breaking international law was the least of his concerns as he clearly demonstrated when he invaded Zaire shortly thereafter – by killing innocent civilians without even eliminating the threat from the insurgents hiding among them.

However, this humanitarian concern was also later ignored by Kagame, as was international law about the sanctity of national borders, when he invaded Zaire shortly thereafter.

Yet pursuit of the rebels was justified, the rationale behind it reminiscent of what Tanzania did in 1979 in response to Idi Amin's invasion of her territory. Tanzania fought back and crossed the border in pursuit of the invaders and forced Amin to flee Uganda after the capital Kampla fell to Tanzanian and anti-Amin forces on 10 April. From Tanzania's standpoint, it was a matter of national security.

That was also the case with Rwanda whose leader, Kagame, was also a great admirer of Tanzanian president, Julius Nyerere and his doctrine of justified intervention in other countries – although he never explicitly said so – who authorised the counterattack against Idi Amin's forces when they invaded Tanzania in October 1978 and annexed 710 square miles of her territory in Kagera Region in the northwestern part of the country bordering Uganda.

Of paramount importance was Rwanda's security when the Rwandan army intervened in Congo. As Kagame himself stated in an interview with *The Washington Post*, 9 July 1997:

"They were insensitive. We told them (the United Nations and world powers) that either they do something about the camps or they face the consequences."[19]

It was time to intervene. The Tutsi Rwandan Patriotic Front Army (RPA) then began training fellow Tutsis, the Banyamulenge, who went to Rwanda for the training, and also established contacts with other groups in Zaire opposed to Mobutu's regime in order to form a united front against one of Africa's most notorious tyrants.

On 18 October 1996, the opposition groups joined forces with the Banyamulenge Tutsis and formed the Alliance of Democratic Forces for the Liberation of Congo-Zaire (ADFL). The ADFL included four main anti-Mobutu groups, divided by ideology, but united in their opposition against a common enemy. They were:

The People's Democratic Alliance whose French acronym was *Alliance Democratique des Peuples* (ADP) led by Deogratias Bugera, a Banyamulenge Tutsi; the National Resistance Council for Democracy (*Conseil National de Resistance pour la Democratie* – CNRD) founded in 1993 by Andre Kisase Ngandu of the National Congolese Movement (*Mouvement National Congolais* – MNC/Lumumba); the Revolutionary Movement for the Liberation of Zaire (*Mouvement Revolutionnaire pour la Liberation du Zaire* – MRLZ) led by Masasu Nindaga; and the People's Revolutionary Party (*Parti de la Revolution Populaire* – PRP) led by Laurent-Desire Kabila who went on to become head of the anti-Mobutu coalition.

In early October 1996, Rwanda learned that the Hutu rebels in Zaire were going to attack the Banyamulenge. Rwandan leaders also learned that the insurgents planned to invade Rwanda with about 100,000 Hutus including 40,000 militiamen.

The threat triggered a joint response from the Rwandan Tutsis and their Congolese kinsmen, the Banyamulenge.

After repeated attacks by Mobutu's soldiers and their local allies (members of tribes including Hutus hostile to the Tutsi), the Banyamulenge fought back. And they won. After routing Mobutu's rag-tag army, they attacked the Hutu refugee camps in eastern Zaire, triggering a mass exodus of hundreds of thousands of Hutus who returned to Rwanda. Hundreds of thousands of others fled west, deeper into the Congo forest, where at least 300,000 of them perished in addition to the 200,000 killed by Tutsi soldiers. The rest fled to Burundi.

In addition to the Hutu threat from Zaire, Rwanda was also deeply concerned about the situation in Burundi, its twin in the south.

Burundi's neighbours had imposed an economic embargo on the country because of a Tutsi-led military coup by Major Pierre Buyoya who ousted constitutionally chosen Hutu President Sylvestre Ntibantunganya in July 1996.

Earlier, Buyoya also orchestrated the abortive attempt to overthrow the government in October 1993 in which President Melchior Ndadaye, a Hutu, was assassinated.

The Tutsi government in Rwanda worried that if the Tutsi lost power to the Hutu in Burundi as a result of economic sanctions and Hutu guerrilla attacks, the Rwandan Hutu rebels would be welcomed by their kinsmen in Burundi who would provide them with a major operational base from which they could launch raids into Rwanda. And if Burundi fell and came under Hutu leadership, it would be only a matter of time before Rwanda did, with the Tutsi government in Kigali

61

collapsing under a combined massive military attack by the Hutu in both countries. In fact, Rwandan and Burundian Hutu rebels have been coordinating their attacks against the Tutsi in both countries for years.

There was also great concern among the Tutsi leaders and their kinsmen in Rwanda that should Burundi fall into Hutu hands, a massacre of genocidal proportions directed against the Tutsi in that country was a very strong possibility, and probably on a scale reminiscent of what happened in Rwanda in 1994, if not worse. To avert such a catastrophe, Rwanda would have to throw its gates wide open to save fellow Tutsis fleeing Burundi before being exterminated.

Some of Burundi's Tutsi leaders, for example former President Jean-Baptiste Bagaza, a hardliner, believed that Rwanda was the only country where fleeing Tutsis could expect to be welcomed, now that it was again under Tutsi leadership after the 1994 genocide.

But it is an assessment not borne out by facts. Rwanda is not the only country where Tutsis could expect to be welcomed if they had to flee Burundi.

Tens of thousands of Tutsi refugees, not just Hutus, from both Rwanda and Burundi, have been welcomed in Tanzania through the years. And tens of thousands of them have acquired Tanzanian citizenship.

They have also been given refuge by other African countries including Uganda. For example, it was from Uganda that the Tutsi Rwandan Patriotic Front (RPF) launched its first – although abortive – invasion of Rwanda on 1 October 1990, including its last and successful one from 8 April – 4 July 1994.

Kenya also has welcomed Tutsi refugees as much as it has Hutus.

But the mere prospect of a massive Tutsi exodus from Burundi, should the Tutsi be ousted from power in that country, was enough to be a matter of serious concern to the Tutsi leadership in neighbouring Rwanda. Such a huge

62

influx would simply lead to another explosion in Rwanda, with Hutus and Tutsis slaughtering each other while fighting over limited space and scarce resources, not even to mention the total collapse of the nation's already overburdened and fragile economy in such a small, desperately poor and overpopulated country.

Therefore, the survival of the Tutsi government in Burundi was seen by the Rwandan Tutsi leaders as critical to the survival of Rwanda itself as a Tutsi ethnocracy and as a safe haven for its dominant ethnic group.

So, it was not just a question of Tutsi ethnic solidarity with their kinsmen in Burundi which motivated the Rwandan leaders to help them stay in power, although ethnic loyalty to each other has always figured prominently in the calculations of both states. It was also a question of Rwanda's survival as a Tutsi ethnocracy, vital to the survival of the Tutsi as a people, that was at stake, as much as Burundi's survival under Tutsi domination was seen as critical to the survival of Tutsis in both countries bound by common destiny.

The Rwanda leaders felt that the threat to their country's security could be best dealt with by supporting the Banyamulenge in their war against their common enemies: the Hutu operating from Zaire, and President Mobutu and his local allies – different tribes – in the eastern part of the country who were equally hostile to the Tutsi in Zaire, Rwanda, and Burundi.

It is true that Rwanda's support for the Banyamulenge and other anti-Mobutist forces – who collectively constituted the Alliance of Democratic Forces for the Liberation of Congo-Zaire – led to the ouster of Mobutu. But it did not lead to the establishment of a friendly regime in Kinshasa – Kabila turned out to be only a temporary ally of convenience – or neutralise the threat to Rwanda's or Burundi's security coming from the Hutu rebels based in Congo.

Security of the two countries can be guaranteed only

when the dominant Tutsi minority – in control of both Rwanda and Burundi – agree to share power with the Hutu majority on the basis of a mutually acceptable compromise. And that includes proportional representation in the government and other areas of national life where power sharing is critical to the survival, wellbeing and prosperity of both groups.

Prospects for Peace

Prospects for a lasting peace in the Great Lakes region are bleak, to say the least. And that will continue to be the case as long as the leaders of Rwanda, Burundi and Congo remain adamantly opposed to devolution of power; and as long as different tribes continue to fight each other and dominate one another.

The twentieth century came to an end without any of the conflicts – in Rwanda, Burundi, Congo, and even in less troubled Uganda – being resolved.

Rwanda and Burundi remained mired in escalating ethnic warfare, with the Hutu vowing to overthrow the Tutsi, and the Tutsi refusing to share power with the Hutu except on their own terms.

Peace in Congo remained elusive even after a peace agreement was signed by all the countries and rebel groups involved in that multinational conflict.

And in Uganda, the government continued to fight its own rebels.

And despite professions to the contrary, Rwanda and Burundi continued to be ruled by quasi-military, not civilian, governments, as the twentieth-first century began; so did the Democratic Republic of Congo whose name is a misnomer in a country without democracy. And all three countries remained deeply divided along ethnic lines.

It is these ethnic rivalries, among other reasons, which African soldiers have always used to justify military coups, claiming that they are trying to inculcate a truly national ethos among the people, while at the same time they continue to maintain the status quo of tribal and regional loyalties. And it is the same ethnic hostilities which have helped to ignite and fuel civil wars in the Great Lakes region through the years in the struggle for power and resources among different groups.

Seizure of power by the military has proved to be the fastest and probably most effective means to achieve this goal, of tribal supremacy, but with dire consequences for the countries involved as the history of military rule in Africa tragically demonstrates.

Military rule has led to institutionalised ethnocracy: for example, by the Kabye in Togo where President Gnassingbe Eyadema, Africa's longest-ruling autocrat in power since 1967, virtually excluded the country's largest ethnic group, the Ewe, and members of other tribes from power and filled the army with members of his tribe – more than two-thirds of the soldiers and army officers were Kabye – from northern Togo; by the Amhara in Ethiopia where Mengistu Haile Mariam seized power in 1977, perpetuating Amharic rule which had gone on for years even before him; by the Tutsi in both Rwanda and Burundi; and by the Hutu in Rwanda since independence in 1962 until they were ousted from power following the 1994 genocide.

Military rule has also led to entrenchment of dictatorship and institutionalisation of corruption as a national virtue, as has been the case under civilian leadership in most African countries. There are many case studies which document this abuse of power across the continent,[20] as the history of military and civilian rule in Africa clearly shows.

Rwanda and Burundi are some of the best case studies of military and civilian dictatorship in Africa whose tyranny plunged the two countries into full-scale civil wars. They also have been the scene of some of the bloodiest conflicts on the continent in the post-colonial period.

We are going to look **at** both in much more detail starting with Burundi.

Chapter Two:

Burundi: A Nation at War

THE African continent has been the scene of many tragedies through the years. But few equal what happened in Rwanda and Burundi in terms of Africans killing fellow Africans. Rwanda and Burundi easily qualify as the killing fields of Africa, two countries of magnificent beauty, with green hills and valleys, soaked in blood.

Even Nigeria's tragedy during the civil war from 1967 to 1970 pales into insignificance by comparison in terms of the number of victims and the magnitude of the violence unleashed.

This is not to ignore the suffering of the Igbos and other Eastern Nigerians in that war. It was a horrendous tragedy. But Northern Nigerians did not slaughter hundreds of thousands of Igbos and other Easterners in

Northern Nigeria as the Hutu and the Tutsi did to each other in Rwanda and Burundi from the early sixties to the mid-nineties alone.

Most of the victims during that tragic period in Nigerian – and African – history died from starvation, a weapon the federal military government deliberately used effectively to starve the Igbos and other Eastern Nigerians into submission. As Chief Anthony Enahoro, the commissioner of information in the Nigerian government under General Yakubu Gowon, bluntly stated at a press conference in July 1968: "Starvation is a legitimate instrument of war, and we have every intention of using it against the rebels."

Chief Obafemi Awolowo, vice chairman of the Federal Executive Council, hence Nigeria's vice president under Gowon who was the head of the federal military government, articulated the same position.

In Rwanda and Burundi, most of the victims were simply slaughtered – hacked, clubbed, stoned, slashed, speared or shot to death. And the carnage continues today.

Although this chapter is about Burundi, it is also about Rwanda because the two countries have so much in common that they literally constitute one country, had it not been for the demarcation line that separates them. At the very least, they are identical twins. The artificial boundary has not changed that. Yet, both are so divided within that each is, tragically, two nations in one, hence four in both: Hutu versus Tutsi.

Formerly known as Ruanda-Urundi, the two countries were a part of what is Tanzania today when all three formed one country called German East Africa (Deutsch-Ostafrika).

The area that came to be known as Tanganyika, what is now Tanzania mainland, is the country that was first named Deutsch Ostafrika (German East Africa). Burundi, then known as Urundi, became part of German East Africa in 1898, and Rwanda, then called Ruanda, in 1899.

After Germany was defeated in World War I, both Ruanda and Urundi were mandated to Belgium by the League of Nations as one territory of Ruanda-Urundi. The territory was administered jointly with Belgian Congo. The administrative centre was Leopoldville, the capital of Belgian Congo which was renamed Kinshasa by President Mobutu in 1966.

Tanganyika, which was the largest part of the East African German colony, became a British mandated territory after Woodrow Wilson, the American president, turned down a request by British Prime Minister Lloyd George to administer it under the League of Nations trusteeship mandate. Otherwise Tanganyika, what is mainland Tanzania today, would have become an American colony or possession, the only one on the continent. Liberia is considered by some people to be a virtual American colony; some even consider it to be America's 51st state. But that is an entirely different subject beyond the scope of this work.

Had the three territories – of Tanganyika, Ruanda and Urundi – remained together and emerged from colonial rule as a single political entity, the history of the Great Lakes region would probably have been different.

It is possible the massacres of the Hutu and the Tutsi which have taken place in both Rwanda and Burundi through the years, including the 1994 genocide, would not have taken place. It is also possible many Hutus and Tutsis would have moved to other parts of the large country – the former German East Africa – instead of remaining crowded in the heavily populated territories of Ruanda and Urundi fighting for scarce resources especially land.

It is also possible there would have been an equitable distribution of power in the larger political entity in which the Hutu and the Tutsi would not have been locked in conflict as they are now in Rwanda and Burundi.

The Hutu constitute the vast majority of Burundi's population, a formidable 85 per cent, and the Tutsi, 14 per cent. The Twa, who are the Pygmies, make up the remaining 1 per cent.

But it is the Tutsi who have always dominated the country and the government. It is this inequity of power, probably more than anything else, which has caused so much bloodshed between the Hutu and the Tutsi through the years.

Other factors, especially shortage of land and poverty, have exacerbated the conflict.

Burundi is one of the poorest countries in the world. It is also the most densely populated country in Africa after Rwanda.

In such a small, desperately poor and overpopulated country, shortage of land may be the country's biggest problem. Had there been enough land, there would have been less conflict which has been an integral part of the country's history since the Tutsi conquered and virtually enslaved the Hutu about 400 years ago and established the kingdoms of Ruanda and Urundi under aristocratic rule.

Even after the end of colonial rule when it was expected that both the Hutu and the Tusti would equally participate in the government of their country, the asymmetrical relationship between the two ethnic groups continued. The Tutsi remained in a dominant position.

On 1 July 1962, the Tutsi-dominated kingdom of Urundi won independence as a monarchy. It was renamed Burundi under the leadership of Mwami (King) Mwambutsa IV.

But independence from Belgium did not usher in a new era of peace and stability for the country. The mid-sixties were marred by violence between the dominant Tutsis and the subjugated Hutus, and by struggle for power among the Tutsi themselves.

The assassination of Louis Rwagasore, a Tutsi and prominent nationalist, on 13 October 1961 by a Belgian just a few months before independence, exacerbated tensions ans intensified competition within the Tutsi elite in their quest for power, with different factions conniving against each other. The factionalism contributed to their defeat in the 1964 parliamentary elections which the Hutu won.

However, even without such intra-ethnic conflict among the Tutsi, the Hutu would probably have won the election, anyway, given their numerical preponderance if the elections were democratic, as they indeed were during the parliamentary contest.

Although the Hutu won the 1964 parliamentary elections, Burundi's head of state, Mwami (King) Mwambutsa IV, refused to appoint a Hutu prime minister to lead the cabinet. And that was at a time when the country was in a very tense political situation because of the intense hostility between the two ethnic groups.

Not long before the 1964 elections, fighting between the Hutu and the Tutsi erupted in December 1963 in which at least 5,000 people were killed following an invasion of Rwanda by Burundi-based Rwandan Tutsis with the help of their Burundian kinsmen in an attempt to overthrow the Hutu-dominated government of Rwanda.

Embittered by their exclusion from power as a result of King Mwambutsa's refusal to appoint a Hutu prime minister after an election they won, the Hutu tried to seize power from the Tutsi.

On 18 October 1965, Hutu insurgents in the Burundi army and gendarmerie in collusion with the Hutu elite and politicians attempted to assassinate Mwami Mwambutsa IV and the Tutsi prime minister he had appointed.

The coup was led by Gervais Nyangoma and succeeded deposing King Mwambutsa. Soon after the king was ousted, Hutus in the police force started killing Tutsis. The police force during that time was led by Antoine Serkwavu, a Hutu.

But the revolt did not last long and was violently suppressed by the Tutsi-dominated army and security forces.

The leader of the counter-coup was Michel Micombero, a Tutsi, who returned to Burundi during the same year after getting military training in Belgium. He had been quickly promoted after his return and was secretary of defence when King Mwambutsa was overthrown.

He mobilised forces in the army whose officers were mostly Tutsi and neutralised the Hutu who ousted the king. The king was reinstated.

Then a wave of violence was unleashed by the army and its Tutsi supporters against Hutus throughout the country.

At least 30 to 40 Hutu soldiers and gendarmes were summarily executed, sending a strong signal to the Hutu that any attempt to oust the Tutsi from power would be dealt with ruthlessly.

The executions were followed by a wave of violence that erupted in the hills above the capital, Bujumbura, formerly known as Usumbura, in which Hutu civilians joined fleeing gendarmes in burning Tutsi homes and other property in retaliation.

The International Commission of Jurists reported that all the elected Hutu members of both houses of parliament, and all the main Hutu leaders, 86 of them altogether, had been shot dead. Many other Hutus were also killed[1] by the Tutsi in an attempt to eliminate any Hutu threat to their hegemonic control of the country in which they were vastly outnumbered. For example, in the central province of Muramvya alone, more than 1,000 Hutu elites were killed by the Tutsi in 1965. And the violence and killings continued.

On 8 July 1966, Mwami Mwambutsa IV was deposed by his son who became Mwami (King) Ntare V in October the same year. The new king was 21 years old. He overthrew his father with the help of Michel Micombero who became the real ruler of the country, with Mwami Ntare being only a figure head.

Mwami Ntare did not last long in "power" even as a mere figure head. He was overthrown less than two months later on 28 November 1966 by Micombero who proclaimed Burundi a republic and became the country's first president. He was 26. He also became brigadier general after promoting himself.

Remarkably, Micombero assumed power after a bloodless coup in a country known for bloodshed. Mwami Ntare had appointed Captain Micombero prime minister on 11 July 1966 because of the role he played in the July 8th coup in which King Mwambutsa IV was overthrown when he was supposedly in voluntary exile in Geneva, Switzerland.

A graduate of the Royal Military School in Brussels, Belgium, Micombero was the army chief of staff when he overthrew Mwami Mwambutsa.

But he later fell out with Mwami Ntare V and accused the new king of failing to discharge his responsibilities. He also accused the youthful, aristocratic ruler of allowing himself to be unduly influenced by his father, the deposed king.

After overthrowing Mwami Ntare V, Micombero formed the National Committee of the Revolution (CNR) entirely composed of army officers. Almost all of them were Tutsi. And the only political party allowed to operate in the country was also Tutsi: the Party of Unity and National Progress (UPRONA). The Hutu party, the Democratic Front of Burundi (FRODEBU), was banned. Captain Micombero was also promoted to colonel and given a seven-year term as president.

The most serious problem Micombero faced when he became president was the presence of tens of thousands of Tutsi refugees, and their king, Mwami Kigeri V, from Rwanda. They fled their homeland between 1959 and 1961 after a bloody conflict – starting with the Hutu mass uprising of November 1959 – in which the Hutu emerged victorious.

Many of the Rwandan Tutsis who had fled to Burundi were also armed. The presence of these Tutsis and their king, in a safe haven in Burundi, was viewed with apprehension by Hutu-dominated neighbouring Rwanda where they were determined to return and restore the Tutsi aristocracy.

Although before independence the Tutsi-dominated kingdoms of Ruanda and Urundi were administered jointly as Ruanda-Urundi by Belgium, they chose to separate after the Belgian colonial rulers relinquished control of their colonial territory.

Rwanda became a republic at independence, and Burundi remained a monarchy until 1966 when the Tutsi aristocracy was replaced by a republican form of government under Micombero.

When Burundi became a republic, her relations with Rwanda also improved. Both countries were now under the same political system. Both were republics. The monarchy in both countries was gone.

Micombero also tried to ease ethnic tensions in Burundi, but only half-heartedly. He imposed harsh rule on the country and silenced his critics within two years of seizing power. Most of those critics were Hutus who had been excluded from power. Therefore, instead of improving relations between the two ethnic groups, he alienated most Hutus. According to *Africa Contemporary Record 1968 – 1969*:

"Political expression in any way critical of the government had remained severely curbed in Burundi.

Six former ministers and parliamentarians were each sentenced to ten years imprisonment on December 26, 1968, for writing and distributing an open letter critical of the president.

Three others arrested in the case in May (1968) were imprisoned from three to seven years, and three were acquitted.

Among those sentenced to ten years' imprisonment was the former president of the Legislative Assemby, Mr. Thadde Siryuyumisi."[2]

In 1969, President Micombero survived a coup attempt by some politicians and disgruntled elements in the army. Following the abortive coup, he consolidated his position by concentrating more power in his hands. And as head of the only legal political party in the country, the Unity and National Progress Party (UPRONA) which was Tutsi, he tolerated no opposition even from fellow Tutsis.

In 1970, Burundi adopted a new constitution. But it did little to liberalise his rule.

One of Africa's bloodiest conflicts erupted in April 1972 when Ntare V returned to Burundi from exile. President Micombero assured him in writing that nothing would happen to him if he returned home.

The deposed king returned to Burundi with dreadful results. An attempt by his supporters to reinstate him failed, and the rebellion was brutally suppressed by government troops. Ntare was "judged and immediately executed."[3]

Mwami Ntare's return coincided with the invasion of Burundi by Hutu exiles mostly based in Rwanda. The invasion was triggered by the brutal purge of Hutus from the military and the government, and by the vicious repression of Hutu peasants across the country by Tutsi soldiers.

There was no direct evidence, circumstantial or otherwise, showing that the Hutu living in Burundi joined the invasion. But given the intense hostility between the two ethnic groups, some probably did, and many undoubtedly supported the idea of dislodging the Tutsi from power by force. However, the invasion failed.

About 10,000 Tutsis were killed in the fighting. But it was the Hutu who suffered the most. The Tutsi-dominated government and army launched a brutal campaign of retaliation and terror against them which amounted to genocide. "The victorious Tutsis proceeded to massacre some 100,000 persons in six weeks, with possibly more slain by summer."[4]

More than 100,000 Hutus fled to Tanzania and Zaire (now Congo) in what had become an established pattern of forced migration in this highly unstable Great Lakes region which has undergone momentous upheavals through the years, with the two countries (Tanzania and Congo) acting as shock absorbers.

However, the refugees, from both Rwanda and Burundi, have never been fully welcome in Congo – in 1981, Zaire under Mobutu stripped the Banyamulenge Tutsis of their citizenship – because of ethnic hostilities and conflicts over land in the eastern part of the country. But they have found better reception in Tanzania. As Professor Harvey Glickman stated in "Tanzania: From Disillusionment to Guarded Optimism":

"Tanzania (has a track record of)...generous treatment of refugees and mediation of disputes that cause refugee flows....

After Zaire, Tanzania hosts the second-largest number of refugees in Africa. More than 700,000 – including a half million from Rwanda and about 200,000 from Burundi – are in camps in the northern and western parts of the country.

Burundians now comprise two generations of refugees. Thousands of Burundians crossed into Tanzania in 1963, fleeing the violence accompanying Burundi's first (abortive) coup. These earliest refugees were resettled and some achieved citizenship.

In 1980 tens of thousands of Rwandan refugees were offered citizenship.

A second wave of refugees from Rwanda entered in 1983, after expulsion from Uganda. Just under 100,000 Burundians have fled the latest surge of violence since

1993 (and sought refuge in Tanzania)."[5]

The ethnic violence will probably continue for years, as it has during the past several decades.

After the abortive April 1972 Hutu invasion of Burundi, the Hutu revolted again in May 1973 against the Tutsi. Another massacre of genocidal proportions followed. Tens of thousands of Hutus and thousands of Tutsis were killed. More refugees, mostly Hutu, fled to Tanzania and Zaire.

In 1976, the Minority Rights Group (MRG), a British organisation, accused Micombero's government of having systematically killed all Hutus who had more than secondary school education.[6]

On 1 November 1976, Lieutenant-Colonel Jean-Baptiste Bagaza overthrew Micombero in a military coup and became president. He was a distant cousin of Micombero. Both were members of the same clan.

A Tutsi himself and Belgian-educated political scientist, Bagaza promised to end civil strife, but with little prospect of success in such a deeply divided country.

In 1979, he was elected to lead the country's ruling party, UPRONA, in a rigged contest and which was almost exclusively Tutsi. The Hutu majority remained virtually disenfranchised.

In 1980, Bagaza established a "civilian government," making the Central Committee of Burundi's sole political party (UPRONA) the main legislative body to approve his decrees, and dissolved his military junta – the Supreme Revolutionary Council – composed of 30 army officers.

Meanwhile, as ethnic violence continued, former Burundian president, Michel Micombero, died of a heart attack in exile in Somalia on 16 July 1983. He was 43. According to *Africa Report*:

"Burundi's former president, Michel Micombero, died of a heart attack on July 16 in Mogadishu, Somalia.

He came to power in 1966 after deposing King Ntare, and he ruled until his ouster in 1976 by Lieutenant-Colonel Jean Baptiste Bagaza, who sent Micombero into exile in Somalia.

Micombero began his career in the military, and then served as minister of defense, secretary of state, and prime minister before installing himself as president.

Once in office, Micombero attempted to reconcile the rift between the Hutu majority and the politically dominant Tutsi minority. He began by freeing Hutu political prisoners, but his rule quickly turned repressive. Following a 1972 attempted coup, his forces turned on the Hutu, killing 100,000 people.

In Somalia, President Mohammed Siad Barre declared a three-day period of mourning for Micombero."[7]

The Hutu-Tutsi conflict also involved the Roman Catholic church which incurred the wrath of the Tutsi-dominated government.

The Catholic clergy was suspected of sympathising with the Hutu majority, a charge which led to the expulsion of many foreign priests and other missionaries in 1985.

The vast majority of the people – Hutu and Tutsi – in both Rwanda and Burundi are Catholic, and the church has great influence in their lives, although it has not been able to resolve the ethnic conflict between the two groups. Ironically, Rwanda and Burundi are the two most Christian countries in Africa.

In May 1987, Major Pierre Buyoya overthrew Bagaza, his cousin. Buyoya was also Micombero's nephew.

The new military ruler introduced reforms intended to reduce ethnic tensions but whose implementation depended on the willingness of the Tutsi to do so.

Buyoya, who went on to rule Burundi for 13 years at different times (1987 – 1993 and 1996 – 2003), became the longest-ruling president in the country's history.

After he overthrew Bagaza, he formed a cabinet to reflect ethnic composition of the country. The majority of the cabinet members he appointed were Hutu. He also chose a Hutu prime minister and encouraged the Hutu to join the Tutsi-dominated army.

But these measures did little to weaken let alone end the Tutsi's hegemonic control of the country. Real power remained in the hands of the military junta which was dominated by Tutsis. The Hutu majority continued to suffer discrimination. They had only limited educational and economic opportunities and remained virtually disenfranchised in a country where they vastly outnumbered the Tutsi 6 to 1.

Burundi again descended into chaos in August 1988 when large-scale fighting between the Hutu and the Tutsi erupted, following an abortive coup attempt by the Hutu whose condition had hardly improved in spite of the reform measures introduced by Buyoya to liberalise the political process and achieve ethnic reconciliation:

"The Tutsi-run military government under Pierre Buyoya massacred an estimated 20,000 Hutus. U.N. Officials at refugee camps near the border with Rwanda told of soldiers chasing, machine-gunning, and bayoneting fleeing Hutus."[8]

Tens of thousands of Hutus fled to Tanzania. But most of them returned to Burundi by mid-1989. However, that was only temporarily, as a new wave of violence engulfed Burundi and the entire Great Lakes region during the 1990s.

On 2 June 1993, Melchior Ndadaye, a Hutu candidate of the Burundi Democratic Front (FRODEBU), won the presidency in the first democratic elections since independence in 1962. He defeated the incumbent military ruler, Pierre Buyoya, who was the candidate of the predominantly Tutsi party, UPRONA.

Ndadaye survived a coup attempt on July 3rd and was sworn in as president on July 10th.

Buyoya had allowed the elections to take place in fulfillment of his pledge to introduce democracy and allow the Hutu to participate fully in the political process. He also believed he was going to win the election because of his liberalisation programme – democratic reforms which had never been introduced before – which may have won him considerable support, so he believed, among the Hutu.

His commitment to egalitarianism, although lukewarm, earned him enemies among his fellow Tutsis, especially hardliners including his cousin Jean-Baptiste Bagaza whom he overthrew in 1987. They saw him as a traitor.

Ndadaye tried to improve relations between the Hutu and the Tutsi and appointed a female Tutsi, Sylvie Kinigi, as prime minister. He also appointed many Tutsis as members of his cabinet. And entire third of the cabinet members were Tutsi. He also granted amnesty to Jean-Baptiste Bagaza who was living in exile and freed political prisoners.

The president also tried to redress the ethnic imbalance across the spectrum and improve living conditions of the Hutu majority who had been deprived of opportunities by the dominant Tutsis through the years. He also introduced reforms in the army and the police to reduce control by the Tutsi. Many Hutus also got government posts originally held by the Tutsi after the landslide victory in the June 1993 election by the predominantly Hutu party, FRODEBU, further infuriating Tutsis.

The freedom of speech Ndadaye allowed also made things worse. Newspapers and the radio provided extensive coverage of the reforms introduced by Ndadaye but in a way that inflamed passions, especially among the Tutsi, who now felt they had been marginalised by the Hutu rulers, although the government was not dominated by Hutus. It was fairly representative of all the people of Burundi and took into account concerns of the Tutsi in a country that was now under a Hutu president, a predominantly Hutu cabinet and parliament for the first time in the nation's history because of truly democratic elections Tutsis have always feared so much since they are vastly outnumbered by Hutus.

The changes Buyoya introduced and tried to implement angered many Tutsis who felt that their privileged position was being threatened by the new policies.

He did not last long in office. He was assassinated within four months, bayoneted to death by Tutsi soldiers on 21 October 1993 in a coup attempt engineered by Tutsi hardliners who wanted to restore Tutsi leadership of the country.

President Ndadaye's assassination infuriated the Hutu. But it also emboldened the Tutsi who saw their loss of power only as temporary.

The result was genocide in which more than 100,000 people, mostly Hutu, were massacred within one year after the assassination, and more than 500,000 fled to Tanzania, Rwanda, and Zaire.

Ndadaye's assassination was a turning point in the nation's history. It marked the beginning of the bloodiest and longest civil war in the history of Burundi. It lasted from 1993 until 2005. More than 300,000 people, mostly Hutu, died in the conflict. Some estimates put the death toll at 500,000.

The war formally ended when Pierre Nkurunziza, a Hutu and former rebel leader who fought the Tutsi, was sworn in as president in August 2005.

A few months after the civil war started in 1993, Cyprien Ntaryamira, another Hutu who had served as the minister of agriculture in the government of Ndadaye, was chosen by the parliament in January 1994 to be the president of Burundi. He was appointed to serve the remainder of Ndadaye's term which was almost the entire term since Ndadaye had been in office for only three months before he was assassinated.

Ntaryamira's appointment as president infuriated the Tutsi. And like his predecessor and fellow Hutu Melchior Ndadaye, he did not last long in office.

He died on 6 April 1994 together with the president of Rwanda, Juvénal Habyarimana, also a Hutu, after their plane was hit by a rocket over Kigali, Rwanda's capital, when they returned from Tanzania where they had participated in peace talks aimed at resolving the ethnic conflict between the Hutu and the Tutsi in both countries:

"The rockets were fired form the immediate vicinity of the Kigali airport, an area controlled by the Rwandan army."[9]

The shooting down of the plane was the beginning of a downward spiral for Rwanda. It was an incident which precipitated an orgy of killings in the Rwandan capital, Kigali, targeting Tutsis and Hutu moderates.

The killings spread rapidly, engulfing the whole country in what came to be one of the most horrific events in the history of mankind towards the end of the twentieth-century history.

The peace talks between the Hutu and the Tutsi which were held in the town of Arusha in northern Tanzania led to an agreement on the establishment of a coalition government in Rwanda. But it was bitterly opposed by Hutu extremists who did not want to share power with the Tutsi. And they are the ones who were suspected of having fired the rocket which hit the plane carrying the two Hutu presidents.

The Hutu blamed the Tutsi for shooting down the plane and, in retaliation for "killing" the two Hutu presidents, started massacring Tutsis.

The downing of the plane may have triggered the massacres, eventually leading to genocide, but the reasons for the genocide can not be explained in such simplistic terms.

And there would have been another major casualty on that plane, with wider implications for the entire region, had fate not intervened.

President Mobutu Sese Seko of Zaire who also attended the peace talks in Tanzania was supposed to have caught the same plane on his way back to Zaire but changed his mind at the last minute and delayed his departure, thus saving his life.

Although Hutu extremists were the prime suspects in the shooting of the plane, Tutsi hardliners were also suspected of having brought the plane down. Like their Hutu counterparts, they also had vehemently denounced the power-sharing agreement as a threat to their security and the very survival of their ethnic group.

It was never firmly established who fired the rocket which brought the plane down. Was it Hutu extremists? Or was it Tutsi hardliners?

What is clear is that circumstantial evidence indicated that it was probably Hutu soldiers who fired the rocket because its trajectory showed it was fired from an area controlled by the Hutu-dominated Rwandan army.

There were Hutu soldiers who were opposed to the concessions made by President Habyarimana at the peace talks in Tanzania and wanted him removed from office, by any means, in order to block implementation of the power-sharing agreement.

But others speculated that the people who killed President Habyarimana and his Burundian counterpart, Cyprien Ntaryamira, belonged to a different opposition group impatient with the delays in forming a coalition government of Hutus and Tutsis and blamed Habyarimana for that.

Whatever the case, the assassination of the two Hutu leaders provided Hutu extremists with an "excuse" to start killing Tutsis – whom they blamed for the murders – and Hutu moderates who wanted to share power with the Tutsi.

Within an hour of the announcement of the deaths of

the two leaders, the killings began, raising suspicion that the massacres had been preplanned.

The tragic incident, shooting down of the plane, not only sparked massive carnage in Rwanda but led to an escalation of violence in Burundi where the Hutu were still enraged over the assassination of the country's first Hutu president, Ndadaye, who was brutally murdered by the Tutsi only a few months before. The assassination of another Hutu president of Burundi, Cyprien Ntaryamira – to the Hutu, by who else? – only stoked the flames.

Before the civil war broke out in Rwanda in April 1994 following the assassination of President Habyarimana, Burundi was in a much worse situation than Rwanda before October 1993 when its first Hutu president, Ndadaye, was assassinated. The country was plunged into chaos following the assassination, and everything was being done by the Tutsi-dominated government to placate and contain the Hutu, employing a combination of diplomacy and brutal suppression.

In September 1994, a power-sharing agreement was reached between the Tutsi-dominated party, the Union for National Progress (UPRONA) which constituted the official opposition, and the predominantly Hutu Democratic Front of Burundi (FRODEBU) which formed the democratically elected government left behind by the two assassinated Hutu presidents, Ndadaye and Ntaryamira.

But the coalition agreement was undermined by Tutsi extremists who denounced the moderate Tutsi prime minister, Anatole Kanyenkiko, as a sellout and finally forced him to leave the predominantly Hutu government.

The situation was further complicated by the fact that former FRODEBU interior minister, Leonard Nyangoma – frustrated by the inability of the Hutu-majority government to govern effectively because of constant undermining by the traditionally powerful Tutsi military and elite – had gone into exile and formed an opposition group.

His group was known as the National Council for the Defence of Democracy (CNDD). It had an armed wing, the Democratic Defence Front (FDD), which started waging guerrilla warfare in northern Burundi from its operational bases in South Kivu Province in eastern Zaire.

The fighting between Nyangoma's Hutu guerrillas and Burundi's Tutsi-dominated army escalated towards the end of 1995 and in early 1996, with the death toll among civilians, mostly Hutu, climbing rapidly. Most of them were killed by Tutsi soldiers in indiscriminate acts of "retaliation."

With the 1994 Rwandan massacre of almost one million Tutsis still fresh in their memories and indelibly etched in their collective psyche, the Tutsi in Burundi feared they would be victims of the same kind of holocaust at the hands of their "historical enemies," the Hutu.

Caught between escalating guerrilla warfare by the FDD Hutu rebels and brutal repression by the Tutsi-dominated army, President Sylvestre Ntibantunganya – another Hutu and FRODEBU's constitutionally eligible successor to his assassinated predecessor, Ntaryamira – was reduced to being no more than a ceremonial head of state, without functional utility, at the mercy of the Tutsi.

It was in the midst of all this that former President Pierre Buyoya, a Tutsi moderate, was returned to power following a Tutsi-led military coup on 25 July 1996 which ousted Ntibantunganya.

But Buyoya himself, although a Tutsi and a soldier and therefore a member of both the dominant ethnic group and the country's most powerful institution (the army), found himself in an untenable position. A moderate who allowed Burundi's first democratic elections to take place in June-July 1993 in which he lost to a Hutu (Ndadaye), he had many enemies among fellow Tutsis who saw him as a traitor for allowing such transfer of power to the Hutu majority. And when he was returned to power in the 1996 military coup, he could not stop the atrocities being committed by the Tutsi army against innocent Hutu civilians.

Hutu support for the rebels also kept on increasing, fuelled by the atrocities being perpetrated against them by Tutsi soldiers. And when Tanzania, Kenya and Uganda imposed economic sanctions on Burundi to punish Buyoya and his Tutsi colleagues for overthrowing the constitutionally chosen Hutu president, Ntibantunganya, who headed a democratically elected although powerless government of the FRODEBU party, the Hutu guerrillas of the Democratic Defence Front (DDF) capitalised on the economic embargo and intensified their military campaign against the Tutsi regime and Tutsi civilians.

The capital itself, Bujumbura, came under attack, raising fears of an imminent holocaust against the Tutsi reminiscent of the 1994 genocide in neighbouring Rwanda.

The economic sanctions imposed on Burundi were producing dividends, however limited, because of the impact they had on the army. But the embargo did not affect the FDD guerrillas who were operating out of eastern Zaire just across the border from Burundi. Even destruction of their bases in South Kivu Province by the Banyamulenge (with the help of Rwanda, Uganda and Burundi) towards the end of 1996 was not enough to neutralise them. Instead, they stepped up their offensive against Burundi's Tutsi regime.

Between July and October 1996, the guerrillas believed that their increased offensive was about to extract concessions from the military junta in Bujumbura whose intransigence led to escalation of the conflict. President Buyoya even started to talk about negotiating with the rebels; a very dangerous move which was strongly opposed by Tutsi hardliners including his cousin Jean-Baptiste Bagaza whom he overthrew in 1987. It could very easily have cost him his life. Yet the economic sanctions seemed to be working, pushing the Tutsi regime towards the conference table. However, towards the end of October, things took an unexpected turn.

After the Hutu rebels were routed from Uvira in South Kivu Province, Zaire, by the Banyamulenge Tutsis on 26 October 1996, their leader Leonard Nyangoma fled to Tanzania where he met with Julius Nyerere, the former Tanzanian president and the force behind the diplomatic initiative to impose an economic embargo on Burundi who had been pushing for a negotiated settlement of the conflict.

But when Buyoya was asked to go to Nyerere's home in the village of Butiama in northern Tanzania for a meeting, he reneged on his promise, saying he had changed his mind and would not participate in any negotiations aimed at resolving the conflict. Tutsi hardliners gave him very little room to manoeuvre even if he had wanted to negotiate with the Hutu.

A few weeks after he refused to meet with Nyerere, he arrested former President Bagaza, his cousin, together with several other Tutsi extremist leaders; a move which gave him more freedom to operate and make his own decisions. However, with the peace process derailed, Nyangoma and his guerrillas stepped up their offensive against Buyoya's government and the Tutsi-dominated army.

The army failed to contain let alone neutralise the guerrillas and started rounding up Hutu civilians in northern Burundi and put them in concentration camps to "isolate" the insurgents; a policy which could partly be attributed to the failure of economic sanctions which had never, from the beginning, been intended to force Buyoya out of power but restore constitutional rule.

Economic Embargo

On 30 September 1996, African regional leaders agreed at a meeting in Arusha, Tanzania, to impose full economic sanctions on Burundi in response to the July 25 Tutsi-led military coup and appealed to the international community for support in enforcing the embargo.

They also demanded immediate talks between all parties within and outside Burundi. But they took no action on a report presented by military planners for armed intervention in the strife-torn country.

The secretary-general of the Organisation of of African Unity (OAU), Dr. Salim Ahmed Salim of Tanzania, confirmed the decision to impose economic sanctions on Burundi after the leaders held a summit meeting to discuss the military coup.

After more than five hours of talks, the leaders said in a statement: "The summit has decided to impose economic sanctions on Burundi and appeals to the international community to support these measures."[10] And as President Benjamin Mkapa of Tanzania put it: "This is a total economic blockade on Burundi. It was a unanimous decision. There was not a single dissenting voice."[11]

The leaders of Tanzania, Kenya, Uganda, Rwanda, Zaire, Ethiopia, Eritrea, Zambia, Cameroon, and OAU representatives led by the organisation's secretary-general, Salim Ahmed Salim, attended the summit. And the measures they agreed upon to punish Burundi's military regime were later formally ratified by the OAU and by the United Nations. Tanzania's President Mkapa who hosted the summit said a technical committee would spell out details when sanctions would start and how long they would last.

Burundi is one of the African countries which is highly vulnerable to such punitive sanctions. A small, desperately poor and landlocked nation, its economy was, even before the sanctions were imposed, already hard-hit by civil war and by the suspension of international aid because of its poor human rights record and the atrocities committed by the Tutsi army against the Hutu, especially since the brutal assassination of President Melchior Ndadaye. Because of its landlocked position, its neighbours could exercise enormous leverage on its government and help bring about fundamental change in the country by simply choking it off. It also relies almost entirely on Tanzania and Rwanda to export its coffee and tea, its main exports, and to import all its fuel and other goods.

But it is highly unlikely that Rwanda, a Tutsi-dominated state, would enforce full economic sanctions against fellow Tutsis in Burundi. And there is humanitarian concern involved in the implementation of punitive measures which hardly affect the economic wellbeing of those in power including their relatives and friends. For example, in 1996 alone, Burundi was in such a bad economic situation because of the civil war that the UN World Food Programme sent it 43,000 tons of food worth $28.5 million (USD) to alleviate the plight.

But sanctions can also be used to weaken and isolate an oppressive regime; encourage its opponents to escalate their campaign against it; turn its supporters against it because of the economic hardship and suffering caused by the sanctions; and force it to make meaningful concessions to its opponents and reach a negotiated settlement. It is in this context that the economic embargo imposed on Burundi must be viewed as an effective bargaining tool in conflict resolution in that embattled country.

The coup which prompted Burundi's neighbours to impose an economic embargo was a direct result of the Tutsi dissatisfaction with the coalition government under Hutu President Ntibantunganya; a dissatisfaction deeply rooted in the animosity and distrust between the two ethnic groups. This was clearly demonstrated by the fact that even power-sharing between them had failed to reduce – let alone end – the ethnic violence plaguing the country.

Many parts of Burundi were so wracked by violence that they were totally out of government control and had become virtually inaccessible. Only the most reckless would even think of going into those areas.

Then the power-sharing agreement, negotiated after the abortive Tutsi-led coup of October 1993 in which Hutu President Melchior Ndadaye was assassinated, collapsed because the Tutsi demanded more power.

On 24 July 1996, the Tutsi political party, UPRONA, withdrew from the coalition with FRODEBU, the Hutu party. The end of the coalition marked the end of the government.

The Tutsi prime minister, Antoine Nduwayo, was rendered powerless by fellow Tutsis; so was the Hutu president, Sylvestre Ntibantunganya, who fled to the American embassy in Bujumbura where he was given sanctuary.

The situation degenerated into chaos as marauding bands of club-wielding young Tutsis took over large sections of the capital Bujumbura with the tacit support of the Tutsi-dominated army which did nothing to stop them.

Then on the following day, 25 July, the army announced that it had seized power and that Major Perre Buyoya, the former military ruler, would be the leader of the new military regime.

The ouster of the coalition government did not come as a surprise. There had been rumours circulating in the capital and elsewhere that Tutsi hardliners in the army were about to execute a coup. The city was gripped with fear, and many people speculated that another genocide was imminent. According to a report from Bujumbura by *The Economist*, 27 July 1996:

"Seasoned visitors to Burundi's capital – which, cleansed of Hutus, now belongs to the 14 per cent

Burundians who are Tutsi – said they had never seen the city so fearful. Not, however, of a coup, let alone a fall of government. Burundians' overriding fear has been that extremists, on either side of the ethnic divide, could send the violence that has killed more than 150,000 people in the past three years spiralling into genocide.

Such fears seemed confirmed last weekend when 350 displaced Tutsis, mostly women and children, living in a settlement at Bugendena in central Burundi, were horribly slaughtered.

Reports by survivors suggest that their attack was masterminded by the rebel Hutu army led by Leonard Nyangoma from just across the border in Zaire, possibly in collusion with elements from the old Rwandan army, also in exile.

On July 23rd, when President Ntibantunganya tried to visit the scene of the massacre, he was stoned by Tutsi protesters and forced to beat a retreat – all the way to the American embassy."[12]

In fact, he was almost lynched and miraculously escaped from the mob.

The Hutu rebel attacks were met with a swift response from the Tutsi army which used them to justify its indiscriminate campaign of terror against Hutu civilians who were targeted mainly because of their ethnicity.

The army also targeted Rwandan Hutu refugees who settled in northern Burundi after they fled their country for fear of reprisals by the victorious predominantly Tutsi Rwandan Patriotic Front (RPF) for the 1994 genocide. And the fact that the refugee camps had some of the perpetrators of the genocide hiding among innocent civilian refugees made the campaign by Tutsi soldiers more credible when they targeted those camps.

However, the presence of Hutu extremists in the camps was also used by the Tutsi government to justify its mass expulsion of Rwandan Hutus from northern Burundi even when there was no need to do so:

"The forcible repatriation of several thousand Rwandan refugees from northern Burundi...began on July 19 (1996) just before the massacre (of 350 displaced Tutsis in a settlement at Bugendena in central Burundi towards the end of July).

Of the estimated 85,000 Rwandans (mostly Hutu) in Burundi, more than 13,000 have so far been crammed into lorries and dumped across the border."[13]

Many of them arrived in Rwanda only to find their homes, farms and property had been taken by Tutsi exiles who were among the one million Tutsis who returned to Rwanda after the genocidal Hutu regime collapsed in July 1994.

But in spite of what happened next door in Rwanda in 1994, a holocaust unprecedented in modern times in terms of magnitude and intensity in telescoped time (one million people slaughtered in 100 days at a rate five times faster than Hitler killed the Jews), the international community did nothing to avert a probable catastrophe in Burundi where low-intensity warfare was claiming countless lives, with a potential for another genocide may be even on a scale equal to or bigger than Rwanda's.

On 22 July 1996, the UN secretary-general, Boutros Boutros-Ghali, asked the Security Council to support a military intervention in Burundi under UN auspices. But his appeal fell on deaf ears.

In Africa itself, a regional East African intervention force – of Tanzanians, Ugandans, and Ethiopians – was being mobilised to cope with the situation. However, nothing went beyond the preparatory stage.

The crisis intervention force could not intervene without Burundi's approval. The Tutsi army itself, the most powerful institution in the country, was in no mood for that. And that was before the coup. Tutsi leaders became even more intransigent after that. Because of its enormous power, the army could veto any decision by the civilian government headed by the Hutu president, Ntibantunganya, and his Tutsi prime minister, Antoine Nduwayo.

The deteriorating security situation in the country had, in June 1996, prompted the civilian government to request military intervention from its East African neighbours before everything spun out of control. But the Tutsi vetoed it, with threats:

"Last month (in June 1996), Mr. Nduwayo was persuaded to join Mr. Ntibantunganya in 'inviting' such a force into Burundi to provide 'security assistance.'

'Traitor,' shouted his fellow-Tutsis. Under this attack, Mr. Nduwayo vacillated, eventually deciding that he resolutely opposed outside intervention, which, he said, would not only fail to prevent massacres but would make the situation worse."[14]

In opposing intervention, Nduwayo had partially rehabilitated himself with his fellow Tutsis many of whom agreed with him when he said the presence of foreign troops would only make things worse.

One main reason for this opposition is that throughout the history of the Hutu-Tutsi ethnic conflict in both Rwanda and Burundi, the Tutsi have repeatedly complained that neighbouring countries – Tanzania, Congo, Kenya, and Uganda (before Yoweri Museveni, of Tutsi ancestry himself, according to some reports, became Ugandan president) – favour the Hutu; a charge without foundation which former Tanzanian President Julius Nyerere dismissed as "nonsense," adding, "we have heard it before," when he was the chief mediator in Burundi's conflict and the main force behind the economic embargo imposed on the Tutsi regime in Bujumbura.

One of the most prominent and outspoken Tutsi leaders

who blamed Nyerere for favouring the Hutu was Charles Mukasi. There were also reports that Tutsi hardliners planned to assassinate Nyerere. A planned visit to Bujumbura by Nyerere during the mediation of the conflict was also cancelled for security reasons cited by the Tanzanian intelligence service.

The underlying argument by the Tutsi – who are Nilotic in origin but who are now also Bantu after centuries of intermarriage with the Hutu majority – is that the people of neighbouring countries take sides with the Hutu because the vast majority of them are Bantu (which is a linguistic designation, not a racial category, since there is no Bantu race) like the Hutu; totally ignoring the asymmetrical relationship between the two ethnic groups in both countries, with the Tutsi minority as the dominant group denying the Hutu majority equal rights and opportunity.

It is an observation that has been made even by foreign missionaries who, because of their sympathy towards the oppressed Hutu majority, were expelled from Burundi in 1985 by the Tutsi military regime led by Jean-Baptiste Bagaza. Many of them had worked there for years.

It was in an attempt to rectify this situation – of Hutu oppression by the Tutsi – that Burundi's neighbours imposed economic sanctions on the Tutsi-dominated state which deliberately functioned as an ethnocracy, for the Tutsi, more than anything else.

Some of the people who were vehemently opposed to the East African intervention force included many Tutsi hardliners in Burundi's army, several of whom were involved in the1993 abortive coup in which President Ndadaye was assassinated. They had an unfinished agenda which would be difficult to pursue in the presence of foreign troops.

Hutu rebels were also opposed to intervention. While their Tutsi enemies vetoed foreign intervention in order to maintain the status quo and preserve Tutsi supremacy, the

Hutu wanted the East African force kept out of Burundi so that they could pursue, without hindrance, their goal to end Tutsi hegemonic control of the country.

The crisis intervention force was supposed to protect government leaders including cabinet members and senior civil servants as well as vital institutions and installations such as banks, the post office, the airport and power plants. But security for the leaders and different establishments in the country would not have stopped the ethnic violence between the Tutsi army and the Hutu rebels. And it would not have saved the lives of innocent civilians, both Hutu and Tutsi, who were being slaughtered at will by the combatants, targeting them purely on ethnic basis.

The regional security force never, of course, intervened in Burundi. It was never invited by President Sylvestre Ntibantunganya and Prime Minister Antoine Nduwayo who had Tutsi hardliners breathing down their necks. And after their government was overthrown, that option was completely ruled out. It was now time to see whether or not economic sanctions would work, since it was obvious that the new Tutsi military regime had no intention of inviting the East African intervention force, let alone giving up power.

The sanctions began to have an impact soon after they were imposed. Within only a few days, many Burundians especially in the capital became fully aware of the stranglehold neighbouring countries, mainly Tanzania, had on their fragile economy.

Rwandan Tutsi rulers, out of solidarity with fellow Tutsis in Burundi, may have wanted to avoid enforcing the sanctions. But their ability to do so was severely limited because their country is landlocked and is itself dependent on Kenya for an outlet to the sea. Burundi, on the other hand, is heavily dependent on Tanzania for that. According to *The Wall Street Journal*, 5 August 1996:

"Gas stations shut down in Burundi's capital after Tanzania closed its border to impose an embargo to force out the new military-installed government. Meanwhile, a U.N. Report says Burundi's army massacred thousands of Hutus in April and May."[15]

The massacres had been going on – on a large scale – since October 1993 when President Ndadaye was bayoneted to death by Tutsi soldiers, plunging the country into chaos. And although the economic embargo did not stop the carnage, it caused a lot of hardship for the army. Fuel shortage restricted the army's mobility, and lack of goods and equipment in general, including spare parts, caused other logistical problems for the military because of the economic sanctions being enforced by Tanzania.

Of all the East African countries, Tanzania was in the best position to enforce the embargo even without the help of other countries because more than 70 per cent of Burundi's imports and exports got through her territory.

The Tanzanian government tightened the noose around Burundi to try to force the Tutsi military junta to relinquish power by blocking oil and tanker trucks and lorries and other vehicles at the border. As a senior Tanzanian official said on 5 August 1996: "The border is closed. Nothing is going in and nothing is going out."[16]

But, in spite of the sanctions, the Tutsi were determined to hang on to power at any cost because of what they believe, rightly or wrongly, to be a threat to their very existence and survival as a people.

Vastly outnumbered by the Hutu, they fear they will perish unless they are the sole rulers of both Rwanda and Burundi; an uncompromising stand – despite professions to the contrary by the Tutsi – which has made power sharing impossible. Any concessions they have made to the Hutu have been minimal and have not loosened their grip on power, thus perpetuating the ethnic conflict.

Therefore any meaningful change has to be pursued

through a combination of punitive measures and diplomacy with the help of the neighbouring countries and the rest of the international community as happened in the case of apartheid South Africa. And that is not a far-fetched analogy.

Tutsi domination and oppression of the Hutu is another form of apartheid; it is black apartheid. But security concerns of the Tutsi as a vulnerable minority if they were to lose power or play a subordinate role in both Rwanda and Burundi where they are vastly outnumbered by the Hutu must also be taken into account.

Tanzania was the first country to enforce the embargo against Burundi, not only to oust the Tutsi military regime but also to help the Hutu actively participate in the political process in a meaningful way. Although the African leaders who imposed the sanctions did not explicitly state that their intention was to remove the Tutsi minority regime from power and replace it with a democratic government, that is exactly what they intended to do when they approved the embargo.

Even Rwanda, a Tutsi state, supported the sanctions, although only symbolically by signing the embargo agreement. In what amounted to no more than a symbolic gesture, Rwanda's foreign affairs minister announced on 5 August 1996 that his country would soon join the sanctions effort. Yet no one took him seriously.

Ethnic solidarity among the Tutsi is paramount and transcends regional interests. The powerful Tutsi minority in Rwanda sympathise with their kinsmen in Burundi and will not do anything to make them suffer regardless of what other regional leaders say.

The immediate effect of the sanctions was petroleum shortage. But the embargo had an impact in other areas as well. Commodities traders said the embargo had doubled the price of salt and other items and pushed up the price of other goods, some of which were no longer available on the market.

Around the same time, South Africa's Deputy President Thabo Mbeki arrived in Tanzania for talks with President Benjamin Mkapa on the Burundi crisis. South African President Nelson Mandela, who had been under increasing pressure to become directly involved in action against Burundi, said his country would act as a part of regional and continental efforts to bring about fundamental change in the landlocked East African country.

On 4 August 1996, Burundi's military ruler Major Pierre Buyoya denied again that he had executed a coup. He went on to say that his action was "an operation to save a people in distress. After all, it is better to face sanctions than to be killed. Countries which have not yet understood the change, particularly Tanzania, will understand."[17]

Buyoya's sentiments on the economic embargo were echoed by the United Nations. On 7 August, the UN made a passionate appeal to Tanzania and Kenya for permission to send food aid to more than 700,000 war refugees in Burundi.

The two countries imposed a tight air, road and water embargo on the landlocked nation which had a major impact because of their access to the sea. Both are bordered by the Indian Ocean. And a sustained embargo – especially by these two countries – could, at the very least, have brought down the Tutsi military junta and paved the way for a return to constitutional order.

As the embargo continued, blockading the coffee- and tea-producing nation to try to force the military regime to restore civilian rule, Major Buyoya said in an interview published on August 7th that he was willing to negotiate with the Hutu if they laid down their weapons. He told the French daily *Le Figaro*: "There will be a national debate. We'll find a solution."

He also pledged to put an end to "abuses and mistakes" after UN observers reported that thousands of Hutu civilians had been killed in recent months: "In a civil war, abuses and mistakes are possible," he said. "We will do all

98

we can to put an end to this. We will use discipline to fight against it."[18]

Buyoya also pledged "all guarantees" for the security of former President Ntibantunganya whom he overthrew and who took refuge in the American embassy in Bujumbura. He said about the ousted president: "I have also suggested he participate in the institutions working for the transition."[19]

UN officials said unless Tanzania and Kenya allowed humanitarian aid to pass to Burundi, the plight of those in need would dramatically deteriorate. In a letter to President Benjamin Mkapa of Tanzania and President Daniel arap Moi of Kenya, the United Nations promised to "put into place a framework that will ensure food reaches only those it is intended for."[20]

Uganda joined the blockade on August 7th, and the state-owned Air Burundi had only one foreign destination, Kigali, the capital of neighbouring Rwanda, another Tutsi-dominated state, which said it would not enforce the sanctions.

Rwanda's vice president and defence minister, General Paul Kagame, the country's most powerful man and *de facto* ruler, told BBC in an interview: "We are going to work with them and help them find a solution."[21].

He was critical of the seven-nation African summit which imposed the economic embargo, saying a mechanism should have been put in place so that the imposition of the sanctions was not done on a country-by-country basis.

But the main and probably only reason why Kagame refused to enforce the embargo was his government's sympathy for fellow Tutsis in Burundi; the kind of ethnic solidarity and ethnocentrism that has helped ignite and fuel tribal warfare in this highly combustible region through the years.

Had he cared about justice, he would have frankly acknowledged Tutsi oppression of the Hutu as the main problem in both Rwanda and Burundi, at the very least as one of the major problems, just as was the case in Rwanda where the Hutu ruled from 1962 to 1994 and discriminated against the Tutsi under a brutal Hutu ethnocracy which also instigated the 1994 holocaust in which almost one million Tutsis perished.

As Buyoya vacillated, without fully committing himself to negotiations with the Hutu for ethnic and pragmatic considerations (Tutsi hardliners could kill him if he made major or too many concessions to the Hutu, and his people, the Tutsi, would be out of power if he re-introduced democracy as he did in 1993), the East African leaders calibrated a graduated response to his initiatives – or lack thereof – to induce him to make fundamental changes short of calling for his ouster.

Not asking him to step down was itself a diplomatic tactic. It was intended to encourage him to cooperate and work with Tutsi moderates to keep Tutsi hardliners at bay; most of the hardliners would like to overthrow him and derail the peace process. However, regional leaders were emphatic in their demand. According to *The Economist*, 3 August 1996:

"They all called for an immediate return to constitutional order in Burundi, with the restoration of parliament and the unbanning of (political) parties.

They stopped short of demanding the reinstatement of ex-President Sylvestre Ntibantunganya...And they also postponed their call for foreign intervention, giving Mr. Buyoya until mid-August to implement the reforms."[22]

Although the regional leaders postponed their call for a crisis intervention force to intervene in Burundi, they still appealed to the international community to support them in enforcing the economic embargo. Buyoya reciprocated by appointing a Hutu prime minister, not only as a gesture of goodwill to the East African leaders who imposed the sanctions, but also as an effort to ease ethnic tensions and initiate meaningful dialogue with the Hutu.

It is a fact of life in relations among nations that countries have temporary friends but permanent interests. That explains why Rwanda and Uganda, both friends of Burundi, joined the call to isolate the Tutsi regime in Bujumbura, although Rwanda's protest was only symbolic.

But it is clear why the other neighbouring countries imposed the economic embargo on Burundi, besides their desire to see a restoration of constitutional order in that embattled nation.

The holocaust in Rwanda which sent waves of refugees pouring across their borders was still fresh in their minds. They could contemplate a scenario similar to that, unfolding in Burundi, if they did not arrest the situation. Otherwise they would have to prepare for the worst: be inundated with an influx of refugees, should Burundi collapse and descend into anarchy.

Therefore it was also purely a matter of national interest why Tanzania and other countries wanted to restore civilian rule in Burundi before millions of refugees started flooding them.

But prospects for a negotiated settlement of the ethnic conflict remained bleak, even as the embargo was being applied to achieve this goal.

The gulf between the two sides had widened even further when the Tutsi army cleansed Bujumbura virtually of all Hutus in 1995. The capital was now inhabited almost exclusively by the Tutsi; hardly a sign of good intentions towards the Hutu majority who have always been excluded from power and denied equal opportunity in all areas.

Even the appointment of Pascal Firmin Ndimira, a Hutu – who had been agriculture minister in 1994, and vice-chancellor of Bujumbura University – as prime minister, did nothing to bring the two sides any closer. "Mr. Buyoya has said he will talk to Leonard Nyangoma's

Hutu rebels who operate from Zaire, controlling large tracts of land in northern Burundi, but only if they first lay down their arms. For his part, Mr. Nyangoma has vowed to go on mobilising the Hutu people until Mr. Buyoya and his Tutsi entourage capitulate."[23]

The Hutu majority had few illusions about Buyoya, despite his professions of good intentions. He was strongly suspected of having instigated the 1993 coup attempt which led to President Melchior Ndadaye's death and that of up to 100,000 other Burundians, mostly Hutu. The suspicion had credibility because it was backed up by UN investigators in Burundi.

And former President Jean-Baptiste Bagaza, who was overthrown by Buyoya in 1987, added fuel to the UN report when he implicated his rival (who was also his cousin) in the October 1993 abortive coup which took place only about four months after Buyoya lost the election to Ndadaye.

But many Tutsis, probably the majority, remained unperturbed by Buyoya's alleged complicity in Ndadaye's assassination, thus adding credibility to the charge that he was indeed involved in the murder in order to neutralise Hutu attempts to gain political power and perpetuate Tutsi hegemonic control of the country. And the Tutsi remained defiant even in the face of a sustained economic embargo. By mid-August 1996, most foreigners left Burundi as the sanctions continued to inflict pain on this landlocked, impoverished nation.[24]

Yet the choices have always been clear in this perennial conflict. The ethnic violence will continue for as long as the Hutu majority are excluded from power; and for as long as the Tutsi minority continue to fear that they will be exterminated.

Economic sanctions could not solve this dilemma and even failed to dislodge the Tutsi from power. But that is mainly because they were not fully enforced on sustained basis even if they had to go on for years to achieve the goal: to choke off the Tutsi-dominated state and enable the Hutu majority achieve equality with the Tutsi minority in a country that equally belongs to them. Therefore, in one way, Tutsi solidarity prevailed.[25]

And there is no doubt that ethnic nationalism will continue to play a central role in the volatile politics of the region for many years and can be contained only when the Tutsi-dominated states of Rwanda and Burundi truly become pluralistic societies with extensive devolution of power probably in a confederation of ethnostates.

The ethnic problems in these two countries require radical and innovative solutions, including separation, which may or may not be applicable or necessary in other African contexts.

Rationale for Intervention

African countries have been pathetically inept at settling their own conflicts through the years since independence in the sixties. They have, instead, relied on foreign intervention to save them – from themselves.

But the involvement of the East and Central African states in Burundi's crisis gave some hope that Africans have the capacity and the determination to solve their own problems without begging foreigners to do that for them, thus making a mockery of their independence.

The intervention by Burundi's neighbours, although limited, was endorsed by the Organisation of African Unity (OAU) – whose solid reputation in conflict resolution rests on its unenviable status as a prestigious debating club and, as Nyerere put it, "a trade union of tyrants" – in a move which was a dramatic departure from its avowed policy of non-intervention in the internal affairs of member states.

Tanzania, Kenya, Uganda, Ethiopia, Zaire, and Zambia, minus Rwanda, severed commercial, air and road links to Burundi; not only to exert pressure on its fragile economy in order to force the Tutsi military regime to capitulate, but also to send a warning to potential coup makers and aspiring military dictators that coups will no longer be tolerated in the region and elsewhere on the continent; and that Africans don't need external intervention to settle their disputes.

Usually, Buyoya's seizure of power in July 1996 would have been virtually ignored or simply accepted by other African states as just another change of government and a ritual of African politics – which was none of their business as long as it took place outside their borders.

Since the founding of the OAU in Addis Ababa, Ethiopia, in May 1963, member states have upheld the principle of non-intervention with religious devotion, and colonial boundaries inherited at independence as sacrosanct. Thus, when Nigeria was plunged into a civil war (1967 – 1970) which could have led to the annihilation of an entire people – the Igbos of Eastern Nigeria who seceded from the federation and declared independence as the Republic of Biafra, had they not surrendered – most African countries, hence, officially, the OAU, refused to exert enough pressure and diplomatic influence on the Nigerian federal military government to induce it to stop the war it was waging against its own people and seek a negotiated settlement. This approach was flatly rejected at the OAU summit of the African heads of state in Algiers, Algeria, in September 1968. According to *Africa Research Bulletin*:

"At a plenary meeting, Tanzania, Zambia, Gabon and the Ivory Coast (the only African countries which recognised Biafra as an independent state) urged that the OAU should demand an immediate ceasefire in the Nigeria war followed by renewed negotiations between the two sides. This view was opposed by many speakers who supported the majority view that the war was an internal

104

Nigerian affair and that Nigerian territorial integrity must be maintained at all costs."[26]

If the massacre of the Igbo in Northern Nigeria and the potential for their extermination during the civil war was Nigeria's internal affair and was a price worth paying to save the Nigerian federation, then the persecution of black people in South Africa under apartheid was equally South Africa's internal affair. Yet other African countries went up in arms, as they vigorously protested and supported the freedom fighters against the apartheid regime.

President Julius Nyerere once addressed this subject with regard to non-intervention in the internal affairs of other countries. He said when an entire people are targeted for discrimination and even extermination, it ceases to be a an internal affair and becomes a matter of concern for all mankind.

That was clearly the case with the Igbos in Nigeria where tens of thousands were massacred and up to 2 million of them perished in the war; it was also the case with South Africa where the apartheid regime espoused the doctrine of white supremacy, oppressing blacks and other non-whites.

And that is clearly the case with Rwanda and Burundi where both the Hutu and the Tutsi have been victims of genocide, only in varying degrees, through the years, killing each other. The crisis calls for intervention whether the rulers, Hutu or Tutsi, like it or not.

But that is not the logic of African leaders. They contend otherwise.

The massacre of about 500,000 – some estimates say 800,000 – people in Uganda under Idi Amin (at least 150 people were killed every day); President Masie Nguema's 11-year reign of terror during which one-third of the population of Equatorial Guinea – about 100,000 people – fled into exile and an estimated 40,000 were tortured and killed; and the 1994 Rwandan genocide were all matters of internal affairs in which other African countries had no business interfering, as indeed was the case. None interfered in those countries, except Uganda when Tanzania got rid of Amin.

In all those cases, other African countries said nothing, and did nothing, to protest or try to stop the pogroms.

By the same criterion, the brutal suppression of the Hutu by the Tutsi army and security forces in Burundi – and in Rwanda by the predominantly Tutsi Rwandan Patriotic Front (RPF) since it seized power in 1994 – is an internal affair to be handled by the Tutsi themselves.

Yet in a complete reversal, the OAU said, "No," in the case of Burundi and supported the initiative by its neighbours to impose economic sanctions on the Tutsi regime to try to force it out of office.

Besides its desire to solve its own problems, Africa is also aware that the rest of the world does not care much about the continent, if at all, except when the interests of the world powers are at stake.

But there are also several reasons for that – why the rest of the world doesn't care about Africa. There is compassion deficit. There is also fatigue, with other people, non-Africans, asking: When are African wars and other major problems – corruption, tyranny, tribalism, poor governance, economic mismanagement, lack of transparency, outright theft by leaders who raid national coffers with impunity, to name only a few – when are all these problems going to end?

There are also considerations of national interest: What do the big powers and other countries have to gain or lose by intervening in or by staying out of African conflicts?

Then there is racism: The victims of ethnic cleansing in Kosovo "look just like us and like our children," unlike those in Rwanda and Burundi. "We even give ice cream to the children in Kosovo. They're happy and even play soccer outside because they are well taken care of, by us," yet "we have no money, we can't afford food for starving

106

African refugees, not even cheap maize flour to make porridge which is a whole meal for them – and which is all they need. They aren't used to anything good like our people in Kosovo."

So Africans have to learn to be on their own – we have to learn to depend on ourselves.

After the debacles of Somalia, Liberia, and Angola, and an almost total lack of interest in the plight of Sierra Leone despite ardent pleas to the international community for help, Africans know that the United Nations will not rush to rescue them.

Sometimes there are legitimate reasons for that.

UN peace keepers were killed and run out of Somalia; they were "exhausted" in Liberia; expelled from Angola; refused to intervene in Rwanda where they could have saved the Tutsi and prevented the genocide; stayed out of Sierra Leone until late in 1999 and, even then, they were mostly Nigerians who were already there constituting the bulk of the West African peacekeeping force and simply changed hats from ECOMOG to UN; and also did not intervene in Burundi and other hot spots across the continent.

After months of delay and lukewarm efforts to find a diplomatic solution to the conflict in Burundi, the UN refused to intervene as the country degenerated into chaos. The Security Council ruled out military intervention but offered no alternative or other options to resolve the conflict; yet another reminder to Africans that you are on your own.

Such UN indifference and OAU's unwillingness or incapacity to act allowed Julius Nyerere, the former president of Tanzania, to take the initiative in trying to resolve the conflict in Burundi; a role which enabled him to exert great influence during the crisis.

For months before the July 1996 coup, he led mediation efforts which brought the two sides together but without resolving the conflict because of the intransigence of both parties, especially the Tutsi who were determined to perpetuate themselves in power. In response to that, he promised "peace enforcement" if the rival parties refused to negotiate and make meaningful concessions. It is this 'peace enforcement" which led to the imposition of economic sanctions on Burundi.

As the sanctions began to bite, Burundi's response was swift, invoking moral arguments as well, to try to undermine the legitimacy and credibility of the embargo as a tool of conflict resolution. But that did not dissuade Tanzania, Burundi's neighbour and direct access to the sea – and probably the most strategically located country in the alliance of embargo supporters, with Kenya being next because of her access to the Indian Ocean like Tanzania but not Burundi's immediate neighbour – from enforcing the economic sanctions.

The other countries also enforced the sanctions in varying degrees, with Uganda doing so only half-heartedly because of her friendship with Burundi, while Rwanda did nothing – besides her symbolic gesture of endorsing the embargo. Without Tanzania's participation, the economic sanctions would have had very little impact on Burundi.

By 10 August 1996, more than 2,000 metric tons of UN food destined for refugee camps in Burundi were being held up in Dar es Salaam, Tanzania, in compliance with the embargo.

The Tanzanian *Sunday News* (the sister paper of the *Daily News*), 11 August 1996, quoted officials in Kigoma, the Tanzanian port on Lake Tanganyika through which most of the Burundi-bound traffic passes, as saying three ships loaded with food had been stopped from sailing to Burundi's capital Bujumbura.[27]

The impact of the sanctions was officially acknowledged by the Burundian government.

Burundi's new foreign affairs minister, Luc Rukingama, said on August 10th in Brussels, Belgium, that the embargo was having a disastrous impact on his country's economy and hurting the most vulnerable people:

"Now it's a matter of explaining, of informing and showing that this embargo is politically without foundation, completely unproductive, morally unacceptable and a catastrophe economically. (Sanctions) work against the children, women, old people and all the men of the country."[28]

Rukingama became minister of foreign affairs in a transitional government formed on 2 August 1996, about one week after President Sylvestre Ntibantunganya was overthrown.

The Tutsi military rulers claimed they seized power to prevent genocide in Burundi. Yet it was their attempt to seize power in October 1993 which triggered the genocide of more than 200,000 (some say 500,000) people, mostly Hutu, within three years after the newly elected President Melchior Ndadaye was bayoneted to death by Tutsi soldiers; an assassination that enraged his kinsmen, the Hutu, who started killing Tutsis, thus provoking an extremely brutal retaliatory response from the Tutsi army which went on the rampage, massacring hundreds of thousands of Hutu civilians including children. No-one was spared. Every Hutu was prime target.

Therefore, there was no reason to believe why a complete takeover by the Tutsi army would stop the very genocide it had started and which it actually had no intention of stopping, as was clearly demonstrated by the extremely brutal repression and continued indiscriminate mass killings of Hutu civilians by Tutsi soldiers even after Buyoya seized power in July 1996.

Since the coup, both sides continued to accuse each other of committing atrocities. And the victims were not getting enough attention, if any, with sanctions compounding the problem.

The international medical charity, Doctors Without Borders, said in August 1996 that the economic embargo was blocking medicine from reaching the victims, and supplies in Burundi were drying up.[29] But in spite of all that, the regional leaders tightened the sanctions.

On August 16th, regional foreign ministers meeting in Kampala, Uganda, banned travel to their countries by the members of Burundi's military regime. Zambia also joined the blockade.

However, the ministers decided to allow medical supplies and food for Rwandan Hutu refugees in Burundi to pass across the border. They also set up a committee, based in Kenya, to coordinate the embargo.[30]

In a coordinated strategy – augmented by the impact of the embargo – to undermine the legitimacy of the Tutsi military regime, Burundi's ousted Hutu president, Sylvestre Ntibantunganya, insisted that he still was the legal head of state, in spite of the fact that he was overthrown and was now a refugee in the American embassy where he was admitted on July 23rd, two days before the coup.

In a statement from him issued by his predominantly Hutu Front for the Democratisation of Burundi (FRODEBU) on August 19th, Ntibantunganya said that Burundi's only legal institutions were his presidency, the National Assembly, and his government.[31]

The statement was released in Nairobi, Kenya, where his party had offices, waging a campaign against the Tutsi military junta. It was a direct response to what Buyoya did after he seized power: he claimed the presidency, formed a government, suspended the National Assembly, and banned all political parties. As Ntibantuganya stated: "The Parliament elected on June 3, 1993, remains the sole legitimate legislative institution."[32]

He thanked neighbouring states for their coordinated effort to punish the Tutsi military regime and force Buyoya to relinquish power.

Their involvement in Burundi's crisis set a precedent in the regional context. No such coordinated effort had been made before to deal with a regional crisis. That is why Idi Amin's reign of terror went unanswered and lasted for more than 8 years (25 January 1971 – 10 April 1979 when the capital Kampala fell), as most of the neighbours looked the other way. And that is why nothing was done by the East African countries to stop the 1994 genocide in Rwanda.

But in spite of such retrogressive isolationism, their 1996 intervention in Burundi had been preceded by another intervention in the region, although on unilateral basis. And that was by Tanzania when Idi Amin annexed 710 square miles of her territory in November 1978, triggering a six-month full-scale war which led to his downfall. He fled on 11 April 1979 in a helicopter and went into exile in Libya.

Economic sanctions against Burundi could have achieved the same objective – ouster of a reprehensible regime – had the two countries in the embargo effort, Tanzania and Kenya, used their strategic location as coastal states to compel the rest to enforce the punitive measures.

Kenya could – and should – have denied both Uganda and Rwanda access to the sea, totally blocking their exports and imports, unless they isolated Burundi entirely. And both Kenya and Tanzania should have blocked Burundi's imports and exports until the Tutsi regime relinquished control and allowed the Hutu majority to share power with the Tutsi minority on the basis of a mutually acceptable formula. Tanzania by herself could have enforced a total blockade of Burundi's exports and imports passing through her territory.

That is probably the only way the Tutsi regime in Burundi could have been forced to capitulate, short of military intervention – an unrealistic scenario in the absence of a regional crisis intervention force.

111

The survival of the Tutsi military regime in Burundi was one more sad chapter in the history of the country and of this highly volatile region. The military rulers only succeeded in perpetuating what is probably the most violent ethnic conflict – Hutu versus Tutsi – on the entire continent.

Its resolution may require bold initiatives unprecedented in the history of post-colonial Africa. The context in which this conflict can be resolved is the subject I have addressed in my other book: *Civil Wars in Rwanda and Burundi: Conflict Resolution in Africa.*

Chapter Three:

Perennial Conflict: The Road to Nowhere

AT THE CENTRE of the Great Lakes crisis is the fate of the powerless Hutu majority whose disenfranchisement guarantees only one thing: perpetual conflict in both Rwanda and Burundi, with its repercussions spreading throughout the region.

Although the Tutsi minority are in power, they are still not secure precisely because they continue to deny the Hutu majority the security they themselves don't have, but which they could have if they conceded the legitimacy of the Hutu demand for equality – one simple word, "equality," whose meaning Tutsi leaders pretend they don't understand or are incapable of comprehending.

The Hutu's subordinate status as a disenfranchised and powerless majority has been clearly demonstrated by the brutal mistreatment they have endured under Tutsi domination through the years, including their predicament as permanent refugees being shuttled back and forth across borders as if they have no country. They belong somewhere, yet they belong nowhere.

The situation in Burundi about a month after the July 1996 military coup is illustrative of their predicament as a "homeless" people. According to a report from Butare, Rwanda, in the *International Herald Tribune*:

"Hundreds of Rwandan Hutu refugees fled Burundi on Tuesday (20 August) for their equally troubled homeland despite assurances from Burundi's new Tutsi leader, Major Pierre Buyoya, that he was opposed to any expulsions.

UN officials said 500 Rwandans had arrived by noon Tuesday at Musenge transit camp outside Butare. A convoy of trucks packed with a total of 1,200 more refugees was also heading from Magara camp on its way to Butare.

The refugees accuse the Tutsi-dominated Burundian Army of harassment and say they fear for their lives.

About 2 million Rwandan Hutu fled their homeland to Zaire, Tanzania and Burundi in 1994 after Tutsi rebels defeated the Hutu-led army and ousted the government, blamed for the genocide of up to a million Tutsi and moderate Hutu.

Major Buyoya pledged Tuesday to protect the refugees after they complained of harassment and beatings from his army....

Shortly after the July 25 coup that brought him to power, Major Buyoya ordered an end to expulsions of Rwandan Hutu refugees."[1]

But the expulsions continued, and the Hutu ended up in their homeland where they found themselves not welcome by the Tutsi who blamed them for the 1994genocide, despite the fact that not every Hutu supported or took part in the massacres.

This is just one case which demonstrates the deep hatred and mistrust between the two groups, and for perfectly understandable reasons in spite of the injustice the Hutu majority have suffered through the years, as did the Tutsi under a brutal Hutu regime in Rwanda – for 32 years from July 1962 to July 1994 – which consolidated a Hutu ethnocracy.

It is a dilemma both groups, in both countries (Rwanda and Burundi), will continue to face for years: how to reconcile legitimate fear of the Tutsi, that they could be exterminated if they relinquish power, with the Hutu's genuine aspirations for equality and power as a legitimate democratic majority. They may not be divided by an implacable wall of hostility, but the perception exists even among themselves that they are, considering the asymmetrical relationship that exists between the two groups in both countries, with the Tutsi perpetuating their dominance.

Under such circumstances, even partition of the two countries along ethnic lines into independent Hutu and Tutsi ethnostates becomes an attractive proposition in order to achieve peaceful coexistence, reprehensible as this option is, especially in the context of Pan-Africanism. But if that is the only way the two countries can end the bloodshed, so be it. Even some African leaders, such as Kenyan President Daniel arap Moi, have endorsed this as a viable solution; Moi said so publicly in 1996. Other leaders have done so quietly.

What is even more repugnant is the willingness of many African leaders to sanction ethnocide – as happened against the Igbos in Nigeria during the civil war, and in Rwanda and Burundi against both the Hutu and the Tutsi – regardless of the cost, just for the sake of African unity: keep African countries united, don't let them break up into smaller, weaker nations, even if we have to loose millions of lives in the name of African unity or just to maintain the territorial integrity of our countries.

That is what has prevented them from recognising Somaliland as an independent state in spite of the fact that it has all the attributes of a sovereign entity as a functional state contrasted with the rest of Somalia which is a wasteland.

In the case of Rwanda and Burundi, it is the Hutu who – despite their weakness as a powerless people – have the capacity to take bold initiatives towards conflict resolution in an ethnic context because of their unassailable status as the vast majority of the population in both countries. And that entails self-determination in the areas they dominate, especially for northwestern Rwanda which could become a microstate and the nucleus of a larger independent Hutu ethnostate, providing impetus and legitimacy to the dynamics of secession in both Rwanda and Burundi.

Both Rwanda and Burundi also can be divided into autonomous regions on ethnic basis, reducing the power of the central government which has caused so much misery for so many people when it is in the hands of one ethnic group or the other.

It will be very difficult to achieve either goal in the context of Rwanda and Burundi because the Hutu and the Tutsi are so integrated in their lives, inextricably linked by geography – living in the same villages; by history and family ties through the centuries, so much so that there are really no "pure" Hutus or "pure" Tutsis, if there ever were.

Yet, for practical purposes, the two groups do exist, tragically demonstrated by bloody conflicts between them on ethnic basis through the years.

But if the people themselves want to do it, they can do it: form independent ethnostates, or create autonomous regions on ethnic basis while maintaining the territorial integrity of both countries.

Outright declaration of independence for northwestern Rwanda, even for southeastern Burundi, or any other Hutu stronghold may be the only way to initiate a vigorous national debate on the status of the two countries as viable political entities or as prime candidates for dissolution on the basis of a mutually acceptable formula which does not rule out the establishment of independent ethnostates or even a confederation of those states.

The Hutu and the Tutsi are no more compatible than the Jews and the Arabs are in Palestine; nor are the Greeks and the Turks in Cyprus, already partitioned by Turkey, despite the refusal by the international community to recognise the Turkish area on the island as a legal sovereign entity.

In the case of the Jews and the Arabs, the national question can be resolved in the context of a dynamic compromise conceding the legitimacy of an independent Palestinian state as the final solution.

The alternative is perpetual conflict, as is the case in Rwanda and Burundi where Tutsi armies and security forces have wreaked havoc through the years, targeting Hutus, for both legitimate and illegitimate reasons: fighting the rebels, and killing innocent civilians for no reason other than that they are Hutu – and therefore rebel "supporters" or "rebels" themselves.

In Burundi, the scale of human devastation was amply demonstrated soon after the July 1996 military coup, belying the claim by the military head of state, Major Pierre Buyoya, and his Tutsi compatriots that the coup was carried out to stop genocide and end the civil war.

The coup made things worse, while the Tutsi cheered. They were glad a Hutu president had been removed from office after being assassinated, and they were now back in power, although they really never lost it, since they were – and have always been – in control of the army which is the most powerful institution in the country.

The Hutu were furious. They saw the coup, and

justifiably so, as an usurpation of power from duly constituted authority, a Hutu president, who had the constitutional mandate to rule.

This clash of perceptions and interests inevitably led to increased bloodshed as tensions escalated.

The Hutu were further enraged when they learned that top military officers – Tutsis including Pierre Buyoya himself – instigated and masterminded the assassination of President Melchior Ndadaye.

The revelation was made during the very same time when Tutsi atrocities before, during, and after the coup were also getting ample media coverage. According to the *International Herald Tribune*:

"The human rights group Amnesty International said Thursday (August 22, 1996) that more than 6,000 people were reported to have been killed in Burundi in the three weeks following the army coup on July 25.

Amnesty, which is based in London, said the human rights situation in Burundi continued to deteriorate despite promises by the new Tutsi military ruler, Pierre Buyoya, to end ethnic killings.

It said it had learned that at least 4,050 unarmed (Hutu) civilians were buried after being executed between July 27 and August 10 by government forces in the central province of Gitega.

In another report issued Thursday, UN human rights observers said 365 people (probably all Hutu) were slain in neighboring Rwanda in July. The report said 226 of the deaths were caused by 'agents of the state,' including members of the (Tutsi) Rwandan Patriotic Army, which killed 182 people during operations against Hutu insurgents. Hutu guerrillas killed 45 people, the report added, while responsibility for the deaths of the remaining 94 could not be established."[2]

Adding fuel to the fire was the revelation that high-ranking Tutsi army officers not only engineered the assassination of President Ndadaye; they did so in order to keep Hutus out of power and perpetuate Tutsi domination of the country and regardless of how may Hutus were killed in the ensuing violence at the hands of Tutsi soldiers.

Although the military ruler, Major Buyoya, denied being involved in the attempted coup which resulted in Ndadaye's death, he was deeply implicated in the plot by a number of fellow Tutsis including his cousin and former president, Jean-Baptiste Bagaza; an assessment given credibility by UN investigators although they did not name him directly as a key conspirator:

"Top officers of the Burundian Army were apparently behind the 1993 assassination of the country's first Hutu president, Melchior Ndadaye, a United Nations report has concluded. 'The planning and execution of the coup was carried out by officers highly placed in the line of command of the Burundian Army,' according to the report. It was sent to the Security Council after Burundi's military ousted the government last month (25 July 1996).

According to the report, the army chief of staff, Jean Bikomagu, ordered the head of the president's bodyguards to Mauritius before the assassination and dismissed reports of unrest among military units that later staged a short-lived coup."[3]

The Tutsi-led abortive coup plunged Burundi into one of the bloodiest and one of the longest civil wars Africa has ever seen, although it went largely unreported by the international media, unlike the 1994 genocide in neighboruing Rwanda.

The killings in Burundi also amounted to genocide. While the genocide in Rwanda was carried out by the Hutu against the Tutsi, the one in Burundi was committed by the Tutsi against the Hutu. Some estimates put the death toll in Burundi's civil war – from 1993 to 1996 alone – at 500,000, most of the victims being Hutu. One of the publications which cited this figure was *The Economist*:

"After years of bloodshed, this country, divided like Rwanda between ruling Tutsis and a Hutu majority, may well face months or years of more – and worse.

Burundi's trouble is not officially organised as genocide, as in Rwanda in 1994. Its Tutsi army was, for practical purposes, in charge even before the coup. But the killing, even if less and less publicised, has been plenty – certainly far worse than anything seen recently in Zaire....

The violence, some estimates say, may have killed 500,000 Burundians in three years."[4]

The estimates seem to be credible, given the magnitude of the conflict and the escalation of the violence, and when the statistics are looked at in another context. For example, at least 10,000 people were killed within the first eight months in 1996; more than 6,000 in three weeks alone, after the Tutsi seized power.[5]

The conflict in Burundi had all the ingredients for another Rwanda, probably with a holocaust of the same magnitude, or worse.

Compounding the problem is the fact that the two enemies are so close to each other, literally and figuratively, yet so far apart. "The two groups still live together on the same hills, share the same language (the Tutsi abandoned or lost theirs when they migrated to the region and became an integral part of the larger Hutu society), culture and economy – and still hate each other."[6]

Added to this volatile mixture was yet another element: within three years (1993 – 1996), two Hutu presidents were murdered, and the third one was forced, by the Tutsi, to seek refuge in the American embassy in Burundi's capital Bujumbura where he was holed up for a long time as if he were a fugitive from the law. Yet he fled from the very same people who broke the law by overthrowing him, seizing power illegally.

This usurpation of power even angered some of Burundi's neighbours, especially Tanzania and Kenya: "Tanzania, which handles 70 per cent of Burundi's imports, including almost all its fuel, closed the border – so enthusiastically at first that food aid destined for 300,000 (mainly Hutu) refugees in Burundi was blocked."[7] It was gunboat diplomacy at its best, African style.

Although the embargo had immediate impact – petrol was severely rationed; some food prices nearly trebled; Burundi's main exports and a vital source of income for the army, coffee and tea, could no longer be exported through Tanzania – there was still skepticism about its long-term effects in terms of bringing about fundamental political change in Burundi.

This was vindicated when the sanctions failed to bring down the Tutsi military regime. Instead, violence escalated across the country, taking Burundi down the road to nowhere, except self-destruction. As former Prime Minister Adrien Sibomana poignantly stated: "(Burundi is) like a truck that has fallen into a ditch. It is a nation of people in despair."[8] And the future does not look bright, as the country continues to be wracked by violence. As Thomas W. Lippman reported in *The Washington Post*:

"Hundreds of Burundians, mostly unarmed civilians, are dying daily in a conflict between the army, led by officers of the minority Tutsi tribe, and insurgent militias of the majority Hutu....

Citing intelligence reports, U.S. officials said the Tutsi-led army was preparing a nationwide campaign against armed Hutu insurgents, a campaign that could lead to large-scale killing of Hutu civilians.

At the same time, these officials said, Hutu militias appear to have received a new infusion of weapons, including heavy mortars, that they are prepared to turn against the Tutsi-populated capital city, Bujumbura.

Members of a Burundian delegation who visited New York and Washington last week (in August 1996) said there was little reason to believe the country could right itself because the level of hatred is so high and the sense of helplessness so profound."[9]

Around the same time, Burundi's ruler, Major Pierre Buyoya, attributed some of the country's plight and deteriorating situation to the economic embargo imposed by some of Burundi's neighbours, especially Tanzania and Kenya.

He warned them that the sanctions could worsen the conflict by causing a human disaster and risking further unrest. In an interview on 2 August 1996, with the Belgian daily newspaper, *Le Soir*, Buyoya said he was ready to meet Hutu opposition leaders for talks to try to build a political consensus provided "they stop behaving like mass killers, whose goal is to kill women, children and old people whose mistake is to belong to such and such an ethnic group."[10]

Yet his Tutsi army was even more notorious for committing atrocities against Hutu civilians, simply because they were Hutu, a fact he never acknowledged but instead blamed only Hutus for the murders and the violence across the country.

That is hardly a basis for meaningful dialogue, especially when he blamed only the Hutu instead of apportioning guilt accordingly. There are no saints in this war.

But it is true, as he said, that the economic embargo aggravated the situation, although the sanctions could not be blamed for the escalation of the conflict.

Hutu rebels stepped up the attacks on their own, emboldened by the sanctions in some respects but not prompted by them. And they inflicted substantial damage on some installations. For example, towards the end of

August 1996, Burundi's capital was without electricity for several days straight after the rebels destroyed power facilities. And lines to buy petrol and other fuel winded through the capital Bujumbura as sabotage by Hutu rebels and the embargo began to take their toll.

The insurgents destroyed four electrical pylons on August 24th which carried power from a northern hydroelectric dam to the capital city of 400,000 people. Hutu political opponents also called on farmers – who are mostly Hutu since they constitute the vast majority of the country's population – not to deliver food to Bujumbura to protest the military coup. Even many Tutsis complied with the "order," afraid they would be targeted by the Hutu rebels if they did not.

The residents of Bujumbura, mostly Tutsi, had become increasingly angry and desperate since the sanctions were imposed a few days after the coup; a situation that worked to the advantage of the Hutu rebels but which was not enough to bring down the military regime.

Hospitals, military bases and hotels filled generators with diesel fuel which would no longer be available because of the embargo. But that was only temporary relief.

Burundi's problems – which caused the embargo, hence the shortages, in the first place – required long-term solutions. Unfortunately, it was impossible to find such solutions as long as the two ethnic groups continued to fight.

Burundi's main rebel group, the National Council for the Defence of Democracy (CNDD, a French acronym), threatened on 28 August 1996 to shoot down any aircraft flying into the nation's capital in violation of the economic embargo. CNDD spokesman, Innocent Nimpagaritse, who was also the group's East Africa representative, said in Nairobi, Kenya:

"We have information some foreign planes are landing

in Bujumbura in defiance of regional sanctions. From today onwards, any plane flying into Bujumbura without clearance from our forces will be shot down."[11]

But a spokesman for Burundi's military regime, Jean-Luc Ndizeye, dismissed the Hutu threats as empty boasts:

"They don't have the technical capacity to do that, and if they do shoot a plane coming in or out of Bujumbura then it will just be another one of their crimes."[12]

During the same time, American envoy Howard Wolpe met with Tanzania's former President Julius Nyerere in Rome and proposed that Buyoya should be recognised as Burundi's president as part of a peace initiative to end the Hutu-Tutsi ethnic conflict. The two leaders met to discuss ways to end the war, and the American proposal was just one of the conceivable scenarios in which peace could be envisioned. The deal would give Major Buyoya six months to restore the National Assembly and negotiate peace between the two sides.

Nyerere held talks with Buyoya on August 25th in Tanzania as part of an effort to mediate an end to the violence. But Burundi's ambassador to Rome, Jean-Baptiste Mbonyingingo, said "the aims of the visits by Mr. Nyerere and Mr. Wolpe to Rome were not known to the Burundian government" and added that no envoys had been sent from Bujumbura to the Italian capital to deliver a message or participate in the talks.[13]

Meanwhile, the economic embargo continued to cause hardship, forcing the capital city to draw upon dwindling fuel stocks to keep water supplies, hospitals and other institutions running. Even the army itself was hit hard by the sanctions. But it continued to commit atrocities against Hutu civilians in pursuit of its scorched-earth policy of hunting down Hutu rebels and punishing their supporters, thus targeting innocent people as well.

As the violence escalated, foreigners started fleeing the country. In the first week of September 1996, renewed fighting flared in the eastern part just outside Bujumbura, prompting the United States and other countries to evacuate their nationals from the embattled East African country. The rebels had taken the war to the capital. According to a report from Bujumbura in the *International Herald Tribune*:

"The Burundi Army was using two helicopter gunships and mortars to repel rebels in some of the fiercest fighting since the July 25 coup.

The rebels lobbed three mortar shells into the capital Tuesday (September 3) and fired rifles into the air from surrounding hills to show the Tutsi residents of Bujumbura that they could come down any time, according to a rebel spokesman."[14]

An American Air Force C-141 plane evacuated Americans and other foreigners from the besieged capital on September 4th, but Tanzania forbade it to use its airspace because of the economic embargo imposed on Burundi. Instead, the plane flew over Rwanda and Uganda to Nairobi, Kenya. With commercial flights banned and borders sealed, Burundi was virtually cut off from the rest of the world.

Shackled by the sanctions, the Tutsi military junta announced on 12 September 1996 that it was immediately lifting bans on all political parties and the National Assembly which were imposed after the coup. If genuine, the changes would have met two of the three conditions stipulated by Burundi's neighbours before lifting the embargo. But the changes were merely cosmetic.

Although Buyoya unbanned political parties, political meetings were forbidden, as were opposition newspapers. And although he reopened the parliament, where the Hutu FRODEBU party had a majority, the members met only to point out that out of 81 parliamentarians, 22 had been murdered. All were FRODEBU members.

The national legislators also said they would do nothing as members of parliament until the constitution was restored.

Buyoya also agreed to unconditional peace talks with all parties, but reneged on his promise.

The third condition for lifting sanctions was unconditional peace negotiations among all parties, including the rebels. But the Hutu insurgents as well as Burundi's main Tutsi and Hutu political parties dismissed the lifting of political bans as a move to loosen the sanctions.

Charles Mukasi, leader of the Tutsi UPRONA party, said lifting bans was meaningless because Burundi's parliament had no real power even before the coup, and would stay powerless. He went on to say, "lifting the ban on Parliament is a cosmetic change simply designed to please Nyerere"[15] who initiated and coordinated the regional sanctions against the impoverished landlocked nation.

What the Tutsi rulers deliberately refused to address was the inequity of power between the two ethnic groups; a conflict deeply rooted in history. Instead, like their ethnic compatriots in Rwanda, they were determined to perpetuate their hegemonic control over the Hutu majority, with dire consequences for the entire region which has literally been engulfed in flames.

The biggest catalyst in this inferno is ethno-nationalism, probably the most potent force in the world today which could change the map of Africa in the twentieth-first century, as it did in Eastern Europe and in the Soviet Union after the collapse of communism towards the end of the twentieth century. As Professor William Zartman stated in his article, "Making Sense of East Africa's Wars," in *The Wall Street Journal*:

"The current round in the unfolding Central African crisis is the result of three countries' (Rwanda's, Burundi's, and Zaire's) attempts at national consolidation on an ethnic basis – the same type of dynamic that has been driving civil wars in the former Yugoslavia (especially Bosnia and Kosovo) and the former Soviet Union (especially Tajikistan."[16]

The intensity of such micro-nationalism in the Great Lakes region has another dimension which makes it even more potent because it is articulated in a "racial" context, although it defies rational explanation contending that the Hutu and the Tutsi belong to different races. And it is sanctioned by the state – the Tutsi ethnocracy – which, by its actions, glorifies it as a virtue at the expense of pluralistic aspirations a heterogeneous society is expected to pursue in order to accommodate its diverse elements on the basis of equality. And tragically, the history of both Rwanda and Burundi is a chronicle of the tribulations of a people divided purely on the basis of what they are or what they perceive themselves to be. But the divisions are real, as are the inequities:

"The relationship between Hutus and Tutsis goes deep into history. It was not always so clear-cut – or deadly.

Hutus tell of centuries of enslavement by Tutsis. Tutsis say that the ethnic divide was invented by colonial rulers, and that Hutus are playing racial politics.

Anyone on the watch for it – and these days everyone is – can spot the difference between Hutu and Tutsi stereotypes. Line up ten people, five Tutsis and five Hutus. The ethnic origin of six would be plain, two could be either, two you would get wrong. Intermarriage has lessened the physical differences; politicians have built up the emotional ones, making the division even sharper than before."[17]

Superficial as they may be in some respects, the differences are real in a very deadly way. That is why almost 1 million Tutsis were slaughtered in Rwanda. Their Hutu enemies did not miss their target – in most cases, they knew who to go after, based on physical features or appearance alone.

They were able to identify Tutsis right away, sometimes even by looking at the shape of their heels (if it was L-shaped, without a curve, "you are Tutsi!"), or at their gums (if they are dark, "you are Tutsi!").

Employing such criteria is indeed arbitrary. But in most cases, they were right on target. Otherwise they would have killed a very large number of their own people, had they simply guessed who was Tutsi and who was not, although they probably also killed an unknown number of fellow Hutus whom they mistook for Tutsis. But probably the most important factor was that they knew the people they killed. They killed their neighbours. They killed their friends and even their own relatives. And they already knew they were Tutsi.

The differences between the two groups are also real in a fundamental respect: allocation of power, hence resources.

It is the Tutsi who dominate. They control the army; they control the government, the economy and everything else. Those who rule set the rules of the game. When their opponents learn the game, they change the rules.

In Burundi, such hegemonic control by the Tutsi has included not only discrimination in the provision of education but also extermination of the Hutu elite, resulting in the intellectual suffocation of an entire people, with appalling results: "If you hire educated people in Burundi's towns these days (in the late 1990s), you hire Tutsis. The divide has become absolute."[18] Therefore the Hutu-Tutsi conflict is also a class conflict.

It is also political because the Hutu are excluded from power; it is also economic, mainly a conflict over land of which there is so little for so many people; and it is, of course, "racial": Nilotic (Tutsi) versus Bantu (Hutu), although there is no Bantu race. Bantus themselves – united only by linguistic affinity and cultural similarities – are different peoples; they are not just one people.

But the Hutu-Tutsi ethnic divide has no parallel in the region. The schism is so wide, and so frightening. Prospects are bleak we will see it closed in the next several decades. It probably never will be. And both sides know that.

What we will probably see in both countries is a *façade* of democracy, accommodating both groups on "equal basis," while in reality one group or the other will always be dominant, exercising power to preserve, protect and promote its own interests at the expense of the other group.

The Tutsi don't want to share – let alone relinquish – power. And the Hutu, once in power as they once were in Rwanda from 1962 to 1994, will probably rule forever if democracy is established on the basis of majority rule. They constitute the vast majority of the population in both countries and are therefore guaranteed to win every election even without rigging. The election of Melchior Ndadaye, a Hutu, in 1993 as president of Burundi clearly demonstrated that. He rode into office on a massive wave of Hutu sentiment, sending shivers down the spine of many Tutsis, probably the majority of them.

It is a cruel dilemma which explains why the two ethnic groups are locked in perpetual conflict.

The search for a solution to this intra-territorial conflict is analogous to the quest for peace and stability in the global arena where equilibrium in the international system is determined by one of two things: domination by one power or by a group of powers united by common interests; or peaceful coexistence between global adversaries. The alternative is chaos.

In the case of Rwanda and Burundi, domination of one

group by the other has failed to bring peace. Peaceful coexistence between the two groups within the same national boundaries has also failed. The result has been war, chaos and anarchy.

War versus Diplomacy

The Tutsi soldiers who seized power from a Hutu president in Burundi in July 1996 only heightened fear among the Hutu that the Tutsi were not interested in peaceful coexistence or power sharing. They clearly showed that they were interested in dominating the Hutu. This led to escalation of the conflict which reached new levels in December the same year, five months after the coup.[19]

And there was mounting evidence showing that the Tutsi national army was waging a vicious campaign of terror against Hutu civilians. The United Nations High Commissioner for Human Rights, Jose Ayala Lasso, gave the evidence on 11 December 1996 showing that Burundi's army had killed at least 1,100 people in two months, including hundreds of Hutu refugees, and urged the country's Tutsi leaders to stop the carnage:

"I appeal to the authorities and all parties to ensure maximum respect for human rights and fundamental freedoms to put an end to killings, arbitrary arrests, destruction of property."[20]

The report, based on UN investigations and testimony by witnesses, said the massacres had taken place in October and November 1996.

The UN human rights office said the biggest massacre during that period took place when Tutsi soldiers killed 200 to 400 Hutu returnees and wounded 200 others in an attack on a church in the village of Murambi in the northwestern province of Citiboke.

The report also stated that Hutu rebels fighting the army may have killed scores of civilians. And it warned that an already alarming situation had been made worse by the influx of more than 50,000 Burundian Hutu refugees who fled a rebellion by the Banyamulenge and other Tutsis – including Rwandan and Burundian Tutsi soldiers – in eastern Zaire.

Killings, disappearances and arbitrary arrests had risen sharply in Burundi since the influx began. The UN report went on state that civilians – mostly Hutu – were bearing the brunt of the increasingly violent confrontations between Tutsi soldiers and Hutu rebels, with the insurgents using mortars and the army striking with planes:

"The human rights situation in November (1996) could be described as alarming, with massacres, arbitrary arrests, pillage and destruction of property perpetrated by the two sides."[21]

But the Tutsi army wreaked more havoc in its campaign of state-sponsored terrorism against the Hutu. The war also amounted to ethnic cleansing:

"Burundi's soldiers have been fighting Hutu guerrillas in a war of terror and counter-terror, with few scruples on either side.

By now much of the northern countryside, if not already guerrilla-controlled, is open to guerrilla attack. Many Tutsis have fled to the towns; often Hutus have fled or been pushed out from them (including the capital Bujumbura which was cleansed of almost all Hutus by the Tutsi)."[22]

The deterioration of the situation was underscored by the promulgation of two decrees in December 1996 which pointed to a bleak future.

One stated that all school leavers and public employees must do a year's army service and be available for "public works," a term whose meaning needed no further explanation in the military language of conscription.

The other decree required all public employees to contribute a month's salary to the military campaign, and all employers to give workers time off for army service.

Burundi's military regime further demonstrated its commitment to a military solution to the ethnic conflict when it refused to participate in peace talks. When Julius Nyerere, the chief mediator in the Burundi conflict, invited the Tutsi military ruler to attend a meeting of all parties in Tanzania in the last week of December 1996, "Mr. Buyoya did not even reply."[23] As one diplomat put it: "This is a complete militarisation of society. They are determined to squash the rebellion."[24]

But this uncompromising stand only fuelled the conflict.

In the first week of December 1996, up to 500 people were killed in attacks in Kayanza Province north of the capital Bujumbura. The killings were attributed to both – Hutu rebels and Tutsi soldiers.

The Tutsi army intensified its campaign when it resorted to resettlement schemes, forcing Hutu peasants to leave their homes and farms and settle in "protective" villages which were no more than concentration camps reminiscent of what the British did in Malaya during the 1950s, and what the Americans did in South Vietnam in the 1960s.

The Tutsi regime claimed that Hutu peasants in war-torn areas were moved to other parts "for their own safety." That was a cruel joke by the regime which was busy killing the same people it claimed it was protecting. Most of the Hutu civilians who were killed – were killed by the Tutsi army, not by the Hutu rebels.

The real motive for moving Hutu peasants into so-called protective villages or areas was to deprive Hutu guerrilla fighters of civilian support from their people, fellow Hutus, and to hold Hutu civilians hostage – in "protective" villages – in retaliation for attacks by Hutu insurgents on Tutsi civilians and soldiers. For every Tutsi killed, so many Hutus would be killed in the concentration camps. Any Hutu who did not relocate or move into a "protective" village was automatically considered to be a rebel and fair game for Tutsi soldiers.

The army was free to do anything it wanted to do because it was the most powerful institution in the country. And it still is.

Even if its leader Pierre Buyoya, the military head of state, wanted to negotiate with the rebels, he would not have been able to do so without army support. As one observer put it: "If he negotiates with the Hutu rebels, he's a dead man."[25]

But it seemed that even he himself had opted for a military solution to the problem even if the army did not exert pressure on him to adopt an uncompromising stand against the peace talks. That is because he thought he could win the war, especially with the isolation of the rebels from their civilian supporters under his resettlement programme which ended up creating some of the most notorious concentration camps on the African continent reminiscent of what happened in Kenya in the 1950s during Mau Mau when tens of thousands of Kikuyus were penned up in barren reserves by the British.

Another reason why Buyoya thought the Tutsi army would win the war had to do with what had just happened right next-door. The Banyamulenge Tutsis in eastern Zaire had just routed the Burundian and Rwandan Hutu guerrillas who had operational bases in that part of Congo, posing great danger to the Tutsi regimes in both Rwanda and Burundi. With the destruction of their operational bases, he felt that this danger had been eliminated or had been greatly reduced, making it difficult for the insurgents to launch raids into Burundi from their bases in Zaire.

133

He also believed that his army could duplicate this success within Burundi itself, considering its performance through the years as a better fighting force than the rebels. But he also underestimated the rebels.

It is true that, more often than not, the Tutsi have demonstrated great ability on the battlefield and have always been proud of their military prowess. And the record speaks for itself, not only in Burundi but also in Rwanda as was clearly demonstrated during the 1994 genocide when the Hutu army was routed by the Tutsi insurgents of the Rwandan Patriotic Front (RPF).

Yet they have not always prevailed against the Hutu even in Burundi itself. The Hutu also turned the tables in Rwanda, first during the 1959 mass uprising in which they ousted the Tutsi aristocracy and killed more than 100,000 Tutsis, forcing hundreds of thousands of others to flee the country; and again in 1994 when they almost wiped out the entire Tutsi population in Rwanda in an unprecedented genocide which claimed about one million lives.

Buyoya was also encouraged to pursue a military solution because the economic embargo which had inflicted a lot of pain on the army as well, was now being circumvented.

But it was a war neither side could win, although the sanction-busters, mostly Francophone African countries sympathetic to another French-speaking country in plight, encouraged the Tutsi military regime in its belief that it could:

"Times are tough: fuel prices have risen sixfold, and building has all but stopped for lack of cement. But there is food in the markets and enough fuel is smuggled from Rwanda to allow life to go on and the army to fight.

The government has been encouraged by feelings building up in French-speaking Africa against sanctions. Sympathy for Mr. Buyoya was plain at two recent high-level meetings (in December 1996) in Congo (Brazzaville) and Burkina Faso; one brought calls for the sanctions to be eased.

The government is losing its former coffee revenues, but, with eastern Zaire's airports now in Tutsi rebel hands, exports may get out by that route (as well as through Rwanda, with Burundi's coffee and tea bags labelled as Rwanda's exports).

With little chance of a political breakthrough, the pattern of war is likely to continue. Hutu fighters attack a school or health clinic, or some group of displaced Tutsi families. The (Tutsi) army moves in, burns (Hutu) villages and murders whatever unlucky Hutus it comes upon. Neither side can win."[26]

And neither side is going to surrender, as the escalation of violence clearly shows.

Yet these are the people who have lived together and who have intermarried through the years, in fact for centuries, without plunging their country into massive violence, until after independence in the sixties.

There had always been hostility between the two groups since the Tutsi conquered and virtually enslaved the Hutu about 400 years ago. But in all those years, the conflict never reached the levels it did from the 1960s to the 1990s.

What went wrong?

The injustices against the Hutu through the centuries undoubtedly had cumulative impact which contributed to the eruption of violence on an unprecedented scale during that period – from the sixties to the nineties. But something else played a role: Hutu politicians and intellectuals with warped minds whipping up"racist" or ethnic sentiments against the Tutsi. As Julius Nyerere stated in his speech to the International Peace Academy in New York in January 1997:

"All violent conditions represent earlier failures of

leadership, either by wrongdoing or by default. They represent failures at local levels, and especially at national levels....

In Africa today, and especially in Rwanda and Burundi, we hear a great deal about ethnic conflicts. Yet these are taking place at particular times and places after members of the different ethnic groups have for long periods lived side by side in the same villages and towns, have worked together and have intermarried. Thus, ethnicity is clearly not a sufficient explanation of conflict.

Ethnicity can, however, be used to conceal the real problems, the genuine economic problems or cultural clashes, behind the easily aroused human fears about those who are unlike ourselves. Ethnicity can also be used to divide and rule. In Rwanda and Burundi, this use of ethnicity was clearly made by Germany and Belgium as colonial powers.

Ethnic conflict will arise when leaders in the society deliberately strengthen the concept of ethnicity, and for their own purposes ignite hostility. In Rwanda and Burundi, conflict has economic roots. The fight for power is mainly a fight for economic resources. Ethnicity is simply being exploited."[27]

The Tutsi control both political power and economic resources. Yet such politics of exclusion will not guarantee security even for the Tutsi themselves in spite of all the power they have. In fact, it has made most Tutsis vulnerable to attack since everyone of them symbolises oppression of the Hutu. That is the way Hutu rebels and their supporters see it.

Therefore every Tutsi, everyone of them, is a target everywhere, not by every Hutu but by Hutu rebels and by other Hutus who use violence against their enemies or against those whom they perceive to be their enemies. And no amount of security by the Tutsi army is going to be enough to protect every Tutsi, in every part of the country,

136

all the time, as the killings of Tutsi civilians by Hutu insurgents tragically demonstrates.

Yet it is this very threat to their survival which Tutsis invoke to justify their determination to hang on to power at any cost and by any means at their disposal including the use of deadly force against any Hutu they think is a threat to them. And that includes innocent civilians who are considered to be dangerous simply because they are Hutu.

It is this threat to Tutsi survival which also compelled the Tutsi military ruler, Major Pierre Buyoya, to start talking to the rebels. And history bears testimony to one brutal fact: It was in Burundi where the Great Lakes crisis started when Tutsi soldiers assassinated the country's first democratically elected president, a Hutu, in 1993, starting a bloodbath which spilled throughout the region and alerted the Hutu in Rwanda as to what would happen to them if the Tutsi also seized power in that country.

The ethnic conflict in both Rwanda and Burundi not only caused more than one million deaths – probably one-and-a-half million – in four years since 1993; it also ignited hostilities between the governments of neighbouring countries and others even further from the region; it displaced millions of people; disrupted trade among the countries in the region and weakened their economies; and plunged the entire region into chaos on an unprecedented scale.

Therefore resolution of the conflict was of paramount concern on the agenda of several countries in the region which wanted to extricate themselves from the imbroglio, as much as it was even for many people in Burundi who felt that neither side could win the war.

In anticipation of the peace negotiations scheduled for September 1997 in neighbouring Tanzania, Buyoya said in an interview in August that the talks could lead to the establishment of a coalition government acceptable to the Tutsi minority. As he put it:

"Democracy is possible, but we have to reinvent our democracy, a democracy adapted to Burundi's realities, that would take into account our culture and experience, our social and political reality. We have to adapt democracy to what we are."[28]

But it was also obvious that a comprehensive peace agreement by Buyoya could cost him his life. That is because he was put in power by Tutsi business leaders and military officers who had the most to lose if the Tutsi relinquished control and democracy was re-established, leading to the election of a Hutu president; which was a virtual certainty, given the tyranny of numbers tipping scales in favour Hutus in this deeply divided country where most people automatically vote along ethnic lines.

Buyoya himself admitted that he probably would be overthrown – and much worse – if he endorsed any peace accord which did not guarantee the Tutsi elite's hold on influence and financial advantage: "I will try to bring a peace accord without causing a coup. You have to manage it so the Burundi people, including the military, are part of the accord."[29]

That is in a country where the Tutsi savagely repressed Hutu uprisings in 1963, 1965, 1972, 1988, 1991, and 1993, at a cost of at least one million lives, mostly Hutu; a holocaust – of several genocides through the years – hardly anyone talks about unlike the 1994 tragedy that befell the Tutsi in Rwanda. It is this kind of disregard for their plight by the international community and by their fellow countrymen, the Tutsi, which rankles the Hutu in Burundi. Throughout this horrendous tragedy, they have largely remained an invisible mass unlike their kinsmen, and unlike the Tutsi, in Rwanda.

Therefore to ask Hutus in Burundi to continue living under Tutsi domination would be equivalent to asking black people in South Africa during the apartheid era to

138

continue enduring white oppression without demanding fundamental change and a complete overhaul of the system.

Yet democracy on the basis of "one man, one vote" is not a realistic solution to the ethnic conflict in Burundi – or Rwanda – because the Tutsi see it as a recipe for catastrophe, leading to genocide against them by the victorious Hutus.

It is difficult to conceive of a scenario in which the Hutu lose an election on the basis of one man, one vote. As Charles Mukasi, the secretary-general of Burundi's Tutsi ruling party, UPRONA, bluntly stated:

"The Tutsi are not scared of elections. They are scared of being exterminated."[30]

The Hutu are not scared of elections, either. And they may not even be scared of being exterminated because there are so many of them, vastly outnumbering the Tutsi. But they are scared of being dominated and of being massacred by the Tutsi.

Both groups have legitimate fears vindicated by history.

But in spite of the hostility and deep resentment between the two groups, each united by fear of the other, neither the Hutu nor the Tutsi always present a united front in pursuit of their goals as ethnic entities. This was best demonstrated during the late 1990s when attempts were made to resolve the ethnic conflict.

There were Tutsi moderates who supported Buyoya's peace initiative, and hawks who were vehemently opposed to it. Hutus were also divided along the same lines.

And although the Hutu rebels were united by their common hatred of the Tutsi, there were times when they also clashed among themselves. One of the worst clashes took place in northwestern Burundi where fighting between rival Hutu insurgents between July and August

1997 left 600 people dead.

In mid-August 1997, about 13,000 Hutus fled their rural homes and sought refuge in Bubanza, a trading town 25 miles north of the capital Bujumbura, to escape fighting between two Hutu guerrilla groups – the National Liberation Front (FROLINA) and the Forces for the Defence of Democracy (FDD) which was the main guerrilla group in Burundi.

A farmer who arrived in a town nearby said many villagers were fleeing because the National Liberation Front "will kill us if we don't give them financial support." A spokesman for the National Council for the Defence of Democracy (CNDD), the political wing of the FDD, denied that factional fighting caused the deaths.[31]

But more than one witness confirmed the fighting. And there was evidence showing that it took place.

However, none of these intra-ethnic conflicts distracted the insurgents from their common goal of trying to oust the Tutsi from power.

But the rebels also targeted their own people, fellow Hutus, for different reasons. Not all Hutus supported the rebels. And not all Hutus believed violence was the solution to the ethnic problem in Burundi. Hutus opposed to guerrilla war were prime targets. Others were killed in raids for food and shelter. Yet others were taken hostage and used as human shields; Tutsi soldiers showed little concern for them.

To them, every Hutu was fair game, and hostages an expendable commodity or just a part of collateral damage, as they carried on their campaign of brutal repression and indiscriminate killings ostensibly to destroy Hutu guerrillas. Anything in their way, including Hutu hostages, was prime target; every Hutu a suspect, to be harassed or arrested, tortured or killed, or interned in a concentration camp.

The plight of one Hutu community of Buraniro illustrates the tragedy that had befallen the rest of their kinsmen in general at the hands of their Tutsi rulers. But it is also a story about the atrocities committed by the rebels themselves against their own people.

Like most Hutus, Mrs. Mary Rose Habyamberi lived in a banana-leaf hut, scratching out a bare living on a plot of land, growing food crops including bananas and vegetables. Yet in the midst of war, poverty was the least of her worries. She was, instead, afraid of the heavily-armed Tutsi soldiers who patrolled around the camp where she had been interned with other Hutus and kept under intense watch.

But she was also scared of the Hutu guerrillas roaming the hills of this densely-populated mountainous country.

In the latter part of 1996, the guerrillas raided for supplies the commune where she lived, killing several people in a hail of gunfire. Among those killed was her 10-year-old son, Olivier. As she sadly recalled in an interview almost a year later in August 1997: "They killed my child. He was fleeing and I never saw him again."[32]

Mrs. Habyamberi became a victim of both sides. But the vast majority of Hutus who were forced into "protective" camps were mostly victims of a vicious campaign by Tutsi soldiers against the Hutu guerrillas.

Mrs. Mary Rose Habyamberi was one of the 13,000 Hutus who had been forced out of their villages by Tutsi soldiers and crowded into a concentration camp around the trading post of Buraniro as part of a scorched-earth policy by President Buyoya's government to neutralise the insurgents.

In August 1997, human rights workers and aid officials said there were at least 44 camps like the one at Buraniro, across Burundi, with about 255,000 people living in appalling conditions. But they also, together with diplomats, conceded that forcing Hutu peasants into the camps had been a successful military strategy. It robbed the guerrillas of supply lines and hiding places, and made it harder for them to recruit young men into the guerrilla force. As Buyoya stated, in justifying this policy: "We are obliged to regroup people to protect them. We have to put them somewhere where they can live together in security."[33]

But the people living in the camps disagreed with that glossy assessment. Life for them was hard. Although some were allowed to go back to their farms during daylight hours, many of them missed the planting season. Even those who had been able to plant could work on their farms for only a few hours a day, thus severely reducing the harvest. Many of them said they were expecting less than half of their normal harvest of yams, cassava and beans.

Therefore, while the concentration-camp policy benefited the military, it also caused famine conditions for Hutu peasants.

But it was a policy not without precedent even in Africa itself. And it was effective.

Hunger has been used effectively as a weapon in many wars to starve people into submission. It was used by the federal military government in the Nigerian civil war to force the Biafran secessionists to capitulate. It was used by UNITA rebels in Angola to try and turn the people against the MPLA government, hoping that they would rise up in a mass insurrection to compel the national leadership to make substantial concessions to the rebels on terms stipulated by UNITA.

Hunger was also used by the brutal regime of Mengistu Haile Mariam in Ethiopia against the peasants opposed to his reign of terror, and by Siad Barre, another brutal despot, in Somalia whose tyranny destroyed the country – it dissolved in anarchy.

Hunger was also one of the weapons – in addition to chopping off limbs, buttocks and ears as well as gouging out eyes – the rebels of the Revolutionary United Front (RUF) used in Sierra Leone to wage war against the democratically elected government of President Ahmad

Tejan Kabbah, although the grisly mutilations and amputations played a bigger role.

President Kabbah was forced to seek peace literally on the rebels' terms which included making the RUF leader, Foday Sankoh, vice president of Sierra Leone, and giving eight ministerial posts – four of which were deputy ministerial – to the RUF rebels and their allies: renegade soldiers who overthrew Kabbah in May 1997. He was reinstated in March 1998 with the help of the West African peacekeeping force (ECOMOG) led by Nigeria.

The difference in Burundi is that it was the Tutsi-dominated military regime which dictated terms to the Hutu majority. Forcing them to live in concentrations camps – or die – was one of those terms. In addition to being interned, the people in the camps were also forced to live in squalid conditions without sanitation. There were hardly any latrines; there was no clean water, not enough food, and much more:

"People...are living on top of one another. Disease is rampant: typhoid fever, dysentery and malaria. And with limited harvests, malnutrition is beginning to take hold in some camps, aid workers said."[34]

The Tutsi military regime painted an entirely different picture. And it continued to say the camps were created to provide security and isolate the rebels who were attacking Hutu civilians as well. Yet hardly any of the interned Hutus said they moved into the camps willingly. Anyone – any Hutu – caught outside the camps at night was automatically considered to be a rebel and could be shot on sight.

There was another intimidating aspect of life in those places which made them qualify as concentration camps. Although none had barbed wire fences or guard towers, they were all garrisoned by Tutsi soldiers in order to prevent the people from leaving the camps.

If the Hutu peasants had settled in the camps willingly or voluntarily, there would have been no need for all those soldiers to be on the premises, worried about Hutus escaping from the so-called protective villages.

Buraniro was one of the few places where people were allowed to return to their farms during the day. In the rest of the camps, Hutu peasants were forced to work collectively on a single tract of land at a time, almost like a prison chain gang. And in some camps, the people couldn't leave at all, because of security problems, the soldiers claimed. Yet nobody, not even the soldiers themselves, was convinced or believed this was really the reason the Hutus were confined to the camps.

The plight of the interned Hutu peasants was highlighted by the predicament of one such farmer, Marcel Nyabenda, a 50-year-old father of nine children, at Buraniro.

His farm was a two-hour walk away, and he had to be back in the camp by 6 P.M., hardly enough time for him to work on the farm. By the time he got there, he was already tired from walking, therefore unable to work as hard as he normally would have. His problem, like that of the other peasants, was compounded by the fact that he was weak from malnutrition and rampant disease in the crowded camp.

His situation got even worse when the Tutsi soldiers guarding the camp did not even allow him to go to his farm in February (1997), the last planting days; many other farmers were not allowed, either. As he explained his plight: "This time I will not harvest because I didn't cultivate."[35]

He went on to explain that he would not dare return to his farm permanently because Tutsi soldiers would shoot him as "a rebel." And the tragedy that had befallen his family as a result of this forced resettlement was enormous.

Since January 1997 when he and other Hutus from his

community of Nyabibuye were moved into the camp, his brother, mother and father died from typhus, one of the diseases endemic in those filthy, highly congested "security" enclaves.

But there were a few Hutus who said they were glad to be in the camps. They said they no longer had to worry about being attacked by the rebels who tortured or killed fellow Hutus who did not support their guerrilla campaign. Anyone who refused to join their guerrilla army or who did not give them food and shelter was fair game.

Ancilla Ndayisenga, a 20-year-old, was one of the residents who was grateful to the government for being given "sanctuary" in the Buraniro "protective" camp: "I like staying here. The rebels find us at our houses and attack us, so the soldiers ask us to come here and protect us."[36]

But the vast majority of the Hutus who were forced to live in the concentration camps did not share that view. Otherwise, they would have moved there willingly.

And from a humanitarian point of view, human rights workers, diplomats and UN officials said forcing people to live in the camps was indefensible regardless of how much the Tutsi regime tried to justify the internment on security grounds. But it is also true that since the military ruler, Buyoya, began moving more and more people into the camps in early 1997, security in the northern and central provinces improved significantly.

By August, the insurgency was confined to the southern part of the country near the border with Tanzania where the rebels used UN refugee camps in western Tanzania as operational bases from which to launch sporadic raids into Burundi.

President Buyoya also enlarged the Tutsi army from 17,000 to 40,000 soldiers, filling the main roads and secondary routes with heavily-armed troops. And in the camps themselves, the military regime launched a propaganda campaign to try to convince Hutu peasants that the Tutsi army was not their enemy but their ally against a common enemy: the rebels.

But none of those tactics – intimidation and internment of Hutus in concentration camps, and indoctrination – helped the army to win the war. As one UN official said dismissively about the anti-rebel propaganda in the camps by the government: "What they are doing in the camps is really brainwashing."[37]

Al that probably only drove many interned Hutus even deeper into the rebels' camp even if they could not then support the rebels' cause with material assistance. As some Hutu peasants – they had not yet been rounded up and put in concentration camps by the Tutsi army – stated in Burarana in northern Burundi in October 1996 when asked in an interview with *The Economist* what caused their misfortune, forcing them to beg for food from the UN World Food Programme, handed out to them by – of all people, as the Hutu saw it – their enemies, the Tutsi, whom they hated and feared:

"The army did this, they chased us from our homes and killed people."

And the rebels?: "Yes, they take our things and our food, but they are our sons, we support them."[38]

In its special report from Burundi, *The Economist* summed up the plight of these huddled masses in the following terms:

"From a distance it looks like a market day. Some 3,000 people are gathered around three small lorries parked on the red earth road at a bend in the narrow valley. Ths is Burarana in northern Burundi.

The trucks, hired by the United Nations World Food Programme, are piled with white sacks of flour.

More people are filing down the steep hillsides to join the crowd; women in bright wraps with babies on their backs, old men with walking sticks. Come closer and you notice that they have a huddled look to them, their own apparel worn and torn. They are afraid. They are Hutus.

A few days earlier, Hutu rebels came through the area. They took food from the people. A day later, Burundi's (Tutsi) army arrived, shot and beat people and burned their huts....The survivors fled towards Burarana. Some have found space in the huts of relatives or friends, others sleep in the open....

The UN workers supervising the unloading of the food are anxious to get going....Three soldiers guard this delivery. All are tall and light-skinned. So are the UN workers supervising the unloading. These are townspeople, dressed in smart jeans and sporting flashy watches. All are Tutsis. Some carry switches to keep back the hungry (Hutu) peasants who need the food but regard its distributors with fear and loathing....

What will these people do now? They shrug. Their homes have been looted and destroyed. They have joined the mass of hungry, homeless humanity, escaping gunfire, seeking food.

There are millions of such people now in Africa's Great Lakes region. Soon there will be many millions more.

The whole region is smouldering. Eastern Zaire has now ignited, catching fire from Rwanda and Burundi. The conflagration threatens to spread even further, even to Uganda and western Tanzania. Eventually, it could affect more than 30 million people."[39]

It did affect all of Rwanda and Burundi where it all started. It affected the entire Congo (formerly Zaire) where Rwandan and Burundian Hutus sought refuge, and when the Tutsi-led rebellion which began in the eastern part of Zaire swept across the country and eventually ousted President Mobutu Sese Seko. It also affected Tanzania where hundreds of thousands of Hutu refugees – and many Tutsis – from both Rwanda and Burundi, and tens of thousands of refugees who fled from the war in Congo, settled in the western part of the country.

They were concentrated in the western regions of Tanzania along the border with the three countries – Rwanda, Burundi, and Congo – which had just exploded, affecting millions of people in the Great Lakes region.

It also affected Uganda where explosions in Rwanda, Burundi, and Congo fuelled anti-government rebellions.

And the fires have not died anywhere in the region. For example, the multinational war in Congo – involving armies from nine African countries – which started in August 1998 in the eastern part of the country and which almost stopped after all the parties involved signed a peace agreement in July 1999, reignited, full-scale, only a few months later in November. According to *The Christian Science Monitor*:

"The fragile four-month-old peace in Congo appeared over as leaders of rival rebel movements said their forces were resuming efforts to topple President Laurent Kabila.

The Congolese Liberation Movement accused Kabila's troops of attacking its positions Friday (5 November 1999) and of using the period since the signing of a truce in July to rearm.

The Congolese Rally for Democracy also said it no longer would observe the truce.

UN experts have been in Congo since October 13 to draw up plans for a peacekeeping mission."[40]

And Burundi's war, which is the least reported, is one of the most protracted and deadliest conflicts on the entire continent in the post-colonial period. The military solution being pursued by both sides to solve this intractable problem not only perpetuates but exacerbates the conflict.

That is one of the reasons – favouring a military solution – why Burundi's Tutsi military regime refused to participate in the peace negotiations in Arusha, Tanzania, in August 1997, despite Buyoya's promise that he would.

The talks began on August 26th when Nyerere, the chief mediator, said he would go on with the meeting despite Buyoya's refusal to take part in the negotiations. Nyerere also dismissed as "stupid" accusations that he was pro-Hutu and therefore unacceptable as a facilitator of the peace process.

Burundi claimed that Tanzania's neutrality had been compromised because it harboured Hutu rebels along its western border. Nyerere was blunt in his response to accusations that he favoured Hutus: "These accusations are not new. These are stupid reasons."[41]

The former Tanzanian president held talks with the representatives of the main Hutu rebel organisation, the National Council for the Defence of Democracy (CNDD); the main Hutu political party, FRODEBU; the radical Tutsi party, PARENA; and two other political parties. But without the participation of the Tutsi military regime, it was obvious that the conflict could not be resolved.

And while the war was going on in Burundi, tensions between Tanzania and Burundi also flared up and escalated into a fiery exchange, although neither side claimed or admitted responsibility for firing first:

"Tanzania was accused of firing across its border at military positions inside Burundi (in October 1997). A Burundi Army spokesman said Tanzanian forces shelled Mugina and Kabonga, killing two soldiers and wounding three others.

Tanzania's Foreign Ministry said it was unaware of any violence.

The two nation's relations have deteriorated in recent months."[42]

Burundi's conflict with Tanzania had to do with failure of leadership within Burundi itself to accommodate and protect the interests of the Hutu majority. Otherwise there would have been no need for Hutus to flee their homeland. And there would have been no Hutu refugees in Tanzania – hundreds of thousands of them. They fled the war which the Tutsi themselves started when they assassinated the country's first democratically elected president, Melchior Ndadaye, a Hutu, in order to perpetuate their hegemonic control of the country.

And their cross-border raids into Tanzania in pursuit of the Hutu rebels inevitably triggered a military response from Tanzania after diplomatic efforts failed to restrain Burundi's Tutsi army from striking across the border, forcing more refugees to flee to Tanzania because of its relentless and extremely brutal repression of the Hutu majority.

It is in this context that Tanzania's retaliatory response must be viewed. The military response was also a warning to the Tutsi military regime in Burundi to desist from launching further provocative attacks on its eastern neighbour. It is also in this context that stepped-up attacks by Hutu insurgents against Burundi's military junta must be looked at as a legitimate response to brutal oppression of the Hutu majority by the dominant Tutsi minority; even if some of their methods, including indiscriminate killings, can not be justified.

But their determination to continue fighting must also be viewed in the overall context of a system of government whose sole existence is on predicated on the politics of exclusion to perpetuate a Tutsi ethnocracy, and not as a savage instinct or morbid desire by the Hutu to exterminate members of a different "race" or ethnic group who "simply don't belong here."

It all boils down to injustice. Unless this injustice is addressed across the spectrum to accommodate conflicting interests of both groups, there will be no peace in Burundi. And the Hutu majority know there is strength in numbers even if the ruling Tutsi minority, blinded by a twisted sense of "racial" superiority, try to ignore this simple

150

reality simply because they have dominated the Hutu for hundreds of years; thus automatically assuming that they have the divine right to rule them.

But it is only a matter of time. They are not going to rule forever. And it will be a horrendous tragedy if the only way they will be compelled to face reality is by force, not by logic. We don't need another holocaust.

Intensified Guerrilla Warfare

Efforts by Hutu rebels to dislodge the Tutsi from power reached a new level on New Year's day in 1998 when the insurgents launched their biggest attack just outside the capital, Bujumbura, since the latest war began in October 1993 following the assassination of President Melchior Ndadaye in that month.

About 1,000 Hutu guerrillas attacked an army base and a village near Bujumbura airport. They fought an hour-long battle in which at least 150 civilians were killed. Colonel Jean-Bosco Darangwe, the commander of the army base, described the attack as the biggest by the Hutu rebels.

He went on to say that the rebels launched the attack as part of a broader and coordinated strategy to destabilise the governments of Burundi, Rwanda, and the Democratic Republic of Congo (DRC). The three countries were then allies against the insurgents until Congo under President Laurent Kabila switched sides in August 1998 when Rwanda, Uganda, and Burundi invaded his country in an attempt to overthrow him.

Colonel Darangwe also said the rebels were pillaging villages as they retreated: "They are attacking anything on their way out. They are killing indiscriminately be it Hutu or Tutsi. They are also forcefully taking people with them as they retreat."[43] But the rebels blamed the army for the massacre.[44]

The army beat back the assault after hours of heavy artillery fire. Lieutenant-Colonel Mamert Sinaranzi told Radio Burundi that 30 rebels and two soldiers were also killed in addition to the civilian casualties.[45]

The rebels retreated north through Rukaramu village, embroiling villagers in the fighting.

Burundi's ambassador to Britain, Jean-Luc Ndizye, said 150 civilian victims were Hutu, like the rebels, and were killed in Rukaramu.[46] But it was not clear who killed the villagers: Hutu rebels or Tutsi soldiers. Bodies of the victims were strewn in the fields of the community.

In the past, Hutu guerrillas have killed Hutu civilians suspected of not supporting their cause. But most of those attacks have been organised strikes on specific locations. However, in the attack on Rukaramu, it appeared that the villagers happened to be in the path of the rebels' retreat.[47] And although rebels regularly strike in northwestern and southern Burundi, two Hutu strongholds, the New Year's attack was the first one on a military target near the capital in two years.

Colonel Darangwe said the army was still finding wounded villagers, and that the death toll could rise as soldiers combed the bush. Many people had life-threatening wounds, he said.[48]

He also said that the Hutu rebels had come from Congo and Rwanda to reinforce their compatriots in Burundi. And Lieutenant-Colonel Sinarunzi said "human losses are very heavy" but still being counted.[49]

The carnage was just one among countless others in a country which has been hobbled by ethnic conflict – in the struggle for power more than anything else – since 1962 when it won independence from Belgium.

The rebels' decision to attack a military base near the capital was undoubtedly intended to achieve maximum impact on the Tutsi military regime and its ethnic supporters by letting them know that they were not safe anywhere in this predominantly Hutu country in spite of

152

the fact that the Hutu majority were powerless.

It may also have stemmed from the fact that the insurgents no longer had much freedom to operate from Congo since Kabila, then Rwanda's and Burundi's and Uganda's ally, became the country's new ruler.

Unlike his predecessor Mobutu Sese Seko who supported the Hutu rebels financially and militarily and allowed them to use Congo (then Zaire) as a launching pad for incursions into Rwanda and Burundi, Kabila was then hostile to the Hutus until he embraced them later as allies in his war against his erstwhile comrades – Rwanda, Burundi, and Uganda – when they invaded his country to try to get rid of him.

But even if the rebels are no longer able to operate from their bases in Congo, they still have the capacity to wreak havoc within Burundi itself, paralyse the government, and extract maximum concessions from any Tutsi-dominated regime by waging a war of attrition indefinitely, sustained by their superiority in numbers as an integral part of the Hutu majority from whom they have always drawn support even though they have alienated some of them with their brutal tactics, especially when they kill fellow Hutus who don't support them as may have been the case with some of the killings on New Year's day in 1998.

As the search for the survivors in the New Year's day attack continued, more casualties were reported. The death toll climbed to 300, including 100 rebels and four government soldiers. And about 7,000 people were displaced when they fled their homes. According to a report from Burundi by Christophe Nkurunziza, a Burundian, in *The Boston Globe*:

"Up to 200 civilians, most of them women and children, died during the assault at Rukaramu settlement and a nearby army camp several miles south of the capital, army spokesman Lieutenant-Colonel Mamert Sinaranzi said....

While international human rights organizations have accused the army of using Hutu civilians as human shields, those aiding yesterday's search (for the attackers) joined voluntarily, said Sinaranzi....

It was unclear whether the civilians were targeted or simply caught in the cross-fire. In other attacks, the rebels...have killed Hutu civilians whom they accuse of denying shelter, money, and recruits to guerrillas....

The army said the Hutu were taking part in yesterday's roundup because they believe they were singled out by the rebels during Thursday's (January 1) attack.

The government's claim was difficult to confirm independently because the army had barred all reporters from the scene except those from state-controlled television, claiming it was too dangerous."[50]

It is doubtful that the survivors joined the search voluntarily, as the army spokesman claimed. Given the army's notorious record of brutality against the Hutu, it is highly probable that any Hutu who did not help the Tutsi army track down the rebels would have been labelled "a rebel" himself, or a rebel sympathiser, and would have risked being shot by Tutsi soldiers.

Another indication that the survivors were coerced into joining the search was the government's decision to bar all reporters from the scene except those working for state-controlled television. If it was dangerous for the other reporters to go to the scene of the massacre, as the government claimed, it was equally dangerous for the state television reporters to go there; and probably even more so, since they worked for the government and would have been prime target for attack by the rebels.

And if the army was able to protect state television reporters, it also could have protected the other reporters as well, had they been allowed to go to the scene of the massacre – as much as it was able to "protect" Hutu

154

civilians who joined the search to help find the attackers.

The state television reporters were allowed to go to the scene of the massacre because, as government employees, they were automatically expected to report favourably on the government and cover up the atrocities committed by the army. As employees of the state-controlled media in a highly repressive state, they could not function as independent reporters but only as megaphones for the Tutsi-dominated regime, echoing what the government wanted to be reported.

But such bias did not change the facts on the ground. The Hutu insurgents were waging a deadly campaign – as were Tutsi soldiers – and continued to do so regardless of how hard the government tried to gloss over the facts, especially regarding its brutal repression of innocent Hutu civilians.

This brutal repression is, only in a more violent way, an extension of the feudal servitude in which the Hutu majority have lived for hundreds of years under the Tutsi. And they will remain at their mercy probably for many years, considering their weakness in spite of their numerical strength:

"Hutus are cynical: though they outnumber the Tutsi six times over, their attempts over the past 30 years to gain power peacefully have been met with murder and repression."[31]

But that is a highly destabilising situation which guarantees only one thing: escalation and perpetuation of the conflict regardless of how many lives the Hutu continue to lose. They still count on their strength in numbers to prevail one day even if it takes 100 years. And they probably will not have to wait that long, may be no more than 30 years.

The New Year's attack which took place shortly before dawn was one of the most daring attempts by the Hutu rebels to strike at the very heart of the Tutsi ethnocracy, the nation's capital Bujumbura and its environs, to demonstrate their commitment to armed struggle as the most effective means to achieve their goal of Hutu emancipation from Tutsi domination, however delusional this may be, right now, considering the country's military might which dwarfs the rebels' capacity to wage war.

But the raid served a psychological purpose of far-reaching consequences. It scared the "invincible" Tutsis. It also dramatised the plight of the Hutu majority which had been largely ignored by the international media except in the case of Rwanda which was highlighted because of the ferocity and magnitude of the 1994 genocide unparalleled in modern history; no other holocaust has claimed so many lives in so short a time, and with so much bloodshed.

The Tutsi – in both Rwanda and Burundi – will never forget that. And any attack by the Hutu rebels reminds them of the fact that there is always a possibility of another holocaust of that magnitude; a fear the Hutu rebels have always exploited by launching more attacks against the Tutsi to create panic throughout the entire community regardless of its unintended consequences, making the Tutsi even more determined to hang on to power out of fear that they will be exterminated if they relinquish control. The New Year's attack was one such raid:

"Shortly before dawn on January 1st, a large group of rebels attacked Burundi's main airport, seizing weapons from the neighbouring garrison. The attack left at least 280 people dead, most of them villagers from nearby Rukaramu.

The army claimed that they had been murdered by the fleeing 'genocidal terrorists.' The rebels say they were killed by the army because of their pro-rebel support. Others say they were caught in crossfire as the soldiers chased the rebels in the darkness.

Most of the bodies seen by independent witnesses had

156

not been killed by bullets but by blows, many of them from hoes or machetes. That points a finger at the rebels. But...why should they kill their own people?

In Burundi's brutal conflict,...civilians, most of them Hutu, are the pawns and victims. The rebels force their support; the army takes revenge and demands their co-operation.

So all three versions of the new year massacre could be true: rebels killing people who refused to help them, soldiers taking reprisal, some people dying in the confusion....

Both FRODEBU, the main Hutu political party, and the National Council for the Defence of Democracy (CNDD), the Hutu guerrilla force, have grown in strength and militancy.

In December (1997) FRODEBU, which lost power in the coup, acknowledged an exile, Jean Minani, as its leader. And the CNDD rebels have linked up with the (Hutu) former members of the Rwandan army and militia; some of the rebels killed in the airport attack were wearing Rwandan uniforms.

Government claims that the group had fled across the border to Congo proved untrue. The rebels camped a few miles north-west of the capital, Bujumbura, launching another attack on January 6th.

That shows a new confidence: they no longer rely on disruptive hit-and-run tactics. But...the Tutsi-dominated army, which ran the country from 1966 until 1993, shows no sign of negotiating itself out of power."[52]

And the Hutu show no sign of giving up the fight.

The 1998 New Year's raid also set a precedent in terms of stepped-up attacks in and around the capital in this perennial conflict, emboldening the rebels to launch more such invasions in the future. The insurgents launched two more raids in the last week of January, belying the government's claim that the Tutsi military regime had everything under control around the capital after the previous attacks on January 1st and 6th. According to an army spokesman on January 21st, the rebels killed 45 people in two separate attacks in the previous 48 hours. All the victims were civilians except one.

Colonel Isaie Nibizi said the insurgents were members of the National Liberation Front (FNL), the military wing of the Party for the Liberation of the Hutu People (PALIPEHUTU). They killed 32 civilians on January 19th during the night in a settlement in northwest Burundi. He also said 13 people, including one government soldier, were killed in a six-hour attack on January 21st in rural Rumonge commune on the shore of Lake Tanganyika 47 miles south of the capital. But it was not clear which guerrilla group carried out the second attack.[53]

However, what was clear was that the guerrillas had intensified their campaign, mainly to extract concessions from the Tutsi-dominated regime and eventually establish a Hutu-majority government.

Although the Tutsi military rulers did not admit it, the guerrilla war compelled them to take some steps towards a political settlement of the conflict. But one such initiative met with disaster. Burundi's defence minister, Colonel Firmin Sinzoyiheba, was killed on 28 January 1998 when his helicopter crashed in poor weather.

According to Burundian officials, Sinzoyiheba, one of the most powerful figures in the military government, and four others died when the helicopter lost visibility and crashed in the Gihinga Hills, a 6,500-foot-high ridge, about 25 miles southeast of Bujumbura, the capital.

He and his entourage were travelling from Bujumbura to Gitega where the defence minister was to meet with Hutu opposition leaders whose political parties were the umbrella organisations of the armed groups waging guerrilla war against the Tutsi military government.[54] Communications minister, Pierre-Claver Ndayicariye, said there were heavy rains in the area when Colonel

Sinzoyiheba flew in the helicopter on his way to an informal meeting with the Hutu leaders to discuss ways of ending the civil war.[55]

Military head of state Pierre Buyoya also flew to Gitega for the informal peace talks but changed his route to avoid the storm, an indication that no sabotage was involved in the defence minister's helicopter crash.

Sinzoyiheba, a retired colonel, kept a low-profile in the Tutsi-dominated military government but was regarded by diplomats in Bujumbura as being almost as powerful as Buyoya. A Tutsi himself like Buyoya, Sinzoyiheba had also served as defence minister under the ousted president, Sylvestre Ntibantuganya, a Hutu, over whom he exerted enormous influence by virtue of his position as a member of the dominant Tutsi ethnic group and the army.

Tanzanian officials, who had tried but failed to mediate in the civil war, described Sinzoyiheba as a hardliner and the man behind the government's refusal to talk to the rebels.

Therefore it is doubtful that he would have made major concessions, if any, to the Hutu opposition leaders had he attended the meeting in Gitega.

But his decision, as well as Buyoya's, to go to the meeting was an indication that the Tutsi military regime had been forced by the guerrilla fighters to face harsh reality: the government can not win the war, and it can not impose its will on the Hutu majority by military means. It has to win their hearts and minds if there is going to be peace in the country. And that can be achieved only if the Hutu majority are given equal rights and are no longer treated as second-class citizens in their own homeland. The alternative is war which is going to bleed the country to death.

The January 1998 attacks had all the elements for such a prolonged war of attrition. The rebels targeted the capital. They raided a military garrison; launched sustained attacks using heavy weapons; blocked the country's main arteries, and were not neutralised by the army, as demonstrated by their tactical retreat when they camped only a few miles northwest of the capital, waiting for another ambush, and showing no fear of government forces who were so near them. According to *Keesing's Record of World Events*:

"Further rebel attacks on the outskirts of Bujumbura continued throughout January. The main road to the centre and north of the country was temporarily closed on January 11 following skirmishes in its vicinity.

Some 42 rebels were reportedly killed at Isale, 10 kilometres from Bujumbura, on January 14, whilst on January 18 rebels targeted a military post at Gikongo, on the northern outskirts of the capital.

Despite claims by military sources that the rebels had been repulsed, further exchanges of gunfire to the south of Bujumbura were reported on January 22."[56]

The attacks were carried out by more than one group, showing the raids were coordinated. The New Year's attack was carried out by the FDD, the armed wing of the National Council for the Defence of Democracy (CNDD); so were some of the other raids.

The rest were carried out by the National Liberation Front (FNL), the military arm of the Party for the Liberation of the Hutu People (PALIPEHUTU).

The attacks continued the following month. On 12 February 1998, at least 24 civilians were killed and 46 wounded when Hutu rebels attacked a village in southern Burundi, witnesses said. Hundreds of rebels descended from the hills around Minago, 30 miles south of the capital, at night, wielding rifles, machetes, hoes, and hammers and knives, according to a report from Minago. As Athanase Nibizi, a 40-year-old priest who hid inside his church during the three-hour attack, stated: "They killed 24 people. I counted the bodies this morning."[57]

160

And in the words of 55-year-old Zacharie Kamwenubusa: "Many, many people were killed with machetes, knives, hoes, hammers, and clubs. I saw a young child...hacked in the neck, head, and hand. Many others were killed in the same way."[58]

Witnesses said the dead included men, women, and children. Most were found hacked to death in their own houses. A few hundred yards behind a church and a camp housing several hundred displaced people, Nibizi pointed to 16 fresh graves topped with stick crosses. He said 8 other bodies were buried nearby.

The villagers in Munago said some of the attackers were singing throughout the mayhem, while others fired off rifles and looted property including chickens, goats and beer. "After killing the people, they looted everything. Everybody tried to hide," Kamwenubusa said. A local military commander who did not want to be identified said at least 46 civilians had been injured.[59]

Besides the carnage, it is the increasing level of sophistication and intensity of the attacks which compelled the authorities, especially the Tutsi army, to acknowledge the magnitude of the guerrilla campaign. According to a Reuters report from Minago, Burundi, in *The Boston Globe*:

"A local military commander...said the wounded were evacuated to hospitals in Bujumbura and further south in the lakeside town of Rumonge. Germaine Nteziyorirwa, a female survivor, showed a Reuters correspondent five machete wounds to her head, neck, arm and hands.

Residents and army officers said the rebels had launched an organized assault, striking simultaneously three separate locations around the village....

The military commander...said his soldiers had chased away the attackers, but as he spoke, the sound of automatic gunfire echoed in the distance.

Hutu rebels stepped up their campaign against

Burundi's Tutsi-dominated army and government last month (January 1998), with a New Year's Day offensive on Bujumbura airport and its environs....The fighting has continued in hills around the capital almost everyday since."[60]

The guerrilla campaign was complemented by the economic embargo to try to compel the Tutsi military regime to make substantial concessions to its opponents. On 21 February 1998, the presidents of Tanzania, Rwanda and Uganda, the prime minister of Ethiopia, and the secretary-general of the Organisation of African Unity, unanimously agreed at a meeting in Kampala, Uganda, to maintain regional sanctions against Burundi until the ruling military junta moved towards civilian rule.[61] However, Rwanda's pledge was only symbolic. The Tutsi quasi-military regime in Kigali, Rwanda's capital, did nothing to honour its pledge and, instead, placed ethnic loyalty – support for fellow Tutsis in Burundi – above democratic principles and regional solidarity.

In yet another deadly attack in April 1998, Hutu guerrillas inflicted heavy casualties in their sustained campaign to destabilise the Tutsi government. It was described as the second-most serious offensive since the January 1st attack in which the insurgents captured and briefly occupied Burundi's main airport just outside the capital.

The latest attack took place on 22 April east of Bujumbura. At least 73 people, including 47 rebels, were killed, according to state radio.[62] The rebels attacked Bandagura and Rubingo hills 12 miles east of the capital Bujumbura, killing 26 civilians and wounding at least 10 others. As the state-run radio put it: "Administrative sources say the death toll has risen to 26 civilians dead, and according to the same sources, 47 assailants were killed."[63] They also stole cattle and escaped to the Kibira forest north of Bujumbura.

The attack near the capital, one among several, was also intended to let the government know that the guerrilla force was a factor to be reckoned with. In spite of the military setbacks the rebels suffered, they made it clear that they were still capable of hitting Bujumbura and its surrounding areas with impunity.

Residents of the capital said they heard gunfire to the east of the lakeside city early in the morning; it's on the northeastern shore of Lake Tanganyika.

The rebels were reportedly killed in ensuring clashes with the army. And, as in previous attacks, the insurgents used hoes and machetes during the dawn raid on April 22nd.

The timing of the raid, at dawn, and its location in the vicinity of the capital, had a significant psychological impact on the city's residents including the military rulers who could no longer dismiss lightly the escalation of the offensive.

Military head of state Major Pierre Buyoya continued to pursue a two-track policy of internal reform and attempts to soften or end the economic embargo imposed on his regime. The military junta also continued to wage war against the insurgents of the National Council for the Defence of Democracy (NCDD) and the Party for the Liberation of the Hutu People (PALIPEHUTU). And the two groups, which represented the Hutu majority, continued to push their demands for military reform, democratic elections, and a new constitution while at the same time continuing to wage guerrilla warfare as a leverage or bargaining tool in any negotiations in order to extract maximum concessions from the Tutsi military regime.

But any major concessions by the government would set a precedent, with the Hutu expecting more, as the Tutsi ethnocracy is eroded gradually and eventually collapses; an inconceivable scenario for the Tutsi. It is unthinkable that they would work for their own destruction. That is what democracy means to them in a country where they are vastly outnumbered.

Yet neither side wants to compromise on the basis of a mutually acceptable formula. This is what has prompted some African leaders to concede that the best solution to the Hutu-Tutsi ethnic conflict is separation of the two groups. Each should have its own independent state, as President Daniel arap Moi of Kenya bluntly suggested. According to a report from Nairobi, Kenya, in the *International Herald Tribune*:

"President Daniel arap Moi of Kenya suggested Thursday (9 April 1998) that the Tutsi of Rwanda and Burundi should live in one country and the Hutu in another, the official Kenya News Agency reported. He linked the suggestion to a warning that tribalism could destroy Africa....

Mr. Moi's proposal brought into the open an idea that has long been discussed behind closed doors, but rejected because of the implications it would have for other African countries where boundaries run through tribal groupings, analysts said....'President Moi said that unless Africans were careful, tribalism will destroy the continent completely,' the news agency said."[64]

Tribalism has inflicted enormous damage on both Rwanda and Burundi, with people being killed everyday because of what they are. For instance, on 18 May 1998, 63 people were killed and 12 wounded when armed Hutus attacked camps in two communes in Burundi's northwestern Cibitoke Province.[65] All the victims were Tutsis. This was one of the attacks the Tutsi military regime used to justify its brutal repression of the Hutu majority, targeting all Hutus for the same reason the Hutu rebels attacked the Tutsi in Cibitoke Province: because of what they are.

It is this kind of bigotry which has fuelled the Hutu-

Tutsi ethnic conflict, one of the bloodiest in the history of post-colonial Africa. Attempts to resolve the conflict have achieved nothing through the years.

But despite the deadlock in the quest for peace, further attempts were made to bring the two sides together and try to end the civil war in Burundi. In early May 1998, negotiators said they would try again in June to hold another peace conference.

The peace talks were tentatively scheduled for June 15th in neighbouring Tanzania. A spokesman for the Organisation of African Unity (OAU) said Burundi's Tutsi-dominated government had agreed to attend the meeting after backing out of an earlier round of talks in August 1997, citing bias and security concerns.[66]

The Tutsi have always accused Tanzania of favouring the Hutu. Tanzania and other countries, as well as human rights workers and missionaries who have worked in Burundi through the years, accuse the Tutsi of oppressing the Hutu; a charge the Tutsi military regime seems to have inadvertently conceded when it promulgated a new constitution in June 1998, mainly as a result of intensified guerrilla attacks and economic sanctions imposed on Burundi by its neighbours in August 1996 but enforced especially by Tanzania and Kenya.

On 6 June 1998, President Pierre Buyoya signed into law a transitional constitution which, theoretically, laid the foundation for sweeping changes in the country's Tutsi-dominated government. The constitution replaced the decree Buyoya passed after he came to power in July 1996.

If implemented, the reform measures embodied in the transitional constitution would have marked the first time in almost two years that the Hutu FRODEBU party, ousted from power in the 1996 military coup, would have started having considerable say in the Tutsi-led government. FRODEBU member of parliament Leonidas Ntibayazi said the transitional accord aimed to "restore peace and make equilibrium in all sectors – in the army, in the economy, in the justice system, and socially."[67]

Members of parliament and other officials said the new transitional constitution provided for a range of institutional reforms including replacing the post of prime minister with two vice presidents, enlarging parliament from 81 to 121, and reducing the overall size of government.

But the new constitution was also a major concession to the Tutsi who engineered and executed the 1996 military coup. It combined some elements of Buyoya's 1996 decree – the edict was tailored to suit the interests of the powerful Tutsi who put him power; otherwise he would not have issued it – with the 1992 democratic constitution which was suspended after the coup.

Peace Process Minister Ambroise Niyonsaba said a government reshuffle was likely to begin the same week the new constitution was signed into law, with Buyoya selecting two vice presidents.[68] Members of parliament said the first vice president responsible for political and administrative affairs was likely to come from FRODEBU. To help reduce hostilities, a Hutu would have to fill such a powerful post. That is why the Hutu FREDOBU party was almost guaranteed to get the job.

The transitional constitution was part of a comprehensive peace initiative led by Tanzania's former president, Julius Nyerere.

But at the peace talks in Arusha, Tanzania, in June 1998, delegates of the Tutsi military junta and the rebel representatives were divided over the question of a cease-fire. In what amounted to a concession to the rebels and to the East and Central African leaders, because of the cumulative impact of the guerrilla campaign and the economic embargo, the Tutsi regime's representatives at the peace talks in Tanzania said they wanted a cease-fire but also an end to the sanctions. However, the rebels of the National Council for the Defence of Democracy (CNDD), the largest Hutu opposition group, rejected the cease-fire and linkage of the two.

The peace talks started on 15 June 1998 under the chairmanship of Julius Nyerere. According to a report from Arusha, Tanzania, in *The Boston Globe*:

"The talks brought together the government and the National Council for the Defense of Democracy for the first time under Nyerere, who has not visited Burundi for two years, in part for security reasons.

In the initial stages of the talks, Nyerere, Tanzania's founding president, is seeking common ground on a cease-fire, the future of sanctions, and a commitment to progress to a second round, delegates said....

The Burundi government delegation said after private consultations with Nyerere it was willing to agree to a 'cessation of hostilities' and was committed to the talks.

Nyerere yesterday (17 June 1998) continued private talks (with political leaders and rebels groups).

Diplomats said the National Council for the Defense of Democracy was opposed both to a cease-fire and to the lifting of sanctions.

Nyerere recognizes National Council founder Leonard Nyangoma as the group's legal representative, even though it remains unclear how much influence he holds over its armed wing, the Forces for the Defense of Democracy, one diplomat said. The rebel group is split and one faction protested yesterday its exclusion from the talks."[69]

The refusal by the National Council for the Defence of Democracy to accept a cease-fire and an end to economic sanctions was deeply rooted in their mistrust of the Tutsi military regime. They did not believe it would honour its commitment to the peace process. They also had history on their side – unfulfilled promises, atrocities against the Hutu which were never addressed and whose perpetrators were never punished – all the way since independence in

1962.

It is a tragic history which includes the assassination of Hutu leaders and the extermination of the Hutu elite – to deprive the Hutu of effective leadership – their colleagues at the peace talks in Tanzania never forgot:

"At one time Burundi's history of ethnic massacres was even more savage than Rwanda"s. So after Rwanda's 1994 genocide, many people assumed that Burundi was on the brink of a similar tragedy....

Out of the 81 members of the 1993 parliament, 23 have been murdered – all of them from the majority, mainly Hutu, FRODEBU party. Many others have fled into exile, some joining militant Hutu movements."[70]

It is these militants – some of whom were moderate before – who took the most uncompromising stand during the peace talks, while some of the most intransigent among them were excluded from the negotiations. On the Tutsi side, there were just as many with an equally inflexible attitude.

The road to peace remained filled with land mines.

Stalemate: Peace without Compromise

In spite of the intransigence of the Tutsi military regime, the peace negotiations in Tanzania were partly facilitated by Pierre Buyoya and his supporters in and outside the government. As soon as Burundi's neighbours imposed economic sanctions on the landlocked nation, Buyoya started working on an agreement with what was left of parliament and its dominant FRODEBU party which won the 1993 elections. It was this agreement which was discussed at the peace talks in Arusha, Tanzania, and which Buyoya hoped would be accepted by Hutu militants, Burundi's neighbours, and by the chief negotiator, Julius Nyerere.

The agreement was endorsed by FRODEBU members of parliament and their Tutsi counterparts, but after a stormy debate in the National Assembly on 4 June 1998. And it was on the basis of this accord that Buyoya had himself formally sworn as president of Burundi, ending his status as a *de facto* head of state.

The new law – transitional constitution – allowed for the creation of a coalition government comprising 22 cabinet members, 11 of whom would come from the opposition; the replacement of the prime minister by two vice presidents, one Hutu and the other Tutsi; and the enlargement of the national legislature, as we learned earlier.

But this constitutionally mandated power-sharing agreement was vehemently denounced by militants on both sides. The chairman of the Tutsi UPRONA party who was also one of the most uncompromising Tutsi hardliners, Charles Mukasi, still refused to talk to the *genocidaires* (as he called them) of the main Hutu FRODEBU party, and did not go to Arusha, Tanzania, for the peace talks. But his party, which supported Buyoya's peace initiative, sent representatives and backed the proposed power-sharing agreement.

On the Hutu side, FRODEBU was also splintered, but the main group supported the peace process. However, the major militant group, the National Council for the Defence of Democracy (CNDD) denounced the agreement as "an act of treason" and vowed it will continue waging guerrilla warfare.

Yet, even the CNDD itself was divided, and its founder Leonard Nyangoma, who led one of the factions, went to Arusha for the peace talks and met Buyoya face-to-face. And two other militant Hutu groups also sent delegates to the peace conference. But given the intractable nature of the problem, prospects for conflict resolution in Burundi remained bleak at best.

169

The warring parties signed a cease-fire agreement in Arusha, Tanzania, on 21 June 1998. But the agreement was violated by both sides. In fact, it was hardly enforced. According to reports from Burundi, about 13,000 people fled renewed clashes between Hutu guerrillas and Tutsi government soldiers in the northern part of the country in the last week of July 1998. President Buyoya conceded that the cease-fire existed only on paper and questioned whether rebel leader Leonard Nyangoma controlled his forces.[71]

Fighting continued throughout the year and, in a rare admission, the government acknowledged its own excesses against civilians. Saying "there were errors and we have to come clean about it," a government spokesman admitted that army troops had killed "around 30" innocent civilians in a clash with Hutu rebels on 3 – 4 November 1998. But he denied reports that 178 civilians had died at Mutambu, 22 miles southeast of the capital.

Although he admitted wrongdoing, this was the only second time that the Tutsi-dominated government had acknowledged responsibility for killing Hutu civilians,[72] whom it has always targeted for reprisals, in retaliation for attacks by the rebels – even if they don't support them. And there was evidence showing that Tutsi soldiers had killed more civilians than the government was willing to admit. According to *Keesing's Record of World Events*:

"Amid continued reports of killings during the month (of November 1998), the Agence France-Press (AFP) news agency reported on November 10 that at least 100 Hutu civilians had been massacred by soldiers of the Tutsi-dominated army at Mutambu, near the capital Bujumbura, in early November.

The killings were said to have been carried out in retaliation for an earlier attack on a camp which was sheltering Tutsis, by fighters of the National Liberation Forces (FNL), the armed wing of the Hutu-based

PALIPEHUTU movement.

On November 14 government officials said three army officers had been arrested in connection with a massacre of 30 civilians at Mutambu, an incident which was described as a botched operation against Hutu rebels.

Severin Ntahomvukiye, the External Relations and Co-operation Minister, said on November 3 that there had been an attempt to form a new group. He did not identify the group but confirmed that a number of people had been arrested."[73]

Then two months later in January 1999, the leaders of the seven African countries which imposed economic sanctions on Burundi agreed to suspend them, pending more progress in ending the civil war.[74] The embargo was really being enforced by Tanzania, more than any other country, because of her strategic position as conduit for Burundi's imports and exports and her determination to help resolve the Hutu-Tutsi conflict.

The decision to suspend sanctions was one of several steps the East African heads of state took at their meeting in Arusha, Tanzania, aimed at increasing cooperation among the countries in the region. The talks specifically sought to achieve integration of Rwanda and Burundi into the East African bloc which was working towards regional solidarity in several areas.

Rwanda and Burundi have really never been an integral part of the East African community of nations, which is mostly Anglophone, because of their civil conflicts and especially their ties to the Francophone bloc. As former Belgian colonies, they have historical ties to Francophone countries and use French as their official language, unlike the rest of the East African countries – Kenya, Uganda and Tanzania – which use English.

Although the economic embargo imposed on Burundi was intended to be a punitive measure, it also drew the country into the orbit as an integral part of the East African bloc. Unfortunately, no significant progress towards ending the civil war – which was the main condition for suspending economic sanctions – was made in the following months to justify continued suspension of the embargo.

In spite of the mutual suspicion between the main parties to the conflict, the parties involved concluded another round of peace talks in Tanzania towards the end of March 1999 and reported "some progress."[75]

The peace process was facilitated in another way when two months later the Tutsi soldiers who assassinated Burundi's first Hutu president, Melchior Ndadaye in October 1993, were convicted of the murder. On 14 May 1999, the Supreme Court of Burundi sentenced five soldiers to death for the assassination. The court convicted 39 people and acquitted 38 in the assassination trial. The Justice Ministry said prison terms handed down ranged from one year to 20 years.[76]

It was this assassination as part of an attempted coup by Tutsi soldiers, just four months after Ndadaye assumed office, which plunged the country into chaos, triggering a wave of massacres and a civil war between the Tutsi-dominated army and the Hutu rebels.

Those sentenced to death were Lieutenant Paul Kamana, in exile in Uganda; Laurence Nzeyimana; Juvénal Gahungu; Sylvere Nduwumukama; and Emmanuel Ndayizeye.[77] They were responsible for one of the most gruesome political murders on the African continent in which President Ndadaye was bayoneted to death.

All the accused, who were Tutsi, pleaded not guilty.[78] Yet the evidence against them was overwhelming, more than enough to justify the sentences imposed on them.

Unfortunately, the real culprits behind the assassination were left untouched because they were powerful individuals in the army and in the country as a whole. And they were all Tutsi like the killers themselves.

Although Ndadaye's assassins were brought to justice, their conviction did not improve relations or bridge the ethnic divide between the Hutu and the Tutsi; nor was it expected to, despite its powerful symbolism as a conciliatory gesture. It was, undoubtedly, hailed by some Hutus as a triumph of justice in this particular case. Yet a comprehensive peace agreement – mandating dispensation of justice across the spectrum for all Hutus, and no less for the Tutsi – would require more than just a few cases of restorative and retributive justice.

The peace process was virtually derailed by the continuation of clashes between the Hutu rebels and the Tutsi army during the following months in what was apparently an escalation of hostilities by both sides to achieve maximum political and military advantages they could use as a bargaining tool in future negotiations. Both sides were losers. There was no winner without peace.

Some of the biggest conflicts took place in August 1999 when Hutu insurgents and Tutsi soldiers clashed outside the capital Bujumbura. Thousands of civilians fled the surrounding areas and sought refuge in the capital.[79] And villagers accused the Tutsi-dominated army of killing 147 Hutu civilians in revenge for a Hutu rebel attack that took place on August 10th. But a Defence Ministry spokesman blamed the rebels for the killings, despite evidence to the contrary and eyewitness accounts by some of the victims who survived the mayhem.[80]

One of the biggest rebel attacks took place on 29 August 1999. It lasted from midnight to dawn, resulting in at least 46 deaths. The offensive, which rocked the capital and terrified tens of thousands of its residents, targeted parts of Bujumbura inhabited by Tutsis – as almost the entire city was, after the ethnic cleansing of the Hutu following the 1996 Tutsi-engineered military coup in which President Sylvestre Ntibantunganya, a Hutu, was ousted.

The August attack came at a critical time as a new

round of negotiations – seen as crucial if the country's fragile peace process were to take hold – drew near in Arusha, Tanzania,[81] and was obviously calculated to disrupt the peace initiative. The attack not only rocked the capital but also spread fear of escalating violence across the country between the Hutu and the Tutsi, and was a major blow to the peace process.[82]

Nyerere Dies

The peace process suffered another major setback within two months of the Hutu offensive when Julius Nyerere, Tanzania's first president and chief mediator in Burundi's conflict, died of leukaemia on 14 October 1999 in a hospital in London, England. He was 77.

His role as a mediator in African conflicts was widely acknowledged. And in the case of Burundi, no other negotiator had Nyerere's stature or could command as much respect as he did from both sides to the conflict.

A scholarly statesman and consummate politician, he was confident of himself in academic circles as much as he was at ease among peasants because of his ascetic lifestyle and genuine commitment to equality and justice for all, from the most humble to the most exalted. He left a void that will be difficult to fill. As *The Economist* stated:

"Although his socialist policies were criticised, his integrity and erudition were much admired....A deeply principled man, Julius Nyerere was that rare – and not always fortunate – sort of idealist who had a chance to put his ideals into practice....He was a preacher as much as a politician....

No one questioned his sincerity, and his integrity was widely admired. Unlike many African leaders of his generation he lived simply and was not corrupt.

He gave Tanzania stability and unity. Under his one-party rule it was politically peaceful and it was spared civil war....

Though honest himself, his moral example was not enough to prevent the widespread theft of foreign aid. A believer in justice, he...(was) as keen on equality as on economic growth....

Compared to some of his neighbours, Mr. Nyerere was an angel....Although late in life Mr. Nyerere did acknowledge that his socialist experiments had failed, his idealism never left him. In retirement, he even tried to reform the ruling party. Finding it inert and ineradicably corrupt, he changed his mind about one-party rule.

Admirers will say that Julius Nyerere was too idealistic for this world and that bad implementation does not negate his dream of equality. To critics, his moral approach to politics masked an arrogance and a refusal to listen to those with shrewder views of what was best for his country.

Tanzanians abandoned ujamaa (familyhood, African socialism) as soon as they could. Yet Mr. Nyerere himself remained extraordinarily popular. His policies had failed, but people admired his sincerity and his ascetic life. His warm and engaging style – in conversation and from a platform – was irresistible....

He bore the title mwalimu or teacher....He was a magnificent teacher: articulate, questioning, stimulating, caring."[83]

And as *Newsweek* put it:

"(Julius Nyerere)...died an international hero....Nyerere's personality was irresistible. Absolute power never corrupted him: he earned $8,000 during his best year. His chosen honorific was Mwalimu – teacher. And under his direction Tanzania's literacy level rose sharply. When Nyerere, 77, died of leukemia last week, the world lost a man of principle."[84]

On a continent no longer under colonial rule but wracked by civil wars, his enormous contribution to the liberation struggle will always be remembered, as much as will his role as a peacemaker and staunch advocate of African unity, for which he will be sorely missed. In the words of *The Christian Science Monitor*:

"His goal of ending white minority rule in Africa, inspired numerous other liberation movements....In retirement, he mediated numerous political crises on the continent."[85]

One of his biggest achievements – besides spearheading the struggle to end white minority rule in Africa probably more than any of his contemporaries besides a few other leaders such as Kwame Nkrumah, Sekou Toure, Modibo Keita, Kenneth Kaunda, and Milton Obote – was the creation and consolidation of Tanzania as a union of two independent states (Tanganyika and Zanzibar), the only such union on the entire continent.

He left behind a stable and peaceful country, a rare phenomenon on this highly unstable and embattled continent. As Keith Richburg, the *Washington Post* Africa bureau chief during the 1990s, states in his book, *Out of America: A Black Man Confronts Africa*:

"One of my earliest trips was to Tanzania, and there I found a country that had actually managed to purge itself of the evil of tribalism.

Under Julius Nyerere and his ruling socialists, the government was able to imbue a true sense of nationalism that transcended the country's natural ethnic divisions, among other things by vigorous campaigns to upgrade education and to make Swahili a truly national language....Tanzania is one place that has succeeded in removing the linguistic barrier that separates so many of

Africa's warring factions.

But after three years traveling the continent, I've found that Tanzania is the exception, not the rule. In Africa,...it *is* all about tribes.

Tribalism is what prompted tens of thousands of Rwandan Hutus to pick up machetes and hoes and panga knives and farming tools to bash in the skulls and sever the limbs of their Tutsi neighbors. Tribalism is why entire swaths of Kenya's scenic Rift Valley lie in scorched ruins, why Zulu gunmen in ski masks mow down Xhosa workers outside a factory gate in South Africa, and why thousands of hungry displaced Kasai huddle under plastic sheeting at a remote train station in eastern Zaire (thousands were massacred, disemboweled, and mutilated in Shaba – formerly Katanga – Province, in 1993). And it is tribalism under another name – clans, subclans, factions – that caused young men in Mogadishu to shell the city to oblivion and loot what was left of the rubble."[86]

And as Philip Ochieng', a prominent Kenyan journalist and political analyst who worked at the *Daily News* in Dar es Salaam, Tanzania, in the early 1970s when I was a news reporter of the same paper, stated in his article, "Mwalimu Nyerere's Bequest to Mkapa a Tall Order," in *The Nation*, Nairobi, Kenya, 16 October 1999, two days after Nyerere died:

"Nyerere...never appointed any official or allowed one to be appointed on any other basis than qualification, inclination and experience. This contributed a great deal to making Tanzania the most united country in Africa.

This unity and sharp national consciousness was contributed to by two other life-works of the Teacher (Mwalimu Nyerere). One was that he insisted on uniform Kiswahili throughout the Republic. During the three years that I worked in Dar es Salaam I rarely heard any tribal language being spoken.

The other was what Mwalimu called *Elimu yenye manufaa*. This 'functional education' was much more than what we in Kenya call *elimu ya ngumbaru* ('adult education'). Though beneficiaries specialised in a technique, education was always holistic. As a result, 'poor' Tanzania has one of the highest literacy rates (almost l00) in the world, many times above that of Kenya."

Ten years after Nyerere died, Ochieng' also wrote the following about the late Tanzanian leader in his article, "Africa's Greatest Leader Was A Heroic Failure," *The East African*, Nairobi, 19 October 2009:

"Julius Nyerere is among the extremely few world leaders who have selflessly attempted great things for their national peoples.
Other African leaders — notably Leopold Senghor and Tom Mboya — have spoken of "African socialism" as a means of restoring human dignity to the African person after a protracted era of colonial brutalisation and dehumanisation. But none has ever offered a plausible definition of 'African socialism.'
Mwalimu Nyerere was the first – probably the only – African nationalist leader to cast a serious moral and intellectual eye upon Africa's "extended family" tradition and weave a practical national development philosophy around it.
Ujamaa had two basic components.
The Ujamaa Village was an attempt to revive traditional rural communalism – bringing groups of villages together, investing collectively in them and running them through modern democratic precepts.
Since the turn of the 21st century, Kenya's own leaders have divided and sub-divided what used to be called districts into veritable village units, claiming a purpose similar to 'Nyerereism' – to bring utilities and social services 'closer to the people.'

178

The second component was much more theoretically shaky – a series of nationalisations intended to bring urban commerce and industry under state control, the state purporting to be the public's trustee.

But the 1967 Arusha Declaration in which this doctrine of "socialism and self-reliance" was enunciated opened a Pandora's box of ideology. Ideas ran from the extreme right to others that were so leftist that, in the circular prism of ideas, they actually bordered on the right!

In a single-party system, all these ideas were forced to contend with one another within that party.

It was no wonder, then, that Marxist-Leninists, Bepari (capitalists) and even Kabaila (feudalists) held central positions both in the party and in government.

This, indeed, was where Nyerere began to reveal his greatness.

In other 'socialist' situations – such as Sekou Toure's Conakry – every thought and activity deemed dangerous would simply have been banned, often on pain of death. Nyerere encouraged even his bitterest opponents to express themselves freely and without fear.

And he often took them on – not by means of such state machinery as our Nyayo House basement, but intellectually, replying to each critic point by point.

The Nationalist (the party's own organ) and *The Standard* Tanzania (the government publication on which Ben Mkapa and I worked – later renamed Daily News) routinely published news, features, columns and letters expressing the most diverse views.

Nyerere demanded only that his detractors produce the facts and figures and weave these into cogent thought.

'Argue, don't shout!' he once admonished his equivalents of the loudmouthed but empty-headed coalition that rules Kenya....

By replacing the colonial educational structure with what he called Elimu yenye Manufaa ('functional education'), he enabled Tanzania to kill up to five birds with one stone.

Tanzanian is the only African country that has totally banished illiteracy, and the Three Rs are solidly linked to vocational interests.

In the process, Tanzania became the African country with the highest degree of national self-consciousness and – through it and through Kiswahili – has almost annihilated the bane of Kenya that we call tribalism....

Any nation that tries to cultivate self-sufficiency, self-efficiency, self-respect and self-pride will find it morally compelling to share these ideals with other nations the world over.

Ujamaa inspired Tanzania into spending much of its meagre resources on liberating the rest of Africa and the world from the colonial yoke.

At a time when Nairobi was drowning in crude elite grabbing, Dar es Salaam was a Mecca of the world's national liberation movements, and a hotbed of global intellectual thought.

From this perspective, it is justifiable to say that Mwalimu Julius Kambarage, son of Chief Nyerere, is the greatest and most successful leader that Africa has ever produced since the European colonial regime collapsed 50 years ago."

Unfortunately, Tanzania's success in combating tribalism and other vices under the leadership of Nyerere has not been emulated by others in the region. In fact, tribalism threatens to destroy Kenya, and even Uganda. And it has almost destroyed other African countries.

It is tribalism which almost destroyed Nigeria during the sixties when the Igbos of the Eastern Province seceded from the federation after tens of thousands of their kinsmen – at least 30,000 – were massacred in the North by the Hausa-Fulani.

Tanzania under Nyerere was the first country to recognise Biafra (Eastern Nigeria) as an independent state on moral grounds as a protest against the massacre of the Igbos – as well as other Easterners – and the unwillingness of the Federal and Northern Nigerian authorities to protect the victims. As Nyerere stated:

"Unity can only be based on the general consent of the people involved. The people must feel that this state, or this nation, is theirs; and they must be willing to have their quarrels in that context. Once a large number of the people of any such political unit stop believing that the state is theirs, and that the government is their instrument, then the unit is no longer viable. It will not receive the loyalty of its citizens.

For the citizen's duty to serve, and if necessary to die for, his country stems from the fact that it is his and that its government is the instrument of himself and his fellow citizens. The duty stems, in other words, from the common denominator of accepted statehood, and from the state government's responsibility to protect all the citizens and serve them all. For, states, and governments, exist for men and for the service of man. They exist for the citizens' protection, their welfare, and the future well-being of their children. There is no other justification for states and governments except man.

In Nigeria this consciousness of a common citizenship was destroyed by the events of 1966, and in particular by the pogroms in which 30,000 Eastern Nigerians were murdered, many more injured, and about two million forced to flee from the North of their country. It is these pogroms, and the apparent inability or unwillingness of the authorities to protect the victims, which underlies the Easterners' conviction that they have been rejected by other Nigerians and abandoned by the Federal Government.

Whether the Easterners are correct in their belief that they have been rejected is a matter for argument. But they do have this belief. And if they are wrong, they have to be

181

convinced that they are wrong. They will not convinced by being shot. Nor will their acceptance as part of the Federation be demonstrated by the use of Federal power to bomb schools and hospitals in the areas to which people have fled from persecution."[87]

There are striking similarities between Nigeria and Burundi – as well as Rwanda – with regard to massacres perpetrated along ethnic lines, while the authorities do nothing to stop the killings. Sometimes they encourage and even help the killers.

It is these pogroms and other atrocities committed by the Tutsi-dominated army against the Hutu in Burundi – and in neighbouring Rwanda – which threaten to destroy the country as a single political entity; a tragedy Tanzania – although a country of 126 tribes – was able to avoid under the astute leadership of President Nyerere. As *The Christian Science Monitor* stated:

"Tanzania is the only country in sub-Saharan Africa, which, thanks to the nationalist policies of Julius Nyerere...forged a sense of national identity strong enough to eclipse tribal affiliation."[88]

Nyerere was eulogised beyond Africa. *The New York Times* hailed his achievements and described him as "an uncharacteristically humble and modest national leader...idealistic, principled." It went on to state:

"Julius K. Nyerere, the founding father of Tanzania,...used East Africa as a pulpit from which to spread his socialist philosophy worldwide....

Mr. Nyerere became one of the most prominent of the first generation of politicians to head newly independent African states as colonialism ebbed, playing a leading role in the debate over economic inequalities between the Northern and Southern Hemispheres.

When he guided what had been the British Trust Territory of Tanganyika into sovereignty in 1961, he was the youngest of the continent's triumphant nationalists, a group that included Kwame Nkrumah of Ghana, Jomo Kenyatta of Kenya, Kenneth Kaunda of Zambia and Felix Houphouet-Boigny of Ivory Coast.

When he stepped down as President 24 years later, he was only the third modern African leader to relinquish power voluntarily on a continent that by then included 50 independent states ((the other two leaders were Ahmadou Ahidjo of Cameroon and Leopold Sedar Senghor of Senegal). He went neither to jail nor into exile, but to a farm in Butiama, his home village, near the shore of Lake Victoria....

After a vast investment in education, literacy rose phenomenally, and 83 percent of Tanzanians were able to read and write. Mr. Nyerere also succeeded in promoting Swahili so that it superseded dozens of tribal tongues to become a true national language....

The debate over Mr. Nyerere's leadership extended beyond his tenure, with academics, politicians and development strategists often dividing sharply over his legacy.

His domestic and international defenders, generally people of the left, praised his emphasis on social investments and his egalitarian economic policies, crediting them with creating a culturally cohesive nation that avoided ethnic conflict while life expectancy, literacy and access to water increased.

His Tanzanian supporters took pride in Mr. Nyerere's reputation as one of the most prominent proponents of a new economic order that would benefit the developing South in economic relations with the industrial North.

Mr. Nyerere also gained international prestige for his principled support of the struggles for majority rule in South Africa, Namibia, Zimbabwe, Mozambique and Angola, and for Tanzania's military counter-offensive against Idi Amin of Uganda, which routed the dictator and sent him into exile.

The Third World honored him, and he won the respect of such Western leaders as Olof Palme, Pierre Trudeau, Willy Brandt and Jimmy Carter.

Still, his critics, who included free-market liberals and conservatives, condemned him for adopting paternalistic and coercive policies like ujamaa....

By the time Mr. Nyerere gave up the last vestiges of political power, when he retired as chairman of the single political party,...almost 70 percent of the people had been prodded to move from traditional lands into paternalistically planned villages – ujamaa – in what became Africa's largest and most debated example of social engineering....

His critics...deplored his insistence on one-party rule and price controls, which they said stultified Tanzania's economy, shrank agricultural production, encouraged corruption and led to vast squandering of foreign aid....

The distance Mr. Nyerere traveled from his birth to political power and to the center of an international polemic on development was enormous, spanning ages as well as years....

He was spotted as an exceedingly bright child by the White Fathers, the priests who ran the (boarding) school, and in 1936 he placed first in the entire territory (of Tanganyika) on an entrance exam for a school in Tabora...which was patterned on private schools in Britain....

He went to Makerere University in Uganda, and...won a scholarship to Edinburgh University, where he earned a master's degree in history and economics....

Mr. Nyerere became the Third World's most assertive exponent of the new economic order in which the economic imbalance between the North and South would be overcome through international law and obligation rather than through markets or charity....

Mr. Nyerere reinforced his reputation abroad by his steadfast support of liberation movements....He provided training camps for the African National Congress from South Africa and...support for national movements fighting in Mozambique and Rhodesia (as well as in Angola and Namibia).

And in 1978, after Uganda annexed a 710-square-mile section of Tanzania, Mr. Nyerere angrily denounced Idi Amin, the Ugandan despot,...(and) with startling bluntness, he added:

'There is this tendency in Africa to think that it does not matter if an African kills other Africans. Had Amin been white, free Africa would have passed many resolutions condemning him. Being black is becoming a certificate to kill fellow Africans'....

After he retired, Mr. Nyerere was often asked whether he had any regrets. In a typical interview, he said he was pleased that 'Tanzanians have more sense of national identity than many other Africans,' and he expressed pride in the nation's high rate of literacy....

'What would I have changed if I had my time again? Not much.'

The white-haired farmer, the Mwalimu, then turned to his attempts to instill his idea of African socialism.

'They keep saying you've failed,' he mused. 'But what is wrong with urging people to pull together? Did Christianity fail because the world isn't all Christian?'"[89]

A true Pan-Africanist, Nyerere died while still in the process of trying to help neighbouring Burundi forge a genuine sense of national identity on the anvil of African brotherhood in one of the most terror-ridden countries on the continent;[90] a country torn by ethnic conflict between the Hutu and the Tutsi – people who are so close, yet so far apart simply because they don't belong to the same "tribe"; although it's hard to find tribes which speak the same language, have the same culture, and the same history for hundreds of years like the Hutu and the Tutsi do.

Prospects for peace in Burundi remained bleak, as the world entered another millennium.

Many Hutu militants remained opposed to peace negotiations; so were Tutsi hardliners. And any settlement that excludes them only spells disaster for Burundi.

Hutu militants – as well as Tutsi hardliners – must be part of the solution. Their concerns, fears and aspirations must be taken into account. Otherwise they will always be a major problem.

As members of the largest ethnic group from which they can draw support because their people are oppressed by the Tutsi minority, Hutu militants have the capacity to wreak havoc across this troubled land for decades. The same fate awaits Rwanda, to which we turn next.

Chapter Four:

Rwanda:
Land of Majestic Splendour
Historical Background

RWANDA'S majestic and spectacular beauty is, indeed, a sight to behold. Like its neighbour Burundi, Rwanda has steep mountains and deep valleys. In the east is a series of hilly plateaus and lakes.

It is also a land of luxuriant vegetation whose fertile, green landscape sparkles with streams of spring water and rivers which water the valleys below.

Like the nearby Ruwenzori mountain range on the Uganda-Congolese border with snow-capped summits, Rwanda's majestic peaks and hilly plateaus are now and then shrouded in mist, presenting an eerie yet captivating sight.

This is also the land of the world-famous mountain gorillas, serene and secure in the dense vegetation of what is one of the most inaccessible parts of the African continent.

If there is any part of the continent which can rightly be called the green hills of Africa, this is it, Rwanda, and its twin, Burundi.

But it is a beauty – the scenic beauty of the landscape and vegetation and the pleasant climate – that sharply contrasts with the history of the country and of the region whose ugly past no one would envy. For, it is here in Rwanda, not in Burundi, where the Tutsi, a tall people who had migrated from the north, first encountered the Hutu about 400 years ago. It was a fateful encounter which was to change the course of history for the entire region. The Tutsi went on to subjugate the Hutu and virtually enslave them for the next four centuries.

Tragically, little has changed in this master-servant relationship despite years of protest and uprising by the Hutu.

It is also here, in Rwanda, where the worst massacre in modern history took place when about one million Tutsis were slaughtered by Hutu extremists in 1994.

The holocaust was unprecedented in one fundamental respect. Never before in recorded history had so many people been brutally murdered in so short a time. The Hutu accomplished their mission in a stunningly short three-month period and almost succeeded in exterminating the Tutsi in this small densely populated East African country.

Rwanda is still reeling from the devastating blows of the genocide, a horrendous tragedy deeply rooted in history whose course has been inextricably shaped by an asymmetrical relationship between the two ethnic groups on terms dictated by the dominant Tutsi minority.

Burundi has fared no better. The history of Rwanda is the history of Burundi, differing only in some respects.

Rwanda has now entered our vocabulary as a synonym for holocaust – "We don't want another Rwanda" – at least in the African context, as much as Biafra symbolised war and famine during the sixties; and as much as Cambodia became synonymous with "killing fields" under the brutal Khmer Rouge regime of Pol Pot in the seventies when more than one million people were executed and starved to death.

Yet Rwanda was one of the least known countries in the world until it exploded on the international scene in 1994 with volcanic fury. Before then, it was virtually unknown even among some educated Africans as I found out in the 1970s. They were students in the United States but born and brought up in Africa. Yet they had never even heard of Rwanda and Burundi, let alone known that the two were African countries. Now almost everybody knows about them, especially Rwanda.

But Rwanda's unspeakable horror is not unique in history. In modern times, the Jewish holocaust in Nazi Germany surpassed it in terms of sheer numbers of the victims who perished; so did Stalin's purges, and Cambodia's "agrarian revolution" which turned plowshares into swords, and farms into killing fields, as did other horrors including the Chinese cultural revolution and even catastrophes in Africa itself where at least 3 million people – mostly blacks – died in Sudan at the hands of the Arabs between 1955 and 1999. And they are still dying today in this racial war.

Also, up to 2 million people, mostly Igbos, died in the Nigerian civil war from 1967 to 1970, mainly from starvation which was effectively used as a weapon by the Nigerian federal military government to starve them into submission. And more than one million people perished in Mozambique's 16-year civil war which ended in 1992.

However, Rwanda's tragedy is unique in Africa in one

189

respect. No other tribe has slaughtered members of another tribe on such a large scale as the Hutu did to the Tutsi in 1994, except, perhaps, the Tutsi in neighbouring Burundi where they killed no fewer than one million Hutus through the years between 1962 and 1996. Between 1993 and 1996 alone, in a period of less than three years, about 500,000 Hutus were killed by the Tutsi in Burundi, according to some sources, as we learned earlier. And the massacres have not stopped, as members of the two tribes continue to kill each other in both countries.

The Colonial Imprint

The imposition of a Tutsi aristocracy – which evolved into a Tutsi ethnocracy – on the Hutu majority preceded the advent of colonial rule by the Germans and the Belgians. Therefore, it would have taken place even if Europeans had never colonised Africa.

But colonialism did accentuate ethnic differences and cleavages. It also exacerbated conflict between the two groups. The Germans, and later the Belgians, invested the Tutsi with authority as the "natural" rulers of the Hutu by virtue of their status as members of a "superior" stock, thus legitimising the conquest and oppression of the Hutu majority which began hundreds of years earlier with the arrival of their conquerors in what is now Rwanda and Burundi.

The Tutsi, who are of Nilotic stock, migrated to the region in the 1400s probably from the southern part of what is Sudan today, a region which is inhabited by Nilotic people. The Maasai, usually called the Masai, are another Nilotic group who also migrated from the same region about 300 years ago and settled in the area that came to be known as Kenya and Tanzania.

However, both have had their origin erroneously placed in Ethiopia whose population and culture is mainly

Semitic – linguistic affinity with other Semitic languages, Arabic and Hebrew, being just one such evidence – and not Nilotic. But it is a mistake which has been sanctioned by folk role as a "historical fact." And some scholars such as Gérard Prunier speculate that the Tutsi may have migrated from the Horn of Africa, thus placing their origin even farther east.

Whatever the case, after the Tutsi conquered the Hutu majority, they went on to consolidate their power through the years and, by the late 1700s, a single Tutsi-ruled kingdom had evolved, occupying most of what is now Rwanda. The kingdom was named Ruanda, only slightly different from the country's current name.

Like its sister state of Urundi to the south, the Ruanda kingdom was ruled by a *mwami*, which means king. He controlled regional vassals who were also Tutsi and subjugated the Hutu on behalf of the king and the entire Tutsi ethnocracy. Thus, both kingdoms had two layers, with the Tutsi on top and the Hutu at the bottom.

Ruanda reached the height of its power and influence under the leadership of Mwami Mutara II who ruled the kingdom in the early 1800s, and under Mwami Kigeri IV who was king from 1853 – 1895. That was the golden era of the Tutsi. Mwami Kigeri established a standing army armed with guns bought from Arab and Swahili traders who travelled to the interior of the Great Lakes region from the coast of what is Tanzania today, selling a variety of merchandise including cloth, beads, and household items, besides guns. He also barred most foreigners from entering his kingdom.

Although the Tutsi kingdoms were independent, their status changed when Europeans went to colonise Africa. In 1890, Ruanda became a German-ruled territory after some resistance which sorely tested the Germans in skirmishes of guerrilla warfare; even today, the Tutsi still have a reputation as formidable fighters.

In 1897, Ruanda became a part of Deutsch Ostafrika,

or German East Africa, which was the territory of Tanganyika. Therefore during German rule, the three territories of Ruanda, Urundi and Tanganyika constituted one country.

But the Germans did not take over Ruanda as an administrative unit until 1899 and assigned a German administrative officer to the colony only in 1907. Urundi was also incorporated late into German East Africa in 1898.

However, the Germans did not have much influence in Ruanda and Urundi as they did in the other part of German East Africa, Tanganyika, which was also the most prized possession. They did not start any major development projects in Ruanda and Urundi as they did in Tanganyika where they established tea and sisal plantations; vigorously encouraged the cultivation of coffee on individual and family farms; built roads and railways, and initiated other projects including the cultivation of cotton.

They wanted to start the same schemes in Ruanda and Urundi, especially the cultivation of coffee and tea, but the outbreak of World War I interfered with their plans. And they had no better land. It is some of the most fertile on the entire continent, endowed with abundant rainfall and an excellent climate, and soil of volcanic origin capable of nourishing a wide variety of crops including export commodities.

In fact, that is one of the main reasons why Rwanda and Burundi are the most densely populated countries in Africa. Their fertile soil and ideal climate at elevations of about 5,000 feet are capable of sustaining hundreds of people per square mile. And most of the land is arable, although not enough for the population. As John Reader states in his book, *Africa: A biography of the Continent*:

"In 1993,...Burundi had a greater proportion of its land surface under permanent cultivation and pasture than any other country in Africa: 87 per cent. Rwanda had less, 59

192

per cent, but even that was equal to the proportion of arable and pasture land in the Netherlands, Europe's most densely populated nation (with 448 persons per square kilometre)."[1]

When the Germans arrived in Ruanda and Urundi as the first colonial masters, they automatically chose the Tutsi to help them facilitate the colonisation of the territory, thus reinforcing their own prejudices about different groups of Africans. Because the Tutsi were already in control, ruling the Hutu, the Germans – and later the Belgians – concluded that they were more intelligent than their subjects who also happened to belong to a different "racial" stock.

Their assessment was based on ethnographic studies by the Germans in the early 1900s which were tainted by racial prejudice. And the German colonial administrators in Ruanda and Urundi accepted this pseudoscience as genuine scholarship and used it to justify their preconceived notions about the Hutu majority as a despicable lot simply because they were generally short and dark, and had been conquered by the tall, "handsome and intelligent" light-skinned Tutsis hundreds of years before.

The stereotypes were reinforced by other differences, real and perceived, between the Hutu and the Tutsi. The Hutu were primarily agriculturalists; the Tutsi, pastoralists. In most African societies, cattle symbolise wealth. Therefore livestock ownership is identified with wealth, or accumulation of wealth, hence upward mobility. It is an attribute that was perfectly in accord with the status of the Tutsi as the rulers of members of "the lesser breed": the Hutu.

Political and economic power was exclusively in Tutsi hands, a monopoly which led the Tutsi aristocracy to conclude that such hegemonic control was a result of divine intent as part of the grand design of the Creator.

And racism among the German colonial masters found a perfect ally in this kind of superstition which was invoked as an article of faith by the Tutsi rulers and not without reason.

Throughout history, aristocrats have "justified" their status as a heavenly mandate even when committing some of the most despicable acts known to man. The Tutsi in Ruanda-Urundi were no exception.

Therefore when the Germans began to consolidate their rule, they filled all native positions in the colonial administration with Tutsi employees, to the total exclusion of the "dull, ugly" Hutus. But by doing so, they only helped to "justify" and solidify inequalities between the Hutu and Tutsi. They also helped to stoke the fires which had been smoldering for centuries and which went on to explode into flames with unconstrained fury a few decades later.

German dreams of a tropical paradise in the misty blue mountains of the Great Lakes regions of East Africa were shattered when World War I exploded in 1914 and the Belgians invaded Ruanda and Urundi from the Belgian Congo in April 1916. They remained in control of Ruanda-Urundi throughout the reminder of the war and were given mandate over it by the League of Nations after Germany lost the war. The rest of German East Africa – the biggest part of the colony – which came to to be known as Tanganyika went to Britain after the United States refused to take it during that nation's period of isolationism under President Woodrow Wilson.

After the Belgians took control of Ruanda and Urundi and consolidated them as one colony of Ruanda-Urundi, they went even further to widen the ethnic divide between the Hutu and the Tutsi. In 1926, they introduced an identity card to distinguish the Hutu from the Tutsi, and vice versa, similar to what blacks were required to carry under apartheid in South Africa.

The difference was that in Ruanda-Urundi, the card

gave legal sanction to the superior status of the Tutsi, who are black people, while in South Africa, it legitimised the inferior status of blacks.

It also gave them even more advantages over the Hutu in education and employment. And it legalised discrimination against the Hutu in a country where the colonial authorities – German and Belgian – had always favoured the Tutsi.

Like their predecessors, the Germans, the Belgian colonial rulers also simply added to the stockpile of fuel for an inferno which almost consumed both countries – Rwanda and Burundi – several years later beginning in the sixties. The fires were still burning when the twentieth-first century began. And history is still fanning the flames. The colonial legacy is not the only culprit but is a major one, a point also underscored by *The Economist*:

"The colonial administrators allowed only Tutsis – albeit few even of them – to attain higher education and hold positions of authority. Christian missionaries undermined the system a little by educating the Hutus.

In the run-up to independence in 1962, the spectre of majority rule began to threaten Tutsi supremacy. In Burundi the Tutsis struck first, slaughtered the Hutu political leaders and kept their hold.

Rwanda's Hutus rose up before independence, and in 1959 murdered thousands of Tutsis, while hundreds of thousands were driven or fled into nearby countries.

The result in Burundi was rule by Tutsi soldiers who massacred Hutus whenever they showed signs of rebellion; in Rwanda, a Hutu regime that discriminated against Tutsis."[2]

The Hutu regime in Rwanda lasted for 32 years, from July 1962 to July 1994, which was a brief shining moment for the Hutu in a nightmare of 400 years of domination by the Tutsi.

Even legitimate protest by the Hutu against such oppression was interpreted by the Tutsi as a rebellion against divine authority from which the Nilotic aristocratic rulers derived their mandate to rule.

Yet, it was not even legitimately constituted authority which derived its mandate from the consent of the people who were being ruled – the Hutu majority. Still, the Tutsi saw themselves as the perfect creation of God, hence the embodiment of all that is best in man, to the exclusion of the God-forsaken Hutus and others. This haughty conceit among the Tutsi was clearly noticed by a number of travellers and missionaries in the region. One such traveller was Hans Meyer who observed the Tutsi phenomenon when he was in Ruanda and Urundi while the two Tutsi kingdoms were still a part of German East Africa (Deutsch Ostafrika):

"One is impressed with the proud reserve of the Tutsi....The tall fellows stand still and relaxed, leaning on their spears while watching the Europeans pass or approach, as if this unusual sight did not impress them in the least....

The Tutsi consider themselves as the top of the creation from the standpoint of intelligence and political genius, (and) to be rich and powerful and to enjoy life by doing nothing is the symbol of all wisdom for the Tutsi, the ideal for which he strives with utmost shrewdness and unscrupulousness."[3]

Thus, when the colonial rulers favoured them in employment and education, the Tutsi automatically assumed that it was their "natural right" to get preferential treatment at the expense of the "inferior" Hutus. In fact, one of the reasons the Tutsi submitted to imperial authority, although not without resistance, was to secure such advantages in order to perpetuate a Tutsi ethnocracy which they felt was threatened by hordes of "backward and primitive" Hutus who vastly outnumbered them.

Such arrogance still rankles the Hutu who now and then through the years have tried to settle scores with the Tutsi by violent means, only to end up losing in most cases, as much as they lost during the colonial era when the Germans and the Belgians simply ignored them while they favoured the Tutsi.

Even when the missionaries tried to help the Hutu a little, the colonial authorities still regarded them as members of an inferior stock unworthy of being educated like the Tutsi. Both colonial authorities, German and Belgian, built some government schools in Ruanda-Urundi almost exclusively for the Tutsi. But it was the missionaries, mostly Catholic, who played a leading role in educating Africans – that is why the majority of Rwandans and Burundians are Catholic, a denomination which played the biggest role in spreading Christianity in the two countries.

However, the primary objective of providing education was not just to educate Africans; the missionaries saw provision of education as the most effective means of winning converts and spreading Christianity.

The white missionaries believed that Africans would be more effective in proselytising among their own people than white foreigners would be.

The Tutsi, on the other hand, defined education almost strictly in secular terms; not as a means of helping spread Christianity but as a way of consolidating their position as the dominant ethnic group. Therefore, they did everything they could to forge close links with the dominant Catholic church and other denominations and strengthened ties with the colonial administrators who were already favouring them.

In the early 1930s, the Belgian colonial rulers reached an agreement with the Catholic church which enabled the missionaries to take over the entire educational system, thus effectively ending the existence of government schools in Ruanda-Urundi. They became mission schools.

But the role of the government in the area of education did not end completely. The government provided money to the Catholic church for all pupils and for all teachers at the mission schools. As a condition for getting the money, the church agreed to enlarge its educational programmes which would include educating Africans who would work for the colonial government mainly as clerks and in other areas, instead of training only missionary workers and teachers for the schools run by the church.

The arrangement was very encouraging. But its implementation was dictated by ethnicity as the answer to this question: Who was to receive such secular education at the mission schools, preparing Africans to work for the colonial government – the Hutu, the Tutsi, or both?

The colonial government and the Catholic church provided the same answer even if it was for pragmatic reasons on the part of the church. As the Catholic bishop, Leon Classe, who negotiated with the colonial authorities on behalf of the church in order to reach an agreement under which the Catholic church would assume control of the schools in Rwanda-Urundi, told his fellow missionaries:

"You must choose the Batutsi because the government will probably refuse Bahutu teachers....In the government the positions in every branch of the administration, even the unimportant ones, will be reserved henceforth for young Batutsi."[4]

It was a typical divide-and-rule tactic by the colonial rulers. And it was blatantly anti-Hutu.

From the early 1930s until after the Second World War, there was no question among the Belgian colonial administrators that the only Africans who should get secular education and missionary training should be Tutsi.[5] They did not care or foresee the devastating impact this

198

kind of discrimination would have on the future of Ruanda-Urundi, as the bloody conflicts between the Hutu and the Tutsi in Rwanda in 1959 and in both Rwanda and Burundi between the two ethnic groups since the 1960s tragically demonstrated.

It was the colonial authorities, not the missionaries, who had the final say on how education should be provided. The Belgian colonial rulers wanted Tutsi employees in the government. If they wanted Hutus, it would have been the same way. The Catholic church simply provided the training, although there were missionaries who were racist just like the colonial rulers were.

The educational arrangement that was agreed upon by the colonial authorities and the Catholic church played a critical role in widening and solidifying the ethnic divide between the Hutu and the Tutsi, compounded by class inequalities. The Tutsi were on top because of their ethnic identity that was also preferred by the colonial rulers, not because they were more intellectually endowed than the Hutu; they also had superior status on the basis of class as the richer and more educated group.

The difference between the two groups was also viewed in a racial context. Bishop Classe foresaw the emergence of a Christian ruling class, a "racial aristocracy," as he put it, meaning Tutsi, supposedly the superior race.

It was the Tutsi who were given the best education, although it was substandard by European standards because Europeans in Ruanda-Urundi – as well as in other parts of Africa – did not really want Africans to get good education lest they start demanding equality with whites in employment and other areas.

It was also the Tutsi, members of a "superior" race, who were entitled to preferential treatment from whites. This was the policy of divide and rule, pitting one tribe against another, which wreaked so much havoc across

Africa during and after the colonial era. And it is still doing so today – Rwanda and Burundi being some of the worst cases – demonstrated by gross inequalities in terms of educational achievements and economic development among different regions or provinces in many Africans countries; inequalities which are also partly fuelled by ethno-regional rivalries.

In the case of Rwanda and Burundi, the Hutu were not completely ignored by the missionaries, although it was obvious that the colonial authorities and the missionaries (not always grudgingly) favoured the Tutsi.

Even the missionaries themselves did not expect much of the Hutu. They saw even educated Hutus – should there be any in the future – playing only a subordinate role, with the Tutsi as the "natural" leaders being entitled to the best jobs. Bishop Classe made a clear distinction between the two ethnic groups and what kind of jobs each should expect to get when he told the Catholic missionary teachers at the schools in Rwanda:

"We must not...neglect the classes of Bahutu young people and children. They also need to be schooled and educated, and they will take up places in mine workings and industry."6

The Tutsi were not expected to work in the mines or in factories as labourers, but the Hutu were. It was one of the most blatant cases of discrimination against the Hutu not only during that period but also years later. They were destined for a peripheral role in society. They were not equal to the Tutsi, their inferior status even acknowledged by the missionaries. The "dark and dull, ugly" Hutus – as whites and Tutsis saw them – were supposed to do "dirty" work, demanding physical labour, while the "pretty," "handsome," "intelligent" light-skinned Tutsis – endowed with "superior" intelligence – stayed on top, "fit" only for clean, intellectually demanding office work.

Therefore, educational opportunities for the Hutu were very limited. They were severely limited even by the church itself in compliance with the decree issued by Bishop Leon Classe.

There were a few Hutus who qualified for training as priests to enable them to spread the faith among their own people. And they knew that seminary training was the only way Hutus could acquire higher education. Other routes to high education for them were closed, except for the Tutsi although even they did not go far enough; they were still colonial subjects like the Hutu, and they were black and African like the Hutu, whose opportunities were limited under colonial rule as was the case everywhere else across the continent.

The Tutsi may have been called "black Caucasians" by Europeans – just like Ethiopians and Somalis have been called 'black Caucasians" – but they definitely were *not* accepted by Europeans as fellow Caucasians. To Europeans, they were just Africans even if different from other Africans – still Africans.

The Hutu used the only means that was available to them to get higher education, seminary training, and some of them did graduate from the seminaries and became priests. And there were those who left the seminaries and went to find jobs in other areas. But there was not much opportunity for them in the secular fields.

There was not even a single African university graduate during that period. The first Rwandan to acquire what was roughly equivalent or close to a university education was Anastase Makuza, a Hutu and former seminary student, who graduated from Centre Universitaire of Kisantu in the Belgian Congo in 1955 with a degree in administration and political science.

But in spite of his distinguished academic credentials, he could not get a job in Rwanda commensurate with his qualifications simply because he was a Hutu:

"His application for a post in the government administration was turned down; a position as research assistant at the Institut pour la Recherche Scientifique en Afrique Centrale was not open to him because, Makuza has said, 'the IRSAC was 150 per cent Tutsi.'

He even looked for a job in Burundi before ending up as a typist in a government office in Kibuye, Rwanda.

In 1957 Makuza was promoted to the rank of administrative assistant and subsequently transferred to Kigali, the Rwandan capital. By then, however, Makuza was already a potential revolutionary."[7]

Instead of silencing him and shunting him into oblivion as they had hoped to, the colonial rulers achieved exactly the opposite as was the case with many other oppressed Hutus.

But to achieve their goals, Makuza's revolutionary potential together with that of his kinsmen would have to be harnessed into a potent force capable of dislodging the Tutsi who were firmly entrenched as the dominant ethnic group favoured by the Belgian colonial authorities and by the missionaries. And that is exactly what the Hutu attempted to do.

From 1956, an increasing number of educated Hutus tried to look for jobs commensurate with their experience and training. But they were virtually locked out of all positions other than menial work and a few posts – as lowly clerks and so on – working under Tutsis who did not even have the necessary qualifications or as much education and training as some of the Hutu who were denied jobs had.

That was the Rwanda of the 1950s which, tragically, was not much different from the Rwanda of the 1990s and thereafter in terms of opportunities for the Hutu following their ouster from power by the predominantly Tutsi Rwandan Patriotic Front (RPF) in July 1994.

During that period, in the fifties, there was only a small

Hutu elite. But it had the potential for cataclysmic change hardly anyone – let alone the Tutsi and their Belgian colonial and missionary supporters – foresaw then. Frustrated by the refusal of the colonial authorities to bring about fundamental change in the system, the highly articulate Hutu elite resolved to end Tutsi domination one way or another. The struggle had to do with the future of Rwanda after the departure of the Belgian colonial rulers.

The Tutsis were already well-positioned. They dominated all sectors of the administration and the economy. They also had advantages in terms of education and training and were well-positioned to assume control of the first African government on attainment of independence from Belgium within five years or so.

The Hutu elite used simple but powerful logic to explain their plight. They attributed the injustices to racial discrimination. The implication was clear. And it resonated well among their people.

Redress the racial imbalance – their plight would end, enabling them to regain the rights they had been denied for so long. And they had an obvious target, the Tutsi, their nemesis for the past 400 years, reinforced by the colonial rulers, both German and Belgian, who left the traditional social structure intact, with the Tutsi on top as aristocrats and the Hutu at the bottom as servants in feudal servitude. The day of reckoning had come.

The end of the Tutsi Aristocracy

In March 1957, the Hutu elite in Rwanda published the *Hutu Manifesto* which called for radical change in the country's power structure and challenged all the premises underlying the asymmetrical relationship between the two ethnic groups.

The Hutu demanded power which would reflect their numerical preponderance and guarantee their rights as the largest racial group in the country. They formed two political parties to articulate their demands and aspirations and achieve their goals. One was the Association for the Social Improvement of the Masses led by Joseph Gitera. The other one was the Party of the Hutu Emancipation Movement (PARMEHUTU) led by Gregoire Kayibanda. The latter became the dominant party and went on to pursue the agenda of the *Hutu Manifesto*.

The *Manifesto* challenged every facet of Rwanda's socio-political-economic system which thrived on the exploitation of the Hutu majority, not as an attempt to reform the system but as a concerted effort to bring about radical change. The Hutu leaders demanded a complete overhaul of the system. They wanted to replace it with an entirely new power arrangement.

The *Hutu Manifesto* identified the fundamental problem which, it said, was "the political monopoly of one race, the Tutsi race, which, given the present structural framework, becomes a social and economic monopoly."[8]

It went on to cite instances of injustice across the political, economic and social spectrum and proposed radical measures to achieve "the integral and collective promotion of the Hutu."

They included an end to class and racial prejudice; the recognition of individual ownership of land, most of which was in Hutu hands but virtually owned by the Tutsi aristocracy, with Hutus working merely as servants under vassals answerable to the *mwami* (Tutsi king); the advancement of the Hutu in the bureaucracy and other areas of the public sector; and the provision of education at all levels to Hutu children.[9]

It was a revolutionary document with echoes of the *Communist Manifesto* in the document's name and in terms of revolutionary language although not in terms of goals – the *Hutu Manifesto* was not communist. But the changes proposed were clearly radical and revolutionary considering the feudalistic nature of Rwanda's traditional system dominated by the Tutsi. And as Professor René Lemarchand states in his work *Rwanda and Burundi*:

"Never before had such a devastating critique of the *ancien régime* been publicly set forth by its opponents."[10]

Yet few people paid much attention to it, in spite of its potential for revolutionary change with far-reaching consequences. The *Hutu Manifesto* strongly urged the Belgian colonial rulers to take "more positive and unambiguous measures to achieve the political and economic emancipation of the Hutu"; a demand which was also an implicit warning of the consequences which would follow if the measures were not implemented. It was also an urgent appeal to the colonial authorities to avert a catastrophe of genocidal proportions. Still, hardly anyone listened.

The *Manifesto* drew only a tepid response from the Belgian colonial authorities. It was not until December 1958, more than a year-and-a-half after the manifesto was issued, that Rwanda's Vice-Governor-General, Jean-Paul Harroy, finally admitted that "the Hutu-Tutsi question posed an undeniable problem."

To help diffuse the potentially explosive situation, he proposed that the terms "Hutu" and "Tutsi" should no longer be officially used by the colonial government.[11] It is a "solution" the government of Paul Kagame has also tried, claiming there are no Hutus and no Tutsis in Rwanda – there are only Rwandans, while ethnic hostilities continue to fester and bubble underneath, with Rwandans who use ethnic labels being accused of promoting "genocidal ideology."

The Hutu rejected the proposal by Jean-Paul Harroy, contending that it was mere "Tutsi obfuscation,"[12] an argument that resonates well among many Hutus in Rwanda even today today who contend that the Tutsi-dominated government of Paul Kagame has made it illegal to use ethnic labels – "Hutu" and "Tutsi" – only to perpetuate Tutsi hegemonic control of the country and cover up inequalities between the two ethnic groups. Under this law, it is reasonable to assume that an entire ministry or department can be filled with Tutsi or Hutu employees, yet no one can complain about discrimination because the employees are just Rwandans and not Hutus or Tutsis. Anyone who complains risks imprisonment for promoting "genocidal ideology."

The Hutu rejected the elimination of ethnic labels in the 1950s, proposed by Vice-Governor-General Jean-Paul Harroy, for understandable reasons. It was also a way for the colonial government to conveniently ignore the demands articulated in the *Hutu Manifesto* – there are no Hutus and Tutsis, only Rwandans.

By remarkable contrast, the Tutsi, already on top and favoured by the colonialists, automatically interpreted government silence and inaction on the *Hutu Manifesto* as an endorsement of their claim to superiority over the Hutu. And that was recipe for catastrophe.

During that period, the traditional power structure was dominated by Mutara III who, as *mwami*, was the effective ruler of Rwanda. The Belgian colonial masters did not want to disturb the traditional equilibrium which was, in effect, a disequilibrium to the detriment of the oppressed Hutu majority.

Mutara III died in July 1958. He was succeeded by Kigeri V.

However, there was a dispute over the succession. And it had far-reaching consequences.

The Hutu complained that Kigeri V had not been properly selected and therefore was not entitled to the throne as the new *mwami*.

Fighting between the Hutu and Tutsi broke out. The Twa (Pygmies) helped the Tutsi fight the Hutu. They had their own grievances against the Hutu who conquered them long before the Tutsi arrived and became the new masters.

After being virtually enslaved for hundreds of years, the Hutu turned the tables in the mass uprising of November 1959 against the Tutsi aristocracy. This was the first time in the country's history that the Hutu had emerged victorious over the Tutsi.

More than 100,000 Tutsis were killed. Hundreds of thousands of them, including Mwami Kigeri V, fled the country. Among those who fled was Paul Kagame, with his parents, when he was about two years old. They fled to Uganda where he grew up as did many other Tutsis.

The majority of the Tutsi including Kigeri V sought refuge in Urundi (as Burundi was then still known before independence) which was still dominated by fellow Tutsis. Others fled to Belgian Congo, and to Tanganyika which became Tanzania in 1964 after uniting with Zanzibar. It was officially named Tanzania on October 29th the same year. Before then, it was known as the United Republic of Tanganyika and Zanzibar.

The 1959 Hutu uprising effectively ended Tutsi domination of the Hutu in Rwanda. It was a humiliating defeat the Tutsi who had ruled the country for hundreds of years never forgot, as they continued to make many attempts during the next several decades to regain power in their homeland.

In place of a Tutsi aristocracy emerged a Hutu ethnocracy which was no more restrained in exploiting ethnic sentiments than its predecessor, and went on to invoke a perverted form of nationalism to justify its incendiary rhetoric against the powerless Tutsi minority.[13] The oppressed had become the oppressor.

Chapter Five:

The Emergence and Consolidation of the Hutu Ethnocracy in Rwanda

THE RISE of the Hutu to power in Rwanda was a turning point in the country's history. But it was also a continuation of the same phenomenon, tribalism, which has plagued the small East African nation for centuries; nor is this phenomenon unique or peculiar to Rwanda and Burundi.

Other African countries including the continent's giants such as Nigeria and Congo as well as Angola have been pushed to the brink of destruction because of tribal conflicts among other things including competition for power and resources fuelled by ethno-regional rivalries. And a race war – it is more than just a religious conflict over *sharia* – threatens to split Africa's largest country, Sudan, in two: predominantly Arab North and Black South.

Hutu versus Tutsi: A Definition

The case of Rwanda – as well as that of its twin Burundi – is problematic in one fundamental respect. Because of intermarriage through the centuries, the Hutu and the Tutsi are not always considered to be distinct tribes, if they are considered to be tribes at all. As Gérard Prunier contends:

" Contrary to a commonly held belief, Hutu and Tutsi are not tribes. They are two social divisions of the Barundi and Banyarwanda tribes who may have had a different racial origin in the distant past but who have lived together, spoken the same language, and intermarried for hundreds of years. Their social conflicts existed before colonization but had never reached the level of open and massive violence that developed in the 1960s and after."[1]

Yet Prunier himself and others who make the same argument that the Hutu and the Tutsi are not two different tribes concede that the Tutsi are Nilotic. Therefore they are not Bantu like the Hutu. Nilotic is a distinct ethnic or "racial" category unlike Bantu which is a collective term designating linguistic and cultural affinity; it is not a racial identity. Members of some Bantu tribes have different physical features although most don't. You can not tell any difference between most of them.

It is true that the Hutu and the Tutsi have intermarried for so long that it seems they no longer exist as distinct tribes. And in many cases, you can not tell the difference between the members of the two groups by simply looking at them; but you also can in a very large number of cases. In spite of the intermarriage between them through the centuries, they really have not ceased to exist as two groups, each with its own identity, even if some people don't want to call them tribes. The differences between the Hutu and the Tutsi are real regardless of how you define them. That is why it is still possible to identify a Hutu or a Tutsi although not all the time.

Some people who look like Hutus are classified as Tutsi not necessarily on the basis of their social status derived from wealth or the class they belong to; they are identified as Tutsi on the basis of lineage as a product of intermarriage. The same standard of judgement applies to Hutus. If your mother is a Hutu and your father is Tutsi, you are a Tutsi; if your mother is Tutsi and your father is a Hutu, you are a Hutu.

And few people would be convinced of the veracity of an outlandish claim such as this one: a group of people, for example 100 or 200 of them, with "typical" Tutsi features – aquiline noses, angular features, thin and tall and with a light complexion – are Hutu.

If they are in Rwanda or Burundi standing in front of you and claim they are Hutu, probably nobody will believe them. So many people, with such distinctive Tutsi features, obviously would not be Hutu. Even an individual with such features most likely is not a Hutu.

And hardly anyone so "well-endowed" would claim such "lowly" status – of Hutu identity – in a society where many Tutsis consider Hutus to be inferior to them. The Hutu-Tutsi distinctions are that brutal, and tragic.

Therefore, in spite of all the intermarriage that has taken place through the centuries, there are still Hutus and Tutsis in Rwanda and Burundi.

What better proof than the massacres which have been committed by both groups, in both countries, through the years? Who is killing who? Tutsis have not been killing fellow Tutsis, nor have Hutus been killing fellow Hutus in cases of deliberate ethnic cleansing. They know whom they are targeting.

That is why the massacres in Rwanda of almost one million Tutsis were carried out with such deadly accuracy. Hutu murderers were right on target, although they killed some of their own people for different reasons including misidentification in a few cases. But most of the time, they knew they were killing Tutsis, their "enemies."

One must therefore acknowledge that the two groups are not mere social categories in the sociological sense. A social category is not an immutable phenomenon. Its existence implies possibility of change from one category to another through social mobility, intermingling and other ways. And because social categories are not permanent by nature, one can expect a Hutu to become a Tutsi and a Tutsi a Hutu, if their identities are mere social constructs and not biological phenomena.

Yet Hutu and Tutsi are fixed categories, which explains why the two groups still exist today with separate and distinct ethnic identities – Hutu versus Tutsi – even after 400 years of living together and intermarrying through the years. Intermarriage between them probably started very early not long after the two met. But it has not entirely eliminated their separate identities.

And that is a global phenomenon. Even in countries where people of different races have intermarried for a long time, and in very large numbers, there are still many people – from the groups whose members intermarry – who continue to exist with their own separate identities as ethnic or racial groups. Racial amalgamation remains unattainable in most societies round the globe. And that includes Rwanda and Burundi.

Although the Hutu and the Tutsi are fixed categories clearly identified by their identities, Hutu versus Tutsi, they are not biological categories, in the absolute sense, because they have shared genes for centuries; so have blacks and whites. The United States is good example. Yet blacks still do exist in the United States in spite of the fact that they have intermingled with whites for centuries since slavery. There are very few blacks in the United States, descended from African slaves, who don't have European genes. Oprah Winfrey is said to be one of them, according to a DNA test in a report on American public television, PBS, by Professor Henry Louis Gates Jr., chairman of the African and African American Studies Department at Harvard University.

Oprah is mostly black African, about 86 per cent, with some of her African roots traced to the Kpelle tribe in Liberia – not the Zulu of South Africa as she originally believed. The rest of her is Native American.

And in spite of the fact that black Americans (African Americans) are a minority in the United States, they have not lost their racial identity from intermarriage and other relationships with whites and members of other races.

The same applies to the Tutsi in Rwanda and Burundi. They are a minority, vastly outnumbered by Hutus. Yet they have not lost their identity in spite of the fact that they have intermarried with Hutus for centuries.

As a very small minority, they could easily have been swallowed up by the Hutu, through intermarriage, and there would hardly be any Tutsis today in Rwanda and Burundi. Yet there are people who are called Tutsis in both countries, not because they are culturally distinct from the Hutu – the two have the same culture and speak the same language after intermingling for centuries – but because they exist as a distinct group.

Call it a social category, an ethnic group, and even a "racial" group. Whatever their identity is, they do exist as a group. And they do identify themselves as a people called Tutsi. They are not Hutu. The Hutu also exist as a group and as a people with their own identity.

The two groups have shared genes for centuries and have a "common" gene pool. But they have not lost their separate identities they had when they first met hundreds of years ago.

The question is: What are these separate identities today if they are different from the ones they had hundreds of years ago before and when they first met? If they are not biological categories, they are social categories, or both. They can no longer be biological categories in the strict sense of the term because of the high rate of intermarriage that has taken place through the centuries. And they can not be mere social categories when, even after hundreds of years, it is easy to identify many Tutsis and many Hutus based on physical features alone just as it is easy to identify blacks in the United States.

There are still whites and blacks in the United States as distinct "biological" entities or categories in spite of their "common" gene pool, just as there are Hutus and Tutsis in Rwanda and Burundi; so are the other distinct racial groups and tribes in other parts of the world in spite of the fact that they have intermarried – therefore have shared genes – for centuries.

All those different races and tribes are not mere social categories. They are a biological fact, clinically verified, for example in the case of racial differences between blacks and whites. Even forensic tests can show that a skeleton, or just a skull, is of a person who was black or white. If the person was of mixed ancestry with a lot of European genes and a lot of Africans genes, it may be difficult to identity his/her racial identity. But experts can conclusively say it was a person of mixed ancestry. That is not a social classification; it is a biological fact.

In the case of Rwanda and Burundi, if "Hutu" and "Tutsi" are mere social categories or designations, what makes them different from each other? Are they different because of different social or cultural attributes?

What makes a Hutu different from a Tutsi? Or what is the difference between the social category of a Hutu and the social category of a Tutsi? If they have the same culture and speak the same language, do they belong to the same social category since culture is a primary attribute of social identity? If they do, does that mean there is only one social category to which both the Hutu and the Tutsi belong?

If they belong to the same social category, with the same social and cultural attributes, why are there two groups who are identified as Hutu and Tutsi, with separate identities, instead of having only one group whose members have the same identity?

Part of the answer may lie in history. The differences between the Hutu and the Tutsi are historical. Historically, the Tutsi have been the rulers; the Hutu, servants of the Tutsi. The Tutsi, as the dominant group, have higher social status; the Hutu don't. Wealth is also associated with the Tutsi, not with the Hutu. And that includes land ownership besides cattle which are one of the most distinctive features of Tutsi identity.

But in many cases, there are also obvious physical differences between Hutus and Tutsis.

Therefore the term "social category" – when it is used to mean that such a category can include people of different racial and ethnic groups who share certain social and cultural attributes – is irrelevant in the Rwandan and Burundian context as a basic definition of what a Hutu or a Tutsi is, except as a designation employed to denote status under a caste system as in India, with the Tutsi as the privileged class and the Hutu being "the untouchables," as was the case under Jim Crow in the United States where blacks were – and in many cases still are – locked at the bottom, with whites on top. As black American legal scholar and law professor, Derrick Bell, states in his book, *Faces at the Bottom of the Well: The Permanence of Racism*:

"Racism is an integral, permanent and indestructible component of this society. Americans achieve a measure of social stability through their unspoken pact to keep blacks on the bottom."[2]

The designation "social category" is inappropriate as a definitive term for the Hutu and the Tutsi not only because it implies possibility of change from one category to another through social mobility, among other ways, hence from Hutu to Tutsi and vice versa; it is also inappropriate for simple biological reasons.

The Tutsi did not get their pointed noses, angular features and light complexion by changing their culture or their social class or by learning to look that way, although not all Tutsis have such pronounced features. You are not going to look Chinese simply because you want to look Chinese or simply because you were born in China, grew up in China, and absorbed Chinese culture just as you can not learn to have a pointed nose anymore than you can learn to be short or tall.

If that were the case, Hutus who desperately wanted to become Tutsis because they were ashamed of the way they looked or were convinced that they were indeed inferior to the Tutsi, would have acquired "attractive" Tutsi features by simply changing their social class once they became rich or married a Tutsi. Many of them did change their identity and became "Tutsi" by registration after they acquired wealth or education. But that did not change their physical features to make them look Tutsi.

They were still Hutu, and looked Hutu, with all their physical features remaining intact – features of "ugliness" and even "congenital idiocy." That is because they were born Hutu, not Tutsi, just as the Tutsi were born Tutsi, not Hutu. Neither can become the other anymore than black American entertainer Michael Jackson became white simply because his complexion changed or was changed to "white" and his black African nose was trimmed or reshaped to look Caucasian.

The Hutu are what they are. They are Hutu and will die

Hutu. So are the Tutsi. They are what they are, Tutsi, and will die Tutsi. And that – this question of identity – brings up the problem of tribalism as an enduring phenomenon in the Rwandan and Burundian context as well as in other parts of Africa.

Tribes do exist; so does tribalism. If there were no tribes, we would not be talking about tribalism in Africa. To pretend that they don't exist is delusional.

And as we have seen in the case of Rwanda and Burundi, the colonial rulers did a very good job of exploiting ethnic differences and exacerbating tensions between the Hutu and the Tutsi. But they were able to do so because tribalism or hostility between the two groups already existed. And in spite of intermarriage between the members of the two groups, the Tutsi knew they were Tutsi, not Hutu, and the Hutu knew they were Hutu, not Tutsi, for centuries long before Europeans set foot on African soil.

The white man did not create the Hutu or the Tutsi anymore than he created the Ashanti, the Ewe, the Hausa, the Xhosa, the Igbo, the Baganda, the Sukuma, the Yao, the Nyamwezi, the Makonde, the Ovimbundu, the Maasai, the Zulu, the Kikuyu, or the Yoruba. When the British fought the Kikuyu in Kenya during Mau Mau, the Ashanti in the Gold Coast, and the Zulu and the Xhosa in South Africa, it was because all these people were already there with their own identities in their African homeland and resented the invaders who conquered them and took their land.

All those tribes and the rest existed before Europeans conquered the continent and even before they knew Africa existed. And they existed as distinct entities, in many cases hostile to each other. In fact, one of the main reasons – besides inferior technology (lack of guns, in place of spears, bows and arrows) – Africans were not able to present a united front against European invaders was tribalism.

They were divided along tribal lines even when they were busy fighting a common enemy, although there were also many examples of different tribes forming alliances to fight Europeans. But in general, they were more divided than united. Not only were they hostile to each other in many cases; they even fought each other long before Europeans came and for reasons which had nothing to do with European imperialism. There were no Europeans in Africa then. But there were tribes.

Didn't the Yoruba speak Yoruba before Europeans came? And don't they even look different from the Fulani, for example, in terms of physical features, although they are all Nigerians?

A tribe is more "biological" than social as a category, although in many cases it is integrationist, one tribe absorbing members of another tribe or other tribes – and therefore acquiring attributes of a social category.

But either way, as a biological phenomenon or as a social construct, the existence of tribes has not been a blessing for Africa because of tribalism which has wreaked so much havoc across the continent. Hence the need for a transcendent nationalism of the Pan-African kind embracing all tribes – be it in Kenya, Nigeria, Congo, or Rwanda and Burundi – as parts of an organic whole sharing only one identity, African identity, as the common denominator, somewhat analogous to Johann Fichte's conception of his Fatherland he forcefully articulated in his *Addresses to the German Nation*[3] he delivered as lectures at the University of Berlin in 1807 – 1808.

In the case of Rwanda and Burundi where the Tutsi are a permanent minority, a truly nationalist movement – in place of divisive, tribal multi-party politics – may be the only appropriate means to achieve national unity, peace and stability. Otherwise, the Tutsi will be perpetual losers, pushed to the periphery of the mainstream. They will never win an election under a multi-party system. They are vastly outnumbered by the Hutu, the majority of whom will probably be motivated by ethnic sentiments when they cast their votes.

Yet, if genuine democracy is not introduced, the Hutu will never stop fighting even if they are quiet for a while. They will start fighting again, sooner rather than later. They could even end up winning on the battlefield, one day, as they did in the mass uprising of November 1959 in Rwanda when they overthrew the Tutsi aristocracy, thus paving the way for the establishment of a Hutu ethnocracy; a system that has proved to be disastrous not only in the case of Rwanda and Burundi but in other countries where it has been instituted at the expense of other groups on this embattled continent.

There is an imperative need to devise a system which can accommodate and satisfy both – the Hutu and the Tutsi in Rwanda and Burundi – without compromising the essence of true democracy, which is equality and justice and full participation of all members of society in the government under which they live.

Hutus' Rise to Power

The 1959 mass uprising in Rwanda was a prelude to the attainment of sovereign status by Rwanda under Hutu leadership.

Unlike in most African countries, the struggle for independence in the Tutsi-dominated kingdoms of Ruanda and Urundi was conducted almost entirely along ethnic lines: Tutsi versus Hutu, Hutu versus Tutsi.

As we learned earlier, ethnic hostility between the two groups didn't just start in recent years; it only got worse, especially since the late fifties and early sixties. And just like everywhere else across Africa, there was tribalism after the colonial rulers left as much as there was tribalism before they came.

Although the colonial administrators exacerbated

ethnic tensions and even instigated tribal warfare in order to divide and rule, they also imposed law and order without which it would have been impossible for them to rule and exploit Africa. In Rwanda and Burundi, the colonial rulers employed the Tutsi to facilitate colonial administration at the expense of the Hutu, a policy which had tragic consequences for the future of both countries.

Colonialism was therefore a paradox. It united tribes in order to create viable colonial entities under one leadership of the colonial government. It also divided in order to rule. Out of this paradoxical situation emerged African nationalism transcending tribalism. As Julius Nyerere said at a symposium at Wellesley College in the United States in 1960 before he led Tanganyika to independence the following year:

"One need not go into the history of colonization of Africa, but that colonization had one significant result. A sentiment was created on the African continent – a sentiment of oneness."[4]

But after nationalism triumphed over colonialism, it was unable to contain let alone neutralise tribalism. With the colonial rulers gone, Africans no longer had a common enemy except themselves. The result is what we see today: Africa in chaos, with Africans slaughtering each other, Rwanda being only one of the most tragic cases, if not the most tragic during the post-colonial era.

The horrendous tragedy that befell Rwanda in 1994 when about one million Tutsis were massacred by their fellow countrymen (Hutu extremists) is a strong indictment against the weakness of the modern African state whose fragility can not be wholly attributed to the partition of Africa by the imperial powers.

It is true that the colonial rulers created unstable countries. But much of Africa's tragedy today is the fault of the Africans themselves. As Adebayo Adedeji, a prominent Nigerian economist who was the Executive Secretary of the UN Economic Commission for Africa (ECA), bluntly put it:

"Quite frankly, African governments have to accept full responsibility....The time has passed when we should lay this blame at the doors of others. If we continue to do that, it means we are not responsible people."[5]

Rwanda's 1994 genocide was one such catastrophe for which Africans did not accept full responsibility let alone try to stop. They waited for outsiders to come and stop the massacres. Some of them even begged outsiders to come and stop the killings while they themselves did nothing, absolutely nothing, to stop the genocide. But the saviours from outside never came and simply watched Africans on television slaughtering one another. They also read about them in newspapers.

The result was one million lives lost for nothing. One million is a lot of people even for a country like China with a population of more than one billion. But percentages depict an even more gruesome picture.

More than 200,000 people were killed in the Liberian civil war from 1990 to 1996, a figure equivalent to about 8% of Liberia's entire population.

In Rwanda, the 1 million Tutsis and Hutu moderates who perished in the genocide constituted 12.5% or one-eighth of the country's total population of 8 million. The magnitude of Rwanda's tragedy in the American context would have been 32.5 million Americans killed by their fellow countrymen. That is equivalent to the extermination of the entire black American population without a single soul spared. And the holocaust had its genesis in the 1959 mass uprising and subsequent rise to power by the Hutu at independence in July 1962.

Before Rwanda won independence, a series of elections were held to prepare the country for the attainment of sovereign status. A Hutu victory at the polls was a foregone conclusion. Numbers were on their side. It was a contest in which the Tutsi were hopelessly outmatched.

The country's transition to independence also got impetus from uncompromising Hutu demands for a rapid transformation of society which compromised the transition process by compelling the Belgian authorities to make hasty preparations for the transfer of power to Africans, in this case Hutus.

Attempts by the colonial rulers to pursue a gradual transition were rebuffed by the Hutu who now had the upper hand in the negotiations as colonial rule was rapidly coming to an end. The Belgians were caught between the Hutus' demands for immediate transfer of power and the Tutsis' refusal to concede the inevitable. So, they had to choose between the two. They decided to go with the winner, the Hutu.

It was a radical switch of "allegiance" by the Belgians tantamount to an act of betrayal. The Tutsi felt betrayed. Throughout the colonial period, the Belgians had sided with the Tutsi. Now they took sides with the Hutu, compelled by historical dictates and contemporary demands of realpolitik in the national interest of Belgium, a departing colonial power that was pragmatic enough not to alienate Rwanda's new masters, the Hutu, whose victory started just before independence when they overthrew the Tutsi aristocracy in November 1959.

From then on, it was obvious they would be the new rulers of Rwanda after the end of colonial rule, unlike in Burundi where the Tutsi remained firmly entrenched in power after they killed the entire Hutu elite – political leaders and educated people including all secondary school students – before independence to prevent the Hutu majority from winning power at the end of colonial rule.

In Rwanda, the Belgians even refused to intervene when Hutu militants instigated violence against the Tutsi.

As one officer commanding Belgian forces in Rwanda during that transitional period explained with startling candour and uncharacteristic bluntness: "Because of the forces of circumstances, we have to take sides. We cannot remain neutral and passive."[6]

One of the first radical measures the Belgians took just before independence was to replace Tutsi rulers. In early 1960, the Belgian authorities began dismissing Tutsi chiefs. They appointed Hutu chiefs to replace them, fully aware of the consequences of such a policy of blatant discrimination against the Tutsi with a potential for violence. If they wanted to be fair, they would have left some Tutsi rulers in power to represent their people and would have created a collective traditional leadership whose composition reflected the demographic realities of the country instead of leaving the Tutsi out completely.

Retaliation by the new Hutu rulers against their former native rulers was inevitable. Many Hutus, if not the majority, equated Tutsi rule with oppression. Therefore removal of Tutsi chiefs was tantamount to freedom from oppression, and retaliation against the Tutsi an inevitable reaction. Yet the colonial administrators did nothing to avert that.

The new Hutu rulers immediately organised campaigns against the Tutsi, causing an exodus of tens of thousands of them. About 130,000 Tutsis fled to Burundi, Congo, Uganda and Tanzania during that period. A large number of them sought sanctuary in Burundi where their kinsmen were still in control.

As the attacks against the Tutsi continued, sending waves of refugees across borders, the Hutu were busy consolidating their position as the dominant group in Rwanda.

In July 1960, communal elections were held across the country and all the parties representing the Hutu and the Tutsi participated in the democratic exercise.

The Hutu parties won and the *Parti du Mouvement de*

l'Emancipation Hutu (PARMEHUTU) emerged as the dominant party. It won control of 210 out of 229 communes, while the Tutsi retained power in 19 of them.

Such victory was inevitable for the Hutu. In any truly democratic election, numbers are on their side.

Only a few months before, the Tutsi controlled the whole country. Now their former subjects who were virtual slaves became the new masters. And they were in a vengeful mood.

As the new rulers of the land and numerically dominant ethnic group guaranteed to win all elections and rule perpetually if democratic contests were to continue, there was nothing that could constrain their fury and passion for vengeance. They went on to institute an oppressive feudalistic system similar to the power structure the Tutsi used for centuries to dominate, suppress, and oppress them.

Following the Hutu victory at the polls, the leader of the dominant party PARMEHUTU, Grégoire Kayibanda, became interim prime minister in the same year.

But the sudden rise to power by the Hutu over their former masters, the Tutsi, led to a deteriorating situation in the country which had the potential to degenerate into chaos similar to what was going on in neighbouring Congo where anarchy reigned following the secession of Katanga Province in July 1960 under the leadership of Moise Tshombe.

To avert such a catastrophe, the United Nations urged Belgium to initiate a dialogue of reconciliation between the Hutu and the Tutsi in Rwanda. But as a senior Belgian official described such an initiative, it was "perfectly useless."

Belgium held a National Reconciliation Conference, anyway, ostensibly to defuse tension between the two ethnic groups. The conference was held in Ostend, Belgium, but led to no settlement. The ethnic divide between the Hutu and the Tutsi was so wide and so deep that it could not have been bridged by one reconciliation meeting. But the Belgian authorities had other plans.

Even when they were organising the meeting, they knew that reconciliation between the two sides was almost impossible. Therefore, they did what they felt was the most practical thing to do. They "colluded with Hutu leaders to arrange what was subsequently described as a 'legal coup.'"[7]

It was a "legal coup" which legitimised the institutionalisation of a Hutu ethnocracy by the Hutu elite.

On 28 January 1961, Rwanda's elected councillors and *bourgmestres*, most of them Hutu, were summoned to a conference for an emergency session on the future status of the country. The meeting was held in Gitarama, the birthplace of Rwanda's interim prime minister, Grégoire Kayibanda, and "the sovereign democratic republic of Rwanda" came into being.

The new republic was proclaimed by acclamation before a mass gathering of 25,000 people, mostly Hutu. With this proclamation as the will of the people, the United Nations was presented with a *fait accompli* and had no choice but to accept Rwanda's *de facto* sovereign status.

Although no referendum took place across Rwanda, and the 25,000 people who gathered at Gitarama barely constituted what could have been described as a significant segment of the country's entire population, Rwandan – mostly Hutu – leaders contended that the decision they had reached was indeed the will of the people. It may have been the will of the people, but those people were mostly Hutu. Most Tutsis did not share or accept that interpretation.

Belgium as the "mother country" was glad to be relieved of the burden of having such a restive population embroiled in ethnic disputes under her tutelage. That was also the period when colonialism in most parts of Africa was coming to an end and the Belgians felt it was also time for them to go.

Rwanda's sovereign status as a republic was confirmed a few months later in UN-supervised legislative elections in September 1961. The elections were a referendum by the Hutu masses which not only ratified Rwanda's status as a sovereign state; they also officially ended the dynasty of the Tutsi aristocracy and the status of the country as a kingdom and instituted a Hutu ethnocracy with the legal mandate to rule as the supreme power in the land which for centuries had been dominated by the Tutsi.

On 1 January 1962, Rwanda won self-government from Belgium and Grégoire Kayibanda became the country's main leader. Independence came on July 1st the same year under a republican constitution, formally ending Rwanda's status as a kingdom which was known as Ruanda. The country's name was also changed from Ruanda to Rwanda.

Kayibanda became Rwanda's first president, ending the era of colonial rule which began in 1890 when Germany acquired the territory and then lost it to Belgium in 1916 during World War I. A new constitution was adopted in November 1962 and Kayibanda was confirmed in his position as president in the general election held that month.

Thus, Rwanda joined the family of African nations as one of the new independent states.

But Rwanda was also a unique case in the history of African nationalism. All the other African countries had fought and others were still fighting to oust a foreign colonial power. Rwanda, like Burundi, had, of course, also been colonised by a European power, Belgium. But the primary focus of the majority of Rwandans, who were Hutu, was on their indigenous rulers, the Tutsi, who would have continued to dominate and exploit them – as they had for centuries – even if Europeans had never conquered and colonised Ruanda-Urundi.

In fact, dislodging this indigenous "racist" regime, the

226

Tutsi aristocracy, took more effort than did the struggle to oust European colonial rulers in some African countries and was bloodier than in most across the continent. However, the Hutu themselves compounded the felony.

Once in power, they went on to espouse and enforce the ideology of "racial" – or ethnic – supremacy, upon which the Tutsi aristocracy was founded, to justify Hutu domination and oppression of their former oppressors as if two wrongs make a right, instead of trying to seek reconciliation and forge national unity on the basis of equality in a pluralistic context.

It was one of the most racist regimes in the history of post-colonial Africa. Soon after independence, the Hutu supremacist regime of President Kayibanda initiated a policy of ethnic quotas based on the country's ethnic composition in order to exclude the Tutsi from most positions in the government, in the economy, in schools and in other areas. It was a broad spectrum of quotas to ensure Hutus dominated every sector of society and every aspect of life.

The new Hutu rulers wanted to make sure that Tutsis did not get equal rights. At the time of independence, the Tutsi constituted about 9 per cent of Rwanda's population. And that became the prime factor in the calculus that was used to determine their fate in a country now dominated by their "enemies," the Hutu.

From then on, the Hutu-dominated regime (with a sprinkling of Tutsi "loyalists" who supported the regime but who had been given positions in the government only as mere tools to be manipulated at will by the Hutu) decreed that it was the official policy of the government that because the Tutsi constituted only 9% of the total population, only 9% of the pupils and students in school should be Tutsi; only 9% of the civil service workers should be Tutsi; and only 9% of the employees in other areas, in all sectors, everywhere across the country, should be Tutsi. No field or sector or area of employment should have more than 9% of this prescribed quota for Tutsis.

That was only fair, the government said, because it simply reflected the demographic composition of the country or the percentages of both groups in the country's total population and ensured proportional representation. But it was clear that the Hutu regime had sinister motives in promulgating and implementing such a policy. And it did so with deadly efficiency.

The policy not only excluded Tutsis from most positions, virtually relegating them to the status of outsiders with no rights in their own homeland; it helped stir up racist sentiments among the Hutu in preparation for a final solution to the Nilotic problem – the Tutsi. It was a solution that inevitably entailed extermination – even if in stages comprising a series of massacres through the years – if the land was indeed to be cleansed of this Tutsi "scourge."

It is a solution that began with the Hutu mass uprising of November 1959 which led to ethnic pogroms in which more than 100,000 Tutsis were massacred in cold blood in an attempt to run them all out of Rwanda and even wipe them out if possible.

There was nothing proportional about it in terms of representation in the quest for equality; it was totally out of proportion. And it fuelled hatred against the Tutsi.

As the quota policy was being implemented, violence against the Tutsi – which began in July 1959 and increased in early 1960 when the colonial authorities began dismissing Tutsi chiefs and other traditional rulers, replacing them with Hutu appointees – continued at an alarming rate, exemplified by these incidents:

"150 Tutsi were killed (around Butare) in September – October 1961, 3,000 houses were burnt down and 22,000 people were displaced. New waves of refugees went on foot to the refugee camps in Uganda."[8]

The killings and arsons had one clear objective: expel all the Tutsi from Rwanda by any means possible, and kill those who resist. The United Nations issued an ominous warning after these incidents, painting a gloomy picture of the country's future:

"The developments of these last eighteen months have brought about the racial dictatorship of one party....An oppressive system has been replaced by another one....It is quite possible that some day we will witness violent reactions on the part of the Tutsi."[9]

That day was not far off. The Tutsi had, in fact, started retaliating as early as the latter part of 1960 when small bands of Tutsi exiles began launching cross-border raids into Rwanda from their refugee sanctuaries in Burundi, Congo, Uganda, and Tanganyika (later renamed Tanzania). The Hutu called them *Inyenzi*, an extremely offensive and derogatory term meaning "cockroaches," and they had one primary mission: overthrow the Hutu regime and re-institute a Tutsi ethnocracy, especially the ousted aristocracy which was still reeling from the humiliating defeat and expulsion from Rwanda only about a year before.

The odds against the Tutsi were great. It was about two years before independence and the Rwandan army was still controlled by the Belgians. Tutsi guerrilla fighters had no chance of winning the war.

But their attacks on Hutu officials were, in many cases, successful. However, the raids provoked a brutal response from the Hutu who exacted retribution for the atrocities. The guerrilla attacks by the Tutsi were launched from outside. But it was the Tutsi within Rwanda who paid the price. The Hutu attacked them indiscriminately and with malicious vindictiveness.

Yet, in spite of such retaliation by the Hutu, attacks by the Tutsi continued through the years. One of the deadliest raids took place around Christmas in 1963, almost one year-and-a-half after independence, about which an international investigating committee had this to say:

"The biggest killings followed a large Inyenzi attack from Burundi on December 23, 1963. Hutu gangs killed an estimated 10,000 Tutsi, while the (Hutu) government executed about 20 prominent Tutsi, some of whose names had been on a list of prospective future ministers in a Tutsi-led government that had been found on the body of one of the attackers."[10]

But repressive as the Hutu regime was, it is clear that it paved the way for fundamental change – even if by bloody means – in the country in the following years. Rwanda was never to be the same again, as tragically demonstrated by the genocide of about one million Tutsis 30 years later, and the continuing civil war through the 1990s and beyond, which may force both the Hutu and the Tutsi to realistically assess their positions with regard to each other on several fundamental issues: the possibility and impossibility of democracy on the basis of universal adult suffrage in Rwanda's highly volatile pluralistic context; the imperative need for a unique form of democracy based on proportional representation, taking into account the realities and historical circumstances of the country; extensive devolution of power preferably under a confederation of autonomous ethnostates; and even partition of the country along ethnic lines into independent states of Hutuland and Tutsiland.

The civil war through the years has clearly shown that this is a no-win situation for either side, unless both agree to compromise and make substantial concessions on the basis of a mutually acceptable formula – or go their separate ways as two sovereign nations on separate territories. The alternative is war and brutal subjugation of one ethnic group by the other, depending on who is power.

The Hutu regime instituted in the early 1960s was responsible for an even more fundamental change. It ended four centuries of Tutsi domination. And that was unprecedented in this Tutsi-dominated region. The rise to power by the Hutu majority in Rwanda, even by constitutional means, would have been impossible had the Tutsi remained politically dominant as was the case in neighbouring Burundi where they remained in power. It took violence and bloodshed to dethrone the Tutsi aristocracy in a mass uprising, the first of its kind in colonial Africa. According to *Africa Contemporary Record*:

"As a result of the peasant revolt in 1959, the Bahutu came to power in Rwanda and several thousand of their rivals, the Watutsi, who once ruled Rwanda, fled the country.

Many thousands of Watutsi were welcomed in Burundi where they armed themselves, and in December 1963, they virtually invaded Rwanda and fought the Bahutu tribesmen in fierce bloody warfare. According to the Rwandan government, at least 750 persons were killed, but unofficial estimates put the number near 5,000."[11]

The 1963 abortive invasion of Rwanda by Tutsi exiles not only triggered a brutal retaliatory response whose ferocity had few parallels in the country's recent history apart from the 1959 Hutu mass uprising and its atrocities the magnitude of which had yet to be surpassed; it also led to the entrenchment of the Hutu regime whose excesses rivalled and even in some cases surpassed the brutalities the Hutu majority had endured for years under the repressive rule of the Tutsi aristocracy; and solidified support for the Hutu ethnocracy, especially among the Hutu elite who were the biggest beneficiaries in the new dispensation.

But how secure was the despotic ethnocratic Hutu

231

regime which exploited racist sentiments and had, as its ideological underpinning, Hutu supremacy and unmitigated Tutsi oppression at any cost?

Subsequent events through the years exposed its inherent weaknesses which were a product of internal contradictions in what was – like its Tutsi counterpart in Burundi and the ousted Tutsi aristocracy in Rwanda – probably one of the most racist, and one of the most brutal and morally bankrupt regimes in post-colonial Africa.

Hutu Entrenchment

The consolidation of the Hutus' dominant position in Rwanda was aided by subsequent invasions of the country by Tutsi exiles through the years. As expected, the invasions triggered intensified repression of the Tutsi minority. But they also helped the regime mobilise support among ordinary Hutus and the elite for its cause of maintaining Hutu supremacy.

Ethnic solidarity was a powerful weapon. It was a clarion call that struck a responsive chord across the nation that was already predominantly Hutu. And it is easy to understand why it resonated well, given the history of 400 years of Hutu oppression by the Tutsi minority.

The fighting which started in December 1963 as a result of the invasion of Rwanda by Tutsi exiles continued well into 1964. The Tutsi launched more but sporadic attacks in an attempt to reinstate their deposed king, Kigeri V, who was still living in exile in neighbouring Burundi. Burundi was then the only Tutsi-dominated state in the region after the Tutsi were ousted from power in Rwanda, a status (as a Nilotic ethnocracy) it has maintained until this day. No other country in the region has been under the domination of a single ethnic group for so long.

Apart from Rwanda where the Hutu ruled for 32 years since independence, which was a relatively brief interruption in the nearly 400-year Tutsi domination of the country, Kenya is another East African country (in addition to both Rwanda and Burundi) that has been dominated by ethnocratic regimes for many years: first, under the Kikuyu from December 1963 when the country won independence until August 1978 when Kenya's first president and Kikuyu patriarch, Jomo Kenyatta, died; and then under the Kalenjin when Daniel arap Moi succeeded him as president (1978 – 2002) and went on to institute one of the most repressive regimes on the continent.

That is what the Hutu (from 1962 to 1994) achieved in Rwanda, also like their predecessors, the Tutsi ethnocratic despots, did for centuries; as did the Kikuyu and the Kalenjin in Kenya, hardly an enviable record yet not surprising on a continent notorious for dictatorship.

People in Africa were tired of being ruled by despots and tribalists. And the dictators themselves in different parts of the continent were insecure and uncertain about their future.

Therefore attempts to reinstate a Tutsi ethnocracy in Rwanda won the Tutsi little sympathy elsewhere across the continent except among the Tutsi within Rwanda itself and in Burundi where their kinsmen were in power. In fact, the 1963 – 1964 invasion of Rwanda by Tutsi exiles mainly those based in Burundi was strongly supported by the Rwandan Tutsi aristocracy, also in exile in Burundi, thus leaving no doubt about the purpose of the invasion.

The invasion was also supported by the Tutsi regime in Burundi which was then still under an aristocracy headed by Mwami Mwambutsa IV. As we learned earlier, the king himself effectively blocked the Hutu from genuine participation in Burundi's government when he refused to appoint a Hutu prime minister and, instead, appointed a fellow Tutsi although it was the Hutu who won the election soon after independence.

But Mwami Mwambutsa's pro-Tutsi sentiments towards his Rwandan kinsmen and fellow aristocrats only enraged the Hutu in both Rwanda and Burundi.

The 1963 – 1964 invasion of Rwanda by the Tutsi triggered a violent response from the Hutu which resulted in the death of more Tutsis than Hutus. The Hutu were in control of the country and the army and other security forces which they used to neutralise Tutsi opposition including the insurgency.

Although the Hutu were now in power, their dominant position could not – in all aspects – be equated with the supremacy exercised by the Tutsi in the preceding years. They had a lot in common in terms of domination and oppression of the other ethnic group. But there was one fundamental difference. Hutu leaders were elected; Tutsi leaders were not. The Hutu government which came to power in the early 1960s was elected in a democratic election supervised by the United Nations. The Tutsi imposed their rule on the Hutu and perpetuated themselves in power – at least for four centuries – without any mandate from the people they ruled until they were overthrown in a bloody uprising in 1959.

In 1965, President Kayibanda was elected to a second term and remained head of the PARMEHUTU ruling party which continued to be predominantly Hutu.

Relations between Rwanda and Burundi were still strained. They were made even worse by differences in the nature of the two governments – the divergent paths the two countries took in choosing their political systems. Rwanda was under a republican constitution. Burundi remained an aristocracy.

However, relations between the two countries later improved considerably when Burundi became a republic in November 1966 following the ouster of the Tutsi aristocracy in a military coup, although the leaders of the two nations belonged to rival ethnic groups.

The new military ruler of Burundi, 26-year-old Captain Michel Micombero, a Tutsi, seized power after a bloodless *coup d'etat* on November 29th when he deposed 21-year-

234

old Mwami Ntare V who earlier on July 8th the same year – with the help of Micombero – overthrew his father Mwami Mwambutsa IV. Soon after the coup in Burundi, Rwanda's President Kayibanda sent a message to Micombero congratulating him for deposing the monarchy:

"In this way, all the Burundi people are freed from the retrograde myth of feudal monarchy."[12]

Also in the same month of the military coup in Burundi, the African heads of state at the OAU summit held in Kinshasa, Congo's capital, asked President Joseph Mobutu (he did not change his name to Mobutu Sese Seko until 1972) of neighbouring Congo to act as mediator between the two countries in their dispute caused by the invasion of Rwanda by Rwandan Tutsi exiles from their sanctuary in Burundi.

Coincidentally, Mobutu himself seized power almost exactly a year before in November 1965 and executed Prime Minister Evariste Kimba but spared President Joseph Kasavubu whom he stripped of all powers, declaring himself president; and he changed his country's name from Congo to Zaire in October 1971.

The dispute between Rwanda and Burundi was also fuelled by the continued presence of Rwandan Tutsi royalists in Burundi who were still determined to overthrow the Hutu government of Rwanda and reinstate their king, Kigera V.

After a three-day meeting in March 1967 between Mobutu, Micombero, and Kayibanda, the three leaders signed an agreement stipulating that the armed Rwandan Tutsi refugees in Burundi should lay down their arms within a month, and that representatives of the two countries should meet regularly under the chairmanship of Mobutu to improve cooperation between the two states. It was also agreed that a permanent commission was to be established to facilitate the return of the Tutsi refugees from Burundi to Rwanda. The refugees were assured that none would be forced to return to Rwanda, and that if they did, nothing would happen to them.[13]

Although Mobutu played an important role in easing tensions between Rwanda and Burundi and was therefore on friendly terms with both countries, his relationship with Rwanda changed later.

On 11 January 1968, he broke off diplomatic relations with Rwanda when President Kayibanda refused to hand over to him white mercenaries who had fled from Bukavu in eastern Congo, near the border between the two countries, to Rwanda in November 1967. Newspapers in Kinshasa criticised Rwanda for giving sanctuary to the mercenaries who had wreaked havoc across Congo, saying the small East African country was still under the "colonialist, neo-colonialist rule of Belgium."[14]

The charge was not entirely unfounded although Congo itself, especially under Mobutu who was a tool of Western powers, was no more independent than Rwanda was. In fact, during Mobutu's reign, the largest CIA station in Africa was in the Zairean capital Kinshasa; and Monrovia, Liberia's capital, was the centre of CIA operations in West Africa during President Tubman's tenure and those of his predecessors.

The refusal by Rwanda to send mercenaries back to Congo to face charges was not an independent decision by the Rwandan government despite claims to the contrary. It was dictated by power politics, an arena in which African countries don't even play a peripheral role a generation after independence except as playgrounds for world powers.

The white mercenaries who caused so much destruction in Congo during the sixties had been an integral part of the invasion force of Belgium, the former colonial ruler of both Congo and Rwanda, which invaded Congo during that period with the support of the United

States – the leader of the Western world – to protect Western interests in Congo, Africa's potentially richest and most strategically located country. As Dr. Walter Rodney, author of the highly acclaimed book, *How Europe underdeveloped Africa*, stated during that time in one of his other works, *The Groundings with My Brothers*:

"Paid white mercenaries have harassed the Congo. Late last year (1967), 130 of these hired white killers were chased out of the Congo and cornered in the neighbouring African State of Rwanda. The white world intervened and they have all been set free.

These are men who for months were murdering, raping, pillaging, disrupting economic production, and making a mockery of black life and black society. Yet white power said not a hair on their heads was to be touched. They did not even have to stand trial or reveal their names.

Conscious blacks cannot possibly fail to realise that in our own homelands we have no power, abroad we are discriminated against, and everywhere the black masses suffer from poverty. You can put together in your own mind a picture of the whole world, with the white imperialist beast crouched over miserable blacks. And don't forget to label us poor. There is nothing with which poverty coincides so absolutely as with the colour black – small or large population, hot or cold climates, rich or poor in natural resources – poverty cuts across all these factors in order to find black people.

That association of wealth with whites and poverty with blacks is not accidental. It is the nature of the imperialist relationship that enriches the metropolis at the expense of the colony, i.e. it makes the whites richer and the blacks poorer....

There is the mistaken belief that black people achieved power with independence, but a black man ruling a dependent State within the imperialist system has no power. He is simply an agent of the whites in the metropolis, with an army and police force designed to maintain the imperialist way of things in that particular colonial area."[15]

That is the kind of predicament Rwanda faced. For all practical purposes in the international arena, it was still a colony. It was powerless. It could neither exercise independent judgement nor extricate itself from the clutches of the imperialist powers to honour its Pan-African commitments.

But Rwanda was also just weak on its own and was not fully committed to the Pan-African cause, unlike its neighbours, Tanzania and Uganda, two of the most militant states on the continent together with Ghana under Nkrumah, Guinea under Sekou Toure, and Mali under Modibo Keita.

When the OAU passed a binding resolution on the mercenaries who had fled to Rwanda, the Rwandan government gave its own interpretation of the resolution and of how the events concerning the mercenaries unfolded. It was an interpretation that may have expressed the collective will of the OAU member states but it did not satisfy neighbouring Congo.

Even other countries may have had reservations about the resolution, since it led to the freeing of the mercenaries instead of having them sent back to Congo to stand trial for the atrocities they committed in that country:

"The Rwandan government denied that the O.A.U. Committee on mercenaries, which met in the previous November (1967), had decided to send the white mercenaries back to the Congo to stand trial.

In Rwanda's view, the Committee, which was led by the O.A.U. Secretary General, Diallo Telli, had 'clearly stated that the mercenaries should be evacuated to their homes through Rwanda,' and that the Congolese request for extradition was a violation of an O.A.U. resolution passed in Kinshasa on 14 September 1967.

President Mobutu agreed on 15 March 1968 to the evacuation of the 119 mercenaries provided that their countries of origin, mainly Belgium and France, gave a guarantee that 'these soldiers of fortune' were never allowed to return to Africa.

The mercenaries were evacuated by air to Europe on April 24.

It was announced in May (1968) that relations between the Congo and Rwanda would be resumed."[16]

Relations were resumed in September 1968 in response to appeals made by President Ismail Al Azhari of Sudan who had been asked by the East and Central African heads of state to act as a mediator between the two countries. And Mobutu could no longer act as mediator in the conflict between Rwanda and Burundi because of his conflict with Rwanda, although he resumed relations with the Rwandan regime.

The 1967 – 1968 mercenary incident did not cause any serious political damage to Rwandan President Kayibanda in his own country. In 1969, he was re-elected to another term – mostly by his fellow Hutus – and went on to further consolidate the Hutu ethnocracy. Perhaps the only major threat to Kayibanda during that period came from neighbouring Uganda.

In 1971 – 1972, relations between the two countries were very bad. Ugandan military dictator General Idi Amin accused Rwanda of helping groups trying to overthrow him. He threatened to invade Rwanda – as he did another neighbour, "I will flatten Tanzania" – and annex the whole territory. The two countries were literally in a state of war, and Rwanda was the underdog.

Amin's threats could not be ignored, as events proved later when he invaded Tanzania in 1978 and announced on November 1st the same year that he had annexed 710 square miles of Tanzanian territory, Kagera Region, in the northwest, bordering Uganda. Tanzania fought back, crossed the border and drove Amin into exile, capturing Uganda's capital Kampala on 11 April 1979. Tanzanian troops began withdrawing from Uganda in July 1979, and Amin never regained power.

The 1971 – 1972 dispute between Rwanda and Uganda which threatened to end Kayibanda's presidency – had Amin invaded the country and removed Kayibanda from power – was followed by another threat to his leadership and the nation's security only a few months later. It was an internal threat but probably just as serious as the danger posed by Amin.

In February and March 1973, fighting between the Hutu and the Tutsi in Rwanda erupted again. Hundreds of Tutsis fled to Uganda. It was reported that 600 of them fled Rwanda. But the actual number was probably much higher than that.

And that marked the beginning of the end of Kayibanda's presidency. The Hutu regime he had presided over since independence was highly notorious for its blatant discrimination against the Tutsi. But Kayibanda also alienated many of his fellow Hutus who constituted the ethnic base of his brutal ethnocracy.

He led a regime that was so autocratic that even the Hutu elite who were its prime beneficiaries bitterly resented Kayibanda's authoritarian ways. And he was aware of the discontent.

To divert attention from his autocratic rule and mobilise support for his regime, he whipped up racist sentiments against the Tutsi, a rallying cry for rabid Hutu ethno-nationalism.

He encouraged Hutu militants to scrutinise schools, the university, the civil service and even private businesses to ensure that the ethnic-quota policy was being implemented in fulfillment of the Hutu aspirations articulated in the *Hutu Manifesto*. As expected, the most ardent supporters of this policy of ethnic cleansing were educated Hutus who would be the greatest beneficiaries. They would automatically take over the jobs which "surplus" Tutsis had been forced to give up after supposedly exceeding their 9% limit.

However, the ethnic cleansing campaign had a profound economic and psychological impact on the country. It inflamed passions among the Hutu against their historical "enemies" and triggered off another mass exodus of the Tutsi who sought refuge in neighbouring countries.

The campaign also had unintended consequences for President Kayibanda. Instead of increasing support for his regime, it helped mobilise increasing opposition to his brutal autocracy, especially among the Hutu elite.

On 5 July 1973, just before the presidential elections scheduled for the following day in which Kayibanda was the only candidate, defence minister, Major-General Juvénal Habyarimana who was also commander of the national guard, overthrew the government and became the new head of state. Like Kayibanda, he was also a Hutu.

Kayibanda was imprisoned and starved to death. And more than 50 of his staunchest allies were killed during the next few years in what amounted to a retaliatory response by the opponents of the regime. Many of them suffered under his brutal subjugation, although they were fellow Hutus.

Like most African leaders across the continent, Kayibanda tolerated no dissent even from his fellow tribesmen which amounted to "betrayal." Those who don't support "their people," their fellow tribesmen in power, are considered to be traitors.

His successor, Habyarimana, tolerated no dissent either. And his nepotism as well as repressive rule became a focal point around which the opposition rallied to mobilise forces against him as much as it did against Kayibanda:

"As with the regime of Kayibanda before him, Habyarimana's 'Second Republic' rapidly became a self-serving institution which fomented dissent among those excluded from the circles of privilege. Especially as rising oil prices and falling commodity revenues brought the economy of the country close to collapse by the late 1980s, and available sources of privilege shrank accordingly."[17]

Soon after Habyarimana seized power, he suspended Rwanda's only legal party, PARMEHUTU, which since independence in 1962 was officially known as the Republican Democratic Movement-Parmehutu.[18] He also dissolved the National Assembly and ruled by decree.

In 1975, he declared his party, the National Revolutionary Movement for Development (MRND), as the only legal political party in the country. It was also still highly ethnocentric, systematically excluding Tutsis.

Although he led a political party, which implied civilian involvement, his government was not civilian. It was, instead, dominated by army officers.

In 1978, a new constitution was ratified and elections were held to consolidate power in the hands of a quasi-military regime entrenched in a Hutu ethnocracy. As expected, Habyarimana easily won the presidency, coasting to victory on a wave of retrogressive Hutu ethno-nationalism and virulently anti-Tutsi sentiments among his fellow tribesmen.

But only a few years later, his regime faced a number of major problems which put a serious burden on the country's fragile economy and threatened to destabilise the government.

In 1982, about 25,000 Rwandan immigrants were violently kicked out of Uganda by members of local tribes with the tacit approval of the Ugandan authorities. Ugandan tribesmen burned their homes and stole their cattle. Thousands fled back to Rwanda, pleading for food and shelter, and the Rwandan government appealed to the international community for help.[18] Most of them were Tutsi, and their return to Rwanda only added to the combustible ethnic cauldron in their homeland.

However, Habyarimana's regime remained securely anchored in power.

In 1983, President Habyarimana was re-elected to another five-year term, but at a time when the country faced serious economic problems.

It had to resettle the 25,000 Rwandans who had been kicked out of Uganda and returned to their native land with nothing. It also had to cope with the potential threat of famine and economic collapse. 1983 was one of the worst years for Rwanda as the country suffered a devastating drought that, together with a dense population which continued to grow at a phenomenal rate, had an enormous impact on economic development in one of the world's poorest countries.

Rwanda's Hutu-dominated regime had to contend with even more problems when in 1988 more than 50,000 Hutus fled Burundi and sought refuge in Rwanda following the massacre of more than 20,000 Hutus by the Burundian Tutsi military government after an abortive coup attempt by the Hutu in August the same year. Tens of thousands of others fled to Tanzania and Congo, what was then Zaire.

It was yet another case of ethnic cleansing in this highly volatile region. However, the spillover of Burundi's ethnic violence into Rwanda did not in any way threaten, let alone erode, Habyarimana's ethnic base.

Thus, when the 1980s came to an end, it seemed to many people that the regimes in both countries were firmly in control of their respective territories. And both were determined to consolidate ethnocratic rule, with Rwanda dominated by the Hutu, and Burundi by the Tutsi.

But while Burundi continued to be ruled by the Tutsi

throughout the 1990s and beyond, as has been the case since independence in 1962, the Hutus' hegemonic control of Rwanda turned out to be, paradoxically, the very cause of their downfall.

The early 1990s witnessed the beginning of the end of one of Africa's most despotic ethnocracies, and probably the bloodiest, culminating in the genocide of almost one million Tutsis and their Hutu sympathisers, a tragedy whose ferocity and magnitude is unprecedented in the annals of ethnic pogroms in modern times.

Chapter Six:

The Rwandan Genocide and Elite's Support of Oppressive Regimes

THE 1994 Rwandan holocaust generated profound ambivalence in the world's reaction to this immense horror.

It attracted world attention yet drew little sympathy for the victims from the very same people who said they were horrified by the unspeakable atrocities and by the magnitude of the tragedy. It was repulsive, yet numbing; shocking, yet tolerable, even if not acceptable.

Equally shocking was the total disregard for human lives and suffering by those who planned and perpetrated the genocide. They included the Hutu academic elite who helped instigate and justify some of the worst massacres in history.

The genocide had its genesis – at least as the immediate cause – in attempts by the Tutsi since 1990 to overthrow President Juvénal Habyarimana's Hutu regime and end Hutu control of the country. The plot to overthrow Habyarimana received a boost from an assessment of Rwanda's internal situation which showed that the Hutu regime was weak and could collapse anytime if the requisite combination of forces was exerted on it to force it to capitulate.

The weakness of Habyarimana's regime became apparent in the late 1980s when Rwanda's economy faced imminent collapse, a prospect which encouraged his opponents within and outside Rwanda to launch a concerted effort to oust him from power. Rwandan refugees in neighbouring countries provided fertile ground for such intrigue:

"Meanwhile (by the late 1980s), refugee numbers in the surrounding states had mounted to at least 400,000, according to the United Nations High Commission for Refugees (UNHCR), and probably as many as 700,000 according to informal sources. From among them, Tutsi leaders and a number of prominent Hutu opponents of the Habyarimana regime collaborated to recruit and arm what they called the Rwandese (sic) Patriotic Front (RPF).

The RPF was preparing to invade, though insisting that its aim was not to reimpose Tutsi hegemony in Rwanda, only to overthrow a corrupt regime and establish democratic government.

In mid-1990 agents in the Rwanda army and government advised that the Habyarimana regime was on the verge of collapse. One push and it would topple, they said."[1]

Although some Hutu opponents of Habyarimana's regime collaborated with their Tutsi counterparts in forming the Rwandan Patriotic Front (RPF), the group was overwhelmingly Tutsi.

And contrary to its declared objectives, it had a hidden agenda to re-institute a Tutsi ethnocracy once Habyarimana was ousted from power, as was clearly demonstrated after the RPF seized power in 1994, leading the establishment of a Tutsi-dominated government with Hutus playing only a subordinate role. Even Rwanda's president in the post-Habyarimana era, Pasteur Bizimungu, a Hutu, was no more than a figure head. Real power was in the hands of the Tutsi in the RPF, especially Paul Kagame.

The RPF was determined to invade Rwanda. And that is exactly what happened, with help from Uganda where it had operational bases from which it launched its first invasion of Rwanda on 1 October 1990.

But it was defeated within days, a victory by the Rwandan Hutu-dominated army attributed to French support, also to Belgian troops sent to Rwanda to "protect their nationals," and to Zairean soldiers whom the weak Rwandan army desperately needed to push back the invaders.

Without that kind of support, especially French and Belgian, the Habyarimana regime would probably have collapsed during the first invasion by the RPF.

The invasion had one immediate impact on Rwanda's defence posture. It galvanised the Hutu regime into action, prompting it to mobilise forces and support in order to enlarge the Rwandan army on a very large scale. Within one year, the army was more than two times bigger than it was at the time of the invasion, and seven times bigger two years thereafter:

"In October 1990 it had comprised about 5,000 men; one year later the number had risen to 24,000 and soared to over 35,000 during 1993."[2]

It was phenomenal growth especially for such a poor country, facilitated by France which made arrangements for the Rwandan Hutu regime to buy a variety of weapons from Egypt in 1992 costing $6 million (USD). Apartheid South Africa also played a critical role in arming the Rwandan army with weapons worth $5.9 million (USD); so did the United States, a long-term supplier, whose arms shipments to Rwanda amounted to $600,000 in 1993 alone.[3]

In relative terms, those were a lot of weapons costing a lot of money for such a small, desperately poor country on the brink of economic collapse. They also provided fire and ammunition for the 1994 genocide but which no-one foresaw at that time.

The invasion of Rwanda by the RPF not only led to the expansion of the Rwandan Hutu-dominated army at the expense of vital social services; it also triggered a retaliatory response against the Tutsi within the country who were automatically suspected of supporting the Rwandan Patriotic Front which was dominated by their kinsmen, and against Hutu "traitors."

These "traitors," collectively known as "the enemy within," came mainly from the southern part of Rwanda and were opposed to Habyarimana's oppressive regime. Habyarimana and many other Rwandan leaders came from the northwest. Regional loyalties played a vital role in national life and southern regional identity was enough to have southern Hutus branded as suspects and collaborators with the Tutsi enemies.

Reprisals against the enemies of the state were swift, although many of the victims were mere suspects, guilty by association because of kinship ties, in the case of the Tutsi, and political affiliation in the case of the Hutu. And they continued for an extended period following the abortive invasion by the RPF from Rwanda.

An International Commission on Human Rights documented some of the abuses by Habyarimana's regime and concluded that between October 1990 and January 1993, about 2,000 Rwandans were killed by the government. Most of them were Tutsis or Hutus belonging to opposition parties. The commission also stated in its report that "authorities at the highest level, including the President of the Republic, consented to the abuses."

But the abuse of power by Habyarimana's regime went beyond that. The International Commission on Human Rights (or Human Rights Commission) also established that the president and his government had orchestrated the violent campaign against the enemies of the state, real and imagined.

Armed Hutu militia groups had been encouraged to take "the lead in violence against Tutsi and members of the political opposition, thus 'privatising' violence formerly carried out by the state itself."[4]

That was no more than a clumsily disguised attempt by the government to divert attention from the regime's pivotal role in the brutal subjugation of its own citizens.

The failure of the first RPF invasion of Rwanda in October 1990 sent its planners back to the drawing table. The new strategy included diplomatic initiatives which bore fruit but without long-term benefits. In August 1993 – as a result of renewed ethnic strife and successful attacks by the RPF forces which drew them closer to the capital Kigali and enabled them to briefly occupy the second-largest city of Ruhengeri in January 1991 – a formal agreement was signed by the Rwandan Hutu government and the Tutsi-dominated RPF at a meeting in Tanzania, formally ending the civil war between the two sides.

The Rwandan National Army – poorly trained, corrupt, and demoralised – proved to be no match for the growing Tutsi guerrilla forces of the Rwandan Patriotic Front; a weakness which forced the Hutu government to make substantial concessions to the rebels under a peace agreement it did not want to endorse. The government would *not* have made such concessions to the RPF had it been militarily strong.

The peace accord was based on a compromise formula calling for mandatory power sharing between the two ethnic groups in a government of national unity. But the anticipated coalition never took place, and both sides went back to war.

The conflict could have been resolved under another compromise agreement in October 1993 had it not been for the uncompromising stand taken by a group of militant Hutu academic intellectuals and other extremist elements of the Hutu elite who were determined to exclude the Tutsi from power by any means at their disposal including murder.

As renewed fighting erupted, it was clear that the Rwandan Patriotic Front (RPF) was ready to fight a long conventional war, or wage a protracted guerrilla campaign if necessary, to oust the Hutu regime from power with the help of Uganda.

The RPF felt it was entitled to Uganda's help because of the critical role the Tutsi – who later formed the RPF – played in helping Yoweri Museveni, himself of Tutsi lineage, seize power in Uganda in 1986. In fact, Paul Kagame, the vice president of Rwanda and most powerful man in the RPF Tutsi-dominated government which came to power in 1994 after the genocide, was the intelligence chief in Museveni's National Resistance Army when it was waging its own campaign to overthrow the Ugandan government led by 72-year-old Lieutenant-General Tito Okello who ousted Dr. Milton Obote in July 1985.

This symbiotic relationship between Rwanda and Uganda became a critical factor in determining the fate of the East-Central African region in ensuing years. Despite occasional squabbles, especially in 1999 over the war in Congo, both were grateful to each other, with Rwandan Tutsis being the greatest beneficiaries. Without Uganda's support, hence without a reliable rear base, the RPF would probably not have been able to overthrow the Hutu regime in Rwanda:

"In Uganda, the children of Rwanda's Tutsi exiles grew up, dreaming of return. Discriminated against by their hosts, they joined the rebel movement of Yoweri Museveni, himself descended from a related Tutsi group. When his army took over in Uganda in 1986, it was largely led by Rwandan Tutsis. Once in power, they plotted their return to Rwanda and in 1990, taking Ugandan army weapons, they formed the Rwandese Patriotic Front (RPF) and invaded their fathers' homeland."[5]

After the failure of the first invasion, the RPF was reorganised into a potent force with the help of the Ugandan armed forces. By the end of 1992, its army had 12,000 soldiers, and more than 25,000 in April 1994 when it launched its final and successful invasion of Rwanda. The final onslaught had been preceded by several successful guerrilla attacks by the RPF in different parts of the country.

The raids had a profound impact on the Hutu who concluded that this was an attempt by their "historical enemies" to re-establish Tutsi domination, a frightening prospect with a potential for catastrophe including massacres of genocidal proportions.

But President Habyarimana's government also realised that – in spite of the help it was getting from France – the Rwandan Patriotic Front could not be ignored, especially after it proved itself on the battlefield to be a force to contend with. And international pressure on the regime to stop extra-judicial killings and the flight of refugees into neighbouring countries played an equally critical role, as did the RPF, in compelling Habyarimana to seek a negotiated settlement to the conflict.

251

The Arusha Accords – endorsed by both parties in Arusha, Tanzania, in August 1993 – called for fundamental change within Rwanda:

"There was to be a transitional government with the RPF guaranteed a share of power; a commission to oversee the safe return of the refugees; and a new army with the RPF contributing 40 per cent of the troops and 50 per cent of the high command."[6]

Hutu militants in President Habyarimana's regime and in the opposition saw this as a sellout and capitulation to the Tutsi, handing power back to their enemies.

To undermine the settlement, state-controlled Radio Rwanda and an independent radio station (Radio/Television Libre des Mille Collines), both based in the capital Kigali, began broadcasting hate propaganda under the direction of Hutu extremists. They denounced the Arusha power-sharing agreement; accused the Rwandan Patriotic Front of trying to re-institute Tutsi ethnocracy; branded all Tutsis as RPF collaborators; and exhorted Hutus to kill Tutsis and any Hutu "traitors" who sympathised with the Tutsi and supported the peace accords.

President Habyarimana and his government did nothing to stop the broadcasts. And any attempt to do so would probably have been futile, enraging Hutu extremists who were determined to intensify their campaign against the Tutsi and the president himself in order to save the Hutu "race."

The government itself was not opposed to such incitement, anyway. That is why the state-controlled Radio Rwanda was used to propagate hate against the Tutsi, obviously with government approval.

This raw-naked bigotry and deep-seated hatred found its most forceful expression among the Hutu elite, many of them highly articulate, and highly educated. They included

252

Casimir Bizimungu, a polyglot intellectual and former minister of foreign affairs:

"The most virulent and effective incitement to hatred and violence... was repeatedly broadcast by Radio/Television Libres des Mille Collines, and was commissioned by Hutu extremists with official connivance in July 1993.

By early 1994 the Hutu propaganda mill was requesting that its sympathizers 'reach for the hatchet' in order 'to fill the unfilled graves with yet more Tutsi' bodies. Incitements to kill were spiced with 'history lessons' of 'well-known' Tutsi treachery and exploitation of the Hutus.

The radio's intellectual braintrust was made up of Ferdinand Nahimana, a professor of history at the Rwandan National University at Butare, and Casimir Bizimungu, the articulate multilingual foreign minister of a former government, and the manager of this 'independent' radio station."[7]

Had the Rwandan Patriotic Front not invaded Rwanda from Uganda in October 1990 and thereafter to try to overthrow the Hutu-dominated government, the Hutu – apprehensive of the future should their ethnocracy collapse and be replaced by a Tutsi regime – would probably not have massacred the Tutsi to eliminate this threat, at least not on the genocidal scale that they did.

No massacres on such a scale to exterminate the Tutsi had taken place in the past because the Hutu felt they were secure in power, as they indeed were since independence. The Tutsi were completely marginalised as if they were not even citizens of Rwanda. They were powerless.

Once they seemed to pose a threat to Hutu hegemonic control of the country, the Hutu became apprehensive. The Hutu whipped up racist sentiments against the Tutsi and tried to wipe them out.

But even the 400-year history of Hutu subjugation by the Tutsi, although understandable as a valid explanation in some contexts of Hutu protests against injustice, could not be used to justify such hate and frenzy of killings which took place in 1994.

Yet Hutu intellectuals invoked it, as a "history lesson," to incite their kinsmen and fuel anger among them in order to accomplish a historical mission of exterminating the Tutsi.

Rwanda was a nation that had gone berserk, inflamed by the incendiary rhetoric of, supposedly, perfectly rational people including university professors to kill their fellow countrymen in a manner reminiscent of the extermination of the Jews in Nazi Germany. As Professor Michael Chege, a Kenyan, stated in his article "Africa's Murderous Professors":

"The catechism of the madness that soon overtook Rwanda was authored not by some African magician extolling the supremacy of the Hutu race in ancient 'tribal' wars, but by accomplished Rwandan professional historians, journalists, and sociologists at the service of a quasi-traditionalist and genocidally inclined cabal....

This elite group was...composed of the Akazu faction of the Hutu ruling class from President Habyarimana's Gisenyi region (in northwestern Rwanda)."[8]

Many documented studies of the chain of events which culminated in the 1994 holocaust amply demonstrate that the most potent weapon in the incitement and mobilisation of anti-Tutsi sentiments among the Hutu was the invocation of the doctrine of Hutu supremacy and the mythology of the Tutsi as the incarnation of evil. And the most effective means of propagating this message of hate was the Hutu-controlled radio whose transmissions penetrated every nook and corner of Rwanda and reached all segments of the population, including the illiterate masses who constituted the largest and most formidable army of foot soldiers mobilised against the Tutsi. Hutu newspapers also played a critical role in the propagation of these "truths," given pseudo-intellectual justification by the Hutu elite as empirically verifiable facts.[9]

In addition to former Foreign Affairs Minister Casimir Bizimungu and history professor Ferdinand Nahimana, other Hutu intellectuals who played a leading role in planning the massacres and inciting the Hutu masses to violence included Professor Leon Mugesira, a prominent national historian at the Rwandan National University at Butare, and faculty member Vincent Ntezimana.

In collaboration with the extremist Akazu faction of the Hutu ruling class which was under the patronage of Agathe Habyarimana, the president's wife, the professors concocted theories of Hutu racial supremacy and pontificated on the evil nature of the Tutsi; and recommended only one final solution to the Tutsi menace: kill the enemy. As Professor Mugesira in what amounted to incitement to violence bluntly told an extremist Hutu meeting in November 1992:

"The fatal mistake we made in 1959 was to let the Tutsi get out....We have to act. Wipe them all out!"[10]

The Rwandan Hutu professors and their colleagues also propagated the old fallacy that the Tutsi originally came from Ethiopia – they actually came down the Nile Valley with their long-horned cows from what is Sudan today – and had overstayed and abused Hutu hospitality. Therefore it was time for them to go back home. How? By shipping them back home via the Nile – as corpses floating down the river.

The Hutu academic elite also contended that because the Hutu constituted the vast majority of the Rwandan population, such ethnic cleansing was entirely justified within the democratic tradition – it was no more than respect for the wishes of the majority, a cardinal principle of democracy. There is no democracy without majority rule.

They totally ignored the fact that true democracy, which is a hallmark of a civilised and humane society, is measured not by how society protects its strongest members but by how it protects the weakest and most vulnerable. Otherwise it is no more than a jungle where only the strongest survive.

In spite of its flawed logic, the intellectuals' message struck a responsive chord among the vast Hutu majority who were ready to do their job of "shipping the Tutsi back to Ethiopia" – dead:

"The flow of mutilated bodies in the Kagera River, televised worldwide..., was testimony to the effectiveness of the Hutu extremist message. The Kagera (which flows from Rwanda through Tanzania and Uganda) empties into Lake Victoria, the source of the Nile, one of whose tributaries rises from the Ethiopian highlands. Thus were the Tutsi 'shipped back home' as planned, a point that eluded Western media coverage."[11]

But it is also a tragedy that could have been avoided had the international community intervened immediately as the crisis was unfolding.

The massacres were triggered by the assassination of President Habyarimana in a rocket attack on his plane over Rwanda's capital, Kigali, on 6 April 1994. The Hutu president of Burundi, Cyprien Ntaryamira, who was on the same plane, was also killed in what some people may have misconstrued as a double strike against Hutu leadership by the Tutsi.

The two leaders had just returned from Tanzania where they participated in peace talks aimed at resolving the Hutu-Tutsi ethnic conflict in both countries. Although despised and reviled by many of his kinsmen for negotiating and reaching a compromise with the Tutsi on power sharing in a coalition government, Habyarimana became an instant martyr to the vast Hutu majority, especially the masses, who automatically blamed the Tutsi for the assassination. They saw the assassination as confirmation of the Hutu intellectuals' assertion that the Tutsi were the embodiment of evil and a mortal danger to the wellbeing ans survival of the Hutu "race."

The Hutu elite – who knew better, yet deliberately blamed the Tutsi for Habyarimana's death, a leader whom they didn't even care about and had earlier denounced as a sellout because of his concessions to the Tutsi-dominated Rwandan Patriotic Front (RPF) – used the assassination as a pretext for inciting the Hutu mases to violence, ostensibly in retaliation for the assassination, but primarily as the final solution to the Tutsi problem.

The violence they instigated led to the extermination of almost the entire Tutsi population of Rwanda: 75% of them were wiped out within 100 days, a record unprecedented in modern times and on a scale of barbarity that has few parallels in recorded history reminiscent of the extermination of the Jews by Hitler and his henchmen. In fact, the Hutu killed the Tutsi faster than Hitler killed the Jews but had the same solution in mind: Wipe them all out including babies to prevent a regeneration of the exterminated race.

The body count tells only a part of the story of this ethnic cleansing in the green hills of Africa. As Keith Richburg, who covered the Rwandan holocaust when he was the *Washington Post* bureau chief in Africa, states in his book, *Out of America: A Black Man Confronts Africa*:

"I watched the dead float down a river in Tanzania...standing at the Rusumo Falls bridge, watching the bodies float past me.

Sometimes they came one by one. Sometimes two or three together. They were bloated now, horribly discolored. Most were naked, or stripped down to their underpants. Sometimes the hands and feet were bound together. Some were clearly missing some limbs....I couldn't take my eyes off one of them, the body of a little baby.

We timed them: a body or two every minute. And the Tanzanian border guards told us it had been like that for a couple of days now. These were the victims of the ethnic genocide going on across the border in Rwanda. The killers were working too fast to allow for proper burials. It was easier to dump the corpses into the Kagera River, to let them float downstream into Tanzania, eventually into Lake Victoria, out of sight, and I suppose out of mind. Or maybe there was some mythic proportion to it as well.

These victims were from the Tutsi tribe, descendants, they say, of the Nile, and more resembling the Nilotic peoples of North Africa with their narrower noses, more angular features. The Hutu, the ones conducting this final solution, were Bantu people, shorter, darker, and tired of being lorded over by the Tutsi. Maybe tossing the bodies into the river was the Hutus' way of sending them back to the Nile....

It was that image, and countless more like it, that I had to live with, and go to sleep with, for three years...that I spent covering Africa as a reporter for the *Washington Post*....Three years of watching bodies, if not floating down the river in Tanzania, then stacked up like firewood in the refugee camp in Zaire, waiting to be dumped into a mass pit. But sometimes the ground would be too hard and there wouldn't be any construction equipment around to dig a hole, so the bodies instead would just pile up higher and higher, rotting and stinking in the scorching African sun until I'd have to walk around wearing a surgical mask over my face."[12]

All this carnage and savagery was partly the product of the Hutu academic intellectuals and their colleagues who masterminded the genocidal campaign and turned Rwanda's green hills into the killing fields of Africa, soaked in blood, and littered with corpses.

Keith Richburg's graphic account is only a part of the picture, a harrowing spectacle that was repeated over and over in every village, and every commune, across Rwanda, every day, all-day long, for one hundred days.

These Hutu intellectuals and their henchmen would have earned medals from Hitler and his fellow Nazis for their efficiency, thrilled at the spectacle of Africans killing fellow Africans.

Yet, for his candour, Richburg, a black American confronting black Africa, was demonised and vilified, rewarded with barbs from many fellow blacks although he also won accolades from just as many others for being brutally frank, exposing the hypocrisy within. As Ghanaian professor, George Ayittey, who also has been greeted with stinging darts for his searing indictment of Africa's brutal despots and their acolytes including academic intellectuals, states in his book, *Africa in Chaos*:

"Writing a book on Africa is a formidable undertaking. Any such book is bound to raise the ire of some group, not to mention that of the corrupt and repressive African governments....

A 'negative' portrayal of Africa, some blacks allege, feeds the racist myth that nothing good can come out of Africa....

Such a fate appears to have befallen Keith Richburg, a black American..., who wrote *Out of America: A Black Man Confronts Africa*. I attended a launch and panel discussion of his book at the Freedom Forum in Rosalyn, Virginia, on 4 March 1997....

After witnessing the savage brutalities and horrific massacres in Rwanda, Richburg had become thoroughly disgusted (with Africa). And he made his feelings known: He was angry and disillusioned. He had taken up an assignment in Africa to learn more about the continent of his slave ancestors. How could he relate to or explain to Americans back home the hundreds of thousands of human bodies – victims of the genocide – floating down rivers in Rwanda?....He was emotionally tormented. To remain 'faithful to his race,' he must advance a sufficiently credible explanation for the slaughter. He could not find any; this time, there were no 'white devils' around to blame....

I went through a similar searing ordeal. Like Richburg, I was also emotionally tormented by the horrific spectacles in Rwanda, forcing me to reexamine...the entire issue of colonialism and independence. Independence was supposed to bring Africans 'freedom,' 'peace,' and 'prosperity,' right? What happened? These questions raced through my mind as I watched television footage of the Rwandan massacres. Of all the pictures and images, two left a gaping gash in my African psyche.

The first was televised footage of a mass burial of the victims of the 1994 Rwandan genocide that claimed at least 800,000 lives. The bodies of hundreds of thousands of slaughtered Tutsis had floated down the Kagera River into Lake Kivu. The human carcasses were collected for mass burial in Gome, Zaire. A bulldozer had dug a deep trench and a front-end loader had scooped up a heap of dead bodies. As it lurched forward to dump its load, a hand twitched. 'It's alive, it's alive!' someone screamed. Relief aid workers frantically pulled the body of a woman out of the heap, but attempts to revive her failed and she died....

Corpses of dead Africans being bulldozed into a mass grave in full glare of Western TV cameras? Whatever happened to 'freedom from colonial rule?' I couldn't bear the thought....

The second image was an award-winning photograph by a Western journalist that showed a severely emaciated child crouching fraily on a dirt road. His eyes were glazed and his mouth open, gasping for air. A swarm of flies hovered around his face and lower lips. In the background, maintaining their distance, was a cackle of vultures, patiently waiting for the child to die."[13]

That is the price Rwanda had to pay in order to be transformed into a veritable Hutu paradise of a pure Hutu ethnostate without the Tutsi as conceived by the warped minds of some of the most brilliant intellectuals among the Hutu elite with the full support of most of their colleagues and the Hutu masses. But in the end, the Hutu themselves ended up paying a heavy price and lost almost as many lives – after the genocide – as the Tutsi did during the holocaust. They also lost power, hence the country itself, to their enemies.

It was this frightening prospect, of the Tutsis' return to power, which may have cost President Habyarimana his life at the hands of his kinsmen. Although he did not participate in the plots by the Hutu elite of the Akazu faction to exterminate the Tutsi – in spite of his notoriety as one of Africa's most brutal dictators, as many African leaders are – in order to usher in a new era of everlasting peace and happiness in a pure Hutu state, he had shown extreme indecisiveness in the 1991 – 1993 negotiations with the Rwandan Patriotic Front. Hutu extremists interpreted his indecisiveness as weakness and capitulation to the Tutsi.

When he returned from peace talks in Tanzania on 6 April 1994, the day on which he was killed, his militant opponents were afraid that he had conceded too much power to the Tutsi at the peace conference and was about to form a coalition government with them based on a constitutional compromise reached at that meeting. The only way they could keep the Tutsi out of the government, they reasoned, was to kill their own president – then blame the Tutsi for his death – and precipitate a national crisis they could use as a pretext to wipe out the entire Tutsi population.

261

The day of reckoning had come. Radio/Television Libre des Mille Collines had for about three months since early 1994 been telling the Hutu masses what to do in fulfillment of their patriotic duty to protect the Hutu nation. And President Habyarimana's assassination signalled the launching of the genocide campaign against the Tutsi.

Groups of Hutu militiamen which had already been formed – ready for the job – went to work with the dedication of religious zealots. The armouries were opened for them under the direction of Colonel Theoneste Bagasora and his colleagues in the defence ministry who provided the militia groups with weapons and ammunition.

The militia groups had different names. But the most famous one was *Interahamwe* which became the collective name for them all, meaning "Those Who Kill Together," or "Unified Assault." Another one was *Ipuzamugambi* which means "Response to Patriotic Duty," or "The Single-Minded Ones."

Most of the militiamen were rural peasants in an overwhelmingly agricultural country where most people, Hutu and Tutsi, live in rural areas. But poor urban dwellers, the dregs of society, also played a major role, a point underscored by Michael Chege:

"Also incited by repeated exhortations of Radio Mille Collines were the teeming urban unemployed, composed of itinerant vendors, laborers, criminals, and assorted hangers-on, who would get drunk and take to arms looting and raping Tutsi women before killing them.

The weapon of choice in the elimination of the Tutsis was the garden machete, but hoes and garden forks were also used. The Hutu perpetrators of this mayhem drew support from nearly the entire Hutu population....As with the Nazis in their genocide against the Jews, special emphasis was placed on eliminating Tutsi children in order

262

to forestall any resurgence of the Tutsi gene."[14]

All these pogroms had the official sanction of the Hutu-dominated government which sponsored the Interahamwe to commit the atrocities. The minister of information himself, Eliezer Niyitegeka, "incited Hutus to kill Tutsis."[15] So did his colleagues in Habyarimana's cabinet including Justin Mugenzi, president of the Liberal Party who was trade and industry minister; Joseph Nzirorera, interim president of the National Assembly and head of late President Habyarimana's National Republican Movement for Democracy and Development ruling party; Pasteur Musabe, director of Rwanda's National Bank, and other Hutu bankers, businessmen, doctors, lawyers, judges as well as others. Even some Hutu priests and nuns were involved. It was total war against the Tutsi, spearheaded by the Hutu elite without the slightest compunction. "For every Tutsi remaining alive, seven had died."[16]

Yet it was a genocide for which even some of its biggest perpetrators refused to acknowledge responsibility let alone apologise, despite their earlier exhortations – sometimes in coded but often in blunt language – to their kinsmen to kill Tutsis. For example, in the October 1995 edition of *Kangura* which was then being published in Nairobi, Kenya, after losing its operational base in Rwanda, its editor Hassan Ngeze was bold enough to state that no genocide had been perpetrated against the Tutsi in 1994, and challenged his critics: "Show me what I wrote that was not good."[17] Yet this was the same editor who had in his editorials and other writings openly called for the extermination of the Tutsi, published the "Hutu Ten Commandments" demanding the isolation of the "evil" Tutsis, and vehemently denounced as an abomination intermarriage between Hutus and Tutsis which he said was polluting "pure Hutu."

More than a year after the massacres, he was not in the slightest apologetic. Instead, he said he wrote nothing bad.

He was also in denial, a form of psychic numbing, not very much different from the Hutu government's refusal, as expected, to admit that may be it was its own soldiers in the Rwandan National Army who shot down President Habyarimana's plane. Instead, the Hutu regime blamed Belgian UN troops in Kigali for firing the rocket which destroyed the plane, killing everyone on board when it exploded over the capital:

"Circumstantial evidence strongly suggests that extremists intent on sabotaging the Arusha Accords were responsible."[18]

Why was the Hutu regime so quick to blame the Belgians if its own people were not the ones who were responsible?

What proof did they have showing that it was the Belgians who shot down the plane? And how did they get the "evidence" right away that pointed to the Belgians as the culprits, thus blaming them?

But also right from the beginning, soon after the plane was shot down, Paul Kagame was strongly suspected of having ordered the downing of the plane. The suspicion lingered on for years until some of his former aides stated publicly that it was indeed Kagame who ordered the plane to be shot down.

What had been lingering suspicion for years came to be accepted as fact by a number of people who had believed all along that it was Paul Kagame himself, not Hutu extremists, who was directly responsible for the tragic incident. According to a report, "Rwandan President Kagame 'Sparked 1994 Genocide'" on BBC News Africa, 4 October 2011:

"A former ally of Rwandan President Paul Kagame has accused him of complicity in the death of a former president which sparked the 1994 genocide.

Theogene Rudasingwa said he heard Mr Kagame boast in 1994 that he ordered the shooting down of the plane carrying President Juvénal Habyarimana.

'By committing that kind of crime Kagame has the responsibility in the crime of genocide,' he told the BBC.

President Kagame has repeatedly denied any involvement in the attack.

Mr Rudasingwa, who lives in the US, has fallen out with Mr Kagame in recent years and was sentenced in absentia in March to a 24-year jail term for threatening state security and propagating ethnic divisions.

'Ridiculous'

Some 800,000 Tutsis and moderate Hutus died in the genocide which began on the evening of 6 April 1994, after Mr Habyarimana and Burundi's leader died in the plane crash.

Hutu militias then began a campaign of orchestrated killing against Tutsis.

One hundred days later, the Tutsi-led Rwandan Patriot Front rebel movement, led by Mr Kagame, captured Rwanda's capital, Kigali, prompting thousands of Hutus, including some of the killers, to flee into Democratic Republic of Congo.

In 2006, a French judge accused Mr Kagame and his allies of killing Mr Habyarimana – an allegation he dismissed as 'ridiculous,' insisting that extremist Hutus shot down the plane and blamed the RPF to provide a pretext for carrying out the premeditated slaughter.

He told the BBC's HardTalk programme in 2007: 'I am not responsible for Habyarimana's death and I don't care, I wasn't responsible for his security and he wasn't responsible for mine either. He wouldn't have cared if I had died and I don't care that it happened to him.'

But Mr Rudasingwa, the RPF's secretary general and a major at the time of the genocide, said in a statement released over the weekend on his Facebook page that despite public denials Mr Kagame was responsible.

He said the RPF leader was aware at the time of the implications of downing the plane.

'He has fully understood that an action like that one might trigger consequences which, as we know, in our country and the Great Lakes region actually produced that crime of genocide,' Mr Rudasingwa told the BBC's Great Lakes Service.

'Lied for too long'

Mr Rudasingwa said he regretted that afterwards as Rwandan ambassador to the US he had promoted Mr Kagame's version of events.

'It is regrettable that I should have been one of the people who was instrumental in explaining and selling this version of the story about the killing of President Habyarimana, the president of Burundi and all the people who perished with them,' he said.

Mr Rudasingwa, with other former RPF members, last year founded the Rwanda National Council, an organisation launched in exile in opposition to President Kagame's government.

He said he had waited a long time before deciding to talk about what really happened.

'I think the most important thing is that finally I have come out with the truth,' he said.

'As to how long it has taken, it is two decades ago, but I think right now let's focus on seeing how this is the truth. But, yes, I've lied for too long.'"

According to another report, "Kagame Ordered Habyarimana Plane Shooting – Former Aide," in a South African newspaper, the *City Press*, Johannesburg, 21 October 2011:

"Nairobi – A former senior aide to Rwandan President Paul Kagame has accused him of ordering the shooting down of the plane carrying former Rwandan president, Juvénal Habyarimana in April 1994.

The crash of Habyarimana's plane, in which Burundian President Cyprien Ntaryamira was also killed, triggered the genocide in which an estimated 800 000 people, mainly Tutsis, were killed.

Kagame has always maintained that the plane was shot down by Hutu extremists, while his opponents have often accused him of being behind the crash.

'The truth must now be told. Paul Kagame, then overall commander of the Rwandese Patriotic Army, the armed wing of the Rwandese Patriotic Front, was personally responsible for the shooting down of the plane,' Theogene Rudasingwa said on his Facebook page. Rudasingwa, who is in exile in the US, confirmed to AFP that he had indeed made that accusation.

'In July 1994, Paul Kagame himself, with characteristic callousness and much glee, told me that he was responsible for shooting down the plane. Despite public denials, the fact of Kagame's culpability in this crime is also a public 'secret' within Rwandese Patriotic Front circles,' Rudasingwa said.

The former chief of staff to Kagame and former Rwandan ambassador to the US said he admitted he had 'enthusiastically sold this deceptive story line, especially to foreigners who by and large came to believe it, even when I knew that Kagame was the culprit in this crime.'

'By killing President Habyarimana, Paul Kagame produced a wild card in an already fragile ceasefire and dangerous situation. This created a powerful trigger, escalating to a tipping point towards resumption of the civil war, genocide and the regionwide destabilisation that has devastated the Great Lakes region ever since.'

Rudasingwa said Kagame should 'immediately be brought to account for this crime and its consequences.'

Rudasingwa, together with other former regime heavyweights now in exile, last year founded the Rwanda National Congress, an opposition party that has been calling on Kagame to leave power.

Other Rwandan opposition parties have accused Kagame of being behind the shooting down of the plane, but their accounts have often lacked credibility."

In his characteristic denial of responsibility for the tragedy, a position he had maintained through the years as much as he does today, Kagame again blamed Hutu extremists a few years earlier in an interview with the BBC in 2007 in which he also said he didn't care about what happened to President Juvénal Habyarimana. According to the report, "Rwanda Leader Defiant on Killing Claim," BBC News Africa, 30 January 2007:

"Rwandan President Paul Kagame, in a rare interview, is asked to respond to allegations by a French investigating judge that he was complicit in the assassination of former President Juvénal Habyarimana in 1994. BBC world affairs correspondent Fergal Keane reports:

At the time of the genocide, most observers believed President Habyarimana had been killed by Hutu extremists opposed to his peace deal with the Tutsi-dominated Rwandan Patriotic Front (RPF).

But French judge Jean-Louis Bruguiere alleges that the RPF leader Paul Kagame – now Rwanda's president – ordered the attack in order to seize total power.

The fact that it is a French judge making the allegation has made this a politically explosive issue.

The French armed and trained the extremists who would later go on to carry out the genocide.

Exile's allegations

I have spoken with several of Judge Bruguiere's witnesses.

They are men who at one time fought alongside Mr Kagame but have since turned against him.

Innocent Marara said he was based at Mr Kagame's headquarters at the time of the shooting down of the plane.

He claims to have overheard the RPF leader discuss the attack on several occasions.

Mr Marara said Mr Kagame was 'collecting advice from people around him' on the president and the plane attack.

I asked what choice Mr Kagame made in the end.

'That was the shooting,' Mr Marara said. You are absolutely sure about that, I asked. 'Yes.'

The Rwandan government accuses Mr Marara of making up the story and says he was involved in criminal gangs. He denies the allegations.

Another witness is Paul Kagame's former defence minister, Emmanuel Habyarimana, now living in exile in Europe.

Emmanuel Habyarimana was once an officer in the Hutu army but defected to the RPF in 1994.

He subsequently fled from Rwanda after falling out with the ruling party.

He told me the Hutu army did not have the missiles to shoot down the plane.

And he claimed he had heard senior RPF officers boasting about having shot down the plane.

'The members of the army – especially officers – didn't hide that they would have had to bring down the plane to take power. They said it loud and clear. They were even proud of shooting down the plane.'

In response, the Rwandan government accuses Emmanuel Habyarimana of being a deserter and says he has a political axe to grind as a leader of an opposition party in exile.

'Political judgement'

I travelled to Rwanda to put Judge Bruguiere's central allegations to President Kagame.

In a defiant response he said: 'I care that there was a genocide here. A million people died – people have been persecuted for decades here in Rwanda.

'I was a refugee for nearly 30 years out of my country as a result of that. Would I care that bloody Habyarimana died, somebody who was responsible for a genocide here, who was a president of a government that discriminated, that persecuted its own people?

'That Judge Bruguiere says this or France says that - I don't give a damn.'

In the aftermath of the genocide, the UN backed away from an investigation of the plane crash.

One investigator alleged the matter was dropped because the UN did not want to confront Paul Kagame.

But could the Bruguiere report provide the evidence for an indictment of Paul Kagame?

The former chief prosecutor for Yugoslavia and Rwanda, Judge Richard Goldstone, thinks not.

'Well I don't think that case has been made at all. It's a very political judgement and I don't believe that it's borne out by the evidence.

'Certainly the witnesses who spoke to Bruguiere allege that those were statements made by President Kagame himself. Whether he did or not obviously is a matter in dispute, in hot dispute, but the political judgement it seems to me is another matter.'

However, in his interview with the BBC, Mr Kagame said he would co-operate with an impartial inquiry carried out by a judge who had nothing to do with Rwanda or France.

Whether any judge would want to take on such a task is quite another matter."

But it was not until Theogene Rudasingwa came forward with revelations that Kagame was responsible for the downing of the plane, hence for triggering the genocide, that the accusations against the Rwandan leader gained credibility among many people including some of his supporters who did not believe he was responsible for such a heinous act.

Rudasingwa's close ties to Kagame as his chief of staff, and to other RPF leaders, as well as his position as secretary-general of the ruling RPF when he was still in the Rwandan government, reinforced this belief and lent even more credibility to his accusations against Kagame.

The accusations by Rudasingwa were also published in a statement in the *San Francisco Bay View*, San Francisco, California, USA, 1 October 2011.

The statement, reproduced below in its entirety, is entitled "Rwanda: Current President Kagame Confessed Ordering Predecessor's Plane Shot Down: Kagame's Former Ambassador to the U.S. Makes Startling Announcement About Event That Triggered Rwandan Genocide":

"On Aug. 4, 1993, in Arusha, Tanzania, the government of Rwanda and the Rwandan Patriotic Front (RPF) signed the Arusha Peace Agreement.

The provisions of the agreement included a commitment to principles of the rule of law, democracy, national unity, pluralism, the respect of fundamental freedoms and the rights of the individual.

The agreement further had provisions on power-sharing, formation of a single National Army and a new National Gendarmerie from forces of the two warring parties and a definitive solution to the problem of Rwandan refugees.

On April 6, 1994, at 8:25 p.m., the Falcon 50 jet of the president of the Republic of Rwanda, registration number 9XR-NN, on its return from a summit meeting in Tanzania, as it was on approach from Dar-es-Salaam to Kanombe International Airport in Kigali, Rwanda, was shot down. All on board, including President Juvénal Habyarimana, President Cyprien Ntaryamira of Burundi, their entire entourage and flight crew, died.

The death of President Juvénal Habyarimana triggered the start of genocide that targeted Tutsi and Hutu moderates and the resumption of civil war between the RPF and the government of Rwanda.

The RPF's sad and false narrative from that time on has been that Hutu extremists within President Habyarimana's camp shot down the plane to derail the implementation of the Arusha Peace Agreement and to find a pretext to start the genocide in which over 800,000 Rwandans died in just 100 days. This narrative has become a predominant one in some international circles, among scholars, and in some human rights organizations.

The truth must now be told. Paul Kagame, then overall commander of the Rwandan Patriotic Army (RPA), the armed wing of the Rwandan Patriotic Front, was personally responsible for the shooting down of the plane. In July 1994, Paul Kagame himself, with characteristic callousness and much glee, told me that he was responsible for shooting down the plane.

Despite public denials, the fact of Kagame's culpability in this crime is also a public "secret" within RPF and RDF (Rwandan Defense Force) circles.

Like many others in the RPF leadership, I enthusiastically sold this deceptive story line, especially to foreigners who by and large came to believe it, even when I knew that Kagame was the culprit in this crime.

The political and social atmosphere during the period from the signing of the Arusha Accords in August 1993 was highly explosive, and the nation was on edge. By

272

killing President Habyarimana, Paul Kagame introduced a wild card in an already fragile ceasefire and dangerous situation. This created a powerful trigger, escalating to a tipping point resumption of the civil war, genocide and the region-wide destabilization that has devastated the Great Lakes region since then.

Paul Kagame has to be immediately brought to account for this crime and its consequences.

First, there is absolutely nothing honorable or heroic in reaching an agreement for peace with a partner and then stabbing him in the back. Kagame and Habyarimana did not meet on the battlefield on April 6, 1994. If they had, and one of them or both had died, it would have been tragic, but understandable, as a product of the logic of war.

President Habyarimana was returning from a peace summit and, by killing him, Kagame demonstrated the highest form of treachery.

Second, Kagame, a Tutsi himself, callously gambled away the lives of innocent Tutsi and moderate Hutu who perished in the genocide. While the killing of President Habyarimana, a Hutu, was not a direct cause of the genocide, it provided a powerful motivation and trigger to those who organized, mobilized and executed the genocide against Tutsi and Hutu moderates.

Third, by killing President Habyarimana, Kagame permanently derailed the already fragile Arusha peace process in a dangerous pursuit of absolute power in Rwanda. Kagame feared the letter and spirit of the Arusha Peace Agreement.

As the subsequent turn of events has now shown, Kagame does not believe in the unity of Rwandans, democracy, respect of human rights and other fundamental freedoms, the rule of law, power sharing, integrated and accountable security institutions with a national character, and resolving the problem of refugees once and for all. This is what the Arusha Peace Agreement was all about. That is what is lacking in Rwanda today.

Last, but not least, Kagame's and RPF's false narrative, denials and deceptions have led to partial justice in Rwanda and at the International Criminal Tribunal for Rwanda, thereby undermining prospects for justice for all Rwandan people, reconciliation and healing. The international community has, knowingly or unknowingly, become an accomplice in Kagame's systematic and shameful game of deception.

I was never party to the conspiracy to commit this heinous crime. In fact, I first heard about it on BBC around 1:00 a.m. on April 7, 1994, while I was in Kampala, where I had been attending the Pan African Movement conference.

I believe the majority of members of RPF and RPA civilians and combatants, like me, were not party to this murderous conspiracy that was hatched and organized by Paul Kagame and executed on his orders. Nevertheless, I was a secretary general of the RPF, and a major in the rebel army, RPA.

It is in this regard, within the context of collective responsibility and a spirit of truth-telling in search of forgiveness and healing, that I would like to say I am deeply sorry about this loss of life and to ask for forgiveness from the families of Juvénal Habyarimana, Cyprien Ntaryamira, Deogratias Nsabimana, Elie Sagatwa, Thaddee Bagaragaza, Emmanuel Akingeneye, Bernard Ciza, Cyriaque Simbizi, Jacky Heraud, Jean-Pierre Minaberry and Jean-Michel Perrine.

I also ask for forgiveness from all Rwandan people, in the hope that we must unanimously and categorically reject murder, treachery, lies and conspiracy as political weapons, eradicate impunity once and for all, and work together to build a culture of truth-telling, forgiveness, healing and the rule of law.

I ask for forgiveness from the people of Burundi and France, whose leaders and citizens were killed in this crime. Above all, I ask for forgiveness from God for

274

having lied and concealed evil for too long.

In freely telling the truth before God and the Rwandan people, I fully understand the risk I have undertaken, given Paul Kagame's legendary vindictiveness and unquenchable thirst for spilling the blood of Rwandans.

It is a shared risk that Rwandans bear daily in their quest for freedom and justice for all. Neither power and fame, nor gold and silver, are the motivation for me in these matters of death that have defined our nation for too long.

Truth cannot wait for tomorrow, because the Rwandan nation is very sick and divided and cannot rebuild and heal on lies. All Rwandans urgently need truth today. Our individual and collective search for truth will set us free. When we are free, we can freely forgive each other and begin to live fully and heal at last."

Then in January 2012, another investigation by the French concluded that Paul Kagame was not responsible for the plane crash in which President Habyarimana was killed. According to a report, "Paul Kagame Allies 'did not shoot down plane' That Sparked Rwanda Genocide," in *The Telegraph*, London, 10 January 2012:

"A French investigation into what sparked the 1994 Rwandan genocide appears to exonerate current President Paul Kagame and his Tutsi allies after Paris had previously accused him of triggering the killing of 800,000 people in 100 days.

Diplomatic relations between Rwanda and France were severed in 2006 when a French judge said Mr Kagame, the rebel leader at the time of the killings, had orchestrated the assassination of Juvenal Habyarimana, the Hutu president, to trigger the bloodshed.

After Habyarimana's plane was shot down, Hutu extremists slaughtered Tutsis and moderate Hutus in some of the fastest mass killings ever perpetrated. Kagame's

Tutsi-led Rwandan Patriotic Front seized power in the aftermath of the genocide.

Mr Kagame has accused former French President Francois Mitterrand's administration of training and arming the Hutu militias responsible for the slaughter.

A team of French investigators, led by two judges, re-examined a dozen eyewitness testimonies to work out where the two missiles that brought down Habyarimana's Dassault Falcon 50 plane were fired from, in an effort to determine final responsibility. Both sides had bases near the airport.

The judges on Tuesday presented their report to Kagame's lawyers, who told media that they had concluded the shots could not have come from a military base occupied by Kagame's supporters. The findings did not specifically point the finger at the Hutus."

The new findings were also reported by BBC. According to its report, "Rwanda Genocide: Kagame 'cleared of Habyarimana crash'," 10 January 2012:

"A report has appeared to clear Rwanda's President Paul Kagame of orchestrating the 1994 assassination of the country's then-leader Juvenal Habyarimana.

The team – mandated by a French inquiry – visited the scene of the attack to work out the trajectory of the missile which shot down his plane.

The crash was one of the triggers that sparked the genocide.

An earlier French probe blamed Mr Kagame and his allies, but they say Hutu extremists killed Habyarimana.

Rwanda's government has welcomed the conclusions of this new report.

The plane crash on 6 April 1994 – in which Habyarimana and Burundi's leader died – triggered the genocide of 800,000 Tutsis and moderate Hutus in just 100 days.

The killings came to an end when the Tutsi-led Rwandan Patriot Front (RPF) rebel movement, headed by Mr Kagame, captured Rwanda's capital, Kigali.

Elite presidential troops

Correspondents say the court on Tuesday concluded that the missile was shot from a distance of up to 1km (more than half a mile) away from the plane, which was about to land at Kigali airport.

At the time this area was held by the Rwandan army – a unit of elite presidential troops.

The experts say it would be very difficult for forces loyal to Mr Kagame to be in this area and therefore shoot down the plane.

They concluded that it would have been much easier for Habyarimana's troops or French troops who were in the area to launch the missile.

In 2006, a French judge accused Mr Kagame and his allies of killing Habyarimana – an allegation he dismissed as 'ridiculous' and which prompted him to break off relations with Paris for three years.

Five years later, in 2011, a former senior ally of the president, Theogene Rudasingwa – the RPF's secretary general and a major at the time of the genocide – also accused Mr Kagame. Mr Rudasingwa fell out with the president and now lives in exile in the US.

Mr Kagame has always insisted that Hutu hardliners – who considered Habyarimana too moderate – shot down the plane and blamed the RPF to provide a pretext for carrying out the premeditated slaughter.

Critics of the 2006 investigation said it failed to visit the area of the attack, or interview the nine high-ranking RPF officers it accused of involvement. It said the missile was shot from a distance of four kilometres away from the airport.

French judge Marc Trevidic headed this latest French

inquiry, launched – with the full co-operation of the Rwandan authorities – towards the end of 2010 because the French crew of the plane also died.

The team has interviewed six of those accused in the 2006 report and conducted a forensic investigation. Two missiles specialists, two air accident experts, a pilot, two surveyors and a sound expert have reconstructed the sequence of the attack.

'Unhappy'

Following this report, Judge Trevidic can either drop the affair or continue his investigations, which could result in a court case.

'Today's findings constitute vindication for Rwanda's long-held position on the circumstances surrounding events of April 1994,' Rwanda's Foreign Minister Louise Mushikiwabo said in a statement.

The lawyer for the Habyarimana family said they are unhappy about the report's conclusions – questioning the credibility of the experts – and they still want someone to be found guilty.

'It does not matter where the shooting took place,' Habyarimana's son Jean-Luc told the BBC's Great Lakes service. 'What matters is who fired the missile,' he said.

Habyarimana's widow, Agathe, told the BBC that she wanted the French inquiry to find out who had bought the allegedly Russian missile that hit the plane – because that would help to identify those behind the attack.

Rwanda has historically been beset by ethnic tension. It worsened under Belgian colonial rule when the Tutsi minority enjoyed better jobs and better education than the Hutu majority.

At independence, following inter-ethnic violence, many thousands of Tutsis went into exile in Uganda from where they eventually launched a civil war in 1990.

A 1993 peace agreement was supposed to usher in a

power-sharing government – but it did little to stop the unrest. "

Still, the new findings by the French did not exonerate Kagame. The testimony by those who were in the inner circle as part of the RPF leadership who maintained that Kagame told them he ordered the plane shot down may be more credible than the findings by the French in the eyes of many people, not just Kagame's opponents.

But, even though the genocide was triggered by Habyarimana's assassination, there is no question that it was planned by Hutu extremists long before it started.

It was such a well-orchestrated campaign and would probably have taken place even if the Rwandan president, Juvénal Habyarimana, had not been killed. And it defies rational explanation that the massacres would have started right away and in such a coordinated fashion right after Habyariman's assassination had they not been well-planned in advance.

This not to absolve Paul Kagame of responsibility for ordering the shooting down of the plane, if he did at all; it simply presents another scenario which could have led to the same tragedy: the massacre of Tutsis on a genocidal scale.

And there is no question that Kagame did not want to implement the power-sharing agreement he and President Habyarimana signed in Tanzania. He wanted absolute power at any cost.

The agreement did not reflect the demographic realities or pattern of Rwanda in terms of power allocation and distribution in a country that is overwhelmingly Hutu. Instead, it gave substantial concessions to the Tutsi minority to allay their fears of being dominated and even of being exterminated by the Hutu majority.

But even that did not satisfy Kagame and his fellow Tutsis who dominated the Rwandan Patriotic Front (RPF). He wanted absolute power at the expense of the Hutu majority and even at the expense of his own people, the Tutsi.

Hutu extremists, equally opposed to power sharing in order to exclude Tutsis and moderate Hutus from the government, also wanted absolute power.

Either way, the result would have been catastrophic. And that is exactly what happened. Both contributed to the genocide.

The extremists who perpetrated the massacres were also notorious for their savagery, "smashing in their neighbors' skulls and chopping off their limbs, and piling up the legs in one pile, and the arms in another, and lumping the bodies together and sometimes forcing new victims to sit atop the heap while they clubbed them to death too,"[19] with nail-studded clubs.

Long nails were the preferred choice:

"(The Hutu militiamen) would carve off your arm first and watch you bleed and scream in pain. Then, if you didn't pass out, they would chop off one of your legs, or maybe just a foot. If you were lucky, they might finish you off with a machete blow to the back of the head. Otherwise, they might carve off your ears, your nose, and toss your limbless torso atop the pile of dead bodies, where you could slowly bleed to death....

I must admit, I too found it hard at first to believe the scope of the horror,...like the story of bodies piled up six feet high outside Kigali's main hospital. Or the story of the ten Belgian paratroopers who were executed while trying to protect Rwanda's prime minister (Agathe Uwilingiyamana who was also brutally murdered by Hutu extremists); first they had their Achilles tendons cut to prevent them from escaping, then they were castrated and the severed organs shoved into their mouths.

These were the stories, repeated over and over again, and I didn't believe them. But now I was seeing it with my own eyes."[20]

This is the hell Hutu extremists created for Rwanda in an attempt to create a Hutu heaven on earth without the Tutsi.

There was nothing that could make them regain their sanity if they ever had any at all.

Injustice breeds injustice. Violence begets violence. It is a vicious cycle.

It is true that the Hutu had been under the heels of their conquerors for hundreds of years. And they were bound to rise up and retaliate against their oppressors one day. But there are also degrees of morality. The atrocities they committed against the Tutsi – some of which the Tutsi themselves committed against the Hutu before – not only defied norms of civilised conduct and standards as all atrocities do; they were unspeakable horrors many people found hard to believe could be perpetrated against fellow human beings.

Yet man is capable of sinking to the lowest depths of moral bankruptcy and doing the unthinkable, hard as it may seem to contemplate the ghastly nature of the atrocities and comprehend the magnitude of his depravity. And seeing is believing. As Keith Richburg states in his book about what he saw in Rwanda:

"A tour of Rwanda's horror show might begin in Byumba town, in the (RPF) rebel-controlled section of northern Rwanda not far from the border with Uganda. A man named Amiable Kaberuka is there....

The Hutu militia entered the school building where he and thousands of others had taken refuge. The attackers told Kaberuka that he must die because he was a Tutsi, and then they used machetes and pangas to hack and club to death his wife and three of his four children. Kaberuka they simply shot, then left him for dead amid a pile of corpses.

Angelique Umutesi is there too. He is only nine years

old, and he survived by running hard and fast. The Hutu militia entered his house and killed his parents and his six brothers and sisters. Then they started on Angelique, first chopping off his left hand with a machete, then taking a chunk out of his right leg. Another machete blow opened a gaping hole in the back of the little boy's head, but he still managed to run to his grandparents' house nearby. Of course, the militia had already been there, and Angelique found everyone in that house dead, too.

So he lay down to die, right there, next to the corpses of his grandparents and others. And he stayed there like that, with the corpses, for four days and four nights, almost bleeding to death until he was rescued by the advancing Tutsi guerrilla soldiers.

And over there is Hassan Twizezimana. He is a Hutu, but even so the madness did not pass him by. His crime is that he was not a card-carrying member of Juvénal Habyarimana's ruling political party. That means, of course, that he must be a secret Tutsi sympathizer, and for that, the Hutu militiamen used their machetes and panga knives to hack to death Twizezimana's father, his brother, and his brother's wife. Twizezimana himself got the back of his head cracked open with a garden hoe, and he, too, lay bleeding to death until he was found and brought to this haven in northern Uganda."[21]

Atrocities like these, committed at the instigation of the Hutu elite including some of Rwanda's most distinguished professors and doctors and eminent priests, became an integral part of the "normal" life for the Tutsi and their attackers across the country.

The pogroms painted the most sordid picture of Rwanda's socio-political landscape which came to reflect the image of the entire continent as one large land mass immersed in blood; as atrocities in other parts of the continent, from west to east and north to south – Liberia, Sierra Leone, Somalia, Sudan, Uganda, Burundi, Zaire,

Congo-Brazzaville, Angola – were being committed during the same time, earning Africa a distinctive appellation, "The Lost Continent," because of its own fault.

Yet, every atrocity had its own gory detail, adding to the macabre scene that never seemed to be complete in its horrifying aspects. There was always something new, as the cases we just cited tragically demonstrate; and much more:

"This is just a small sampling of it, a few random snapshots, individual faces and stories lifted from the entire grotesque tapestry. Press on, because there's much, much more. Like the the three little girls, six to eight, whose heads and eyes are swollen because they have been buried alive up to their necks in a mass grave that contained the mutilated bodies of their parents. I find them in Byumba, still dazed, unable to speak or walk properly, still vomiting dirt.

And there's the old woman who was hiding in a church in Butare, in western Rwanda, when the militiamen burst in and killed nine people in her family, including all but one of her children. They chopped off all the fingers of the old woman's hand. And just for spite they slashed her across her face....

There's another stop on our grisly tour, the Catholic church in the town of Gafunzo, in Rwanda's far southwest, near Lake Kivu. The large crucifix bears silent witness to the atrocities committed here; the life-size figure of Christ is framed with bullet holes, the altar swash with blood. Some ten thousand people packed into this church and the surrounding buildings, the schoolhouse, the rectory. They fled here in April when the massacres began....But this once-holy place now screams out with the souls of those who died in the search and slaughter. Handprints of dried blood along th wall give witness to the struggle; blood trails from the ceiling tiles where some, in vain, sought to

283

hide before the panels were ripped away. Two mass graves flank the church on either side."[22]

While all these killings were going on, the Hutu elite escalated their rhetoric several decibels, whipping up their kinsmen into a frenzy to commit even more massacres, and faster, in order to accomplish their mission in record time and usher in a new era of a Hutu paradise in Rwanda's Garden of Eden.

It was Rwanda's Garden of Evil. One of the same rivers, the Kagera, watering the green hills of Africa in picturesque Rwanda is the same river in which thousands of corpses, perhaps tens of thousands, floated towards lake Victoria. The daily count alone was horrifying: "Several hundred each day. And it has been this way for several days," as *Washington Post* reporter Keith Richburg once observed in northwestern Tanzania through which the Kagera River flows from Rwanda on to Lake Victoria.[23] Every corpse floating down the river was an echo chamber of the deadly broadcasts coming from Radio Mille Collines, owned by President Habyarimana's brother-in-law Seraphim Rwabukumba, exhorting Hutus to kill more Tutsis.

And everyone of these bloated, discoloured bodies conjured up images of the genocidal Hutu elite huddled in their secret chambers planning more massacres of their fellow countrymen who happened to members of another "race" or "tribe," and whose Hutu sympathisers were equally condemned to death by Rwanda's court of instant mob justice administered by Hutu extremists almost all of whom knew many of their victims as friends and as neighbours, and even as relatives. But because they were Tutsi, they had to go. It was a job that had to be done to clear the land of this "vermin."

The Hutu militiamen were well-organised into small cells in every village across Rwanda. And every cell leader had a list of the names of all the Tutsi in his village, making it brutally simple to get rid of them. "At the local level, the slaughter was directed by the gendarmerie, the préfets, the bourgmestres, sundry civil servants and sympathizers."[24]

The massacres began in the capital, Kigali, during the night of President Habyarimana's death. Within 36 hours, the 1,500-man presidential guard had killed most of the prominent Tutsis and Hutu moderates in the capital. They included politicians, journalists, human rights activists including missionary workers and others. A significant number of Hutu moderates – synonymous with "traitors" – were targeted. But most of the victims were Tutsi.

And across the country, militia groups specially organised for this purpose and which had a total of at least 50,000 members, received their order to kill Tutsis through a chain of command that extended from the highest levels of government all the way down to the *préfets*, bourgmestres, and local councillors.

Rape, torture, and mutilations were common before the victims were killed; tens of thousands of them suffering a slow, excruciatingly painful death and other cruelties. Mothers were forced to watch their children bludgeoned or hacked to death before being killed themselves. Children were forced to kill their own family members – parents, brothers and sisters – and parents their own children, and in-laws their own in-laws, often in the most revolting manner with some of the crudest weapons. As *The Economist* reported on some of these atrocities:

"Brutality here does not end with murder. At massacre sites, corpses, many of them those of children, have been methodically dismembered and the body parts stacked neatly in separate piles."[25]

And as Gérard Prunier states in his book *The Rwanda Crisis: History of A Genocide*:

"The vast majority of the civil servants carried out their murderous duties with attitudes varying from careerist eagerness to sullen obediency."[26]

But the genocide could not have been carried out on such an immense scale without the active participation of countless peasants and other ordinary people across the country. Some of the biggest killers were Hutus who killed their Tutsi neighbours, relatives and friends, a pattern that was repeated from village to village, in every commune, and every part of the country. And as *The Economist* stated about the Hutu-Tutsi conflict in Rwanda and Burundi where Tutsis in both countries also kill Hutus as they have for years:

"The conflicts are marked by attempts not just to defeat but to annihilate. Killing (by both Hutus and Tutsis) is often referred to as a task, work which must be completed. Neighbours kills neighbours; sometimes there is even killing within mixed families."[27]

There are no saints here, although the Hutu were the villains in the 1994 Rwandan genocide.

Although the massacres were triggered by the assassination of President Habyarimana, there is ample proof, including testimony from some of the perpetrators of those heinous crimes, showing that the killings had been planned well in advance.

Hutu intellectuals had for years been preparing for a final solution to the Tutsi problem almost in the same way Hitler and his henchmen did with the Jews. They blamed the Tutsi for all the nation's problems. Perhaps they even blamed them for bad weather if there was crop failure and famine stalked the land.

The only way these problems – including land shortage, although the Tutsi, being a minority, occupy only a small percentage of it – could be solved was by getting

286

rid of the Tutsi as Professor Leon Mugesira openly advocated in his highly inflammatory speech before an extremist Hutu gathering in November 1992 in which he urged his kinsmen to "wipe them all out!." The same incendiary rhetoric also came from other members of the Hutu academic elite at different times up to the time of the holocaust.

Ironically, Rwanda's – and Burundi's – problem of land shortage could be solved, not by expelling or by killing the Tutsi who constitute only a very small minority, but by kicking out a very large number (may be 3 to 4 million from each country) of the very same people who have overpopulated the country. And that is the Hutu who constitute the vast majority of the population, at least 85%, in each of the two countries.

But where are they going to go even if that many people want to leave willingly? That is the same question the Tutsi ask. Why are they going to go if the Hutu kick them out? Neither the Hutu nor the Tutsi have anywhere else to go – unless neighboring countries open their borders and welcome them to settle in those countries; which is a viable option Julius Nyerere once suggested in a larger context about Africa in general – before the genocide in Rwanda – when he said African countries should open their borders to welcome fellow Africans. He said it was a shame for Africans to be refugees in Africa.

In spite of the fact that neither of them has anywhere else to go, the Hutu in Rwanda said the Tutsi could not live there anymore. They were determined to exterminate them as the final solution to the nation's problems including land shortage – and even poverty. They blamed them for everything.

The Hutu-controlled media, especially Radio Mille Collines and newspapers such as *Kangura* and *La Medaille* magazine, had since early 1994 been exhorting Hutus to get their weapons ready in order to start killing Tutsis. The massacres started within an hour of the announcement of the downing of the plane carrying President Habyarimana and his Burundian counterpart and fellow Hutu, Cyprien Ntaryamira, a participant in the peace talks in Tanzania. There is no way the killings could have started within so short a time, after Habyarimana's assassination, and on such a large scale of genocidal proportions across the country, unless they had been planned well in advance. The killings were timely, and methodical, with surgical precision.

The genocide also had other unmistakable features pointing to a major Hutu conspiracy of Tutsi extermination. The massacres were systematic and well-coordinated across the country, thus entirely ruling out any possibility that they were spontaneous or merely the work of only a few deranged individuals. And they were carried out with brutal efficiency; yet another proof of a well-orchestrated campaign formulated and masterminded by the Hutu elite. No ordinary Hutu citizen or citizens could, with military precision, have mobilised forces across the country on such a large scale and high level of coordination.

Everything pointed to a conspiracy and to the Hutu elite including the military and their perfidy in playing an indispensable role in the conception and execution of this master plan of genocide. And nothing – not even the 400 years of oppression by the Tutsi – can exonerate them of responsibility for this holocaust, although the volcanic fury of the Hutu masses as well as the intellectuals themselves can be explained, but not justified, in a historical context of the injustices they have endured for centuries in feudal servitude at the hands of their Tutsi conquerors.

During the genocide, Rwanda degenerated into anarchy, making it possible for the Rwandan Patriotic Front (RPF) to take over the country in July 1994 without any difficulty. The Hutu Rwandan National Army was in tatters, having virtually destroyed itself as an institution during the holocaust. It was easily routed in a 14-week blitzkrieg by the RPF forces as they swept across the country and went on to seize the capital.

The Hutu elite not only helped ruin their country; they also – with the genocide they instigated and masterminded – destroyed themselves and paved the way for the Tutsis' return to power from which the aristocratic rulers were ousted in the mass uprising of 1959.

Elite Hypocrisy:
Continental Phenomenon

What happened in Rwanda in terms of elite involvement in the genocide is a continental phenomenon.

In most African countries the elite, that arrogant class of the "enlightened" who think they know more than anybody else what is best for the country as much as dictators claim they do, have played a critical and very destructive role through the decades defending dictatorship and justifying some of the worst excesses of tyranny across the continent "in the name of the people."

Yet these are the very same people who claim to be the best custodians of the nation's values and uncompromising defenders of human rights and equality for all.

Some of them have even found refuge in other African countries where they have been allowed to operate with impunity, as they continue to propagate their dogmatic views in an attempt to undermine fledgling democratic institutions in their home countries, or spread their message of hate against particular groups.

That is what happened in the case of some members of the Rwandan Hutu elite who found sanctuary in Kenya and continued to demonise the Tutsi – instead of campaigning for true democracy and pluralism – with the blessings of President Daniel arap Moi, himself a tribalist favouring his fellow Kalenjins, and one of Africa's most brutal dictators. Through the years, Moi has been notorious for and adept at mobilising tribal sentiments against his opponents to perpetuate himself in power like the Hutu – and even the Tutsi themselves before them – did in Rwanda from 1962 to 1994.

Rwanda's tragedy is that the country is once again in the hands – and at the mercy of – another hypocritical and racist elite; this time, the Tutsi, who are back on top. They promised to introduce democracy whey they seized power in 1994. But they continue to exclude the Hutu from meaningful participation in the government. Many Hutus have been given token posts, while the Tutsi have remained in control of the levers of power to manipulate them at will. For example, Rwanda's president since 1994 all the way through the decade and beyond was a Hutu – Pasteur Bizimungu. Yet he was no more than a figurehead in a Tutsi-dominated government.

The most powerful man and *de facto* ruler was the vice president and defence minister, Paul Kagame, a Tutsi, in a country that is overwhelmingly Hutu and bitterly polarised along ethnic lines.

Probably one of the most tragic consequences of the 1994 Rwandan genocide is that the Tutsi never learned from the holocaust.

The Hutu majority can not continue to be denied meaningful participation in the government of their country in a way that reflects their demographic status and composition as the nation's largest ethnic group.

And ethnic conflicts in Rwanda can not be solved by pretending that Hutus and Tutsis no longer exist, only Rwandans do. People know better than that.

It would, indeed, be wonderful if Hutus and Tutsis considered themselves to be just Rwandans without ethnic differences which lead to conflict. But that is not the case. There are still Hutus and Tutsis in Rwanda just as there are other ethnic groups in other parts of Africa. Their ethnic identities, differences and problems are not going to disappear by simply wishing them away or by pretending that they no longer exist.

Also, the Tutsi can not live in a country where they are not considered to be citizens, or equal citizens, simply because they are a minority who supposedly don't even belong there but where they came from, wherever that is.

We all came from somewhere, sometime in the past. The Hutu, like the Tutsi, also came from somewhere. It was the Hutu who found the Twa (Pygmies) in the area that is now Rwanda and Burundi. They conquered and oppressed the Twa. The Twa have not forgotten that. Then came the Tutsi who conquered the Hutu.

Regardless of where they all came from, including the Twa themselves who are considered to be the indigenous people or the original inhabitants of the land, Rwanda belongs to them all; so does Burundi.

Chapter Seven:

After the Genocide: Its Implications and Repercussions

RETRIBUTION for the massacres of the Tutsi by the Hutu was one of the most prominent items on the agenda of the Tutsi-dominated Rwandan Patriotic Front (RPF) when its forces took over the country in July 1994. But it was not acknowledged by the RPF as one of the objectives it would pursue once in power.

Equally important, and probably even more so, was the establishment and consolidation of a Tutsi ethnocracy to prevent another genocide. However, the real intention was to re-establish Tutsi domination to ensure Tutsi survival.

But the Hutu were equally uncompromising. They

were determined to resist domination by an ethnic group they vastly outnumber at least by 6 to 1. The result was a continuation of war between the two groups which went on for several years and devastated the country as much as it widened the ethnic divide in a nation already deeply divided along ethnic lines. And the war never stopped completely.

It is a perennial conflict which, together with those in Burundi and Congo, could redraw the map of Africa's Great Lakes highly volatile and combustible region with serious implications for the entire continent; even if newly created *de facto* borders in this embattled region are frozen in place by a balance of power to establish stable, autonomous or independent ethnostates.

The impact of this reconfiguration will be no less destabilising in other parts of Africa where different ethnic groups also want to have their own autonomous or independent states.

In Rwanda, the establishment of a Tutsi-dominated state by the RPF could propel the country in that direction. Some Hutus, unable to dislodge the Tutsi from power or achieve equality for their people, may declare independence, for example, in the Hutu strongholds of Gisenyi and Ruhengeri provinces in the northwest which could also constitute a nucleus of a larger Hutu homeland. Others may pursue accommodation and peaceful coexistence of the two ethnic groups, while the rest – and probably the most dangerous elements – will continue to wage war in an attempt to exterminate the Tutsi or expel them from the country.

However, despite the temptation to retaliate, the RPF was at first restrained in its dealings with the Hutu when its troops rode into Kigali and seized power in 1994. But such restraint was only a temporary tactical manoeuvre because it was politically expedient, enabling the Tutsi-dominated regime to consolidate itself and acquire legitimacy as an ethnically representative government. The

RPF also wanted to deflect criticism that the regime was essentially Tutsi.

The Tutsi, who dominated the RPF, were clever enough to give most cabinet posts to the Hutu to disprove any charges that they wanted to re-establish Tutsi domination over the the Hutu majority. And some people including a number of Hutus were duped into believing that. When the Rwandan Patriotic Front formed the first post-genocide government in Kigali and announced it on 18 July 1994, 16 of the cabinet members including the president himself were Hutu. That was an impressive majority in a 22-member cabinet.

But the regime was still dominated by the Tutsi. And it degenerated into a murderous clique when it launched retaliatory strikes, most of them indiscriminate, against the Hutu civilian population.

Yet even almost two years after the 1994 holocaust – obviously in an attempt to burnish its image after many killings of innocent Hutu civlians – the RPF tried to show that it was committed to justice whether the accused were the actual killers or mere accomplices. According to *The Economist*:

"For a long time the government vowed to execute all killers. Now it threatens death only for the planners and leaders – priests not least. Others will be offered a plea bargain."[1]

Pragmatic considerations also figured prominently in this calculation. As Deputy Justice Minister Gérard Gahima bluntly put it: "If we had to try all the suspects, it would take thousands of years."[2]

He was not far off the mark. For those already in custody by 1996 (and more were still being arrested), it would take at least 500 years to try them individually, confirming the old saying that the wheels of justice do indeed turn slowly.

295

But even after all those attempts to dispense justice, the government was still dogged by suspicion that it was bent on re-establishing Tutsi domination to re-institute a Tutsi ethnocracy. The suspicion was partly confirmed when several Hutu ministers were expelled from the cabinet – the rest resigned – not long after the government was formed, thus leaving behind what was a predominantly Tutsi clique to rule the country:

"Seth Sendashonga, a Hutu sacked as interior minister, has accused it (the Rwandan Tutsi government) of trying to murder him when he was shot in the shoulder in Nairobi, the Kenyan capital.

'If we'd wanted him dead,' says one minister, 'we wouldn't have missed.'

But Kenyan police arrested a Rwandan diplomat found near the spot, they say, with a gun and bullets.

Mr. Sendashonga, who is forming a new party, now supports the...charge of a former prime minister, Faustin Twagiramungu, another sacked Hutu, that the new regime has killed 300,000 Hutus."[3]

A conservative estimate showed that the new Tutsi rulers had killed more than 10,000 Hutus within Rwanda itself by the end of 1997, and more than 200,000 in neighbouring Zaire where they went in hot pursuit of the perpetrators of the 1994 genocide who were hiding in the refugee camps among their kinsmen.

But it was also out of malicious vindictiveness, since the vast majority of those killed were innocent civilians including women and children, and the elderly. Countless were slaughtered as they fled deeper into the jungle, away from advancing Tutsi soldiers who had crossed the border and gone into Zaire just to kill Hutus who fled Rwanda after the RPF seized power.

But in spite of all those atrocities committed by Tutsi soldiers in both Rwanda and Zaire, their scorched-earth policy of hot pursuit could be comprehended and partly justified in a regional context involving Rwanda's security. Hutu extremists – including the ousted Hutu government which sponsored the holocaust, the Hutu Rwandan National Army and other perpetrators of the genocide – had re-established themselves in Zaire by seizing Masisi District in the eastern part of the country close to the border with Rwanda, and threatened to expand into neighbouring countries and eventually topple the Tutsi-dominated regime in Kigali.

They had basically succeeded in establishing a mini-state in Zaire, one of those enclaves in a region with fluid borders where warlords were able to establish fiefdoms, without any fear of being dislodged by the weak Zairean army, because of the wars going on in that part of Africa. It was open territory. Any powerful group could seize a big chunk of it and set up its own "government."

Major-General Augustin Bizimungu was the military commander of the ousted genocidal Hutu regime operating out of bases in eastern Zaire. The leadership included Theodore Sindikubwabo, Rwanda's political leader (virtual president) during the 1994 genocide, and Robert Kajuga, head of the Interahamwe militia which continued to pursue its genocidal campaign against other ethnic groups in eastern Zaire, including Zairian Tutsis, in order to create a virtually autonomous Hutu state in the occupied enclave:

"Though the Hutus in exile maintain a well-stocked army apart from the nearby refugee camps, the conflict in eastern Zaire is primarily waged by civilian militia (the Interahamwe and other groups) who target undefended villages. For almost a year they have been descending on these tiny settlements, killing or burning out the residents....

They have 'cleansed' one ethnic group, are doing battle against four indigenous populations, and have pushed thousands of new Zairian refugees into two neighboring

297

countries.

Their impact is region-wide and spreading....They are already aggravating the existing violence in nearby Burundi to the point of all-out war, and pose security problems for Uganda's current stable southern region... (and) the new, relatively moderate government of Rwanda....

'The perpetrators of the Rwandan genocide have rebuilt their military infrastructure...in Zaire,' the Human Rights Watch concluded nearly a year ago....

Two years ago (in 1994), the ousted regime, composed primarily of ethnic Hutus, fled to exile in Zaire with its 30,000-strong military and a brutal civilian militia known as the Interahamwe....

During the past two years, the exiled regime has masterfully manipulated its refugee followers, exploiting them as pawns to attract humanitarian aid – more than $1 million a day supplied by 100 agencies – and using the refugee camps to camouflage military incursions into Rwanda."[4]

The Hutu extremists launched a military campaign in 1995 – 1996 to seize the 2,000-square-mile Masisi area of eastern Zaire only 35 miles from the border with Rwanda. It was a strategic location which would enable them to launch cross-border raids in an attempt to overthrow the Tutsi-dominated regime in Kigali. By mid-1996, their ethnic cleansing campaign in eastern Zaire – to clear the area of the indigenous people in order to establish an autonomous Hutu enclave there – uprooted as many as a quarter of a million people from their homes in Masisi District.

The situation was different in Rwanda. The Hutu rebels were not a major force or threat to contend with. The danger they posed came from, not inside Rwanda, but from their cross-border raids launched from their operational bases in Masisi District and other parts of

298

eastern Zaire. Yet even the danger from Zaire was not serious enough to destabilise let alone oust the Tutsi-dominated government in Kigali, at least not in the short-term.

But the raids had profound implications for Hutu civilians within Rwanda who were routinely targeted for reprisals by the Tutsi army for the attacks by their brethren across the border. And the civilian Hutu refugees in eastern Zaire were afraid to return to Rwanda for the same reason: reprisals. There was a high probability that the Tutsi regime in Kigali would retaliate against them indiscriminately for the 1994 genocide.

In August 1996, Zaire and Rwanda agreed to repatriate more than a million refugees who fled to eastern Zaire in mid-1994 as the Rwandan Patriotic Front (RPF) advanced towards Kigali after its successful sweep across the country from its bases in Uganda. About 1.3 million Rwandan Hutu refugees had been living in more than 30 camps in Zaire.[5]

Besides fear of retaliation for the massacres if they returned to rwanda, the refugees were also threatened by the perpetrators of the genocide hiding among them if they wanted to return home.

The killers were against the mass repatriation because they would lose this human shield and be arrested once they themselves were forced to return to Rwanda with the rest of the refugees. But no mass repatriation took place soon after Zaire and Rwanda agreed in August to empty the refugee camps.

In October 1996, the American secretary of state, Warren Christopher, said in Arusha, Tanzania, during his visit to a number of African countries that it was safe for the Hutu refugees to return to Rwanda, and that their camps in Tanzania and Zaire should be closed: "We believe it is time to close the camps closest to the Rwandan border that pose the greatest security threat."[6] He made that statement after talks with African leaders about

Rwanda and Burundi.

In a written statement later, the American secretary of state asserted that the "refugees should be encouraged to return voluntarily to Rwanda," and that the American view was that most refugees "can now do so safely."[7]

Christopher's statements were an endorsement of the Rwandan government's position that it was safe for the refugees to return home. He spoke after a meeting with President Benjamin Mkapa of Tanzania, President Daniel arap Moi of Kenya, President Yoweri Museveni of Uganda, and Julius Nyerere, Tanzania's first president who was the chief mediator in Burundi's conflict.[8]

In 1995, Zaire forcibly sent 15,000 refugees back to Rwanda. Tanzania also wanted the hundreds of thousands of refugees in the western part of the country to return to Rwanda, but had not yet forced them to do so. However, in October 1996, Zaire issued a one-week ultimatum for 200,000 Hutus to leave the country.[9]

Warren Christopher also said that after a meeting with President Mkapa, the Tanzanian leader had responded positively to a call for the creation of a crisis response force to deal with conflicts across the continent, including the civil war in neighbouring Burundi. African countries would provide the troops under the auspices of the United Nations.

It was this kind of intervention force which African countries should have mobilised on their own under the collective leadership of the Organisation of African Unity (OAU) during the 1994 Rwandan genocide, instead of waiting for outsiders to come in and stop the holocaust; which they never did. The failure, unwillingness or refusal for outsiders to intervene was a form of shock therapy which should have been enough to galvanise Africans into action to start settling their own conflicts without external intervention. But it never worked, as other wars continued to rage across the continent.

Within Rwanda itself, conflict resolution between the

Hutu and the Tutsi after the genocide entailed dispensation of justice – at least a semblance of it – in the conventional way. And memories of the holocaust were still fresh; its enormity sometimes incomprehensible. As *The Economist* described the magnitude of the tragedy:

"It was not the biggest mass killing of the 20th century, but was the fastest."[10]

The other trials of the Rwandan Hutu suspects for crimes against humanity opened before a United Nations war crimes tribunal in Arusha, Tanzania, in October 1996.

It is ironic that the very same organisation that refused to intervene to stop the massacres in Rwanda is the same one that was now conducting trials for the genocide.

The lingering question is whether or not the international community could indeed have prevented the holocaust or would have merely delayed it even if for a number of years. "Yes," is a plausible answer. The United Nations could have prevented the genocide, at least then, based on reports coming from Rwanda itself long before the massacres started.

In the months before the genocide, senior UN officials were warned of the impending catastrophe. In a series of internal reports, the officials were told in no uncertain terms that Hutu extremists had a plan to exterminate hundreds of thousands of Tutsis and kill UN Belgian peace keepers in Rwanda. One report was sent to the UN headquarters in New York from Rwanda four months before the massacres began.

Collectively, the reports provide a chilling forecast of the extermination of the Tutsi by the Hutu to accomplish a historic mission which was defined by its proponents as a patriotic duty for all Hutus to fulfill in the service of the motherland belonging to the Hutu nation free from the "Inyenzi"; a highly offensive term applied to the Tutsi meaning "cockroaches." But senior UN officials simply ignored the warning.

Detailed reports of the genocidal conspiracy by Hutu extremists started to circulate in UN military circles in early 1994. The Canadian commander of the UN peacekeeping forces in Rwanda, Major-General Romeo Dallaire, sent a cable to UN headquarters on 11 January 1994 warning that a Hutu informant who was a leading member of a Hutu political party in charge of training Hutu militiamen had told him of a plot to wipe out the Tutsi. According to the cable, the informant "has been ordered to register all Tutsi in Kigali," Rwanda's capital. "He suspects it is for their extermination. Example he gave was that in 20 minutes his personnel could kill up to 1,000 Tutsi."[11]

The report to the UN also described an unrealised plot to provoke Belgian peace keepers during a rally in Kigali in January 1994, and "if Belgian soldiers resorted to force a number of them were to be killed and thus guarantee Belgian withdrawal from Rwanda."[12]

Major-General Dallaire took the warnings by the Hutu informant seriously and made repeated requests to the UN for reinforcements to beef up his small peacekeeping force. He also asked for permission to use his troops to seize Hutu weapons caches, according to documents and Colonel Luc Marchal of Belgium, second-in-command of the UN peacekeeping troops in Rwanda, who interviewed the informant.

The credibility of the warnings was enhanced when UN Secretary-General Boutros Boutros-Ghali wrote in the introduction to a UN study on Rwanda that there was an internal document – at the UN headquarters – warning of massive violence and recommending a strong UN response. "Such action went beyond UNAMIR's mandate," he wrote of the UN peacekeeping mission in Rwanda.[13]

Although the assassination of Rwandan President Juvénal Hyabirimana when his plane was shot down on 6

302

April 1994 provided the pretext for the massacres of the Tutsi whom Hutu extremists blamed for the tragedy and for which they themselves were probably responsible, there is no question that extermination of the Tutsi would still have taken place even if President Habyarimana had not been killed. Planning for the massacres preceded his assassination. In fact, it had been in the making for a number of years at least since October 1990 when the Tutsi-led Rwandan Patriotic Front (RPF) first invaded Rwanda from Uganda, an invasion which scared Hutus who now felt that the Tutsi were coming back to rule them again.

The Hutu Rwandan National Army and the militia groups – Interahamwe and Impuzamugambi – massacred the Tutsi and 10 Belgian UN peacekeepers with an efficiency and high level of coordination which convinced Colonel Marchal that his informant had been right.

In early 1996, Boutros-Ghali said he had sent a special adviser, Chinmaya Gharekhan, to brief the UN Security Council on 12 January (1994) on the Hutu plot. But Security Council members later denied that claim. However, the UN Secretary-General's claim was backed up later when an assistant to Kofi Annan, who was then the undersecretary-general for UN peacekeeping operations and who went on to succeed Boutros-Ghali as UN secretary-general, conceded that he had seen a document signed by Annan concerning the request for more UN troops in Rwanda to avert an impending catastrophe, but nothing was done about it. He made the concession after Annan became UN secretary-general and when culpability for international inaction during the massacres was being placed on the UN by an increasing number of critics.

But even before Kofi Annan's deputy in the UN peacekeeping mission made that statement, there had been more reports about the United Nations' deliberate inaction during the Rwandan genocide. A UN official admitted in the last week of November 1996 that Chinmaya Gharekhan told the UN Security Council only about the deterioration of the security situation in Rwanda and about the distribution of weapons and ammunition to the Hutu militiamen before the massacres started, and not about the detailed plot for genocide.

That alone should have been enough warning for the Security Council to take action, although this official did not concede that much. However, the same official also said that Western powers in the region during that time – the United States, France, and Belgium – were informed of the plot described in the UN communique.[14]

And according to American intelligence officials cited in the media, the CIA and the DIA (Defence Intelligence Agency of the U.S. Defence Department) had also warned the United States government about a plot to exterminate the Tutsi in Rwanda.

Yet President Bill Clinton refused to intervene, contending that it would not help him politically, and that it was not in America's national interest to do so; especially after the debacle in Somalia in 1993 when 18 American soldiers were killed by Somali militiamen. Some of the dead Americans were dragged through the streets of Mogadishu, the capital, speeding up America's and the UN's exit from the devastated country.

Therefore the Americans were extremely cautious about another involvement in an African civil war, or in any other foreign venture, especially when such involvement or intervention was not in the best interest of the United States.

It is also obvious that a small, desperately poor African country like Rwanda, even without the Somalia fiasco, would have been of no interest to the United States or any other major world power – except France which backed up the tottering genocidal Hutu regime to protect its Francophone zone in Africa from Anglophone encroachment – especially after the end of the Cold War

304

when the West no longer had to compete with the East in an ideological and geopolitical rivalry to win client states in the Third World.

The logic of the Cold War was simple: Every country counts. Today, most don't. And they are mostly African, including Rwanda.

Even the plight of millions of refugees from the Rwandan holocaust did not get the attention it deserved from the world powers and other members of the international community. There were several reasons for this: lack of national interest, racism, donor fatigue, and the endless cycle of violence and other perennial conflicts on the African continent defying external solutions.

But it must also be conceded that – and this is a credit to the international community we Africans criticise so much for not helping us when we do nothing to help ourselves and one another – without UN help and relief from other international organisations, African war victims would have nothing, absolutely nothing. The Organisation of African Unity (OAU) has been utterly impotent in resolving African conflicts, let alone in helping war victims on this embattled continent.

So, it was with UN help that the Rwandan Hutu refugees in neighbouring countries, especially Zaire and Tanzania, were able to eat, get shelter and eventually return home two years after the 1994 genocide. But hundreds of thousands of them in western Tanzania refused to go home when the repatriation started. According to a Reuters report from Ngara in Kagera Region, northwestern Tanzania, in the *International Herald Tribune*:

"Up to 320,000 Rwandan refugees have abandoned their camps in northwestern Tanzania, rejecting a plan to repatriate them to Rwanda by the end of the year, United Nations officials said Thursday (12 December 1996)....

UN officials said two camps that had held more than

290,000 refugees on Wednesday were now almost empty, apparently because Hutu extremist militiamen had intimidated the refugees into refusing to follow the repatriation plan.

UN refugee agency officials said 35,000 people abandoned other camps at Kitale, Lukole and Keza overnight and headed southeast in hope of reaching Zambia and Malawi. About 15,000 refugees fled earlier this week from camps close to the Ugandan border. About 560 of them crossed the Kagera river by canoe to reach Uganda.

The exodus started on a small scale Sunday (8 December) and began to steamroll as word spread through the camps that refugees in other areas had headed into the bush.

Members of the Hutu militia do not want to go home for fear of persecution or reprisals for the massacre of Rwandan Tutsis in 1994. They want other refugees to stay with them, believing that there is strength in numbers.

The mass exodus Thursday brought to 320,000 the number of refugees who have fled. That is more than half the 540,000 Rwandans in the 13 Tanzanian camps."[15]

There were other reports stating that some of the Hutus who fled Rwanda even wanted to go as far as Nigeria, walking, since they believed that is where they originally came from. Bantu tribes in East and Southern Africa migrated from Cameroon and the eastern part of Nigeria about 2,000 years ago. West Africans themselves originated from the Great Lakes region and other parts of East Africa about 5,000 years ago.

Regardless of where they wanted to go, it was clear that many Hutus were desperate and would have accepted asylum anywhere, although some of them said they did not want to live outside Africa.

But even without intimidation by the perpetrators of the genocide in the refugee camps in Zaire and Tanzania, many Hutu refugees had already decided on their own not to return to Rwanda, afraid that they would be punished by the Tutsi-dominated government simply because they were Hutu and therefore suspected of having participated in the massacre of the Tutsi.

The United Nations High Commission for Refugees (UNHCR) had hoped that it could, together with the Tanzanian government, persuade the refugees to return to Rwanda willingly, but failed to do so. There was now fear that countless refugees would end up wandering in the bush across Tanzania, just as their brethren were, during the same time, in the forests of Zaire after more than 600,000 others had returned to Rwanda from the eastern part of that country since mid-November 1996.

The refugees in Zaire fled their camps in October 1996 after Rwanda, together with the Tutsi-led Congolese rebels, attacked the camps to destroy them and flush out the perpetrators of the 1994 genocide who were hiding among the civilian refugees and launching cross-border raids into Rwanda in an attempt to overthrow the Tutsi-dominated government. After the camps were destroyed, most of the extremists and other Hutus fled deeper into the jungle in Zaire, while the rest went back to Rwanda in one of the largest migrations in modern history.

And in Tanzania, there was a sudden change in the movement of the refugees as tens of thousands of them headed back towards the camps on 13 December 1996. According to a report from Rusumo, northwestern Tanzania, they had abandoned the camps just the day before, and this dramatic reversal indicated that they were willing to return to Rwanda:

"Aid workers said 400,000 refugees who had been heading east toward a Tanzanian game reserve turned around and began heading west, toward the camps and toward the Rwandan border....

Tanzania has given refuge to 535,000 Rwandan Hutu,

more than any other Central African country since the exodus of refugees out of Zaire last month, and the Tanzanian government has given them until December 31 to leave."[16]

The change came after Hutu militants lost control of the mass of refugees they used as a cover to avoid being forcibly returned to Rwanda where they would face retribution for the 1994 genocide.

Yet another dramatic development took place when about 300,000 refugees walked back to Rwanda on 15 December 1996 after they were forced out of the largest camp in Tanzania by the army, according to reports by UN relief workers in Rusumo, northwestern Tanzania:

"Refugees said the Tanzanian soldiers, who entered the Beneco camp at midday on Sunday (15 December), herded the refugees along the road to the nearby Rusumo border crossing into Rwanda. The soldiers forced them out by using sticks and batons."[17]

Many of them, if not the majority, were apprehensive of the future as they headed back to live under a Tutsi-dominated government. Aware of this concern, Rwandan President Pasteur Bizimungu, himself a Hutu, went to the border to welcome the refugees back home and guarantee them safety: "I came to reassure them that nothing bad will happen to them."[18] He also said that groups of Hutu intimidators were blocking other refugees from crossing into Rwanda, threatening them with physical harm if they attempted to do so.

The stream of refugees was a solid mass stretching for at least 8 miles on the road to the Rusumo border crossing. Lines of UN trucks and other relief agencies waited on the Rwandan side of the border to carry some refugees to their distant villages.

About 200,000 of the refugees originally came from

villages within 30 kilometres – about 18 and a half miles – of the Rusumo crossing, and they were expected to walk back to their former homes, if they could find them unoccupied by some of the 1 million Tutsi exiles who returned to Rwanda after the Tutsi-dominated Rwandan Patriotic Front (RPF) took over the country in July 1994. Many of the returning Tutsis seized land and property left behind by fleeing Hutus who left the country in fear of reprisals by the victorious RPF army.

At least 1,000 people were crossing the Tanzanian-Rwandan border every hour in the second mass repatriation in five weeks. The exodus followed talks between UN camp leaders and officials of the Tanzanian government who said all 540,000 Rwandan Hutu refugees had to be out of the country by 13 December 1996, despite protests by different critics against the expulsion order.

Tanzanian soldiers and policemen turned back refugees who had earlier tried to flee inland into Tanzania from their camps and told them to walk towards the Rwandan border. Anne Willem Bijleveld of the United Nations High Commission for Refugees said the soldiers walked with the refugees but "in a humane manner" and even assisted the needy.[19]

UN aid officials said they believed a rush away from the Rwandan border by hundreds of thousands of refugees on 12 December 1996 broke the grip of the Hutu militants who had threatened them with physical harm if they tried to go back to Rwanda.[20]

The UN High Commission for Refugees supported Tanzania's decision to send the refugees back to Rwanda, but was strongly criticised for doing so. In fact, both had departed from the long-standing opposition to forced repatriation of refugees. And for decades, Tanzania had been a haven for exiles and had the largest number of refugees on the continent for many years. They included freedom fighters of all the liberation movements in Southern Africa when Dar es Salaam, Tanzania's capital, was the headquarters of the Organisation of African Unity (OAU) Liberation Committee and of all the liberation groups on the continent.

Many people were therefore surprised when Tanzania reversed her long-standing policy, although the change turned out to be only temporary and was caused by logistical problems. After this brief interruption, refugees once again flowed into Tanzania and were allowed to stay during the following years when the Great Lakes region was embroiled in conflict. They came from three countries: Rwanda, Burundi, and Congo, formerly Zaire.

However, the United Nations High Commission for Refugees' endorsement of Tanzania's expulsion order in December 1996 drew sharp criticism from some human-rights groups. "It is a compromise," a senior UN official said in Geneva, the UN agency's headquarters. But he and several officials said the agency's support for the return of the refugees in Tanzania was a bow to the "new realities."[21]

One of those new realities was that Western governments had reduced funding for Western operations and were demanding even more drastic cuts to force the refugees to return to their homeland. The Rwandan refugee camps in Tanzania cost about $2 million a day, and the United States had for months been pressuring the refugee agency to close them.

The Clinton Administration went so far as to strongly argue that food deliveries to the camps should be drastically reduced, and then stopped, to force the refugees to go back to Rwanda. And it got strong support from the Rwandan government in this repatriation policy, since the Tutsi-dominated regime in Kigali wanted the camps in Tanzania closed – as much it did those in Zaire – because anti-government rebels were operating from those camps, posing a big security threat to Rwanda.

Senior UN officials in Geneva explained how the forced repatriation of the Rwandan Hutu refugees began

310

with a police operation set up by Tanzanian authorities to force rebel soldiers and paramilitary units out of the camps, in order to enable the refugees to decide on their own whether they wanted to stay in Tanzania or return to Rwanda.

Yet that did not settle the matter. However well-intentioned and whatever the geopolitical realities, the refugee agency's endorsement of the repatriation order by the Tanzanian government prompted several human rights groups to criticise the agency strongly for what they believed was a wrong and cruel decision. Human Rights Watch accused the UN agency of having "shamefully abandoned its responsibility to protect refugees." Amnesty International took a similar position.[22]

But the former director of disaster-relief operations in former American President Ronald Reagan's Administration, Julia Taft, dismissed such critics as being unrealistic. Taft, who during the Rwandan crisis was president of the Washington-based Interaction, a coalition of non-governmental relief and development agencies, responded by saying:

"One can be a purist if one wants. But you also have to be a realist. You have to make hard decisions. Where are people better off, in the hell of the camps, or back in Rwanda? The answer is Rwanda."[23]

That was also the position of the UN High Commissioner for Refugees, and apparently Tanzania's. As Viera de Mello, senior assistant to the High Commissioner for Refugees, explained:

"We believe that the conditions in Rwanda have evolved in a positive and encouraging manner, so that the refugees can return in safety and dignity."[24]

While the return of the refugees may have been a

positive step towards their long-term resettlement in their homeland, it was also bound to exacerbate tensions between the two ethnic groups whose members would have to live together again as neighbours within only a short period after the 1994 genocide. Yet reconciliation, if such a goal could indeed be achieved in Rwanda's extremely hostile environment, would be impossible without repatriation. The two, killer and victim, had to come face to face.

And what the perpetrators of the genocide feared most if they returned to Rwanda, did not happen. The repercussions of the genocide were only beginning to be felt within Rwanda when the two groups came face to face after the return of the refugees. Even the apprehension of the mass killers was a matter for concern among the Hutu who feared they could be targeted for retribution, as many of them indeed were, for no other reason than that they belonged to the same ethnic group as the murderers.

On 29 December 1996, UN aid officials announced that the repatriation of the Rwandan refugees from Tanzania had ended, with nearly half a million back in Rwanda in the same month. As Justin Cockerell, a delegate of the International Committee of the Red Cross in the northwestern Tanzanian town of Ngara, put it:

"The operation is winding down; overall, it is finished....There no longer appear to be any large refugee groups. We see one or two sporadic family groups. We will be mopping up, as clearly some people remain somewhere, but it will be nothing like the same scale as before."[25]

And Ephreme Kabayija, director of Rwanda's commission for the repatriation of refugees, said all refugees who had fled to Tanzania in 1994 had returned to their homeland by 28 December 1996.[26] Rwanda Radio quoted him as saying that no refugees remained in

Tanzania and that none were still travelling after 480,000 returned since the repatriation operation began on 14 December.[27]

As the repatriation ended, genocide trials began. People convicted of murder faced the death penalty. As Deputy Justice Minister Gérard Gahima out it: "Those on trial are accused of playing a very serious role in the genocide."[28]

More than 2,300 Hutus who returned from Tanzania in December 1996 and from Zaire in November the same year were detained on suspicion of involvement in the genocide. But a Hutu refugee lobby group, the Rally for the Return of Refugees and Democracy to Rwanda, said the detained returnees had been falsely accused by people who wanted their property, and dismissed the trials as "a mockery of justice."[29]

The first trials in Rwanda began on 27 December 1996 in the southwestern town of Kibungo where Deo Bizimana, a former medical assistant, and Egide Gatanazi, a former local administrator, pleaded "Not guilty" to organising massacres. And the first genocide trials in the Rwandan capital Kigali opened on 30 December.[30]

The trials in Kigali, like the ones in Kibungo, also involved two defendants. One suspect was Francois Bizimana, and the other one was said to be a former Speaker of Rwanda's parliament whose name was not given right away. The trial of Silas Munyageshali, a former prosecutor in Kigali, was adjourned because a three-man panel of judges headed by Judge Juriel Rutaremara ruled that it would be unfair to try Munyageshali in the same court he previously served as prosecutor.

The trial of Theodomir Ruzirabwoba, a 50-year-old former administrator in Kigali, was adjourned until 3 January 1997.

Deputy Justice Minister Gahima announced that more genocide trials would take place on December 31st in the northern town of Byumba.[31]

With these first trials, the process of retributive justice against the perpetrators of the genocide and their accomplices, hence the tortuous road towards reconciliation of the two ethnic groups after the holocaust, had officially begun.

Whether or not retribution would lead to reconciliation was an entirely different matter. Yet without retribution, there probably would be no justice even if there had to be no reconciliation.

The bigger question Rwanda still faces is whether or not there can be peace without reconciliation and justice. Injustice only breeds contempt for the law and for the victims, and is therefore a threat to peace even if it is tolerated to achieve reconciliation by granting full pardon to the guilty as happened in many cases during the Truth and Reconciliation Commission hearings in post-apartheid South Africa.

In the case of Rwanda, retribution prevailed when the first Rwandans to stand trial for genocide, Deo Bizimana and Egide Gatanazi, were sentenced to death by firing squad on 3 January 1997. They were the world's first convictions for genocide first defined in the 1948 Genocide Convention after World War II. According to a report from Kibungo, Rwanda, the two men "were convicted on 11 charges, including organizing massacres and raping and pillaging their Tutsi neighbors."[32]

And in neighbouring Tanzania, the International Criminal Tribunal for Rwanda (ICTR) – set up by the United Nations – opened its first genocide trial in the northern town of Arusha on 9 January 1997.

Besides logistical problems including poor communications facilities in Arusha, hiring unqualified personnel because of nepotism, one of the biggest obstacles to conducting trials was the reluctance by African countries to cooperate with the tribunal in arresting Rwandan suspects – who had sought refuge there

– and transferring them to Arusha. Cameroon topped the list of those countries.

The first defendant in Arusha was Jean-Paul Akayesu, a former mayor of a commune where 2,000 Tutsis were massacred by the Hutu between April and June 1994. He was charged with genocide and crimes against humanity.

And among four indicted Rwandans who were being held in Cameroon at that time was Colonel Theoneste Bagosora who spearheaded the massacres and distributed weapons to the militia when he opened up the armouries in his capacity as a senior official at the ministry of defence. As Alison DesForges of Human Rights Watch Africa said about Bagosora: "He gave the military orders in the first 24 hours (to kill Tutsis)."[33]

The president Cameroon, Paul Biya, refused for months to surrender Bagosora and other Rwandan suspects to the international court in Arusha partly out of solidarity with fellow members of the African Francophone bloc. Although Rwanda was not a former French colony, it is a French-speaking country like Cameroon and had nothing but contempt for the court proceedings in Arusha.

But unlike Cameroon, it wanted Bagosora in its custody so that he could get the maximum penalty of death by firing squad. The most he could get in Arusha was life imprisonment. The international criminal tribunal – in order to get bigger criminals – had no death penalty; one of the reasons it earned contempt from the Rwandan authorities.

Yet, unlike the trials in Rwanda, the Arusha proceedings were conducted within the bounds of law based on internationally accepted norms of justice guaranteeing adequate legal representation and fairness for the accused.

In Rwanda, there was not even a semblance of justice despite professions to the contrary, although the accused were probably guilty in many, if not in most, cases. But the way the trials were conducted, and who presided over the proceedings, raised serious questions about the fairness of the courts; the convictions of the first defendants being a prime example:

"Each of the Kibungo defendants was delivered, handcuffed, to the courtroom in a truck. The audience applauded as a prosecutor read out the charges. Children gathered on the window ledges outside, peering in at the suspects as they stood at the bench in their pink prison uniforms. Relations of their alleged victims lined up to lay claim to the defendants' belongings.

Each trial lasted about four hours.

The three judges refused to let one defendant, Deo Bizimana, speak in French, though it is a national language. Neither defendant had a lawyer, or much time. The closest either came to confronting his accusers – whose statements to investigators were read, not presented in person – was when a young man in the audience stood up to show the machete scars on his neck and the stubs of three fingers....

Out in Bizimana's village, his Tutsi ex-neighbours say he was guilty, no question. Hutus do question it. One woman who listened to the proceedings on the radio stops short of calling him innocent, but says some details presented in court were wrong. She says investigators never questioned her, and that many Hutus are afraid even to attend a court, let alone present evidence challenging the prosecution.

If the judges seemed unseasoned, it is because they are. All three grew up in Zaire, where one was a teacher, another studied banking and the third ran a business. Over 80 per cent of Rwanda's old legal officials were killed or fled during the genocide; many took part in it.

The new Tutsi-dominated government advertised for judges on the radio, and the top scorers in a general-knowledge test – typical question: 'What is the largest desert in the world?' – won a four-month training course in

Rwandan law, modelled after Belgium's system. A few of the new judges are Hutus, some are Tutsis who lost their families. But most are Tutsis born in exile."[34]

The first most senior official to go on trial for genocide in Rwanda was Froduald Karamira, a Tutsi. He became a "Hutu" later in life after meeting certain qualifications and was one of the strongest proponents of Hutu power.
He was a vice president of the extremist MDR-Power party under the former Hutu-dominated government of Juvénal Habyarimana and went on trial in Kigali on 14 January 1997.

He was accused of being a founder and ringleader of the Interahamwe militia which led the attacks in the capital, Kigali, and was allegedly responsible for inciting genocide through broadcasts – on Radio Rwanda, which was government-owned, and on privately-owned Radio Mille Collines – to kill his own people; a role equivalent to what some Jews allegedly did as willing executioners, helping Hitler to exterminate fellow Jews, as some writers contend. Also on trial together with Karamira were four Hutus.[35]

It was also alleged that he killed 13 members of his own family and hundreds of other Tutsis.

He was executed by firing squad, together with 21 others convicted of genocide, at Nyamirambo Stadium in Kigali on 24 April 1998.

The event, marked by a carnival atmosphere, was attended by tens of thousands of people, mostly Tutsi, who cheered when the convicts were executed. As James C. McKinley stated in his report from Kigali, "As Crowds Vent Their Rage, Rwanda Publicly Executes 22," in *The New York Times*, 25 April 1998:

"The policemen led the four prisoners in pink prison clothes out under a slate-gray sky at 10:30 A.M. and tied them to four posts sunk into the red earth of a soccer field.

Tens of thousands of Rwandans who had gathered to watch the first executions of people convicted of genocide pressed forward. Many stood on tiptoe to see the four former political leaders -- a businessman, a prosecutor, and two school administrators -- meet their deaths. The policemen put black hoods over the prisoners' weary faces, trussed their heads back with ropes and hung bibs bearing rectangular targets on their chests.

For 20 minutes the prisoners, three men and a woman, remained blindfolded and bound to the poles as the crowd jeered and grew more impatient. Suddenly two police Land Rovers roared onto the soccer field. A captain and four policemen in black masks with assault rifles leapt from the back of one car. Each policeman rushed up to a prisoner, aimed at the chest and fired several shots. Then they traded places and fired again.

The crowd surged forward. Many people cheered. One woman held her baby up to see. An old man thrust his hand in the air and cheered. Others just smiled and walked away.

Then the police captain walked down the line of bodies. He fired a pistol twice into each hooded head. The smell of gun smoke and excrement drifted on the air.

'This is justice,' said a young man perched on top of a goal post. 'They killed and they have to be killed.'

Brushing aside appeals for a stay of execution from the Pope, the European Union, the United States and several human rights organizations, the Government of Rwanda today shot 22 people convicted in local courts of genocide crimes.

The shootings today were carried out before large crowds here and in four other towns -- Gikongoro, Nyamata, Murambi and Kibungo. The condemned were the first to be convicted by local courts in the massacres here in 1994, when more than 500,000 Tutsi and moderate Hutu were killed in a campaign orchestrated by the previous Government, which has since been overthrown in a civil war.

Human rights advocates say many of the trials failed to meet international standards of justice. In some cases, they assert, defendants were not represented by a lawyer or given adequate time to prepare their cases. But the Government is under pressure from survivors of the massacres and hard-line Tutsi politicians who complain about the slow pace of justice and to press ahead with prosecutions. One of the people executed here today was Froduald Karamira, a prominent businessman and the prime ideologue behind the extremist Hutu Power movement. During the spring of 1994, Mr. Karamira's daily hate broadcasts on the radio encouraged Hutu to take part in mass killings of Tutsi.

Rwandan officials have defended the rulings of their courts as fair and just. They have argued that the executions must go forward to send a message to Hutu guerrillas, who have continued over the last four years to kill hundreds of Tutsi in the countryside and have stepped up their attacks in recent months.

Government officials have also said they hoped the executions would establish the rule of law in Rwanda and finally end the cycle of ethnic bloodshed that has plagued this country since independence in 1962, costing hundreds of thousands of lives.

'We are not sadists,' Cabo Ninyetegeka, a presidential aide, told The Associated Press today. 'But there is a legacy of political ruthlessness and now justice must be done.'

Of the 346 people who have been tried in Rwandan courts, about a third have been sentenced to death and another third have been given life in prison. The rest have received lesser sentences. Only 26 have been acquitted. There are about 125,000 people still awaiting trial.

Despite the backlog, the speediness of the Rwandan trials stands in stark contrast to the United Nations tribunal in Arusha, Tanzania, which is investigating the same crimes.

After two years of proceedings, the tribunal has yet to convict any of the suspects it has in custody, including several high-ranking former Government officials. The tribunal does not have the power to impose a death penalty.

But human-rights advocates point out that the trials in Rwanda have been conducted in an inconsistent manner. For instance, Dr. Deogratias Bizimana and Egide Gatanazi, former local government officials who were executed in the town of Kibungo today, were convicted and sentenced to death after a four-hour trial in January 1997. They had no lawyer and no witnesses were called in their defense.

'Revenge is not justice,' Marc Saghie of Amnesty International told The Associated Press.

Most of the Tutsi people who came out to witness the executions in the capital today saw the situation differently. Many had lost several members of their families in the massacres, and few in the crowd seemed to have any doubt about the guilt of the four people executed at the Tapis Rouge soccer field, which is in the Nyamirambo neighborhood.

Like Mr. Karamira, the three other people shot here today were also well-known government officials accused of directing Hutu militias that carried out massacres around the capital. They were Silas Munyagishari, a former Kigali prosecutor; Elie Nhimiyimana, a school director, and Virginie Mukankusi, a school inspector in Kigali.

'Both my parents were killed by those militias and those condemned today were with the militias too,' said Ismael Gatete, a taxi driver from Kigali. 'Even if they didn't kill, they ordered the killing.'

At times the crowd seemed gripped with blood-lust. When Mrs. Mukankusi was brought out of a pickup truck holding the prisoners, cheers and jeers went up from the mass of people, who were pressed up against one another in a large semicircle about 50 yards from the prisoners, jostling to get a better look while soldiers held them back. As the tension deepened, several foreign journalists, who had been barred from bringing cameras or recording devices to the soccer field, were harassed by spectators.

Two men tore up a reporter's notebook and said he would be shot if he wrote down anything. Another reporter was stoned by a crowd who accused him of sympathizing with the prisoners.

After the executions, several people who had watched said they felt a confused and bittersweet sense that justice had been done. Many expressed a hope that the executions would deter Hutu extremists from further massacres. Others said that putting the ringleaders of the 1994 killings to death was the only way to begin rebuilding the divided country.

'That's the way they killed my family," a man who gave his name only as Gerard said after the shooting. 'I cannot be satisfied. I can't get my family back. But they have to know that life is precious. I'm not happy to have somebody killed, but I lost all my family that way. I'm afraid they will do it again.'

Stephen Mazowera, a 40-year-old accountant whose brother and sister were slain in 1994, said survivors of the massacres were hungry for the kind of justice dispensed today. Public executions gave them a way to vent their immense anger, he said.

'My family won't be back because these four people died,' he said. 'But it's the first time in this country somebody has been executed because he killed Tutsi. We hope it's the end of impunity and we hope that now somebody out there will think twice before committing this crime.'

It remains to be seen, however, if the executions will bring reconciliation or fuel the conflict, diplomats said.

Most Western governments have supported Rwanda's

current leaders since they came to power in July 1994, mostly because the Tutsi rebel army that drove the former Hutu-led regime into exile, ended the massacres and restored order.

But the Government remains at heart a military regime controlled by former Tutsi rebel leaders. The Hutu insurgents, many of whom took part in the massacres and have little to lose, show no sign of giving up.

Instead, armed Hutu bands have been stepping up terrorist attacks and ambushes in the countryside since December, killing hundreds of civilians. The predominantly Tutsi army has struck back, waging counterinsurgency campaigns in which some Hutu civilians have been killed, human rights officials said. Diplomats and human rights officials fear the fighting will only intensify after the executions today.

For their part, Rwandan officials are defiant in the face of international calls for clemency and warnings that executions will only deepen divisions. On Thursday, Anastase Gasana, the Foreign Minister, said the executions served 'an educational and pedagogical purpose.' Today, Patrick Mazimhaka, a Cabinet minister, rebuffed the Pope's call for mercy, saying in 1994 'I didn't hear the Pope call for forgiveness then.'

These politicians may be playing to a domestic audience. As the streets of Kigali returned to normal after the traffic jams this morning, several survivors of the massacres said they were relieved the executions had begun.

Rose Mukamusana, a 31-year-old mother, spent three months in hiding around Kigali during the 1994 massacres, in which her husband and dozens of members of her extended family were killed. Much of the time, she was huddled with her children in an orphanage just a few blocks from the field where the executions took place today. In those days, Tutsi bodies littered the streets of that neighborhood every morning.

'This is a sign that law is working here in Rwanda,' she said. 'Those people killed people and they have been killed. It will be an example to anyone else who thinks to do so.'

But others who also lived through that time were not as sanguine. 'This will not finish it,' Mr. Gatete, the taxi driver, said after leaving the soccer field. 'It is not over.'"

One of the repercussions of the genocide – especially of the re-imposition of Tutsi hegemonic control of the country which itself was a product of the holocaust – and of the trials was increased guerrilla warfare by Hutu extremists, many of whom were forced to go back to Rwanda after the refugees were repatriated from Zaire and Tanzania, respectively, in November and December 1996.

Some of the victims of the violence were foreigners. A group of about 10 Hutu gunmen killed three Spanish aid workers and several Rwandans and severely wounded an American in northwestern Rwanda on 18 January 1997. The attack was directed at a cluster of aid centres in the town of Ruhengeri where thousands of Hutu refugees returned from Zaire and sought help from international relief agencies. The aid agencies included Doctors Without Borders, Doctors of the World, and Save the Children. The three Spaniards who were killed worked for a Spanish unit of Doctors of the World.[36]

Several soldiers were also killed and many Rwandan civilians were injured when the guerrillas exchanged rocket and machine-gun fire for about 90 minutes with the Tutsi-dominated Rwandan Patriotic Army (RPA) which intervened after the attack was launched by the guerrillas. The attackers were believed to be former members of the Hutu Rwandan National Army or the Interahamwe and Impuzamugambi militia groups which carried out the 1994 massacre of Tutsis and moderate Hutus.

The attack on Ruhengeri was not the first one. According to Rwanda Radio, the guerrillas had launched several raids in the region before. But the attack was the worst carried out against international relief agencies in the province. The UN High Commissioner for Human Rights suspended the agency's activities in the Gisenyi prefecture's six communes in northwestern Rwanda a few days before the January 18th ambush "after a group of armed men beat, robbed and threatened to kill a team of UN human rights observers there. On January 11, a hospital was attacked and its pharmacy was pillaged at Kabaya in the same prefecture. Three Rwandans were killed."[37]

Thus, tragically, the end of the 1994 genocide did not end the ethnic conflict in Rwanda; nor would the trials and execution or imprisonment of the perpetrators of the genocide. For all practical purposes, Rwanda had not even started out on the road towards reconciliation, if such an option was indeed viable in the country's highly polarised and explosive situation where the two ethnic groups are divided by an "implacable" wall of hostility.

The attacks on Ruhengeri underscored this problem that was inextricably linked with attempts by the rebels to sabotage the judicial process involving genocide trials; a concerted effort by the insurgents which entailed targeting some of their own kinsmen for elimination:

"More than 60 people, including three Spanish aid workers, were murdered in Rwanda. Many of the dead were returned refugees who were potential witnesses in genocide trials."[38]

Many of the trials were nowhere close to what would be considered to be impartial judicial proceedings, a shortcoming the guerrillas tried to use to justify their attempts to sabotage them. Thus, while the victims of the genocide deserved justice, and the enormity of the crime could not be disputed by fair-minded people, the government's impatience and desire to punish the guilty seemed to compromise the judicial process and impede reconciliation by conducting proceedings in a haphazard manner. A senior Western diplomat derisively dismissed the trials in Rwanda by saying: "This meets our standards for a kangaroo court."[39]

Such kangaroo justice would hardly help the reconciliation process. As John Keys, country director of the International Rescue Committee, said: "Justice is not the only ingredient necessary for reconciliation. But it's absolutely key."[40] Alison DeForges, of Human Rights Watch/Africa and who had studied Rwanda for 30 years, also condemned the proceedings, saying: "The trials will lack credibility if things don't change. Serious prosecution appears not to be a top priority for this government."[41]

The top priority for the Tutsi-dominated government in those proceedings was swift retribution with malicious vindictiveness. By the end of January 1997, eight defendants had been condemned to death in proceedings which lasted only a few hours.

Rwanda's Deputy Justice Minister Gérard Gahima admitted that the trials "could be better conducted....The magistrates are new to their job. They're not sure what to do."[42] That was a chilling admission, an implicit admission that some people were being convicted unfairly and may be were even condemned to death when they should not have been.

But he also said that Rwanda's critics were being unfair. He explained that the trials were being conducted under the same system the country used before the genocide. Then, as now, trials frequently proceeded without defence lawyers because only 3 per cent of the defendants could afford them. John Keys also defended Rwanda, contending:

"The standard is both unrealistic and unfair. To level these complaints against Rwanda doesn't take into account the demands placed upon a very poor country."[43]

As the trials were going on, Hutu guerrillas continued to wage their campaign of terror against innocent civilians in order to destabilise the Tutsi regime in Kigali. And the United Nations was forced to evacuate its staff, while most relief groups scaled back their missions as mourners bade farewell to four human rights monitors who were killed by the rebels on 4 February 1997 in Karengera, 180 miles southwest of Kigali. They included a Briton, a Cambodian, and two Rwandan aides. A third Rwandan in their entourage died hours later of gunshot wounds.

The United Nations suspended its operations in western Rwanda and moved to the capital Kigali. It urged other foreigners to do the same.[44] And the arrest of more genocide suspects only made things worse across the country as Hutu guerrillas vowed to continue and escalate their campaign. One such suspect was Alfred Musema, wanted by the UN International Criminal Tribunal for Rwanda in Tanzania. Once the director of a tea factory in Rwanda, he was arrested in Switzerland in February 1995 and extradited to Tanzania on 20 May 1997. Musema was accused of organising the massacre of Tutsis who worked at the plantation of which he was in charge.[45]

One aspect of the Rwandan tragedy that many people may not know about is the involvement of women including nuns. Most of the murders were committed by men. But thousands of Hutu women also participated in the massacres. And many of them ended up in jail during the round-up of suspects among the refugees who returned home from Zaire and Tanzania.

Although the government officially welcomed the refugees, it did not trust them, a tragic legacy of the holocaust which will probably endure for many years with serious implications for the unity and stability of the country. The government's position was clear from the beginning when the refugees returned:

326

"Jails (are) crammed with hundreds of men and women accused of taking part in the 1994 killings....Officially, the government welcomes them back. But it also knows that many of them joined armed Hutu gangs on their return. The authorities watch the young men who come back, such as Jeremiah, carefully.

Gangs ambush military vehicles and attack government offices and even schools. Two UN workers were murdered this week (in June 1997). The army, already stretched, is unable to contain the attacks, but claims to have killed many militiamen. It also kills civilians suspected of helping them....In both Burundi and Rwanda the (Tutsi) armies respond to guerrilla attacks by taking revenge on (Hutu) civilians."[46]

That is one of the biggest obstacles to peace and reconciliation in Rwanda – as well as Burundi. As long as the government continues to target civilians simply because they are Hutu and therefore automatically guilty, the rebels will continue to find fertile ground for recruiting fighters who are ready to join their guerrilla armies. And as long as the insurgents continue to fight, the government will always find excuses to target Hutu civilians. It is a dilemma and a vicious cycle of violence that feeds on itself. And it can be broken only when both sides make substantial concessions on the basis of a mutually acceptable formula in order to achieve peace and stability, unity and progress, in this war-ravaged, impoverished country where the Hutu and the Tutsi have the misfortune of living together.

And they will continue to live together, whether they like it or not, unless they choose to separate; which is highly unlikely, although some African leaders have suggested that, as we learned earlier.

It is a misfortune – of the two antagonistic groups being forced to lived together by dictates of geography and history – that foreshadowed the cataclysmic event of

1994. The genocide actually never stopped. Hutu extremists continued to kill Tutsis, although in small numbers. Their operations were only restricted by retaliatory responses from the predominantly Tutsi national army. But they were determined to continue killing Tutsis..

Equally guilty was the Tutsi-dominated government which took over the country and whose army started killing Hutu civilians with impunity. Yet, in spite of its military superiority, it failed to defeat the rebels who continued to launch deadly raids from across the border in Zaire and within Rwanda itself.

One of the deadliest attacks by the insurgents took place on 22 August 1997. According to *The Wall Street Journal*: "18 Tutsi refugees died in a suspected Hutu attack in Rwanda Friday."[47] The rebels showed no signs of de-escalating their campaign in spite of the reprisals against Hutu civilians by Tutsi soldiers. According to a report from Gisenyi, a Hutu stronghold in northwestern Rwanda, by *The Economist*:

"In a chilling way, the attack awoke memories of the 1994 Rwandan genocide. Hundreds of Hutu militiamen surged into a Tutsi settlement last month (August 1997), singing and chanting, swinging machetes and clubs with nails sticking out of them. Their target was Mudende, a refugee camp near Gisenyi, in north-west Rwanda; their victims ethnic Tutsis from the Masisi region in eastern Congo, who had fled across the border after being attacked by Hutus in 1995. After returning from Congo, they are still being pursued and killed – 130 of them died in the Mudende attack – by Hutu extremists.

According to the Rwandan government, many Hutu soldiers from the defeated army of the late President Juvénal Habyarimana, together with their allies in the militia, have returned to the country over the past eight months – along with a million or so refugees. Extremists

328

among them still hold to the racist creed that fed the genocide: get rid of all Tutsis.

Since May (1997), they have stepped up their attacks in the northwest, the heartland of Hutu extremism. Using the banana plantations around Gisenyi as cover, they launch attacks on government troops and on local officials, beating drums and blowing whistles. The army strikes back.

A UN humanitarian report estimated that more than 2,000 civilians were killed in army operations in May and June....(And) over 110,000 people are languishing in appalling jails awaiting trial for genocide...."[48]

Around the same time the United Nations issued its humanitarian report condemning the massacre of Hutu civilians by Tutsi soldiers, a Belgian legislative panel published its findings saying the UN could have prevented the 1994 genocide. According to *The Washington Post*:

"A Belgian legislative commission investigating the 1994 genocide...has gathered strong evidence that U.N. peacekeepers in the central African country could have prevented or at least hindered the extermination campaign but were thwarted by superiors at the world body's headquarters in New York."[49]

The Belgian legislators were concerned about what happened in Rwanda because Belgium was the colonial power that once ruled Rwanda; also because 10 Belgian soldiers who were a part of the UN peacekeeping force were tortured and killed by Hutu militiamen in the first days of the genocide.

Just as the Hutu genocide planners had anticipated, the murder of the Belgian peace keepers prompted the Belgian government to withdraw all 400 of its soldiers – the best-trained and best-equipped in the UN contingent in Rwanda – only five days after the massacres began; a withdrawal whose impact was compounded by the UN's refusal to send more troops to the embattled country.

Even the request by the UN peacekeeping forces commander in Rwanda, Major-General Romeo Dallaire, to confiscate arms caches – intended for the massacre of Tutsis – within 36 hours of his urgent plea, and grant asylum to the Hutu informant (who told about the massacre plot) and his family, was denied by his superiors at the UN headquarters in New York; thus raising serious doubts about the UN's commitment to its peacekeeping operations in Rwanda.

The Belgian government itself was culpable. After withdrawing its troops from Rwanda, it urged the United Nations to drastically reduce its peacekeeping force from 2,500 troops to about 270. The UN did exactly that, without delay.

The world's major powers, especially the United States, were behind the decision not to send more UN troops to Rwanda. But other officials at the UN, including Kofi Annan who was then in charge of peacekeeping operations worldwide, were also responsible for the tragedy:

"A spokesman for Annan, Fred Eckhard, says that all senior officials at the U.N. peacekeeping directorate were behind the decision to refuse Dallaire's request.

'We're taking a bum rap on this....We had to work within the limits of the mandate,' Ekhard says. 'We bent over backwards to give Dallaire a scheme where he could participate in an arms-seizure operation but from a distance...[by forming] a cordon sanitaire around the area of operations while the (Hutu) government went in,' and seized the arms caches, Ekhard says. 'Of course it had no interest in doing that.'"[50]

Since the UN officials already knew that the Hutu government would not seize the weapons from its own people (Hutu extremists), there is no reason why they did not send additional troops to Rwanda, and why they even told Major-General Dallaire that he could participate in the arms-seizure operation, but only from a distance, knowing full well that he could not fulfill such a weak mandate, especially with the few and poorly-trained soldiers he had. If he had the capability to seize the weapons with the troops he had, he would not have asked for additional troops. It is easy to understand why the Rwandan government and many Rwandans in general were angry and blamed the UN for refusing to intervene and stop the massacres even before they started.

Belgian Senator Alain Destexhe, a former head of Doctors Without Borders, said the refusal by the UN peacekeeping office to back Major-General Dallaire's plan of a preemptive strike against Hutu extremists to neutralise the genocidal offensive also included instructions to Dallaire to convey the informant's intelligence, along with the UN's decision not to act on it, to Rwandan President Juvénal Hyabarimana and his ruling political party.

The party was virulently anti-Tutsi although it had some Tutsi members whom it used for public relations purposes and as puppets.

The Belgian senator said in disbelief about the UN's instructions to Dallaire to tell Hutu leaders what he already knew and that the UN was not going to do anything to stop the genocide:

"They were the ones preparing the massacres. It's like informing a terrorist that you know how he's preparing his terrorism and assuring him you're not going to do anything about it."[51]

The UN set a precedent in the African context with its refusal to prevent the massacres in Rwanda; a dereliction of duty and abdication of moral responsibility by the world body that was repeated in Sierra Leone. When the UN finally intervened in Sierra Leone, it was too late. The damage had been done by the rebels, with tens of thousand dead, just as many with their limbs, buttocks, lips and ears chopped off, and hundreds of thousands left homeless.

The UN and the world's major powers who control the UN did nothing to stop the massacres in that West African country even after repeated pleas for help were made. As Mrs. Victoria Kajue, who saw her six children mowed down when they were lined up against the wall by the rebels of the Revolutionary United Front (RUF) in Sierra Leone's capital Freetown, bitterly remarked amid tears:

"The world seems to seek justice in Kosovo. Are we on a different planet? Are my children worth less than the children in Kosovo? Why don't we get the same treatment?....

I saw them execute all my children and a two-year-old grandson. And I have nowhere to lay a complaint. I have no justice."[52]

And in the words of Sierra Leone's democratically elected President Ahmad Tejan Kabbah whom the rebels forced to share power with them, Sierra Leone endured years of the "most brutal warfare in the modern world." [53] Reverend Alimamy Koroma who played a critical role, as did President Kabbah, in reaching a peace agreement with the rebels, stressed the critical importance of international intervention in ending such conflicts. As he said about the war in his country Sierra Leone:

"This war has gone on for eight years – for eight years we have been on our own – and I'm sure there are actors out there who could have stopped it."[54]

The Tutsi in Rwanda were victims of the same kind of neglect, including neglect by fellow Africans, and expressed the same collective sentiment during the 1994 genocide as did Sierra Leoneans when the civil war was raging in their country.

And they knew why nobody – not even fellow Africans – came to their rescue, although pictures of mutilated bodies of thousands of their kinsmen as well as many Hutus who sympathised with the Tutsi were being televised worldwide everyday. As Marie Manyeh, a local aid worker in Freetown, said about the victims of the civil war in Sierra Leone:

"It's like the world believes that we as black people can absorb more horror than the white race."[55]

Even many African diplomats at the United Nations, setting diplomatic etiquette aside, raised charges of racism as the primary factor in the international community's lack of vigorous response to Africa's plight characterised by complex emergencies of perennial conflicts, crumbling state institutions and decaying economies, the AIDS epidemic, and drought and famine – all rolled into one. As Andre Mwamba Kapanga, the representative of the Democratic Republic of Congo, pointed out, a Congolese was no less deserving of help than someone in Kosovo or East Timor, and added: "The color of his skin does not make him a substandard being."[56]

And Nigerian representative Ibrahim Gambari asked the UN Security Council to compare the world's response to the Kosovo crisis – where he said the international community spent $1.50 per day per refugee – to the response to conflicts in Sierra Leone and Rwanda where he said the daily expenditure per refugee was 11 cents.[57]

In the middle of the Kosovo crisis, children in the embattled region were even given – and seen on television eating – plenty of ice cream, a luxury few can afford in such a situation, while some of the war victims in Sierra Leone were scooping up maggots to eat, as reported by *The Christian Science Monitor*. Not everybody was eating maggots – Corinna Schuler, *The Christian Science*

Monitor reporter, witnessed this, people eating maggots – but the contrast between what the international community gave to Kosovo and what went to Sierra Leone and Rwanda and other war-torn African countries, is glaring and morally repugnant.

There are, of course, those who may argue that children in Kosovo were given ice cream in addition to better food because that is something they are used to, unlike Africans who are not used to that, except a simple maize meal or something similar to that with nothing else to go with it except salt and water. If they are given anything better than that, it is time for them to celebrate – "Do they eat that in their African villages besides maize, cassava and other foods similar to that?" Some international donors may ask that kind of question.

But that is not even the main issue, although it is important to highlight to show that African victims of war and other catastrophes are not treated the same as other victims.

The larger question that has yet to be addressed is what can be done to help them, besides giving them the same kind of help which has failed to produce positive long-term results of alleviating or ending misery in African countries. Some of the answers are disturbing. Yet they may be the only solution to Africa's perennial plight in a number of areas.

It is true that strife-torn African countries have not always been helped by the international community for a number of reasons including racism. But there is another dimension to this crisis response, or lack thereof, in the African context.

More than anybody else, it is Africans themselves who are at fault. They are the ones who are responsible for the wellbeing of their own people. And they are the ones who set themselves on fire – and then scream for help to put out the fire.

And it is African countries themselves that are to blame

for not helping each other or one another, for not solving their own problems, and for destroying themselves. Many of them have descended into hell and have virtually ceased to exist as functional entities, an assessment underscored by Nigerian President Olusegun Obasanjo. As he bluntly put it:

"Everywhere in Africa the evidence is of dereliction and decay. We are rapidly becoming the Third World's Third World."[58]

Probably the most important lesson we Africans can learn from the Rwandan tragedy and other horrors across the continent is that we can not and should *not* count on the international community to come to our rescue whenever we cry, "Help! Help!" We are on our own.

It is wrong for other countries not to help when they can. We are a part of the human family. But many people don't consider us to be a part of them because of what we are: black. Although it is wrong for them not to help us when they are ready to help other people, it is also wrong for us to beg all the time. We beg too much.

Denying us help when we are desperately in need, when millions are starving and dying, is shocking. It is living hell. Look at eastern Congo where more than 3 million people died within five years or less since 1998 because of conflict in that region, the bleeding heart of Africa. There was hardly any international response to the crisis, and hardly any mention of it in the international media. It was as if the people who were dying didn't even exist and never even existed.

Yes, it is shocking, all these tragedies in Africa, and the lack of response from the international community. But that may be the only form of shock therapy that can galvanise us into action to help ourselves and solve our own problems.

Otherwise our national flags will be no more than

pieces of cloth fluttering under the tropical sun symbolising nothing.

Chapter Eight:

War as a Means to an End

BOTH SIDES to the Rwandan conflict in the post-genocide era chose war, instead of dialogue, as a policy to achieve their long-term objectives.

The Tutsi-dominated regime wanted to impose peace and stability on Rwanda and maintain national unity by force, using ferocious internal repression to control and intimidate the Hutu majority into submission.

Hutu rebels also believed that only force would enable the Hutu majority to win their rights in a country dominated by the Tutsi minority.

And, tragically, the position taken by both sides has been vindicated by history in different parts of the world, although without achieving lasting peace and stability when some parties to the conflict have been excluded from power or meaningful participation in the political process and government of their country.

War may be the bloodiest means to achieve one's goals. But it is also the most effective one, especially when one side wins a quick victory by inflicting maximum damage on the enemy and minimising loss for the winner.

When looked at in terms of cost-benefit, one can find many cases in history to show the advantages of a quick victory in war. Only a Pyrrhic victory may not be worth the cost.

But war can also be the costliest and least effective means to achieve one's objectives especially when both sides take an uncompromising stand and continue to fight, waging war of attrition. Again, there are cases throughout history in different parts of the world to prove the absurdity of this approach as a sound strategy and policy to achieve national goals or advance a rebels' cause.

Tragically, in the Rwandan context as in several others throughout history, both sides subscribe to this notion, victory without compromise, at a terrible cost to the nation. And history can be invoked to justify this approach in both cases, government versus rebels and vice versa, even in Africa itself during the post-colonial period.

Since 1955, the rebels of southern Sudan have waged war but have failed to win autonomy, let alone independence, from the country's Arab rulers in the north in what is unquestionably Africa's oldest and bloodiest civil war in the post-colonial era. By mid-1999, the war had already cost 3 million lives. Most of the victims were black southerners. And they continued to suffer the heaviest casualties as the war went on. Their misery was compounded by another tragedy: outright enslavement of black Africans by the Arabs throughout the war and even before then.

In Nigeria, full-scale war by the federal government effectively ended Biafra's secession after two-and-a-half years of bitter conflict and mass starvation from 1967 – 1970. It was the bloodiest conflict in modern African history up to that time. Up to 2 million people, mostly Igbos of the secessionist region of Eastern Nigeria, died during the war, mostly from starvation. And 30 years after the war, Igbos still face discrimination despite earlier and successful – though short-lived – attempts to re-integrate them into the Nigerian society soon after the war ended. As Chinua Achebe, an Igbo and author of the classic novel *Things Fall Apart* who is also probably Africa's best known writer, stated in an interview with *The Christian Science Monitor*:

"There are three major ethnic groups in Nigeria. The Hausa, the Yoruba, and the Ibo. But the Ibo have been forgotten....

There is great sadness. This is a country that has ceased to work....Even arriving at the airport in Lagos is depressing. You suddenly felt that something was wrong. There was a lack of smoothness in the runaway....

Regulations say there should always be a wheelchair on board (Achebe was left paralysed from the waist down in a car accident on the Lagos-Ibadan expressway, Nigeria, on 22 March1990). First, you wonder why this airline would disregard the rule on this flight. Then you realize – it is because they are going to Nigeria....

I would like to go back to my village. I would like to go back and retire."[1]

Such pessimism coming from one of Africa's most renowned writers who has won international acclaim, is depressing, although it is a blunt appraisal from his perspective of what Nigeria, the continent's giant and black Africa's best hope, has failed to be. His contention that his kinsmen, the Igbo, are victims of discrimination is not a lone voice in the wilderness; nor does it come only from the Igbo. It is an assessment shared by other people including Ghanaian economics professor, George Ayittey, who states in his book *Africa in Chaos*:

"In Nigeria, this insidious tribalism has retrogressively evolved into what Nigerian columnist Igonikon Jack called a 'full-blown tribal-apartheid,' in which people of a particular tribal, regional, or religious origin enjoy more privileges than their fellow indigenous compatriots, the Christian Ibos of the Southeast. The Ibos, who lost the Biafran War, are the most disadvantaged and discriminated against."[2]

Although Nigeria won the war against the Igbo secessionists, it came perilously close to falling apart because of tribalism. And secessionist sentiments even today in the Niger Delta and among some Yoruba groups and others elsewhere across the country may plunge Nigeria into chaos, unless the federal government fully implements the principal of dual sovereignty – federal and state – through extensive devolution of power to the states and local communities, while retaining enough power at the centre to maintain the territorial integrity of the federation as a single supra-national entity.

War saved Nigeria during the sixties. But not all African countries have prevailed against rebel forces by sheer might.

In Mozambique, the government failed to crush the rebels of the Mozambique National Resistance, known by its Portuguese acronym as RENAMO, after 16 years of civil war which cost one million lives. The conflict ended only after the two sides signed a peace agreement in 1992. The agreement worked because, right from the beginning, both sides were determined to uphold it. And both sides knew neither could win the war and achieve its objectives only by military force.

In Angola, after 25 years of civil war since 1975, the government was still fighting the rebels of UNITA (Union for the Total Independence of Angola), although the insurgents were on the verge of defeat at the end of 1999, the first time in a quarter of a century they had been pushed to the brink of destruction. They continued to fight as the year 2000 came in, in a war that had also spilled into neighbouring Namibia, but with little prospect of sustaining the insurgency as they had done in the past. The war ended after UNITA leader, Jonas Savimbi, was shot and killed by government troops on 22 February 2002.

By contrast, in Sierra Leone, the rebels of the Revolutionary United Front (RUF) shot their way into office when they forced an elected government to share power with them after leaving a trail of blood, body parts including chopped limbs, and tens of thousands dead during an eight-year civil war, one of the most brutal, and most gruesome, in modern history.

Rwanda may be headed in the same direction, although it is now locked in a protracted conflict with no clear winner emerging any time soon. Neither side is willing to compromise to avert a national catastrophe which may lead to another genocide reminiscent of the 1994 holocaust.

There are other parts of Africa where rebels have won war against governments or have come close to victory during the post-colonial period.

In 1991, rival factions in Somalia overthrew a tyrannical regime, plunging the country into anarchy in a violent power struggle that turned Somalia into a wasteland. Somalia still had no government and was the only stateless state in the world at the dawn of the 21st century.

In neighbouring Ethiopia, insurgents overthrew another brutal dictatorship in the same year (1991), only to be replaced by another repressive though less brutal regime, at least in the beginning.

And earlier in 1990, rebel factions in Liberia ignited a civil war – it was actually started by Charles Taylor on

Christmas Eve, 1989, when his rebel group invaded the country from the Ivory Coast – which consumed the government. President Samuel Doe was captured and executed by one of the rebel factions – led by Prince Yormie Johnson – in September 1990.

The war went on for seven years. That was the first Liberian civil war which ended in 1996. It devastated the country, leaving it virtually stateless. The second Liberian civil war started in 1999 and ended in 2003 with the forced resignation of President Charles Taylor who went into exile in Nigeria.

One rebel uprising which had ripple effects in its region was the insurgency in Uganda during the 1980s. In 1986, the rebels of the National Resistance Movement overthrew the Ugandan government and installed rebel leader Yoweri Museveni as president. From 1990 – 1994, Museveni backed the Rwandan Patriotic Front (RPF) which overthrew the genocidal Hutu regime in Kigali that orchestrated the massacre campaign against the Tutsi and their Hutu sympathisers. And together with the Rwandan Tutsi rulers, Museveni also sponsored the uprising in Zaire which overthrew President Mobutu Sese Seko, a highly notorious tyrant, in 1997.

And in the island nation of the Comoros in the Indian Ocean, the national army failed to suppress the secessionist insurgency on Anjouan Island which declared independence in 1997. The secessionist impulse also propelled the island of Moheli, the smallest in the federation, in the same direction. The two islands declared independence as one state. Although no country recognised them as a sovereign entity, they remained defiant, and Comoros' government remained helpless, unable to reclaim them.

Probably the best approach towards resolving this conflict would be for the Comoro federal government to concede their *de facto* independence as a *fait accompli*, and then try to form a confederation with them. It could also be the best option for Rwanda – short of total independence for its provinces – if the country were to be restructured in order to establish autonomous ethnic enclaves or entities to guarantee safety for the Tutsi minority and maximum self-rule for the disgruntled Hutu majority.

But even after the 1994 tragedy, an exercise in ethnic cleansing unparalleled in recorded African history, the Rwandan Tutsi-dominated government did little to allay fears of the Hutu majority as an oppressed group. It continued to pursue a scorched-earth policy against the rebels instead of trying to resolve the conflict through extensive devolution of power to the regions – Hutu strongholds in the west and northwest such as Gisenyi and Ruhengeri; a concession to the Hutu majority that could have robbed the insurgents of support from the civilian population, without which they would not be able to sustain a military campaign against the state.

The mass trials of those accused of genocide also drove the two ethnic groups even farther apart because of the perceived injustice in these hasty proceedings. Many Hutus, probably the majority, did not believe in the fairness of the trials.

By November 1997, about 120,000 Hutus had been arrested since 1994 on genocide charges. Since January 1997, the Rwandan courts had tried more than 200 people before the end of the year.

About 40 per cent of them were sentenced to death. At least 30 per cent were given life imprisonment, and about 1 in 20 defendants was acquitted.[3] And there was no guarantee that any of them got a fair trial in this deeply divided nation:

"The Government's relative success in...bringing cases to trial has not eased the legal crisis here, nor has it brought about reconciliation between the two ethnic groups, aid workers, lawyers and diplomats say.

With ethnic war raging in this hilly nation's western provinces, the police and the Tutsi-dominated military continue to arrest more than 1,000 Hutu a month on various genocide charges, shoving them into already teeming prisons, where most await hearings without formal charges lodged against them.

At the present rate of trials, it would take 500 years to try all the defendants."[4]

Rwandan officials hoped that they would speed up the trials after they passed a law in 1996 offering people who participated in the genocide but who were not ringleaders shorter prison terms if they confessed and apologised for their crimes. But only 45 people – out of more than 120,000 who had been arrested – had confessed by October 1997. Some of them remained tight-lipped because they hoped that their kinsmen would storm the jails and free them during guerrilla raids as they had done before.

But there were other and even more compelling reasons why Hutu prisoners refused to cooperate with the government. Most of them did not even recognise it as legitimate. It was Tutsi-dominated. It was oppressive. And they did not vote for it.

Many Hutu prisoners also argued that no genocide took place in Rwanda in 1994 but instead described the massacres as no more than a part of the civil war between the Hutu and the Tutsi. They flatly denied that the pogroms were a deliberate attempt to exterminate the Tutsi. As one worker with an international relief agency described the difference in perception:

"You have a war on. So the concept that justice could bring about national reconciliation is invalid. I'm not sure that most Hutu agree that a judgment meted out today wouldn't be motivated by revenge."[5]

Most Hutus languishing in prison said they were framed or falsely accused. Nonetheless, Deputy Justice Minister Gérard Gahima seemed to be more interested in extracting confessions through plea bargaining than he was in dispensing justice:

"We intended to deal with most of these cases through the confession program. It has not picked up and in the ministry (of justice), we are still trying to see how we can jump-start it."[6]

One of the main reasons the government was unable to get confessions from a significant number of Hutu prisoners, let alone from the majority of them, had to do with ethnic solidarity.

Among the prisoners were many politicians, military officers and other members of the Hutu elite who had planned and led the massacres. They were among the hundreds of thousands of Hutu refugees who returned to Rwanda from Zaire and Tanzania, hoping to evade detection by the authorities in such a huge wave of migration. These are the people who faced the death penalty, and they discouraged their kinsmen facing less severe charges from bargaining with the prosecutors for shorter sentences. And it was not hard to convince them not to do so, given the strong ethnic bond between them as Hutus who felt that they were being victimised by the Tutsi minority. As Gahima conceded:

"The intelligentsia with whom the idea of genocide started are there in prison and they guide the mood of the prisoners."[7]

The case of Clavier Nkulikiyinka, a 46-year-old veterinarian from the town of Byumba in northern Rwanda was typical of the rest among the Hutu elite locked up in the Gokondo prison in Kigali, a former warehouse.

Nkulikiyinka was arrested in June 1996, accused of leading a group of militia members who massacred people in the capital Kigali. He faced the death penalty and, like many of the 7,000 Hutus locked up in the warehouse prison, he maintained that he hid in a house during the massacres and did not take part in the genocide.

After five appearances in court, he said he had no faith in the judicial system under the Tutsi. They had already determined he was guilty even before the trial was over; his Hutu lawyer was arrested on genocide charges; and he did not know who the prosecution's witnesses were or how he would defend himself. He went on to say: "I don't think it's going to be a fair trial. There are some people who died on my street, and they say I participated in these killings. I never did."[8]

It was a standard denial, hard to prove either way in many cases in this highly-charged atmosphere, made even worse by Rwanda's toxic politics of ethnicity.

And defence counsel was out of the question in most cases. There were only 44 trained lawyers in the whole country after the genocide, and most of them refused to represent the accused. By the end of 1997, there were only five foreign lawyers working for an international aid organisation, Lawyers Without Borders. They represented more than 70 defendants. But they were stretched thin and, because of the on-going civil war, could not go to all the courthouses in the rural areas where they would be exposed to violence. As Marielle Hallez said on behalf of Lawyers Without Borders: "It's not possible to defend them all. That's clear."[9] To which Gahima retorted: "Can you say that we should not punish genocide just because our country doesn't have enough lawyers?"[10]

Yet few people, including Gahima himself as well as his colleagues in the Tutsi-dominated government, would like to be tried in a court where they could not be guaranteed a fair trial even if they knew they were guilty of the crimes they were accused of committing. The fact that many of the Hutus – if not the majority – who were in prison awaiting trial were probably guilty, did not justify arbitrary dispensation of justice in these proceedings by the Rwandan authorities.

Such injustice only intensified hostility between the two groups in a country that was already embroiled in conflict which caused immense suffering across the land. Some of the biggest victims of the war were children, many of whom ended up as orphans, a tragedy that cut across ethnic lines. As Jurate Kazickas, a member of the Women's Commission for Refugee Women and Children who visited the embattled East-Central African Great Lakes region, wrote in *The Christian Science Monitor*:

"While the international community continues to commit vast amounts of aid to Bosnia (and later to Kosovo as well), there are many more orphaned, homeless children in Rwanda, Congo, and Burundi....

In Gisenyi (Rwanda), my group saw dozens of lost and orphaned children who had returned from the refugee camps near Goma (Zaire), being shuttled from one center to another to escape periodic shellings. The supervisor said he had no emergency plan to evacuate them if the situation worsened. The genocide of 1994...left an estimated 400,000 children separated from their parents....

Many of these children watched as their parents were slaughtered by immediate neighbors. UNICEF says two-thirds of the children have seen someone killed, and 80 percent have lost at least one family member.

In one center in Giterama (Rwanda), I saw dozens of infants, lying wide-eyed and listless on plastic sheeting in stifling, airless rooms. Nearly 300 more wandered in a dusty courtyard, waiting for the most meager dinner of potatoes and rice."[11]

The lack of response to their plight by the international community, especially the rich Western countries including the United States which have benefited enormously from cheap African labour and the continent's abundant natural resources they have mercilessly exploited through the years and even for centuries in some cases, can not wholly or even largely be attributed to donor fatigue. Had such catastrophe hit Europe, the United States would not have ignored it, let alone invoked donor fatigue, but would instead have rushed to help the victims as the Americans did after World War II when they helped Germany rebuild under the Marshall Plan; nor would Europeans have ignored Americans, let alone fellow Europeans, seeking help in the midst of disaster.

The unwillingness by the world's richest countries to help African victims of war is no different from their neglect of the millions of AIDS victims on this forgotten continent. "They are nothing to us," is the Western response. And that is racism, a fact conceded even by some American officials. According to *U.S. News and World Report*:

"It's one of the dirtiest whispers of all: racism. But U.S. officials are conceding that attention to the widespread AIDS epidemic in Africa has been uninspired because, well, it's largely black. 'We'd be naïve to say race doesn't play a part,' Clinton AIDS czar Sandra Thurman tells us. 'Our response has been slow.'"[12]

During the 1994 genocide, there was none, for the same reason. And Africa should not expect much help in trying to solve her problems, the Rwandan conflict being one among several.

Tragically, the combatants themselves have done little to resolve the conflict which could end up destroying Rwanda as a nation.

What continues to fuel the war is the determination by the Tutsi to perpetuate themselves in power; the relentless struggle by Hutu militants to oust the Tutsi from power –

348

even expel them from the country if possible; and vengeance, especially by the Tutsi, for the 1994 genocide which led to another genocide, this time against the Hutu, in neighbouring Congo then known as Zaire:

"The Rwandans (who backed Laurent Kabila and helped him overthrow Mobutu Sese Seko) were also fighting a war of revenge, one deeply intertwined with ethnic conflicts between Hutu and Tutsi groups that have tormented this region. The Tutsi troops from Rwanda and Congo who made up the core of Mr. Kabila's army had a powerful motive for vengeance, since thousands of Hutu refugees in the camps had taken part in the slaughter of more than half a million Tutsi in Rwanda in 1994....

Congo's human rights groups and Catholic missionaries say they have received numerous accounts of massacres across the breadth of Congo....Hutu refugees and Congolese villagers assert that rebel groups hunted down and killed thousands of unarmed people....

The roots of Congo's civil war lie in the 1994 genocide in Rwanda....The (Congolese Rwandan-backed) rebels attacked the Hutu's (refugee) tent cities again and again, driving them deeper into the rain forest in Congo's interior where the refugees, relief groups and local Congolese say, were hunted down and hundreds died of disease or drowned trying to cross rivers as they fled.

For the majority of refugees who were not Hutu guerrillas, the long flight through the jungle was a trail of tears....'We will never go back to Rwanda; the Tutsi are trying to kill us, and will certainly get rid of us there,' said Marie-Claire Muanyogoga, 13, at Tingi Tingi (in north-central Congo) in February (1997), when she and her sister, Sophie, 12, had become separated from their parents....

Hundreds drowned trying to cross the broad, powerful (Congo) river, infested with crocodiles (as they fled the rebels who attacked their refugee camps deep inside

Congo)....

One high-ranking United Nations refugee official said: 'We do have clear facts. It's clear that there have been killings with impunity by alliance troops.'"[13]

Just as the 1994 genocide triggered a retaliatory response against the Hutu refugees in Congo by the Rwandan Tutsis and their Congolese clients whom they had sponsored to oust Mobutu Sese Seko from power and with whom they collectively constituted the alliance troops, the massacre of the Hutu in Congo helped fuel the conflict in Rwanda where Hutu rebels indiscriminately killed Tutsis – and selectively targeted Hutus who did not support their cause or give them food or shelter – and continued to wage war in an attempt to overthrow the government.

But even without the massacres in Congo, the Hutu insurgents would still have declared war on the Tutsi-dominated government in Rwanda. And the Tutsi regime itself launched a prolonged military campaign against Hutu civilians within Rwanda, as it did against Hutu refugees in Congo, in retaliation for the 1994 genocide.

It was a vicious cycle of violence that fed on itself, and both parties to the conflict were guilty of genocide and other acts of wanton violence throughout the late 1990s. And they continued to kill as the ethnic violence continued into the 21st century. But the nineties were the most violence years. More Tutsis were killed in Rwanda in 1994, but the death toll among the Hutu refugees in Congo at the hands of the Rwandan Tutsis and their Congolese allies – especially Congolese Tutsis – in retaliation for the genocide, was equally appalling:

"Something horrible happened to Rwandan refugees in Congo's forests....A UN team arrived in Kinshasa (Congo's capital) in a renewed attempt to investigate the disappearance of about 200,000 Rwandan refugees, thought to have been killed earlier this year (1997)....

A report by Human Rights Watch...alleges that aid agencies and their food supplies were used as bait by the (Tutsi) Rwandan army and the (Congolese) Tutsi rebels to bring the refugees out of the bush. They were then murdered."[14]

As the ethnic conflict in Rwanda continued three years after the 1994 genocide, Hutu rebels tried to free hundreds of their kinsmen from jail in one of the most daring raids against a government facility.

About 1,500 rebels stormed a jail in northwestern Rwanda in a coordinated attack which began on 17 November 1997 near the border with Congo. Most of the inmates were awaiting trial for genocide. Almost 300 people died in the ambush.[15]

But the rebels failed to free their fellow tribesmen. As Claude Dusaidi, a government official and close aide to Rwanda's *de facto* ruler Major-General Paul Kagame, said about the insurgents and their deadly raid on the jail: "These so-called rebels are the same people who committed atrocities in 1994. Three years later, they are still trying to finish off what they started."[16]

The implication was obvious. The rebels were trying to accomplish their mission of exterminating the Tutsi, although that may have been an overstatement by Claude Dusaidi, considering the logistical problems Hutu rebels faced now that the country was under Tutsi control. But there is no question that if they had the means and the opportunity to achieve their goal, they definitely would have wiped out the Tutsi.

The Hutu rebellion intensified at a time when the Tutsi-dominated government was trying to resettle hundreds of thousands of Hutu refugees who returned in 1996, fleeing civil war in what was then known as Zaire. The rest returned from the Tanzania the same year.

But genuine reintegration of the refugees was more

apparent than real in a country where the Tutsi rulers adopted a policy which they described as "control at all cost" over the vast Hutu majority. It was an apt description of the policy by the Tutsi elite which alienated even Hutu moderates.

Control of the Hutu majority by the dominant Tutsi minority was intended to perpetuate Tutsi domination. But it also fuelled the insurgency against the government and Tutsi civilians across the country. The mistreatment of the Hutu returnees also inflamed passions among them and their kinsmen. Most of them were confined to the hills to "practice basic peasant agriculture."[17]

They included educated Hutus. Most of them could not get the jobs for which they were qualified because of discrimination by the Tutsi-dominated government. The result was virtual monopoly of the economy by the Tutsi elite. As Gérard Prunier stated in a November 1997 report about the uncompromising positions of the two ethnic groups which the Tutsi used to justify discrimination against the Hutu:

"For the Tutsi, it is: 'Unless we maintain absolute control, they will finish us the next time.'

And for the Hutu: 'We only have to wait, numbers will play in our favor and the so-called international community will neither want nor be able to stop us.'"[18]

Few would disagree with this assessment, given the tense if not outright hostile relationship between the two groups, especially after the 1994 extermination of almost the entire Tutsi population in Rwanda by the Hutu and the massacre of more than 200,000 Hutu refugees in Zaire by the Tutsi. And the continuing civil war only made things worse. As one Western observer in Rwanda put it:

"The worst thing that could have happened in the world happened in Rwanda. The country has a long way to

352

go....At the same time, Rwandans know that they are all together on a small boat, and it's leaking."[19]

And what some saw as attempts to repair the boat or keep it afloat were interpreted by others as attempts to sink it. The genocide trials were among these "noble" or "sinister" attempts, depending on how one looks at the situation.

Even among the Tutsi, there were those who dismissed the trials – especially the international war crimes tribal conducting proceedings in Tanzania – as a circus and no more than a slap on the wrist for the Hutu accused of genocide, except the cases which ended in death sentences.

The Hutu saw the trials as a witch hunt.

One of the biggest defendants being tried by the International Criminal Tribunal for Rwanda (ICTR) in Arusha, Tanzania, was Jean-Paul Akayesu, the former mayor of the Rwandan commune of Taba. His trial started in January 1997 and he was the first defendant to go before the court.

By the end of the year, his trial had not yet ended. At that rate, it would take more than 20 years just to try the 35 people who had been indicted for war crimes by the international court.

Three years after the genocide, the court had not yet convicted a single defendant. And most of those who had been indicted had not yet been arrested. They were hiding in other countries.

The suspects in Arusha included some of the most prominent officials in the former Hutu-dominated government which was ousted in 1994. Prime Minister Jean Kambanda, and Deputy Defence Minister Theoneste Bagosora were the highest-ranking officials facing trial.

The slow pace of the proceedings drew strong criticism from the Tutsi regime in Rwanda and other governments around the world. Many diplomats said for reconciliation

353

to take place, justice must be administered quickly.

The Arusha trials were also being watched by some people who wanted to see a permanent international court for genocides established. As Agwu Okali, the registrar of the International Criminal Court in Arusha, said: "This is the first time the international community has really geared up with determination that it is no longer going to allow these kinds of crimes."[20] And in the words of the chief judge of the tribunal, Laity Kama of Senegal, who also explained the importance of the proceedings: "The entire world will be looking to our decisions."[21] And that included the ability to arrest those who had been indicted by the court.

In July 1997, investigators raided several homes in Kenya and arrested seven prominent suspects including former Prime Minister Kambanda and two high-ranking military officers. And in October the same year, responding to criticism from several feminists and human rights groups, Bernard Muna, the deputy prosecutor for the international war crimes tribunal, submitted a new indictment in Akayesu's case, charging him for the first time with ordering the rape and sexual mutilation of Tutsi women.

Others on trial included Clement Kayishema and Obed Ruzindana, two officials from the town of Kibuye. They were charged with leading and participating in the massacre of thousands of Tutsis. And the trial of of George Anderson Rutaganda, a prominent Hutu businessman who operated a hate – anti-Tutsi – radio and who was a high-ranking official in the Hutu militia, began on 18 March 1997.[22] The "racist" broadcasts played a critical role in inciting the Hutu masses to violence against the Tutsi.

As the trials went on, Hutu rebels also continued to wage war against the Tutsi-dominated regime. On 3 December 1997, they attacked a prison in Bulinga, 30 miles northwest of the capital Kigali and freed 507 jailed compatriots. It was the second jail raid in two days. On

December 2nd, about 400 rebels freed 103 prisoners at Rwerere prison near the border with Congo.

The raid on December 3rd was the boldest attack since 2 million Hutu refugees returned to Rwanda from Zaire, Tanzania, and Burundi. Rwandan officials said since the return of the exiles, barely a week passed without a rebel attack on a prison or a road ambush in what appeared to be a new military strategy by the insurgents in their campaign against the government.[23]

But the government itself was partly responsible for the escalation of the violence and human rights abuses. The United Nations High Commissioner for Human Rights, Mary Robinson who was also the former president of Ireland, visited Rwanda in December 1997 and criticised the government for its abuses. She said after a fact-finding mission that she left Rwanda disappointed with Rwandan leaders because of their abuse of human rights and unwillingness to pursue national reconciliation.

She acknowledged an upsurge in violence by the rebels. But she also said she had noticed an increase in abuses by the Rwandan Patriotic Army (RPA):

"Political power and decision-making have become more and more concentrated....There appears to be an absence of a committed policy of reconciliation and there are a number f very serious human rights violations."[24]

The abuses she cited included arbitrary arrests, prolonged detentions and serious overcrowding resulting in inhumane conditions in the prisons.

Rwandan officials said Robinson's criticism of the government was "unfair," but a diplomat in the Rwandan capital welcomed the statement because it drew attention to serious problems which required a response from the international community. Yet, like just before and during the 1994 genocide, the international response to Rwanda's plight was muted at best. As the American Secretary of

State Madaleine Albright said about the genocide in a speech to the Organisation of African Unity (OAU) in Addis Ababa, Ethiopia, during her trip to Africa in December 1997:

"We, the international community, should have been more active in the early stages of the atrocities in Rwanda in 1994 and called them what they were: genocide."[25]

Massacres at a Refugee Camp: Ethnocide as Policy

Just as the 1994 genocide was a means to an end, the ethnic violence which continued after the holocaust was also a means to achieve several objectives, including demoralisation of the government and its army by the rebels who intensified their attacks on jails and other targets.

During the night of 10 – 11 December 1997 beginning at 11 P.M., Hutu guerrillas ambushed a Tutsi refugee camp with grenades, guns and machetes in one of the bloodiest attacks since the genocide. Early reports said at least 231 people were killed and more than 200 wounded, according to United Nations officials and aid workers in Rwanda.[26] UN spokeswoman Paula Ghadini said the rebels raided about 100 tents in the camp at Mudende in northwestern Rwanda which had about 17,000 refugees from the Masisi area in neighbouring Congo.[27]

Before the raid, Rwandan Tutsi soldiers had recently massacred Hutu civilians ostensibly to contain and possibly neutralise the insurgency.

The attack on the Tutsi refugees at Mudende, 15 miles north of the town of Gisenyi on the border with Congo in the northwestern region (also called Gisenyi and a Hutu stronghold), underscored the fragility of the peace and reconciliation process in the country. It also clearly showed that the Tutsi-dominated Rwandan Patriotic Army (RPA) faced a formidable task of trying to bring stability to the embattled region.

Northwestern Rwanda had the most intensive guerrilla activity in the whole country which, if unchecked, threatened to engulf the entire nation. Yet the government itself fuelled the conflict:

"The army has massacred (Hutu) civilians in their attempts to defeat the Hutu guerrillas....(And) in recent weeks, the guerrillas have not only killed hundreds of Tutsi civilians but have also begun distributing racist propaganda and broadcasting radio messages like the ones that fueled the mass killings three years ago.

In the attack before dawn today (11 December 1997), the guerrillas raided the camp at Mudende, sending 17,000 inhabitants fleeing into the hills and leaving the ground covered with bodies, United Nations refugee officials said. It was the second time the camp had been attacked. In August, 148 people were killed during a similar assault attributed to the Hutu rebels....

As Hutu militants have drifted home among the refugees, many have taken up arms again. Since May (1997), when Mr. Kabila took power in Congo, the Hutu guerrillas here have stepped up their attacks, killing Tutsi civilians, ambushing cars and attacking prisons to free jailed Hutu. In response, the Tutsi army has also committed atrocities, killing...Hutu civilians, diplomats and human-rights groups say."[28]

The attack on the Mudende refugee camp took place only hours after the rebels raided a jail holding their kinsmen for genocide. According to a report from Gisenyi, Rwanda, in *The Boston Globe*:

"The rebels set fire to 200 huts and attacked the refugees with machetes, hand grenades and guns. In addition to those killed, at least 227 refugees were wounded, most with severe head wounds caused by machetes and nail-studded clubs....

Hutu rebels...slaughtered at least 234 Tutsi refugees, a military spokesman said."[29]

But that was not the final death toll.

The head of the northwest military region, Colonel Nyamwasa Kayumba (who later fell out with Kagame and sought asylum in South Africa), said Hutu rebels also raided a jail at Mutura on December 11th and an unknown number of Hutus – rebels and jail inmates – were killed during the ambush. It was the third attack on the jail in the month of December alone.

However, Colonel Kayumba conceded that the massacre at the Mudende refugee camp, which was within shouting distance of the jail, took his small garrison by surprise.[30]

It was these ambushes, in addition to intensified guerrilla activity in general, which sent shock waves throughout the entire Tutsi community and even had the government worried about the escalation of the conflict. The Tutsi-dominated regime was virtually besieged in the escalating conflict which continued to defy a military solution.

Yet perhaps out of desperation because of its inability to defeat the rebels, but probably mainly as part of a deliberate campaign of ethnocide, the Tutsi-dominated government committed some of the worst murders in the post-genocide period which amounted to another genocide. But the rest of the world knew nothing about it. Tragic and vicious as the rebel insurgency was, it paled into insignificance when compared to what the Tutsi army did to the Hutu in Gisenyi Province with the full support of Rwanda's Tutsi rulers who were united with their brethren in the military by indispensable bonds of ethnic solidarity in a country where nothing else matters.

According to a report from Gisenyi by *The Economist*:

"There was a stench at the mouth of the cave and human remains were just visible in the rubble. People had certainly died here at the Nyakimana caves, 16 kilometres – ten miles – east of Gisenyi....

Last month (November 1997), a Brussels-based opposition group accused the Rwandan army of killing more than 8,000 civilians sheltering in these caves in late October....

The caves, according to the government, had been used by Rwandan Hutu militiamen in their war against the regime. A military spokesman, Major Richard Sezibera, said the army had sealed all the entrances to the caves except one, but had no idea how many people had been inside. Some of the dead, he believed, might have drowned; some could have starved to death when the caves were sealed off. Others might have been militiamen killed at the cave entrance.

The report from Brussels accused the army of shelling the caves, killing thousands of locals who had taken refuge. Some shelling could certainly have taken place, as the roof had fallen in, blocking one entrance. Nearby houses had been abandoned and there was an eerie emptiness in the normally densely populated countryside.

Accusations of mass killings by the Rwandan army, and of other indefensible behaviour by the authorities, are growing loud. They reached a crescendo last weekend when Mary Robinson, the UN's new high commissioner for human rights, launched a stinging attack on the government.

At the end of her three-day visit, she called the situation 'bleak,' citing arbitrary arrests, prolonged detentions and inhumane prison conditions, as well as continued killing by the Rwandan army....Mrs. Robinson (also) criticised the government for making no headway on reconciliation."[31]

The extermination of thousands of Hutus by Tutsi soldiers in the Nyakimana caves was undoubtedly motivated by ethnic hatred, although in pursuit of political objectives. But the massacre of the Tutsi by Hutu insurgents at the Mudende refugee camp – even if in pursuit of political aspirations – was also equally inspired by hate and tribalism and was reminiscent of the 1994 genocide in terms of brutality. The carnage claimed even more lives than the initial count. The final death toll was at least 272, with more than 227 injured. According to a report from Mudende in *The Boston Globe*:

"Most had been beaten with nail-studded clubs or chopped with machetes.

Mothers were rolled up with their children in plastic roof sheeting and set ablaze; a group cowering in a tractor shed were slashed to death, their hands and arms chopped off as they tried to protect themselves."[32]

Some Tutsis and many Hutu rebels were also killed when the insurgents exchanged grenades and gunfire with Tutsi soldiers who tried to fend off the attack. As Colonel Kayumba said about the attack: "This is genocide, pure and simple. They were killed only because they were Tutsi."[33]

Colonel Kayumba said 72 soldiers of the Rwandan Patriotic Army (RPA) were on guard at the refugee camp when it was ambushed. Another 120 soldiers from a nearby garrison rushed to help them in a battle that lasted about 6 hours until 5 A.M.

But some survivors gave a slightly different version of what happened. They said the soldiers who were supposed to be protecting the refugees fled when the rebels attacked the camp, and seem to have fought back only when reinforcements came hours later.

It was a brutal massacre. As one man who lost a son in

the attack described the carnage: "They came while we were sleeping and we had no chance to escape. They just started chopping, chopping, chopping."[34]

One woman was chopped vertically in half. Survivors said they were attacked by 80 to 300 rebels. But the army said more than 1,000 Hutu guerrillas were involved in the ambush.

Most of those killed were women and children. And the number of casualties may have been much higher than what was reported, especially as days went by; many of them succumbing to illness and infections because of the wounds inflicted on them during the raid. International human rights monitors and survivors of the attack said more than 1,000 refugees may have been killed at the camp. All spoke on condition of anonymity.[35]

Most of the remaining 17,000 refugees fled to Nkaramira where they sought refuge. And several of them told the American war crimes envoy David Scheffer, who visited Nkaramira, that at least 1,500 people were killed in the ambush.[36] Few, if any, disputed the death toll. And all those who were interviewed gave graphic accounts of what happened:

"From Gisenyi, Rwanda, one woman gave this account: Screams of agony ripped through the silence in the Mudende camp as darkness fell and hundreds of rebels wielding machetes, guns, and nail-studded clubs set upon the refugees, most of them asleep in tents of plastic.

Rangwida Ugiriwabo watched in horror as her husband and four children were shot to death, then she ran for safety to a nearby bush. But the attackers spotted her feet and began to chop at her with machetes, slashing her heels and lacerating her legs. 'They did not have pity on me. How can I forgive?' Ugiriwabo asked Saturday (13 December 1997) a she lay on a bed in a tent ward at Gisenyi hospital, 60 miles northwest of the Rwandan capital, Kigali."[37]

The Mudende massacre was only one of several incidents in the upsurge of violence by the Hutu rebels in northwestern Rwanda. And the message was clear. They had not given up their campaign, and they would not hesitate to kill innocent civilians to destabilise the country in order to force the Tutsi-dominated regime to capitulate to their demands which amounted to one thing: Power.

That would be the end of Tutsi domination, a concession the government would never make. It would be suicidal, leaving the Tutsi minority at the mercy of the vast Hutu majority. So the war had to go on. But as it went on, it kept on driving the two groups farther and farther apart, claiming more and more lives including the most vulnerable:

"The little girl's head had been split by a machete. A long ragged suture ran from her left eye across her ruined skull. Her breath fluttered shallow and light, and her frail body seemed to cling to the world of the living with no more than a butterfly's strength.

'We found the baby between the bodies of the parents,' the girl's aunt, Esperance Dusabi, said, wiping blood from the child's head in the green light of a hospital tent. 'They killed my younger sister, her husband, their children. This is the only survivor. I don't know how I can describe them. These are people who want to exterminate all mankind.'

The 4-year-old girl, Alice Mukeshimana, was one of 227 wounded people who were brought to the Gisenyi hospital after Hutu guerrillas attacked a Tutsi refugee camp (at Mudende) in northwestern Rwanda three days ago, killing at least 272 people and leaving nothing but burning tents and leaflets preaching genocide in their wake."[38]

The violence escalated in the last six months of 1997 to unprecedented levels since the 1994 holocaust and turned

362

the northwestern province of Gisenyi into a deadly combat zone where no one felt safe. The region was completely militarised. The Hutu guerrilla force grew bigger and bigger as the refugees including perpetrators of the 1994 genocide returned to Rwanda. And the tactics – brutal though they were – which the insurgents employed also had a clear political objective. According to a report from Gisenyi by *The New York Times*:

"In recent months, the guerrillas have stepped up a campaign aimed at making Rwanda ungovernable. They have assassinated local officials, laid ambushes on the roads, massacred scores of Tutsi civilians in their homes and attacked jails, freeing hundreds of Hutu men who were awaiting trial on genocide charges.

They have also begun distributing racist literature and broadcasting hate radio messages from a pirate radio station in the Congo, echoing the propaganda technique that fueled the 1994 genocide."[39]

Such violence, including reprisals by the Tutsi-dominated Rwandan army, made reconciliation impossible. Escalation of the guerrilla campaign also underscored the futility of the government's attempt to pursue a military solution to the conflict.

But the Rwandan government disputed the political nature of the guerrilla campaign, contending that it was no more than a murderous rampage. As Colonel Nyamwasa Kayumba, the military commander of Gisenyi Province, put it: "We are not fighting war here. The people who did this have no political agenda, no economic agenda. It is genocide, pure and simple."[40]

It was not only the second attack on the Mudende refugee camp but also one of the deadliest since the 1994 genocide, and one of the most well-publicised.

The buildings at the camp belonged to a university campus that was destroyed during the 1994 genocide.

Military analysts conceded that the insurgents appeared to be better organised and more brazen than in the past, often moving in groups of 500 to 1,000 and hitting targets in broad daylight. Compounding the problem for the government was the fact that the 40,000-man Rwanda army was stretched thin and its soldiers were tired, according to diplomats in Kigali and other observers. And according to UN human rights monitors, between April and December (1997) alone, the war had claimed more than 6,000 lives,[41] and it continued to escalate.

Another major problem for the army was that the rebels had a lot of support from their kinsmen in the province which is probably the strongest and most fiercely independent Hutu region in the country.

The late President Juvénal Habyarimana came from Gisenyi Province; so did most of the soldiers in the former Hutu-dominated national army.

Most of the militiamen, who together with the soldiers perpetrated the 1994 massacre of the Tutsi and Hutu moderates, also came from Gisenyi Province, a region which in the 1800s was a Hutu kingdom that fiercely resisted conquest by the Tutsi aristocracy based in the southern part of the country. And they were the ones who were waging a ferocious campaign against the Tutsi Rwandan Patriotic Army (RPA) in the province.

In fact, the province has all the attributes of a semi-autonomous or an autonomous entity because of its history, fiercely independent spirit, and a solid Hutu ethnic base which could make it play a very important role in the reconfiguration of Rwanda if the country were to be restructured under a new political system such as confederation in order to achieve lasting peace between the Hutu and the Tutsi. It also probably constitutes the nucleus of the Hutu "nation" and could exercise enormous leverage in negotiations with the Tutsi if the two ethnic groups were to agree to separate, although that is an unlikely prospect.

The Hutu from this region of Gisenyi constituted the bulk of the guerrilla force and had many relatives and friends in the villages and communes throughout the province. As Epimaque Ndagijimana, the governor of Gisenyi Province, conceded:

"We have to bear in mind that this region was primarily occupied by the former militiamen and army. The most crucial thing about this crisis is that the attackers are always related to the local people. They are their cousins, brothers, uncles."[42]

And their hatred was unmistakable, motivated by tribalism and racism as much as by anything else including ethnic solidarity; an enduring phenomenon deeply rooted in the nation's history and which therefore can not be explained exclusively in a political context as no more than a struggle for power by the Hutu elite in contemporary times.

It is true that the Hutu elite orchestrated the 1994 massacre of the Tutsi in their quest for Hutu supremacy, and that this quest is therefore of relatively recent origin especially since October 1990 when Ugandan-based Tutsis started invading Rwanda, thus threatening Hutu hegemonic control of the country. But tribalism, or racism, or intense ethnic loyalty is nothing new in the history of Rwanda or of any other African country. It is also worth remembering that although it is true that violence of this magnitude is unprecedented in the country's history, the very nature of the asymmetrical relationship between the Hutu and the Tutsi had a tribalistic – or racist – component which even the Tutsi aristocracy itself invoked to justify its supremacy.

The fact that the Hutu did not rise up against their Tutsi masters before – until the mass uprising of November 1959 as independence approached – did not make the system then any less abhorrent or any less tribalistic or racist.

Rwandan politics even during the precolonial era of Tutsi hegemony has always been driven by tribalism (or racism). Therefore the post-genocide guerrilla campaign by the Hutu, although infused with a potent political message as a struggle for the rights of the powerless Hutu majority, was also prosecuted in a context that was no less tribalistic or racist than the past one was. And it was articulated in stark terms, as the attack on the Tutsi refugee camp at Mudende tragically demonstrated:

"Some of the attackers yelled racist slurs as they descended on fleeing refugees with guns, clubs, hoes and machetes. Some women were rolled in plastic sheeting and burned to death, survivors said. Others were dismembered by machete blows.

'They started firing at us while they shouted,' James Nzabanita, a 43-year-old farmer, said. 'Wherever we tried to escape, we found they had already blocked the way. They shouted: 'Kill the cockroaches! Kill the cockroaches!"[43]

The Tutsi, vilified as *Inyenzi*, which means "cockroaches" in the Kinyarwanda language, had become the target of a brutal campaign that was no different in intent from the 1994 genocidal rampage.

The conflict rekindled fears that Rwanda would be faced with the same kind of violence that had engulfed neighbouring Burundi since October 1993 when the assassination of President Melchior Ndadaye (a Hutu) by Tutsi soldiers triggered a full-scale civil war between the Hutu and the Tutsi. And there were indications that the country could indeed degenerate into chaos as the violence continued to spread.

The Hutu guerrillas who attacked the Tutsi refugee camp at Mudende, which was only five miles from the Rwandan-Congolese border, fled back to eastern Congo just across the border where they were based. But as they fled, they spread terror in the region.

Their compatriots also attacked the southwestern town of Cyangugu when they crossed into Rwanda from Bukavu, a Congolese city located near the border between the two countries. As Simon Munzu, the acting chief of mission for the UN Human Rights Field Operation in Rwanda, described the situation in the country: "It's becoming a more tense situation when you think of the number of attacks reported in the [northwest.]" He also underscored the brazen nature of the raids, saying before the guerrillas stepped up the attacks, they were content with ambushing a government official in his house or a farmer in his field. But they were now hitting bigger and more visible targets, frequently raiding prisons, "which are usually well-guarded, and those choices are quite significant."[44]

It is obvious the attacks had a profound psychological impact on the government. Tragically, both were fighting a war of attrition, with neither side winning the conflict.

Many diplomats and other observers were surprised that the Rwandan Tutsi army, one of the best in Africa, had failed to defeat the rebels. But like in any other guerrilla campaign, conventional tactics and weapons used by regular armies don't work very well against elusive enemies who easily hide in the general population and look like ordinary civilians, a problem acknowledged by the Rwandan authorities.

The war was not being fought in the conventional theatre. As Patrick Mazimhaka, the minister of state in the president's office, said:

"[The problem is that the rebels] are operating within a population....They're using family homes. They put on civilian clothes in the day; they go from village to village at night....It's like the Vietnam War."[45]

And their determination to wage war was clearly demonstrated even months before, in July the same year (1997), when thousands of Hutu rebels tried to capture Gisenyi, the capital of the northwestern province, but were repulsed within hours. As they became more organised, they started to coordinate their attacks which became increasingly successful, although not decisive. For example, the December attacks on Mudende in the northwestern province and on Cyangugu in the southwestern part of the country occurred within 24 hours of each other, showing that they were well-coordinated.

Although the guerrillas did not have the means to defeat the Rwandan army, their prolonged military campaign – even if haphazard in many cases – had the potential to drain the country of energy and resources, making it impossible for Rwanda to rebuild its infrastructure and rejuvenate the economy. The war also thwarted whatever efforts – lukewarm at best – the Tutsi-dominated regime was trying to make to achieve reconciliation between the two ethnic groups. As one diplomat in Kigali bluntly put it:

"Everything that means political progress is paralyzed because of insecurity. That's the cornerstone. As long as they don't have the situation controlled in the north, there is no way they can achieve anything else."[46]

The insurgency in northwestern Rwanda and violence in other parts of the country was a continuation of the civil war that started in October 1990 when the predominantly Tutsi Rwandan Patriotic Army (RPA) – the military wing of the Rwandan Patriotic Front (RPF) – invaded Rwanda for the first time from its bases in Uganda in an attempt to overthrow the Hutu-dominated regime in Kigali. It was this invasion and subsequent incursions into Rwanda by the RPA forces – especially the 1991 military campaign that brought them to the verge of victory and compelled the Hutu regime to agree to power sharing – which alarmed the Hutu to the danger of a Tutsi takeover of the country.

The Hutu elite exploited this fear of the Tutsi's return to power and whipped up virulently anti-Tutsi sentiments to a frenzy among the Hutu majority which eventually led to the 1994 genocide, a holocaust that was also "justified" by the Hutu as a concerted effort to stop the Tutsi from re-establishing domination over them.

Therefore when the Hutu lost power to the Tutsi in 1994, they felt vindicated in their fear of the Tutsi's reconquest of the country and in their earlier attempts to resist such usurpation of power – "We told you so! The Tutsi are coming back to dominate us and oppress us again" – and even tried to justify the 1994 genocide in that context. It is the same rationale Hutu guerrillas used to justify their campaign of terror after the holocaust as a continuation of the same war, against the same enemy, which the Tutsi themselves started when they first invaded Rwanda from Uganda in 1990 in order to overthrow a Hutu government in a predominantly Hutu country.

As the guerrilla war continued, human rights abuses by the Rwandan army also increased in direct proportion to the escalation of the conflict which, the government said, was an attempt by the Hutu rebels and their civilian supporters to exterminate the country's remaining Tutsis. The Tutsi regime used this threat to justify its indiscriminate campaign against Hutu civilians, leading to gross violations of their rights. It also led to an increase in violence as the insurgents retaliated against the government for its brutal repression. According to a report from Ruhengeri, northwestern Rwanda:

"In the latest attacks, 35 civilians were killed in two separate raids this week, the Rwandan News Agency reported yesterday (24 December 1997). Among the dead was the family of a Protestant minister in Nayakabanda, in central Rwanda.

The army faces a thorny dilemma: how to protect refugees while aggressively pursuing the rebels, who pose no immediate political threat to the Tutsi-dominated government but keep it off-balance and, according to critics, make it prone to human rights abuses."[47]

But human rights abuses cut across ethnic lines. Hutu rebels were no less guilty of such violations than the Tutsi-dominated army. While the army targeted Hutus, the insurgents attacked Tutsis as well as fellow Hutus who did not support their cause.

One of the most tragic aspects of the Rwandan civil war was betrayal. Some of the most trusted people turned out to be some of the biggest villains in this conflict. The role played by some members of the clergy in the 1994 genocide clearly showed how even the most "religious" members of the community could be so evil. One such "saintly" character was Elizaphan Ntakirutimana, a Hutu Seventh-day Adventist (SDA) pastor who, under his cloak as a clergyman, lured hundreds of Tutsis to their deaths. According to the *International Herald Tribune*:

"In the days after the ethnic slaughter broke out in Rwanda in 1994, when neighbor had turned against neighbor, people (including Hutus) in the town of Mugonero say the local Tutsi still trusted one pastor enough to hide in a church and hospital compound at his urging.

Once men, women and children had gathered there, however, the clergyman, Elizaphan Ntakirutimana, came back with a well-armed band of Rwandan (Hutu) soldiers and militiamen to add hundreds more Tutsi victims to the genocide's gruesome tally, according to an indictment issued against him by an international tribunal (in Arusha, Tanzania).

He was arrested in 1996 in Texas, where he had fled to

live with a son....

Mr. Ntakirutimana, 73,...a prominent member of Rwanda's Hutu majority, was president of the Seventh-day Adventists in the Kibuya region of western Rwanda....

One of Mr. Ntakirutimana's sons, Gerard, 40, an American-educated physician, has been charged with the same crimes as his father. The younger Ntakirutimana is in the custody of the Arusha tribunal."[43]

The pastor's role in the massacres may have shocked many people, probably even more so than that of the Hutu militants whose extremism left no doubt about what they intended to do. But even the involvement of the clergy in the genocide did not come as a complete surprise to some people for the same reason the participation of ordinary Hutus didn't. It all boils down to man's capacity for evil regardless of one's status or station in life, an argument that was eloquently expressed by one Rwandan clergyman as much as it has been by many other people throughout history.

Speaking in May 1996, almost two years after the holocaust, Laurien Ntezimana, a Catholic theologian, admitted that he was shocked by the massacres but not astonished. People live behind a mask, he said, which the winds of history occasionally blow aside. The genocide was shocking, but only those who are naïve about human nature could be astonished: "I have the impression that you have not yet discovered man, either in his grandeur or in his misery; he can always surprise us."[49]

During the genocide, Rwanda was a nation that had descended into hell.

French Role in the Genocide

Another tragedy during the 1994 genocide, besides the magnitude of the suffering and regional implications of the war, was the internationalisation of the conflict.

Uganda sponsored the Rwandan Patriotic Front (RPF) whose invasion of Rwanda – from the beginning in October 1990 – paved the way for the holocaust as Hutu militants sought to block the establishment of a coalition government in order to exclude the Tutsi from power and to prevent them from re-establishing Tutsi domination should they win the war. And the Hutu regime itself got support, mainly weapons, from France, Zaire, Egypt, and South Africa. Zaire under Mobutu Sese Seko was a bitter enemy of the Tutsi throughout the entire Great Lakes region for years and even stripped Zairian Tutsis of their citizenship in 1981.

But it was France which played the most important role in backing up the genocidal Hutu regime. The French government provided political and military support to Hutu politicians and the Hutu national army even in the midst of the holocaust itself when Hutu extremists – sponsored by the Hutu regime that was being supported by France – were busy killing Tutsis at a torrid pace unparalleled in recorded history.

French leaders had a close relationship with President Juvénal Habyarimana and other Rwandan Hutu leaders including army officers. They knew – even before the massacres started – that Hutu extremists who went on a genocidal rampage had received special training and indoctrination from the Hutu elite espousing the ideology of Hutu supremacy. President Habyarimana's ruling party, the National Republican Movement for Democracy, sponsored the Interahamwe. The Coalition for the Defence of the Republic, which was even more extremist, sponsored the Impuzamugambi, another extremist group. And the French knew that.

The two political parties – the National Republican Movement for Democracy and the Coalition for the

Defence of the Republic – had overwhelming support among the Hutu across the country, enabling them to mobilise strong anti-Tutsi sentiments among their supporters.

In August 1993, the same month the Hutu government and the Tutsi-dominated Rwandan Patriotic Front agreed to form a coalition government after signing the Arusha Accords in Tanzania, Radio Television Libre des Milles Collines was launched in preparation for the genocide.

It was started by Ferdinand Nahimana, former director of the state media under President Habyarimana who was fired by the president for his virulently anti-Tutsi and extremist views. One journalist called it "Rwanda's Killer Radio"[50] because of its hate message urging Hutus to exterminate the Tutsi.

The French government knew about all that. Yet it continued to support the Hutu regime, hence its genocidal army, paramilitary forces and anti-Tutsi propaganda machinery fully aware that the Tutsi were about to be exterminated by the government and the army it supported.

Even when Rwanda's acting president, Dr. Theodore Sindikubwabo, a pediatrician who succeeded the late Habyarimana, publicly thanked the murderers during the genocide and even promised them help to kill more Tutsis, France continued to support the murderous Hutu regime. Other Hutu leaders and members of the elite including mayors, policemen, teachers, university professors and students, perpetrated the the massacres with impunity to cleanse the land of Tutsis in preparation for a Hutu nirvana.

They were not in the least worried about any kind of retribution, as their compatriots cheered them and the rest of the world looked the other way. It was absolute madness.

Even some of the most cold-hearted people, full of hate, may have felt moral inhibitions against chopping up children into pieces. But that was not the case with these murderers, swinging machetes, hoes, and nail-studded clubs at their helpless victims who were bludgeoned to death while begging for their lives. They terrorised the land as angels of death and turned the whole country into a slaughterhouse.

No part of Rwanda was left untouched. And every Rwandan, Hutu and Tutsi, has a story to tell about what happened in that blood-soaked part of Africa.

Among the butchers were the leaders themselves. Men of social standing including pastors were some of the most notorious, urging men and women, boys and girls, to kill their fellow countrymen including their relatives and neighbours whose only crime was that they were born Tutsi or partly Tutsi. What happened in Nyakizu is a case in point; a microcosm of the hell that Rwanda had become. As Neil Kressel states in his book, *Mass Hate: The Global Rise of Genocide and Terror*:

"The genocide had two phases: First, within minutes after the crash of Habyarimana's plane, the Presidential Guard set up roadblocks in Kigali, while troops arrested and killed moderate Hutu officials – including Prime Minister Agathe Uwilingiyamana – and Tutsi politicians. During this phase, extremist leaders distributed lists of targeted people to the death squads.

Then, after about two days, the militias were given license and encouragement to kill every Tutsi they encountered – first in the capital and, then, throughout the country. Some Hutu civilians, unaffiliated with the militias, also joined the massacre. They were incited to do so by a barrage of radio broadcasts, but the seeds of hatred had long been present.

In Nyakizu, Rwanda, frightened Tutsis and Hutus went to their mayor, asking what might be done to prevent the spreading slaughter from reaching their town. He reassured them that nothing would happen, because the troublemakers were members of the Interahamwe militia and that they did not exist in the area.

Several days later, two hundred Hutus approached the town. The armed mob included several policemen, a school superintendent, teachers, university students, and, at its head, the mayor himself. He told Tutsis who had gathered on parish grounds that they need not worry. They should put down their staffs. They did, and the mob attacked.

Using axes, stones, spears, and guns, they murdered Tutsis wherever they could find them. The killings continued for several days. When the deputy mayor, the director of an adult education program, and several other Hutus tried to intervene, the mayor had them killed.

A few days after the killings began, Rwanda's acting president, Theodore Sindikubwabo, a pediatrician, came to town; he thanked the Hutu townspeople for their accomplishments and offered to send help for the next phase.

If we are to understand the origins of the genocide in Rwanda,...we must understand the mindset of these Hutu killers, a mindset forged over several centuries of Hutu-Tutsi relations but also owing much to the years and months preceding the massacre....

Many Hutus who participated in the massacres probably did believe that they were defending themselves and their families against a potential Tutsi assault. But reality squares better with the conclusions of a United Nations report issued in the late fall of 1994.

According to this report, 'Overwhelming evidence indicates that the extermination of Tutsi by Hutu had been planned months in advance of its actual execution. The mass exterminations of Tutsis were carried out primarily by Hutu elements in a concerted, planned, systematic and methodical way and were motivated out of ethnic hatred'....

Although it has become a habit in some circles to

blame most of contemporary Africa's problems on colonialism, the roots of Hutu-Tutsi animosity originate squarely in the pattern of relations between the groups that evolved well before the arrival of the Europeans in the late nineteenth century."[51]

The past is never in the past. It is always with us because it determines the present. And it will always be with us because it shapes the future.

The animosities between the Hutu and the Tutsi are real. The two groups have earned the dubious distinction as some of the most bitter enemies on the African continent.

But mass hate in both Rwanda and Burundi is a relatively recent phenomenon; a product of manipulations by the Tutsi and the Hutu political elite who have exploited these animosities and ethnic differences to advance their own political interests by inciting mass violence in the name of ethnic solidarity. That is why there were no massacres, on a very large scale, until the late 1950s and early 1960s when the Hutu and the Tutsi political elite emerged on the political scene to replace the Belgian colonial rulers who left both countries – Rwanda and Burundi – in 1962.

It has been hell ever since, although this should not be misconstrued as an endorsement of imperial rule as an era of paradise on earth for Africans. It is, instead, a searing indictment against African leaders in both Rwanda and Burundi – as well as in other parts of the continent – who have failed or who refuse to transcend their ethnic differences for the sake of national unity, thus exacerbating ethnic tensions and igniting warfare.

The taproot of the problem, or the root cause of the conflict, is inequity of power between the Hutu and the Tutsi. And it is deeply rooted in history. When Rwanda exploded in 1994, culminating in genocide, the tragedy was a historical inevitability, clearly determined by the past.

The Tutsi may not have expected it. And that may be one of the reasons why they ignored early warnings about the impending disaster, a disaster that would affect them directly. The Hutu minced no words about it – what they were preparing to do. So, it was really not surprising that they did what they said they were going to do to the Tutsi. What was surprising was the speed of the massacres. That is what surprised everybody, including some of the most seasoned historians and other observers. As Alan Kuperman stated in his article, "Rwanda in Retrospect," in *Foreign Affairs*:

"Perhaps the most remarkable aspect of the genocide was its speed.

According to survivor testimonies gathered by African Rights and Human Rights Watch, the majority of Tutsi gathering sites were attacked and destroyed before April 21, only 14 days into the genocide. Given that half or more of the ultimate Tutsi victims died at these sites – churches, schools, hospitals, athletic fields, stadiums, and other accessible spaces...[where] they sought refuge – the unavoidable conclusion is that a large portion of Rwanda's Tutsi had been killed by April 21 – perhaps 250,000 in just over two weeks. That would be the fastest genocide rate in recorded history....

By late April, only three weeks after the president's plane crash, almost all the large massacres were finished. The rebels themselves acknowledged on April 29 that 'the genocide is almost completed.'

Human Rights Watch concurs that 'in general, the worst massacres had [been] finished by the end of April.' By that time, it notes, 'perhaps half of the Tutsi population of Rwanda' – some two-thirds of the ultimate Tutsi victims – already had been exterminated. Killing of the remaining Tutsi continued at a slower pace for another two and half months until halted by the rebels' military victory....

After the genocide and civil war, some 150,000 Tutsi survivors were identified by aid organizations....The number of Hutu killed...range(s) from 10,000 to well over 100,000."[52]

Someone should have intervened to stop the madness. No one did.

Most Tutsis and Hutu moderates who were massacred were killed in the first three weeks of April; an incredible record Hitler would have been envious of.

Belgium, the former colonial power which still had close ties to Rwanda, did nothing to stop the massacres. African countries themselves did nothing. Yet all this was going on in their own backyard. The UN peacekeeping force – known by its acronym UNAMIR (UN Assistance Mission for Rwanda) – did nothing. And it could not do anything, given its weakness and limited mandate. And France, of course, did nothing to stop the genocide. Instead, this champion of Francophone Africa was busy arming the killers, some of the most cold-blooded murderers in history. When survivors of the genocide confronted them, they showed no remorse:

"During the 1994 massacre of Tutsis, Sam Gody hid in a septic tank for six weeks and lived off a crate of church wafers. Six brothers and sisters were massacred. Now, he says, their killer has returned. When Mr. Gody confronted the man, a farmer he had known for years, the killer professed his innocence: 'I only cut off your brother's hands. Others came and killed him'....

[Another man], Apollinaire Nsabimana, 25, beat a man to death with a stick. He was following solders' orders, he says: 'They told me they didn't want to waste bullets.'"[53]

A lot of those bullets, and weapons, came from France. According to a French newspaper, *Le Figaro*, France supplied a large quantity of arms and ammunition to the

378

Hutu government during the same time when the massacres were going on, thus fuelling the genocide. French officials denied the report. But there was substantial evidence to prove the charge.

The conservative daily newspaper also quoted a "high military official" in France who said French planes kept on flying arms to the Hutu even after France voted in favour of a United Nations arms embargo against the genocidal regime in Kigali. The paper went on to state: "France persevered in its policy of cooperation with the Rwandan regime, with those who made the genocide possible,...at least until the end of May 1994," nearly two months after the massacres began.[54]

France sent a peacekeeping force to Rwanda in June 1994, too little, too late.

The paper contended that President Francois Mitterand, a socialist, pursued the policy – of virtual unconditional support of and cooperation with the murderous Hutu regime – in order to thwart American penetration of Francophone Africa. He was supported by Prime Minister Edouard Balladur, a conservative, in a spirit of solidarity that transcended ideological differences in pursuit of French national interests.

Around the same time the paper published the report in mid-January 1998, the ethnic violence continued to destroy many parts of the embattled Great Lakes region. In Rwanda, the Tutsi army killed 18 Hutus near the border with Congo. A military spokesman said they were all rebels, although it's possible innocent civilians were among the victims as was the case many times when the government claimed its army killed only Hutu rebels.

And in neighbouring Burundi, at least 55 people were killed on January 11th and on January 12th in battles between Tutsi solders and Hutu guerrillas just outside the capital, Bujumbura,[55] which is only about 10 miles from the Congolese border, hence within striking range of the rebels from their bases in eastern Congo.

Publication of the report by *Le Figaro* about the role of France in the Rwanda during the 1994 genocide fuelled criticism of the French government for its involvement in the holocaust and thereafter; for, it was the French, using their troops in Rwanda, who secured a corridor which enabled the perpetrators of the genocide to escape to Zaire, another French-speaking country in the Francophone zone. But the French government was emphatic in its denial, insisting that it did not help the Hutu government and the rebels during the genocide. French leaders also said they did not help the killers escape to Zaire.

According to the *International Herald Tribune*, France categorically denied on 12 January 1998 that she authorised arms exports to Rwanda until 30 May 1994, nearly two months after the genocide started. The deputy spokesman at the Foreign Affairs Ministry, Yves Doutriaux, said France had stopped sending weapons to the Hutu government even before the United Nations imposed an arms embargo on the murderous regime on 17 May 1994.[56] The French government denied "most categorically" that France authorised arms shipments to Rwanda after 4 August 1993.[57]

But *Le Figaro* quoted sources saying that President Mitterand told aides during the summer of 1993 that "in such countries, genocide is not too important."[58]

It was a callous remark, making it clear that France cared only about France even if that meant sacrificing the lives of hundreds of thousands of black Africans – almost one million Tutsis in Rwanda – just to secure and promote French national interests in the heart of Africa and keep Rwanda securely anchored in the Francophone zone instead of allowing it to fall into the hands of other Western powers. According to *Le Figaro*:

"(French cooperation with the Hutu regime) continued at least until the end of May, or nearly two months after the start of the extermination and about two weeks after the United Nations vote on an arms embargo....

On May 3,1994, or nearly a month after the start of the genocide, an aircraft transporting arms for the Rwandan armed forces worth $942,680 landed in Zaire. The company Dyl-Invest, then based at Cran-Gevrier, played the role of intermediary to charter this flight, paying $450,000, with the rest of the payment made by the (Hutu) Rwandan Embassy in Cairo.

(At the beginning of May, the French arms export company Sofremas) confirmed an $8,028,000 arms order from the Rwandan Embassy in Paris. (*Le Figaro* has evidence showing that) on July 18, a flight transporting $753,645 worth of arms landed at Goma in Zaire. The Rwandan Embassy in Paris financed this flight with the sum of $175,000 and the Rwandan Embassy in Cairo with the sum of $578,645."[59]

The articles documenting French official implication and involvement in the 1994 Rwandan genocide were written by Patrick de Saint-Exupéry, an African specialist at *Le Figaro*. He quoted aid workers, officials and soldiers, together with evidence gathered by the United Nations in Rwanda and by a Belgian legislative commission which also investigated the massacres.

The newspaper went on to state that French soldiers secretly fought the Rwandan Patriotic Army (RPA) from 1992 and thereafter when the predominantly Tutsi rebel group invaded Rwanda from Uganda. French troops were at the frontline, leading and supporting the Hutu national army. They were also in Rwanda during the holocaust as virtual accomplices of the Hutu in the extermination of the Tutsi.

This work exonerates nobody who was involved in the genocide and other atrocities. I wrote the book to tell the truth. That was more than ten years ago. More than ten years later, I maintain the same position.

Even Tutsi soldiers committed atrocities after the

genocide. But Hutu extremists were the biggest offenders because of their involvement in the extermination of the Tutsi. And they did get some help from France.

The Hutus' numerical preponderance as the largest ethnic group, and their natural right to rule as the democratic majority, were – ostensibly – the prime determinants for French intervention in Rwanda. But the real motive was different.

The driving force behind the venture was what Patrick de Saint-Exupéry called the "Fashoda syndrome": President Mitterand's geopolitical assessment of the Tutsi invasion of Francophone Rwanda from Anglophone Uganda as an integral part of a grand design by the United States to end French influence in Africa.

When Patrick de Saint-Exupéry cited the "Fashoda syndrome," he was drawing a historical analogy between the Franco-American rivalry in East-Central Africa in the 1990s and the Anglo-French rivalry in Sudan in the 1890s.

In 1898, the Anglo-French rivalry in Sudan culminated in the famous Fashoda Incident. The two powers came to the brink of war over the control of the Upper Nile region in pursuit of their imperial ambitions.

Britain wanted to establish a continuous belt of colonial possessions from Cape to Cairo – C to C – as an integral part of the British empire. France wanted to establish an overland route across the African continent from the Red Sea to the Atlantic Ocean.

To validate their claim, the French sent a small military force from Brazzaville (capital of French Congo-Brazzaville) to the region in spite of British warnings not to do so. The French expeditionary force arrived in the village of Fashoda – now Kodok – on River Nile in southern Sudan on 10 July 1898. The contested region is close to the source of the Nile.

The British responded by sending their own troops to Fashoda and claimed the village for Egypt which was then under their jurisdiction.

It was a classic demonstration of imperial might.

The French resisted for a short time, but, fearing war, withdrew their forces on 3 November 1898. In March 1899, France renounced her claim to the Upper Nile region and accepted part of the Sahara as compensation.

Almost exactly a century later, the French – who have always sought grandeur as a major power beyond continental Europe, a vision forcefully articulated by Charles de Gaulle – saw striking parallels between their frustrated ambitions and humiliation at the hands of the British in Sudan in 1898 and the American encroachment in the 1990s on what they have always considered to be their sphere of influence in the Francophone region of East-Central Africa: Rwanda, Burundi, and Congo.

It is their quest for this lofty status and their determination to protect their sphere of influence which led them to support one of the most murderous regimes in history at a cost of almost one million lives in Rwanda alone, and hundreds of thousands more in Congo and Burundi, a genocide they could have stopped had they intervened, given their enormous influence over the Hutu regime in Rwanda which would have collapsed much sooner had it not been for French support to this clique of brutal autocrats through the years.

But the invasion of Rwanda by the Tutsi from their bases in Uganda did not help the situation in a country where the government was already virulently anti-Tutsi. The invasion only provided an excuse for Hutu militants to start killing Tutsis to prevent them from taking over the country.

The killing of Tutsi civilians began in early 1992 as part of an orchestrated campaign by the Hutu elite – including priests and nuns, doctors and university professors, lawyers, businessmen and politicians of all ranks and stripes – to eliminate them.

The Belgian intelligence service was aware of this sinister plot and reported in the same year (1992) the existence of a secret Hutu government command charged with "exterminating the Tutsi of Rwanda...in order to make a final solution to the ethnic problem, and also to crush the (moderate) Hutu political opposition."[60]

Western ambassadors in Kigali reportedly expressed their concern to the Rwandan Hutu government about the murders of Tutsi civilians, but the French ambassador refused to do so, and lightly dismissed the reports of the massacres as "only rumors."[61]

Around the same time, a leader of the Tutsi who was based in Uganda, probably Paul Kagame, went to Paris to complain about the killings and the support France was giving to the anti-Tutsi regime in Kigali. But he got no positive response from the French government. According to *Le Figaro*, he was told at the Foreign Ministry that unless the Ugandan-based Tutsis stopped invading Rwanda, "your brothers and families...will all be massacred."[62]

The massacres continued and, in February 1993, an international commission denounced "acts of genocide" in Rwanda.[63] It was not long after this that President Mitterand callously remarked to an associate during summer: "In countries like that, a genocide is not very important."[64]

There is a slight difference in wording, exactly what the French president said, according to different sources I have cited here, but the content of the message was the same.

Almost exactly one year later, about one million Tutsis were slaughtered between April and July 1994 with the full connivance of the French government. It was as if the French were saying to the Tutsi during the genocide, "We told you so!"

France's collaboration with the Hutus continued for at least another month after the genocide.

As late as July 18th (1994), long after the United Nations imposed an arms embargo on Rwanda to stop all arms shipments to the ousted genocidal Hutu regime and its army, weapons were still flowing into the country from France and going to the murderers via Goma, a town on the Rwandan-Zairian border.

Thousands of these murderers who had sought refuge in Zaire were also being rearmed by France and Zaire in preparation for a counter-invasion of Rwanda. A French military intervention had been launched at the end of June, ostensibly as a humanitarian mission, while the real intention was to provide cover and protection for Hutu political leaders, soldiers and militiamen as they fled to safety just across the border in Zaire; saving the very same people who had instigated and perpetrated some of the worst atrocities in history in the name of justice through ethnic cleansing.

Just a week after the *Le Figaro* series of articles on French complicity in the Rwandan holocaust appeared, Hutu rebels struck again, although there probably was no connection between the publication of the articles and the rebel attacks and their timing.

On 19 January 1998, the rebels attacked a bus carrying workers to a brewery in northwestern Rwanda, killing 34 people and wounding 25 others. The bus was taking the workers to the country's only brewery outside Gisenyi, the capital of Gisenyi Province, the most violent region in Rwanda after the genocide.

Colonel Nyamwasa Kayumba, the military commander of the region, said the guerrillas first shot and killed the bus driver, then they threw gasoline on the bus and set it on fire. Seven people were burned to death, another 27 were killed by the rebels as thy jumped out of the bus and tried to escape the inferno, and five escaped.[65]

The killers were some of the very same people who were trained by French soldiers before the 1994 holocaust and perpetrated some of the worst massacres during the genocide. As William Pfaff stated about French complicity in the Rwandan tragedy:

"France's involvement now has public confirmation from witnesses, participants and official inquiries by the United Nations and the Belgian Parliament....

Patrick de Saint-Exupéry, the journalist who revealed secret French implication in events which culminated in the murder of something like a million Tutsi civilians, report(ed) that France obstruct(ed) the work of the UN War Crimes Tribunal on Bosnia because it fear(ed) that the second UN War Crimes Tribunal, concerned with Rwanda, might demand testimony from French officers."[66]

French involvement in the Rwandan genocide was tragic enough. But even more tragic is the fact that the genocide never ended when it was supposed to have ended in 1994. Like the other countries in the Great Lakes region – Burundi, Congo, and Uganda – Rwanda was sucked into the vortex of an immense crisis which had profound implications for peace and stability across the entire continent.

Fractured along ethnic lines, and locked in a brutal war of attrition, Rwanda, like its twin Burundi which also has two "nations" – Hutu and Tutsi – within its borders, may have to take bold, radical initiatives to end the violence and maintain its integrity as a single political entity, a subject I have addressed in my other book, *Civil Wars in Rwanda and Burundi: Conflict Resolution in Africa*.

It will require enormous concessions by both sides to achieve lasting peace.

Chapter notes

Chapter One

1. Leon Mugesira, quoted by Michael Chege, "Africa's Murderous Professors," in *The National Interest*, No. 46, Washington, D.C., Winter 1996/97, p. 34.

2. Hassan Ngeze, editor of *Kangura*, a Hutu newspaper, Gisenyi, Rwanda, ibid.

3. *La Medaille*, Kigali, Rwanda, February 1994, ibid.

4. Michael Chege, Ibid. See also Emmanuel Bugingo, quoted by Robert Block, "Labour of Love at a School of Hate," in *The Independent*, London, 8 January 1995; *Rwanda: Massive and Systematic Violation of Human Rights from October 1990*, Paris: International Human Rights Foundation, 1993; Gérard Prunier, *The Rwanda Crisis: History of A Genocide* (New York: Columbia University Press, 1997); Philip Gourevitch, *We Wish to Inform You That Tomorrow We Will Be Killed with Our Families: Stories from Rwanda* (New York: Farrar, Straus & Giroux, 1998); Rosamond Halsey Carr with Ann Howard Halsey, *Land of A Thousand Hills: My Life in Rwanda* (New York: Viking, 1999).

5. René Lemarchand, "The Fire in the Great Lakes," in *Current History: A Journal of Contemporary World Affairs*, May 1999, p. 196. See also R. Lemarchand, *Burundi: Ethnic Conflict and Genocide* (New York: Cambridge University Press, 1996).

6. Philip Gourevitch, "The Psychology of Slaughter: In Uganda, An Echo of the Rwandan Horror," in *The New*

York Times, Op-Ed Sunday, 7 March 1999, p. WK-15. See also P. Gourevitch, *We Wish to Inform You That Tomorrow We Will Be Killed with Our Families: Stories from Rwanda*, op. cit.

7. R. Lemarchand, "The Fire in the Great Lakes," op. cit., p. 198. See also George B. N. Ayittey, Africa in Chaos (New York: St. Martin's Press, 1998), pp. 54 – 57.

8. R. Lemarchand, ibid., p. 197.

9. *Rwanda in Reader's Digest Almanac and Yearbook: 1986* (Pleasantville, New York: Reader's Digest Association, Inc., 1985), p. 639.

10. Vincent Gasana and Alfred Ndahiro, "Zaire Crisis Provokes Cry of Tribalism," in *Africa Analysis: The Fortnightly Bulletin on Financial and Political Trends*, No. 259, London, 1 November 1996, p. 15. See also *Broadcasting Genocide – Censorship, Propaganda and State-Sponsored Violence in Rwanda 1990 – 1994* (London: Article 19, 33 Islington High Street, 1996).

11. Godfrey Mwakikagile, Chapter Three: Ethnic Cleansing in Rwanda and Burundi: In Search of An Alternative to The Modern African State, *The Modern African State: Quest for Transformation* (Huntington, New York: Nova Science Publishers, 2001), pp. 73 – 107; G. Mwakikagile, *Africa After Independence: Realities of Nationhood* (Dar es Salaam, Tanzania: New Africa Press, 2009); Colin Legum and john Drysdale, eds., Africa Contemporary Record: Annual Survey and Documents 1968 – 1969 (London: Africa Research Ltd., 1969), p. 442. See also Jorge G. Castañeda, *Compañero: The Life and Death of Che Guevara* (New York: Alfred A. Knopf, 1997), pp. 276 – 325, 326 – 338, 346 – 347, 356, 367, and 386; Madeleine G. Kalb, *The Congo Cables: The Cold War in Africa – From Eisenhower to Kennedy* (New York: Macmillan, 1982); David Gibbs, *The Political Economy of Third World Intervention: Mines, Money and U.S. Policy in the Congo* (Chicago: University of Chicago Press, 1991).

12. Crawford Young, "Zaire: The Unending Crisis," in *Foreign Affairs*, Fall 1978, p. 178. See also C. Young, *Politics in the Congo* (Madison: University of Wisconsin Press, 1978); Otto Klineberg and Merisa Zavalloni, *Nationalism and Tribalism Among African Students* (Paris: Mouton, 1969).

13. Che Guevara, quoted by R. Lemarchand, "The Fire in the Great Lakes," op. cit., p. 199. See also Che's diary on the Congo, Ernesto Che Guevara, *Pasajes de la guerra revolucionaira* (el Congo), 1966; Rolando E. Bonachea and Nelson P. Valdes, eds., *Che: Selected Works of Ernesto Guevara* (Cambridge: Massachusetts, MIT Press, 1969).

14. Che Guevara, *Pasajes de la guerra revolucionaira* (el Congo), quoted by J. G. Castañeda, *Compañero: The Life and Death of Che Guevara*, op. cit., p. 164. See also G. Michael Schartberg, *Mobutu or Chaos? The United States and Zaire: 1960 – 1990* (New York and Philadelphia: University Press of America/ Foreign Policy Research Institute, 1991); G. Madelaine Kalb, The Congo Cables (New York: Macmillan, 1982).

15. Gérard Prunier, "The Great Lakes Crisis," in *Current History: A Journal of Contemporary World Affairs*, May 1997, p. 195. See also G. Prunier, *The Rwanda Crisis: History of A Genocide* (New York: Columbia University Press, 1997).

16. "Zaire Rebels Aim to Oust Mobutu," in *Africa Analysis*, op cit., p. 1.

17. Paul Kagame, cited in *The Washington Post*, 9 July 1997, p. A-1.

18. Ehud Barak, quoted by Amos Elon, "Exile's Return," a review of Edward W. Said, *Out of Place: A Memoir* (New York: Alfred A. Knopf, 1999), in *The New York Review of Books*, 18 November 1999, p. 12. Se also Edward W. Said, "The One-State Solution," in *The New York Times Magazine*, 10 January 1999.

19. Paul Kagame, quoted in The Washington Post, op.

cit., p. A-18. See also Marina Ottaway, "Africa's 'New Leaders': African Solution or African Pproblem?," in *Current History: A Journal of Contemporary World Affairs*, May 1998, pp. 209 – 213.

20. Godfrey Mwakikagile, *The Modern African State: Quest for Transformation*, op. cit.; George B.N. Ayittey, *Africa in Chaos* (New York: St. Martin's Press, 1998); G.B.N. Ayittey, *Africa Betrayed* (New York: St. Martin's Press, 1992); Seyoum Y. Hameso, *Ethnicity and Nationalism in Africa* (Commack, New York: Nova Science Publishers, Inc., 1997); Wole Soyinka, *The Open Sore of a Continent: A Personal Narrative of the Nigerian Crisis* (New York: Oxford University Press, 1996); Fergal Keane, *Season of Blood: A Rwandan Journey* (New York: Viking, 1996); Chinua Achebe, *The Trouble with Nigeria* (Enugu, Nigeria: Fourth Dimension Publishing, 1985).

Mahmood Mamdani, *Imperialism and Fascism in Uganda* (Lawrenceville, New Jersey: Africa World Press, 1984); David Lamb, *The Africans*, (New York: Random House, 1982); Samuel Decalo, *Coups and Army Rule in Africa: Studies in Military Style* (New Haven, Connecticut: Yale University Press, 1976); W.F. Gutteridge, *Military Regimes in Africa* (London: Methuen, 1975); Anton Bebler, ed., *Military Rule in Africa: Dahomey, Ghana, Sierra Leone, and Mali* (1973); Jeffrey T. Strate, *Post-Military Coup Strategy in Uganda: Amin's Early Attempts to Consolidate Political Support in Africa* (1973); Henry Kyemba, A State of Blood (1973); Godfrey Mwakikagile, *Military Coups in West Africa Since The Sixties* (Huntington, New York: Nova Science Publishers, Inc., 2001).

René Lemarchand, *Burundi: Ethnocide as Discourse and Practice* (Cambridge: Cambridge University Press, 1994); Gebru Takeke, *Ethiopia: Power and Protest* (1991); Amii Olara-Otunnu, *Politics and The Military in Uganda: 1890 – 1985* (1987); Robert A. Dibie, *The Military-Bureaucracy Relationship in Nigeria: Public*

Policy and Implementation (Westport, Connecticut: Praeger Publishers, 1999); Larry Diamond, Anthony Kirk-Greene, and Oyeleye Oyediran, *Transition Without End: Nigerian Politics and Civil Society under Babangida* (Boulder, Colorado: Lynne Rienner, 1997); Howard Adelman and Astri Suhrke, ed., *The Path of A Genocide: The Rwanda Crisis fro Uganda to Zaire* (Piscataway, New Jersey: Transaction, 1999).

Ken C. Kotecha and Robert W. Adams, *The Corruption of Power: African Politics* (Washington, D.C.: University Press of America, 1981); Victor LeVine, *Political Corruption: The Ghana Case* (Stanford, California: Hoover Institution Press, 1975); Jean-Francois Bayart, *The State in Africa: The Politics of the Belly* (London: Longman, 1984); Richard Sandbrook, *The Politics of Africa's Stagnation* (New York: Cambridge University Press, 1993); David Waller, *Rwanda: Which Way Now?* (Oxford: Oxfam, 1993); G. E. Boley, *Liberia: The Rise and Fall of the First Republic* (New York: St. Martin's Press, 1983); Peter Anyang' Nyong'o, ed., *Popular Struggles for Democracy in Africa* (London: Zed Books, 1987); Robert E. Jackson and Carl G. Rosberg, *Personal Rule in Black Africa: Prince, Autocrat, Prophet, Tyrant* (Berkeley: University of California Press, 1982).

Nelson Kasfir, *The Shrinking Political Arena: Participation and Ethnicity in African Politics, with a Case Study of Uganda* (Berkeley: University of California Press, 1976); Crawford Young and Thomas Turner, *The Rise and Decline of the Zairian State* (Madison: University of Wisconsin Press, 1985); Jean-Francois Bayart, Stephen Ellis, and Beatrice Hibou, *The Criminalisation of the State in Africa* (Bloomington: Indiana University Press, 1999); Ngugi wa Thiong'o, *Barrel of Pen: Resistance to Repression in Neo-Colonial Kenya* (Lawrenceville, New Jersey: Africa World Press, 1983); Thomas P. Ofcansky, *Uganda: Tarnished Pearl of Africa* (Boulder, Colorado: Westview Press, 1995); Viva

Ona Bartkus, *The Dynamics of Secession: An Analytical Framework* (New York: Cambridge University Press, 1999).

Chapter Two

1. Burundi, Colin Legum and John Drysdale, eds., *Africa Contemporary Record: Annual Survey and Documents 1968 – 1969* (London: Africa Research Ltd., 1969, p. 141.

2. Ibid., p. 142.

3. Ntare V in *Information Please Almanac: 1998* (Boston: Houghton Mifflin Co., 1997), p. 160; *The Columbia Encyclopedia* (New York: Columbia University Press, 1993), p. 402.

4. *Information Please Almanac 1998*, ibid. See also George B.N. Ayittey, *Africa in Chaos* (New York: St. Martin's Press, 1998), p. 56; *Daily News*, Dar es Salaam, Tanzania, April – July 1972. I was a news reporter of the *Daily News* in Dar es Salaam when the massacres were taking place in Burundi during that period, forcing tens of thousands of refugees, mostly Hutu, to flee to Tanzania. We covered the crisis extensively and our newspaper became a valuable source of information about what was going on Burundi. I left for the United States in November, the same year, to attend college.

5. Harvey Glickman, "Tanzania: From Disillusionment to Guarded Optimism," in *Current History: A Journal of Contemporary World Affairs*, May 1997, p. 218. See also Harvey Glickman, *Ethnic Conflict and Democratization in Africa* (Atlanta, Georgia: African Studies Association Press, 1995); Gérard Prunier, *The Rwanda Crisis: History of A Genocide* (New York: Columbia University Press, 1997); René Lemarchand, *Burundi: Ethnic Conflict and Genocide* (New York: Cambridge University Press, 1996); R. Lemarchand, *Burundi: Ethnocide as Discourse and*

Practice (Cambridge: Cambridge University Press, 1994); Philip Gourevitch, *We Wish to Inform You That Tomorrow We Will Be Killed with Our Families: Stories from Rwanda* (New York: Farrar, Straus, and Giroux, 1998); Rosemond Halsey Carr with Ann Howard Halsey, *Land of A Thousand Hills: My Life in Rwanda* (New York: Viking, 1999).

6. Burundi, in *Reader's Digest: Almanac and Yearbook: 1986* (Pleasantville, New York: Reader's Digest Association, Inc., 1985), p. 517.

7. Michel Micombero, in *Africa Report*, September – October 1983, p. 35; *Daily News*, Dar es Salaam, Tanzania, 17 July 1983; *Daily Nation*, Nairobi, Kenya, 17 July 1983; *Le Monde*, Paris, 19 July 1983; *The New York Times*, 18 July 1983.

8. G.B.N. Ayittey, *Africa in Chaos*, op. cit., p. 56. See also G.B.N. Ayittey, *Africa Betrayed* (New York: St. Martin's Press, 1992).

9. *The Washington Post*, 17 April 1994, p. C – 2.

10. African leaders at a meeting in Arusha, Tanzania, in a statement quoted in "African Chiefs Seek Blockade of Burundi in Coup Protest," in the *International Herald Tribune*, 1 August 1996, p. 8.

11. Benjamin Mkapa, ibid.

12. "Burundi's Woe: Anybody There?" in *The Economist*, 27 July 1996, p. 37.

13. Ibid.

14. Ibid.

15. Burundi, in *The Wall Street Journal*, 5 August 1996, p. A-1, and 6 August 1996, p. A-1.

16. Tanzanian official, quoted in "Tanzanian Move to Block Oil Deliveries to Burundi," in the *International Herald Tribune*, 6 August 1996, p. 2.

17. Pierre Buyoya, ibid.

18. P. Buyoya, in *Le Figaro*, Paris, 7 August 1996; and in "UN Appeals to Africans to Allow Burundi Aid Shipments," in the *International Herald Tribune*, 8 August

1996, p. 2.

19. Ibid.

20. United Nations statement, ibid.

21. Paul Kagame, in an interview with BBC, quoted ibid.

22. "Burundi After the Coup," in *The Economist*, 3 August 1996, p. 35. See also Burundi, in "African Action," in *The Economist*, ibid., p. 4.

23. Ibid., p. 35.

24. Burundi, in *The Economist*, 17 August 1996, p. 4.

25. Ibid. See also Rwanda and Burundi, in *The Economist*, 10 August 1996, p. 4: "Rwanda's Tutsi-dominated government said it would not join other East African countries in imposing sanctions on the new Tutsi-led military regime in Burundi. The Burundian army was accused of massacres of Hutu civilians in a UN report."

26. "Organisation of African Unity (OAU) Conference: Resolution on Nigeria," in *Africa Research Bulletin*, Vol. V, London, September 1968, pp. 1171 et seq.; *Africa Contemporary Record: 1968 – 1969*, op. cit., p. 620.

27. Tanzanian officials, cited in *Sunday News*, Dar es Salaam, Tanzania, 11 August 1996; "UN Aid for Burundi Blocked at Port," in the *International Herald Tribune*, 12 August 1996, p. 7.

28. Luc Rukingama, quoted in "UN Aid for Burundi Blocked at Port," in the *International Herald Tribune*, ibid.

29. Doctors Without Borders, cited ibid. See also "Nations Send an Important Message to Burundi – and to Africa," in the *International Herald Tribune*, 17 August 1996, p. 6.

30. "Stronger Sanctions Placed on Burundi," in the *International Herald Tribune*, ibid., p. 7.

31. Sylvestre Ntibantuganya, cited in "Ousted Leader Assails Regime in Burundi," in the *International Herald Tribune*, 20 August 1996, p. 10.

32. Ibid.

Chapter Three

1. "Hutu Flee Burundi Despite Assurances," in the *International Herald Tribune*, 21 August 1996, p. 2. See also *The Economist*, 24 August 1996, p. 4: "Thousands of Rwandan Hutu refugees fled from camps in Burundi claiming persecution by the army. Thousands of Zairean Tutsis, their citizenship denied, were driven out of eastern Zaire."

2. "Burundi Toll After Coup Put at 6,000," in the *International Herald Tribune*, 23 August 1996, p. 8.

3. Ibid.

4. "Bloodshed in Burundi: The Other War in Central Africa," in *The Economist,* 14 December 1996, p. 43.

5. "Don't Forget Burundi: Behind It Hovers the Spectre of Rwanda," in *The Economist*, 24 August 1996, p. 12.

6. Ibid.

7. Ibid.

8. Adrien Sibomana, quoted in "Fragile Burundi, 'Nation in Despair': U.S. and Aid Groups Cite Fears of a Surge in Mass Killings," in the *International Herald Tribune*, 26 August 1996, p. 9.

9. Thomas W. Lippman, on Burundi, in *The Washington Post*, 25 August 1996; and in "Fragile Burundi, 'Nation in Despair,'" in the *International Herald Tribune*, ibid.

10. Pierre Buyoya, quoted in *Le Soir*, Brussels, Belgium, 27 August 1996; and in "Burundi's Leader Cautions Neighbors on Embargo," in the *International Herald Tribune*, 28 August 1996, p. 8.

11. Innocent Nimpagaritse, Hutu rebel spokesman, quoted in "Hutu Rebels Vow to Down Planes Flying into Burundi," in the *International Herald Tribune*, 29 August 1996, p. 2.

12. Jean-Luc Ndizeye, Burundi's military regime

spokesman, ibid.

13. Jean-Baptiste Mbonyingingo, ibid.

14. "Battle Forces Foreigners to Flee Burundi Capital,"in the *International Herald Tribune*, 5 September 1996, p. 1.

15. Charles Mukasi, quoted in "Foes Play Down Burundi's End of Two Key Bans," in the *International Herald Tribune*, 14 September 1996, p. 2.

16. I. William Zartman, "Making Sense of East Africa's Wars," in *The Wall Street Journal*, 15 November 1996, p. A-14. See also "Africa's Approaching Catastrophe: Death Shadows Africa's Great Lakes....Why Are Hutus and Tutsis So Ready to Kill Each Other?" in *The Economist*, 19 October 1996, p. 45: "Genocide consumed Rwanda in 1994. Now, in another form, it threatens Burundi, maybe Zaire. Why are Hutus and Tutsis so ready to kill each other?....The relationship between Hutus and Tutsis goes deep into history....Hutus tell of centuries of enslavement by Tutsis. Tutsis say that...Hutus are playing racial politics." See also pp. 45 – 47, and 18, ibid.

17. "Africa's Approaching Catastrophe: Death Shadows Africa's Great Lakes," in *The Economist*, ibid.

18. Ibid.

19. Burundi, in *The Economist*, 7 December 1996, p. 4. See also Burundi, in *Current History: A Journal of Contemporary World Affairs*, December 1996, p. 443: "October 28 – The Tutsi-dominated army admits that its soldiers killed at least 50 Hutu civilians in the southern province of Bururi on October 13; aid workers say more than 100 civilians were killed."

20. UN High Commissioner for Human Rights, Jose Ayala Lasso, in "UN Reports 1,100 Killings by Burundi Army and Asks Halt," in the *International Herald Tribune*, 12 December 1996, p. 8.

21. Ibid.

22. "Bloodshed in Burundi: The Other War in Central Africa," in *The Economist*, op. cit., p. 43.

23. Ibid.

24. Unnamed diplomat, ibid.

25. Ibid.

26. "Bloodshed in Burundi: The Other War in Central Africa," in *The Economist*, ibid., p. 44.

27. Julius Nyerere, "No Peace Without Justice, Which Is More Than Democracy," reprinted in the *International Herald Tribune*, 15 January 1997, p. 8. See also Nyerere in *The New York Times*, 14 and 15 January 1997.

28. Pierre Buyoya, in "Blood Rivalry Thwarts Burundi's Peace Quest," in the *International Herald Tribune*, 12 August 1997, p. 2. See also James C. McKinley, his report from Bujumbura, in *The New York Times*, 11 August 1997.

29. Ibid.

30. Charles Mukasi, ibid.

31. "Hutu Rebels Are Said to Clash in Burundi," in the *International Herald Tribune*, 13 August 1997, p. 1.

32. Mary Rose Habyamberi, in "Burundi Interns Hutu in Camps: Farmers Become the Victims of Crackdown on Guerrillas," in the *International Herald Tribune*, 14 August 1997, p. 2.

33. P. Buyoya, ibid.

34. "Burundi Interns Hutu in Camps," ibid.

35. Marcel Nyabenda, ibid.

36. Ancilla Ndayisenga, ibid.

37. UN official, ibid.

38. Quoted in "Africa's Approaching Catastrophe: Death Shadows Africa's Great Lakes," in *The Economist*, op. cit., p. 45.

39. Ibid.

40. "Fragile Four-Month Old Peace in Congo Appears Over," in *The Christian Science Monitor*, 8 November 1999, p. 24.

41. Julius Nyerere, quoted in "Talks Start Without Burundi," in the *International Herald Tribune*, 27 August 1997, p. 7.

42. *The Christian Science Monitor*, 28 October 1997, p. 2.

43..Jean-Bosco Daradangwe, in "Burundi Army Tracks Hutu Attackers," in the *International Herald Tribune*, 2 January 1998, p. 7.

44. *The Economist*, 10 January 1998, p. 4.

45. Mamert Sinaranzi, cited in "Hutu Raid Army Base in Burundi: At Least 150 Civilians Reported Killed in Battle," in *The Boston Globe*, 2 January 1998, p. A-2.

46. Jean-Luc Ndizye, ibid.

47. "Hutu Raid Army Base in Burundi," in *The Boston Globe,* ibid.

48. J.B. Daradangwe, cited in "Burundi Army Tracks Hutu Attackers," in the *International Herald Tribune*, op. cit., p. 7.

49. M. Sinaranzi, ibid.

50. Christophe Nkurunziza, "Survivors Aid Burundi Search for Attackers," in *The Boston Globe*, 4 January 1998, p. A-18.

51. "Africa's Approaching Catastrophe," in *The Economist*, op. cit., p. 47. See also the Tutsi in *Africa Analysis: The Fortnightly Bulletin on Financial and Political Trends*, No. 259, London, 1 November 1996, p. 15.

52. "Burundi's Cruel Civil War: Pawns in the War," in *The Economist*, 10 January 1998, pp. 37, and 38.

53. "Hutu Rebels Kill 45 in Two Burundi Attacks," in the *International Herald Tribune*, 22 January 1998, p. 6.

54. "Burundi Official Killed in Crash," in the International Herald Tribune, 29 January 1998, p. 11.

55. Pierre-Claver Ndayicariye, cited in "Copter Crash Kills Burundi Defense Chief, Four Others," in The Boston Globe, 29 January 1998, p. A-6.

56. Burundi, in *Keesing's Record of World Events*, January 1998, p. 41991. See also pp. 41950, and 41897.

57. Athanase Nibizi, in "Burundi Rebels Said to Kill 24 in Attack on Village," in *The Boston Globe,* 12 February

1998, p. A-23.

58. Zacharie Kamwenubusa, ibid.

59. Ibid.

60. Reuters, ibid.

61. Burundi, in *Current History: A Journal of Contemporary World Events*, April 1998, p. 189.

62. "73 in Burundi Reported Dead in Hutu Rebel Raid," in *The Boston Globe*, 23 April 1998, p. A-24.

63. Ibid.

64. Daniel arap Moi, cited in "Moi Urges Separation of Tutsi and Hutu," in the *International Herald Tribune*, 10 April 1998, p. 6.

65. "63 Reported Killed in Burundi Camps," in the *International Herald Tribune*, 20 May 1997, p. 6.

66. Burundi, in *The Christian Science Monitor*, 8 May 1998, p. 2.

67. Leonidas Ntibayazi, in "Signing of Constitution Sets Stage for Burundi's Reforms," in *The Boston Globe*, 7 June 1998, p. A-27.

68. Ambroise Niyonsaba, ibid.

69. "Burundi Military and Rebels Disagree Over a Cease-fire," in The Boston Globe, 18 June 1998, p. A-28.

70. "Burundi on the Brink of Peace?," in *The Economist*, 20 June 1998, p. 49.

71. "Refugees Flee Burundi Crashes," in The Boston Globe, 1 August 1998, p. A-7. See also Burundi, in *Current History: A Journal of Contemporary World Affairs*, September 1998, p. 289.

72. Burundi, in The Christian Science Monitor, 13 November 1998, p. 2.

73. "Burundi: new Spate of Killings," in *Keesing's Record of World Events*, November 1998, 42599. See also p. 42540.

74. East Africans Drop Burundi Sanctions," in the *International Herald Tribune*, 25 January 1999, p. 4; *The New York Times*, 24 January 1999; *The Economist*, 30 January 1999, p.4.

75. *The Economist*, 20 March 1999, p. 6.

76. "Five Sentenced to Death in Burundi Murder," in the *International Herald Tribune*, 15 May, 1999, p. 2.

77. Ibid.

78. "Burundi: Convictions in President's Death," in *The New York Times*, 15 May 1999, p. A-4; *The Economist*, 22 May 1999, p. 6.

79. *The Economist,* 14 August 1999, p. 4.

80. "Burundi's Army Killed Hutu, Villagers Say," in the *International Herald Tribune*, 13 August 1999, p. 1.

81. *The Christian Science Monitor,* 30 August 1999, p. 20.

82. *The Economist*, 4 September 1999, p. 10. See also, "In Burundi, 9 Die in Attack on UN Convoy," in the *International Herald Tribune*, 13 October 1996, p. 6:

"Nine people were killed Tuesday (12 October 1999) when Hutu rebels attacked a UN relief convoy in southern Burundi, a spokesman for the Burundi Army said....An extremist Hutu organization known as PALIPEHUTU has recently warned all expatriates in Burundi to leave the country or face attack.

It was not clear which rebel group carried out the attack, but Colonel Longin Minani said he was certain that the attackers had come from their base in neighboring Tanzania.

Several Hutu rebel organizations that operate out of both Congo and Tanzania are trying to oust the Tutsi-dominated government of President Pierre Buyoya. Since the Hutu rebels recently stepped up their attacks in areas outside the capital (Bujumbura), the government has forcibly moved at least 250,000 Hutu civilians from their homes and into what it calls 'protected sites.'

Colonel Minani has said the Hutu civilians are being transferred to the camps to protect them from rebel pressure to support their cause as well as to clear the way for the army to flush out the rebels.

Both the European Union (EU) and the United States

have criticized the forced relocation of civilians, and the World Food Program said last week that it was distributing food to the camps on a 'critical need basis.'"

See also "UN Workers in Burundi Were Slain on a Whim," in the *International Herald Tribune*, 14 October 1999, pp. 1, and 8: "The Burundi government, which is dominated by an elite sliver of the minority Tutsi population, has responded (to rebel attacks) by moving large numbers of Hutus off their land while the army sweeps the countryside. More than a quarter of a million people have been confined to 'regrouping' camps. Conditions are said to be wretched, and international agencies have pressed for relief."

See also Burundi, in *Current History: A Journal of Contemporary World Affairs*, October 1999, p. 348.

83. Nyerere, in *The Economist*, 16 October 1999, p. 4; "Obituary: Julius Nyerere, Africa's Failed Idealist," in *The Economist*, 23 October 1999, p. 101.

84. "Nyerere: A Good Heart," in *Newsweek*, 25 October 1999, p. 8.

85. "Julius Nyerere Dies in London," in *The Christian Science Monitor*, 15 October 1999, p. 24. See also Nyerere, in the *International Herald Tribune*, *The Washington Post*, 15 October 1999.

86. Keith B. Richburg, *Out of America: A Black Man Confronts Africa* (New York: Basic Books, Harper Collins, 1997), p. 241.

87. Julius Nyerere, "Why We Recognised Biafra," in *The Observer*, London, 28 April 1968; reprinted in Colin Legum and John Drysdale, eds., *Africa Contemporary Record: Annual Survey and Documents 1968 – 1969* (London: Africa Research Ltd., 1969), pp. 651 – 652.

88. "Room for Optimism in a Churning Africa," in *The Christian Science Monitor*, 18 October 1999, p. 10.

89. Julius Nyerere of Tanzania Dies; Preached African Socialism to the World," in *The New York Times*, 15 October 1999, p. B-10.

90. "Burundi's Even Uneasier Peace: Murder and Manhunts," in *The Economist*, 23 October 1999, p. 50:

"The fighting nowadays is low-intensity but it remains vicious, marked by massacres and arbitrary killings....

(When) President Pierre Buyoya seized power, for the second time, in 1996,...he presented himself as a model military reformer, committed to building an alliance of moderate Tutsis and Hutus, isolating the extremists on both sides.

Peace talks were started in Arusha, Tanzania, under the chairmanship of Julius Nyerere. Sanctions were lifted in January (1999), and hopes rose for a settlement by the end of the year, after Mr. Buyoya's promise of a 'government of partnership' and a transition to civilian democracy.

But the death last week of Mr. Nyerere casts doubt on the prospects for peace, which had already been badly undermined by violence. The government blames the two main rebel groups, the Forces for the Defence of Democracy (FDD), and the Party for the Liberation of the Hutu People (PALIPEHUTU). Moderate wings of both movements have been brought into the Arusha negotiations, but the militants remain outside them."

Without the inclusion and participation of the militants in the peace process, there will be no peace in Burundi. The leaders of my country, Tanzania, should know that. The same applies to Rwanda. In Burundi alone, several thousand people were killed in 1999. And more people are going to be killed.

False accusations also help fuel the conflict. For example, not long after nine people were killed on 12 October 1999 in an attack on a UN relief convoy in the southern part of Burundi, relief workers disputed the government's claim that it was certain the attackers were Hutu rebels who had come from their base in neighbouring Tanzania. Instead, the international relief workers and their Burundian counterparts blamed the Tutsi-dominated government for the cold-blooded murders of the UN relief workers.

See "Crackdown on Burundi Rebels Forces 350,000 Hutu into Camps," in the *International Herald Tribune*, 28 December 1999, pp. 1 and 4:

"On October 12, two UN workers, one with the World Food Program and the other with UNICEF, were executed in southeastern Burundi. The government identified several rebels as the killers, although many aid officials suspect the (Tutsi) army itself"; cf., "In Burundi, 9 Die in Attack on UN Convoy," in the *International Herald Tribune*, 13 October 1999, p. 6.

Chapter Four

1. John Reader, *Africa: A Biography of the Continent* (New York: Alfred A. Knopf, 1998), p. 617; World Resources Institute, *World Resources: An Assessment of the Resource Base that Supports the Global Economy* (New York: Basic Books, 1986), pp. 256 – 257.

2. "Africa's Approaching Catastrophe: Death Shadows Africa's Great Lakes," in *The Economist*, 19 October 1996, p. 46.

3. Hans Meyer, quoted in René Lemarchand, *Rwanda and Burundi* (London: Palm Hall, 1970), p. 42; and John Reader, *Africa: A Biography of the Continent*, op. cit., 633. See also Rene Lemarchand, Burundi: *Ethnocide as Discourse and Practice* (Cambridge University Press, 1994).

4. Leon Classe, quoted in Ian Linden, *Church and Revolution in Rwanda* (Manchester, England: Manchester University Press, 1977), p. 163.

5. R. Lemarchand, *Rwanda and Burundi*, op cit., p. 74; J. Reader, *Africa: A Biography of the Continent*, op. cit., p. 634.

6. L. Classe, quoted in Ian Linden, *Church and Revolution in Rwanda*, op cit., p. 164.

7. Anastase Makuza, in John Reader, *Africa: A Biography of the Continent*, op. cit., p. 635; R. Lemarchand, *Rwanda and Burundi*, op cit., p. 139.

8. *Hutu Manifesto*, cited in J. Reader, *Africa: A Biography of the Continent*, ibid.

9. Ibid.

10. R. Lemarchand, *Rwanda and Burundi*, op cit., p. 149.

11. Jean-Paul Harroy, quoted in R. Lemarchand, ibid., p. 152.

12. Cited by I. Linden, *Church and Revolution in Rwanda*, op cit., p. 250; J. Reader, *Africa: A Biography of the Continent*, op. cit., p. 636.

13. Africa Rights, *Rwanda: Death, Despair and Defiance* (London: Africa Rights, 1995); International Human Rights Foundation, *Rwanda: Massive and Systematic Violation of Human Rights from October 1990* (Paris: International human Rights Foundation, 1993); David Waller, *Rwanda: Which Way Now?* (Oxford: Oxfam, 1993).

See also Guy-Vassall-Adams, *Rwanda: An Agenda for International Action* (Oxford: Oxfam, 1994); "Rwanda: No End In Sight," in *The Economist*, 23 April 1994; W. R. Louis, *Ruanda-Urundi: 1884 – 1919* (Oxford: Clarendon Press, 1963); A.I. Asiwaju, *Partitioned Africans: Ethnic Relations across Africa's International Boundaries 1884 – 1984* (London: Hurst, 1983); Human Rights Watch, *Divide and Rule: State-Sponsored Ethnic Violence in Kenya* (New York: human Rights Watch, 1993).

Chapter Five

1. Gérard Prunier, "The Great Lakes Crisis," in *Current History: A Journal of Contemporary World Affairs*, May 1997, p. 195. See also G. Prunier, *The Rwanda Crisis: History of A Genocide* (New York:

Columbia University Press, 1997).

2. Derrick Bell, Faces at the Bottom of the Well: The Permanence of Racism (New York: Basic Books, 1992), pp. 1, 3, 10, and 152. See also Andrew Hacker, *Two Nations: Black and White, Separate, Hostile, Unequal* (New York: Ballantine Books, 1992).

3. Johann Fichte, *Addresses to the German Nation*, University of Berlin, 1807 – 1808. See also Fichte in K.R. Minogue, *Nationalism* (Baltimore, Maryland, USA: Penguin Books, 1970), pp. 7, 61, 62 – 69, 76, and 141.

4. Julius Nyerere, "Africa's Place in the World," Wellesley College, *Symposium on Africa* (Wellesley, Massachusetts, USA, 1960), p. 149. For a brief analysis of Nyerere's argument, see also Ali A. Mazrui, "Why Does an African Feel African?" in *The Times*, London, 17 February 1962, reproduced in *The Globe and Mail*, Toronto, Canada, 22 February 1962; Ali A. Mazrui, *Towards A Pax Africa: A Study of Ideology and Ambition* (London: Weidenfeld & Nicolson, 1968), p. 46.

5. Adebayo Adedeji, in Margaret A. Novicki, "Adebayo Adedeji: Executive Secretary, (UN) Economic Commission for Africa," an interview, in *Africa Report*, September – October 1983, p. 14. See also Adebayo Adedeji, quoted in "Africa for the Africans: A Survey of Sub-Saharan Africa: The Democratic Habit," in *The Economist*, 7 September 1996, p. 5 of the survey.

6. Quoted in G. Prunier, *The Rwanda Crisis: History of A Genocide*, op. cit., p. 49.

7. John Reader, *Africa: A Biography of the Continent* (New York: Alfred A. Knopf, 1998), p. 672. See also G. Prunier, *The Rwanda Crisis*, op. cit.; René Lemarchand, *Rwanda and Burundi* (London: Pall Mall, 1970); Ken C. Kotecha and Robert W. Adams, *The Corruption of Power: African Politics* (Washington, D.C.: University Press of America, 1981); Robert H. Jackson and Carl G. Rosberg, *Personal Rule in Black Africa: Prince, Autocrat, Prophet, Tyrant* (Berkeley: University of California Press, 1982).

8. Quoted in G. Prunier, *The Rwanda Crisis*, op. cit., p. 53; J. Reader, *Africa: A Biography of the Continent*, op. cit., p. 673.

9. United Nations report, quoted ibid.

10. Africa Rights, *Rwanda: Death, Despair and Defiance* (London: Africa Rights, 1995), p. 12.

11. Colin Legum and John Drysdale, eds., *Africa Contemporary Record: Annual Survey and Documents 1968 – 1969* (London: Africa Research Ltd., 1969), p. 193.

12. Grégoire Kayibanda, in his November 1966 message to Michel Micombero, congratulating him for overthrowing the Tutsi monarchy in Burundi, quoted, ibid.

13. Ibid.

14. Collective sentiment expressed by Congolese newspapers against Rwanda in 1968 for giving safe haven to white mercenaries who had devastated Congo, cited ibid.

15. Walter Rodney, *The Groundings with My Brothers* (London: The Bogle-L'Ouverture Publications, 1969), pp. 19, and 18. See also Walter Rodney, *How Europe Underdeveloped Africa* (Dar es Salaam, Tanzania: Tanzania Publishing House (TPH), 1974; Washington, D.C.: Howard University Press, 1982).

16. *Africa Contemporary Record*, op. cit, pp. 193 – 194.

17. J. Reader, *Africa*, op. cit., p. 764. See also G. Prunier, *The Rwanda Crisis*, op. Cit.

18. Rwanda, in *Reader's Digest Almanac and Yearbook: 1986* (Pleasantville, New York: Reader's Digest Association, Inc., 1985), p. 639. See also *The Columbia Encyclopedia* (New York: Columbia University Press, 1993), p. 2385.

Chapter Six

1. John Reader, *Africa: A Biography of the Continent*

(New York: Alfred A. Knopf, 1998), p. 674; Gérard Prunier, *The Rwanda Crisis: History of A Genocide* (New York: Columbia University Press, 1997), p. 63.

2. J. Reader, *Africa*, ibid., p. 675.

3. Ibid.

4. Guy Vassall-Adams, *Rwanda: An Agenda for International Action* (Oxford: Oxfam, 1994), p. 25; J. Reader, *Africa*, op. cit., p. 675. For comparative analysis, see Robert H. Jackson and Carl G. Rosberg, *Personal Rule in Black Africa: Prince, Autocrat, Prophet, Tyrant* (Berkeley: University of California Press, 1982); Ken C. Kotecha and Robert V. Adams, *The Corruption of Power: African Politics* (Washington, D.C.: University Press of America, 1981).

5. "Africa's Approaching Catastrophe: Death Shadows Africa's Great Lakes," in *The Economist*, 19 October 1996, p. 46. See also Tom Stacey, "African Realities," in *National Review*, New York, 19 May 1997, pp. 30 – 32.

6. J. Reader, *Africa*, op. cit., p. 675. See also *Daily News*, Dar es Salaam, Tanzania, August 1993; *Daily Nation*, Nairobi, Kenya, August 1993; *Times of Zambia*, Ndola, Zambia, August 1983; *The Observer*, London, August 1993; The Economist, August 1993.

7. Michael Chege, "Africa's Murderous Professors," in *The National Interest*, No. 46, Washington, D.C., Winter 1996/97, p. 34.

8. Ibid., p. 33. For similarities of this phenomenon of the intellectuals' role in fomenting mass violence in several countries, for example in Nazi Germany, czarist Russia, early 20th-century Japan, imperial China, and colonial India, see Barrington Moore, *The Social Origins of Dictatorship and Democracy* (Boston, Massachusetts: beacon Press, 1966), also cited by Michael Chege.

In the late 1990s, especially between 1998 and 1999, we saw the same phenomenon during the ethnic cleansing of Albanians in Kosovo whose expulsion by Serbs – the Yugoslav army and paramilitary forces – was justified by

Serbian intellectuals and politicians in nationalist terms. The Kosovo Albanians turned the tables when they reclaimed the contested province after Yugoslav President Slobodan Milosevic and his armed forces capitulated following several weeks of intense bombing by NATO.

In Africa, the Rwandan Hutu elite were preceded – in this murderous role – by the Afrikaner Broederbond whose intellectuals and stormtroopers were in league with Hitler's anti-Semitic elite and Brown Shirts in the late 1930s and early '40s in full support of the doctrine of Aryan racial supremacy and provided pseudo-scientific justification for apartheid.

They were also preceded by the Hausa-Fulani aristocracy and intellectuals who instigated the massacre of tens of thousands of Igbos and other Eastern Nigerians – at least 30,000 of them – in Northern Nigeria in 1966 which led to the secession of Eastern Nigeria as the independent Republic of Biafra in 1967, plunging the country into a civil war that claimed up to 2 million lives, mostly Igbo, between 1967 and 1970 when the secessionist forces capitulated to Federal might on January 15th.

It is this Northern clique which perpetuated Northern domination of the Nigerian Federation for almost 40 years since independence in 1960, most of those years under brutal military dictatorship. Wole Soyinka bitterly denounced this "infinitesimal but well-positioned minority" in his book *The Open Sore of a Continent: A Personal Narrative of the Nigerian Crisis* (New York: Oxford University Press, 1996), p. 8:

"In denouncing the activities of this minority, described variously as the Sokoto Caliphate, the Northern Elite, the Kaduna Mafia, the Hausa-Fulani oligarchy, the Sardauna Legacy, the Dan Fodio Jihadists, et cetera, what is largely lost in the passion and outrage is that they do constitute a minority – a dangerous, conspiratorial, and reactionary clique, but a minority just the same. Their tentacles reach deep, however, and their fanaticism is the secular face of religious fundamentalism."

The Rwandan Hutu elite which instigated the 1994 genocide also had parallels to the Tutsi ethnocracy in neighbouring Burundi which was responsible for the massacre of hundreds of thousands of Hutus – probably no fewer than one million – through the years since independence in 1962 including the systematic extermination of all Hutus who had secondary school education and beyond. Students were among those who were massacred. This wholesale murder of Burundi's Hutu elite, hence decapitation of the Hutu body politic, by the Tutsi took place between 1972 and 1976.

See also George B. N. Ayittey, *Africa Betrayed* (New York: St. Martin's Press, 1998).

9. African Rights, *Rwanda: Death, Despair, Defiance* (London: African Rights, 1994); Danish Ministry of Foreign Affairs, *International Response to Conflict and Genocide: Lessons from the Rwanda Experience* (Copenhagen: Danish Ministry of Foreign Affairs, 1996); Gérard Prunier, *The Rwanda Crisis*, op. cit. See also "Rwanda: The Legacy of Inequality" in Neil Jeffrey Kressel, *Mass Hate: The Global Rise of Genocide and Terror* (New York: Plenum Press, 1996); "Rwanda and Burundi: When Two Tribes Go to War?" in Jack David Eller, *From Culture to Ethnicity to Conflict: An Anthropological Perspective on International Ethnic Conflict* (Ann Arbor: University of Michigan Press, 1999).

10. Leon Mugesira, quoted in International Human Rights Foundation, *Rwanda: Massive and Systematic Violations of Human Rights from October 1990* (Paris: International Human Rights Foundation, 1993), cited by M. Chege, "Africa's Murderous Professors," in *The National Interest*, op. cit., p. 34.

11. M. Chege, ibid., p. 35.

12. Keith B. Richburg, *Out of America: A Black Man*

Confronts Africa (New York: Basic Books, Harper Collins, 1997), pp. Ix, and x. See also pp. 90 – 99, 102 – 104, and 241.

13. George B. N. Ayittey, *Africa in Chaos* (New York: St. Martin's Press, 1998), pp. xii, xiii, and xiv. See also pp. 54 – 57; G.B.N. Ayittey, *Africa Betrayed* (New York: St. Martin's Press, 1992).

14. M. Chege, "Africa's Murderous Professors," in *The National Interest*, op cit., p. 36.

15. G.B.N. Ayittey, *Africa in Chaos*, op. cit., p. 355. See also *Africa News Weekly*, Charlotte, North Carolina, 5 May 1995, p. 3.

16. J. Reader, *Africa*, op. cit., p. 676.

17. Hassan Ngeze, quoted by M. Chege, "Africa's Murderous Professors," ibid., p. 37.

18. J. Reader, *Africa*, op. cit., p. 676. G. Prunier, *The Rwanda Crisis*, op. cit., pp. 213 – 229. See also *The Washington Post*, 17 April 1994, p. C-2: "The rockets were fired from the immediate vicinity of the Kigali airport, an area controlled by the Rwandan army....The assailants could have been extremists within the Rwandan Army who wanted to remove Habyarimana before the transitional government took power. They could have been soldiers linked to the internal opposition, impatient with the delays in implementing the peace accords. Whatever the circumstances, it provided extremists within the ruling group with the long-sought pretext for wiping out their opponents. Within an hour of the announcement of Habyarimana's death, the elite presidential guard launched a search-and-destroy mission." President Habyarimana and Burundi's President Cyprien Ntaryamira flew together from Rwanda to Arusha, Tanzania, on 4 April 1994 and returned on April 6th, only to be killed.

19. K. Richburg, *Out of America: A Black Man Confronts Africa*, op cit., p. 91.

20. Ibid., pp. 96 – 97.

21. Ibid., pp. 97 – 98.

22. Ibid., p. 98.

23. Ibid., p. 101.

24. J. Reader, *Africa*, op cit., p. 676.

25. *The Economist*, 1994, quoted in G. Prunier, *The Rwanda Crisis*, op cit., p. 256.

26. Ibid., p. 246; J. Reader, *Africa*, op cit., p. 677. See also African Rights, *Rwanda: Death, Despair, Defiance* (London: African Rights, 1994).

27. "Africa's Approaching Catastrophe: Death Shadows Africa's Great Lakes....Why Are Hutus and Tutsis So Ready to Kill Each Other?" in *The Economist*, 19 October 1996, p. 45. See also Godfrey Mwakikagile, "Chapter Three: Ethnic Cleansing in Rwanda and Burundi: In search of an Alternative to the Modern African State," *The Modern African State: Quest for Transformation* (Huntington, New York: Nova Science Publishers, Inc., 2001), pp. 73 – 107; Seyoum Y. Hameso, *Ethnicity and Nationalism in Africa* (Commack, New York: Nova Science Publishers, Inc., 1997); Fergal Keane, *Season of Blood: A Rwandan Journey* (New York: Viking, 1996); David Waller, *Rwanda: Which Way Now?* (Oxford: Oxfam, 1993); Howard Adelman and Astri Suhrke, eds., *The Path of A Genocide: The Rwanda Crisis from Uganda to Zaire* (Piscataway, New Jersey: Transaction, 1999).

Chapter Seven

1. "Rwanda After the UN," in *The Economist*, 23 March 1996, p. 37.

2. Gérard Gahima, quoted ibid. See also "Trials Near in Burundi," in the *International Herald Tribune*, 12 August 1996, p. 7; *The Economist*, 17 August 1996, p. 4: "More than 80,000 people (have been) imprisoned on suspicion of genocide."

3. "Rwanda After the UN," ibid.

4. "Where Ethnic Cleansing Goes Unchecked: Hutu

Refugees from Rwanda Continue to Slaughter in Eastern Zaire," in *The Washington Post*, National Weekly Edition, 22 July 1996, p. 22.

5. "UN Left Out of Rwanda Refugee Accord: 'Panic and Chaos' Are Predicted If Deal With Zaire Goes Ahead," in the *International Herald Tribune*, 24 August 1996, p. 7.

6. Warren Christopher, quoted in "To Christopher, Rwanda's Safe: He Asks Refugees in Tanzania and Zaire to Return," in the *International Herald Tribune*, 12 October 1996, p. 5.

7. Ibid.

8. Ibid.

9 .The Economist, 12 October 1996, p. 4.

10. "Punishing Rwanda's Genocide: Punishing the Guilty, Maybe," in *The Economist*, 12 October 1996, p. 48.

11. Quoted in "UN Knew of '94 Plot to Kill Tutsi," in the *International Herald Tribune*, 30 November 1996, p. 4; *The Boston Globe*, 29 November 1996.

12. Report to UN headquarters in New York from the commander of the UN peacekeeping forces in Rwanda, quoted ibid.

13. Boutros Boutros Ghali, ibid.

14. An unnamed UN official, cited ibid.

15. "Rwandans Fleeing Camps in Tanzania," in the *International Herald Tribune*, 13 December 1996, p. 7.

16. "Refugees Head Back Toward Home," in the *International Herald Tribune*, 14 December 1996, p. 3. See also "U.S. Dims Chance of Relief Force for Rwandans," ibid.

17. "Tanzania Ousts Rwandan Horde," in the *International Herald Tribune*, 16 December 1996, p. 7.

18. Pasteur Bizimungu, quoted ibid.

19. Anne Willem Bijleveld, ibid.

20. UN officials, ibid. See also "Zaire and Rwanda: A Tale of Two Homecomings," in *The Economist*, 21 December 1996, p. 51: "Rwanda's Tutsi-led government is

412

happy to see the refugees home. For all the problems, it would rather have them there than in camps in Tanzania or Zaire controlled by remnants of the Hutu extremist regime which it ousted two years ago."

21. United Nations High Commission for Refugees (UNHCR) officials, cited in "Refugee Agency's Rwanda Policy Is Assailed," in the *International Herald Tribune*, 23 December 1996, p. 7.

22. Ibid.

23. Julia Taft, ibid.

24. Viera de Mello, ibid.

25. Justin Cockerell, quoted in "Rwanda Starts Its Genocide Trials," in the *International Herald Tribune*, 30 December 1996, p. 9.

26. Ephreme Kabayija, cited ibid.

27. Ibid.

28. Gérard Gahima, ibid.

29. Rally for the Return of Refugees and Democracy to Rwanda, a Hutu refugee lobby group, quoted ibid.

30. Ibid.

31. "More Rwandan Trials Signaled," in the *International Herald Tribune*, 31 December 1996, p. 5.

32. "Death Penalty for Rwandans," in the *International Herald Tribune*, 4 January 1997, p. 5; "Justice for Genocide: Rwandan-Style," in *The Economist*, 11 January 1997, p. 39.

33. Alison DesForges, quoted in "UN's Rwanda Genocide Court: Is It Fit to Judge?" in the *International Herald Tribune*, 9 January 1997, p. 1.

34. "Justice for Genocide: Rwandan-Style," in *The Economist*, op. cit., p. 39.

35. "Rwanda Politician Goes on Trial on Charges of Inciting Genocide," in the *International Herald Tribune*, 15 January 1997, p. 2. See also Julius Nyerere, "No Peace Without Justice, Which is More Than Democracy," in the International Herald Tribune, 20 January 1997, p. 9. See also Nyerere. in *The New York Times*, 19 January 1997.

36. "Three Aid Workers Killed in Rwanda," in the *International Herald Tribune*, 20 January 1997, p. 9.

37. Ibid.

38. Rwanda, in *The Economist*, 25 January 1997, p. 6.

39. Western diplomat, quoted in "Rwanda and UN Tribunals Hampered: Justice, Too, on Trial in Genocide Courts," in the *International Herald Tribune*, 31 January 1997, p. 2; *The Washington Post*, 30 January 1997.

40. John Keys. Ibid.

41. Alison DesForges, ibid.

42. Gérard Gahima, ibid.

43. J. Keys, ibid.

44. "Danger in Rwanda," in the *International Herald Tribune*, 7 February 1997, p. 7.

45. "Swiss Extradite Rwandan for Trial," in the *International Herald Tribune*, 22 May 1997, p. 6.

46. "Rwanda's Legacy to the Region: The Great Lakes – Legacy of Genocide," in *The Economist*, 21 June 1997, p. 48.

47. *The Wall Street Journal*, 25 August 1997, p. A-1.

48. "Rwandan Killing, Resumed: Too Familiar," in *The Economist*, 13 September 1997, p. 47.

49. "The Trail of Blood: A Belgian Panel Suggests the U.N. Could Have Prevented Rwandan Killings," in *The Washington Post*, National Weekly Edition, 6 October 1997, p. 14.

50. Ibid. See also Rwanda in *The Globe and Mail*, Toronto, Canada, October 1997. Belgian Senator Alain Destexhe told Toronto's *Globe and Mail* that the findings of the Belgian legislative commission on the Rwandan genocide would be released at the end of October 1997.

51. Alain Destexhe, quoted ibid.

52. Victoria Kajue, quoted in "Sierra Leone's 'See No Evil' Pact,"in *The Christian Science Monitor*, 15 September 1999, pp. 9, and 1.

53. Ahmad Tejan Kabbah, in "Faith's Unbreakable Force: As Sierra Leone Takes Courageous Steps in

Peacemaking After Almost a Decade of Civil War, The Country's Religious Leaders Have United to Help End the Conflict and Lay a Foundation for National Reconstruction," in *The Christian Science Monitor*, 23 December 1999, p. 11.

54. Alimamy Koroma, ibid.

55. Marie Manyeh, in "Sierra Leone's 'See No Evil' Pact," ibid., p. 9.

56. Andre Mwamba Kapanga, in "Foreign Aid: Is the U.S. Stingy? Who Helps the World? In an Age of Prosperity, the U.S. Foreign Aid Budget Is Shrinking," in *The Washington Post*, National Weekly Edition, 13 December 1999, p. 7.

57. Ibrahim Gambari, ibid. see also Robert M. Press, *The New Africa: Dispatches From A Changing Continent* (Gainesville, Florida: University of Florida Press); "The Politics of Freedom in Africa: Stories of a Continent's Struggles from a Western Reporter," in *The Christian Science Monitor*, 30 December 1999, p. 21.

58. Olusegun Obasanjo, quoted by Jonathan Yardley in his book review of Graham Boynton, *Last Days in Cloud Cuckooland: Dispatches From White Africa* (New York: Random House, 1997), in *The Washington Post*, National Weekly Edition, 25 August 1997, p. 33. See also "Holbrooke Sets African Course for UN: Crisis-Ridden Continent Is to Top Agenda of U.S.-Led Security Council," in the *International Herald Tribune*, 22 December 1999, pp. 1 and 8; Colin Legum, *Africa Since Independence* (Bloomington, Indiana: Indiana University Press, 1999); Sakah S. Mahmud, ed., *Africa Today: Conflict and Resolution in Africa*, Vol. 43, No. 2 (Bloomington, Indiana: Indiana University Press, 1999); Florence Bernault and Thomas Spear, eds., *Africa Today: Crisis in Central Africa*, Vol. 45, No. 1 (Bloomington, Indiana: Indiana University Press, 1999); Godfrey Mwakikagile, *The Modern African State: Quest for Transformation* (Huntington, New York: Nova Science

415

Publishers, Inc., 2001).

Chapter Eight

1. Chinua Achebe, quoted in "Going Home Was a Sad Awakening: Interview with Chinua Achebe," in *The Christian Science Monitor*, 6 January 2000, p. 17. See also Achebe in "Chinua Achebe Has a Story, Still, to Tell," in the *International Herald Tribune*, 11 January 2000, p. 20:

"Chinua Achebe...has been unable to move back to Nigeria (he teaches African literature at Bard College in the state of New York) not just because the country was, until recently, in the grip of a corrupt dictatorship (under General Sani Abacha – 'that hideous tyrant,' in Achebe's words), but also because the civil order – including a health-care system that can tend to his needs – has all but collapsed....

(In) 1990,...a car accident outside Lagos left him paralyzed from the waist down....He was flown to London for surgery immediately after his accident. Six months later he was invited to Bard....

The country (Nigeria), he said, is like a wobbly tripod, and its three major ethnic groups – the Hausa, Igbo and Yoruba, who frequently contest one another for power and turf – are its three unwieldy legs. 'Nigeria,' he observed, 'refuses to stand on three legs.'

'I'm still very emotional about it,' he said of his five-week sojourn (when he returned to Nigeria for a visit). 'It's really a wonderful experience (after being away for nine years) to connect again to people who share this culture, this land of Igbo, and to be with people who have been treated very badly by rulers."

See also Chinua Achebe, *The Trouble with Nigeria* (Enugu, Nigeria: Fourth Dimension Publishing, 1985), p. 3:

"The fear that should nightly haunt our leaders is that

they may already have betrayed irretrievably Nigeria's high destiny.

The countless billions that a generous Providence poured into our national coffers in the last ten years would have been enough to launch this nation into the middle-rank of developed nations and transformed the lives of our poor and needy. But what have we done with it? Stolen and salted away by people in power and their accomplices. Squandered in uncontrollable importation of all kinds of useless consumer merchandise from every corner of the globe. Embezzled through inflated contracts to an increasing army of party loyalists who have neither the desire nor the competence to execute their contracts....

The trouble with Nigeria is simply and squarely a failure of leadership. There is nothing basically wrong with the Nigerian character. There is nothing wrong with the Nigerian land or climate or water or air or anything else. The Nigerian problem is the unwillingness or inability of its leaders to rise to the responsibility, to the challenge of personal example which are the hallmarks of true leadership....

We have lost the twentieth century; are we bent on seeing that our children also lose the twentieth-first? God forbid!"

See also Chinua Achebe in African News Weekly, Charlotte, North Carolina, 1 October 1993, p. 32:

"One of the most urgent matters for Nigerians to address when they settle down to debate the National Question is the issue of collaboration by professionals and technocrats with corrupt and repressive regimes. We must devise effective sanctions against our lawyers and judges and doctors and university professors who debase their professions in their zealotry to serve as tyranny's errand-boys, thus contributing in large measure to the general decay of honesty and integrity in our national life."

2. George B.N. Ayittey, *Africa in Chaos* (New York: St. Martin's Press, 1998), pp. 170 – 171.

3. "Massacre Trials in Rwanda Have Courts on Overload," in *The New York Times*, 2 November 1997, p. Y-3.

4. Ibid.

5. Aid worker, quoted ibid.

6. Gérard Gahima, ibid.

7. Ibid.

8. Clavier Nkulikiyinka, ibid.

9. Marielle Hallez, ibid.

10. G. Gahima, ibid. See also "Justice for Rwanda's Genocide May Require a Plea Bargain with Killers," in *The Christian Science Monitor*, 6 November 1997, p. 7.

11. Jurate Kazickas, "Central Africa's Lost and Orphaned," in *The Christian Science Monitor*, 7 November 1997, p. 18.

12. "AIDS Race," in *U.S. News and World Report*, 17 January 2000, p. 10.

13. "Uncovering the Guilty Footprints Along Zaire's Long Trail of Death: Hidden Horrors," in *The New York Times*, 14 November 1997, pp. 1, and 12.

14. "Murder Inquiry in Congo: Who Killed Whom?" in *The Economist*, 15 November 1997, pp. 44, and 4.

15. *The Christian Science Monitor*, 21 November 1997, p. 2.

16. Claude Dusaidi, quoted in "Genuine Ethnic Accord Still Eludes Rwanda," in *The Christian Science Monitor*, 24 November 1997, p. 6.

17. Gérard Prunier, quoted ibid.

18. Ibid. See also Gérard Prunier, *The Rwanda Crisis: History of A Genocide* (New York: Columbia University Press, 1997).

19. Western observer in Rwanda, quoted ibid.

20. Agwu Okali, quoted in "On 1994 Blood Bath in Rwanda, Tribunal Hews to a Glacial Pace," in *The New York Times*, 21 November 1997, p. A-10.

21. Laity Kama, ibid.

22. "The Rwanda Killings, Court Hews to Glacial

Pace," ibid.

23. "507 Hutu Are Freed in Rwanda Jail Raid," in *The New York Times*, 4 December 1997, p. A-13; *The Economist*, 6 December 1997, p. 4.

24. Mary Robinson, quoted in "Robinson Critical of Rwandans," in the *International Herald Tribune*, 8 December 1997, p. 7.

25. Madeleine Albright, quoted in "Albright Touts Trade, Not Aid, on Africa Tour," in *The Boston Globe*, 10 December 1997, p. A-18; "Albright Says U.S. Was Slow in Reacting to Rwanda Terror," in *The New York Times*, 10 December 1997, p. A-10; "Albright Turns a New Leaf in Central Africa," in the *International Herald Tribune*, 10 December 1997, p. 7.

26. "As Albright Starts a Peace Visit, Rebels Kill 231 in Rwanda Raid," in *The New York Times*, 12 December 1997, p. A-1.

27. Paula Ghedini, cited in "Albright Finds Hope in Rwanda," in *The Boston Globe*, 12 December 1997, p. A-10.

28. "As Albright Starts Visit, Hutu Rebels Raid a Camp," in *The New York Times*, p. A-9.

29. "Hutu Kill Rwanda Refugees," in *The Boston Globe*, 13 December 1997, p. A-5.

30. Nyamwasa Kayumba, cited ibid.

31. "The Killing in Rwanda: Terrible, Anyhow," in *The Economist*, 13 December 1997, pp. 39 – 40, and 4.

32. "Old Hatreds Tied to Slaughter in Rwanda," in *The Boston Globe*, 14 December 1997, p. A-33; "Albright's Visit Draws US Scrutiny to Tutsi Massacre," in *The Boston Globe*, 15 December 1997, p. A-4.

33. Nyamwasa Kayumba, in "Old Hatreds Tied to Slaughter in Rwanda," ibid.

34. Survivor of the massacre, ibid.

35. "Albright's Visit Draws US Scrutiny to Tutsi Massacre," in *The Boston Globe*, ibid.

36. David Scheffer, ibid.

37. Rangwida Ugiriwabo, ibid.

38. "Machete Returns to Rwanda, Rekindling a Genocidal War," in *The New York Times*, 15 December 1997, p. A-1.

39. Ibid., p. A-8.

40. Nyamwasa Kayumba, ibid.

41. "Killings in Rwanda Defy Effort at Healing," ibid.

42. Epimaque Ndagijimana, ibid.; "Again, Hutu Genocide Against Tutsi Tears at Rwanda," in the *International Herald Tribune*, 16 December 1997, pp. 1, and 4.

43. "Killing in Rwanda Defy Effort at Healing," ibid.

44. Simon Munzu, quoted in "Rekindling the Horror in Rwanda: Tutsi Refugees from Congo Are the Target in the Most Recent Ethnic Massacre," in The Washington Post, Weekly Edition, 22 December 1997, p. 15.

45. Patrick Mazimhaka, ibid.

46. A diplomat in the Rwandan capital Kigali, quoted in "Killings by Hutu Frustrate Hope of Nation-Building in Rwanda," in the *International Herald Tribune*, 23 December 1997, p. 2.

47. "Rwandan Army Is Criticized for Abusing Rights: Troops Also Rapped for Not Protecting Refugees," in *The Boston Globe*, 25 December 1997, p. A-24.

48. Elizaphan Ntakirutimana, in "U.S. Judge Frees Hutu Tied to Killings: He Rules That Right to Extradite Is Missing," in the *International Herald Tribune*, 31 December 1997, pp. 1, and 6; "Rwandan Goes Free," in the *International Herald Tribune*, 6 January 1998, p. 8. See also "Heart of Rwanda's Darkness: Slaughter at a Rural Church," in *The New York Times*, 3 June 1994, p. A-1; "Clergy in Rwanda is Accused of Abetting Atrocities," in *The New York Times*, 7 July 1995, p. A-3.

49. Laurien Ntezimana, quoted by Lindsay Hilsum, "Rwanda: The Betrayal," on "Witness," Channel 4 TV, London, 16 May 1996, cited by John Reader, *Africa: A Biography of the Continent* (New York: Alfred A. Knopf,

1998), p. 682. See also Burundi, where the Hutu-Tutsi ethnic conflict continued to take its toll as in Rwanda, in David Schorr and Natacha Scott, "The Huddled Masses in Tanzania: A Case in Point," in *The Christian Science Monitor*, 2 January 1998, p. 18:

"The conflict between Hutus and Tutsis in Central Africa has triggered some of the most horrifying events of recent times....But the human toll of this conflict extends beyond these episodes, and beyond the borders of the two republics (Rwanda and Burundi). The refugee camps in western Tanzania, where we recently visited, are a good place to glimpse the repercussions for the region and its people.

A string of 11 refugee camps – home to over 200,000 Burundians, 70,000 refugees from Congo, and an unknown smaller number of Rwandans – stretch along Tanzania's border with Burundi....

Most of the Burundian refugees in Tanzania are Hutus, running away from a repressive Army dominated by Tutsis. We heard descriptions of family members being killed, the capture of all the males of certain villages – whose fate is unknown, and the torching of houses and fields. These recent arrivals from various regions of Burundi paint a horrific picture of a terrorized citizenry. One man described the relief at reaching the camps: 'People were afraid to sleep,' he told us, 'here at least they can sleep'....Whatever the abuses of the Hutu rebels, the apparently widespread violence by the military against noncombatants is a central problem of the conflict....

Burundian, Congolese, and Rwandan nationals have lived in Tanzania for years, even decades....Tanzania has a long record of welcoming immigrants from neighboring countries, even inviting earlier waves of refugees to become citizens."

David Schorr and Natacha Scott wrote the article after they visited Tanzania in their capacity as senior associate and consultant, respectively, for Refugees International, an independent humanitarian advocacy group.

See also Dennis McNamara, "Needed: A Recommitment to Refugee Protection," in *The Christian Science Monitor*, ibid:

"The past year (1997) has witnessed a greater loss of refugee life, especially in the Great Lakes region of Central Africa, than in any comparable period since the human rights declaration was adopted (by the United Nations in 1948).

The international failure to protect civilian refugees during the Great Lakes crisis of the past three years has brought into sharp focus some basic dilemmas. It has shown that unless governments are prepared to provide muscle to support refugee rights, refugees will not be protected. When governments openly violate fundamental principles with apparent impunity, the system itself is threatened."

Dennis McNamara wrote the article when he was director of the Division of International Protection, Office of the United Nations High Commissioner for Refugees (UNHCR), Geneva, Switzerland.

Escalation of the conflict in Burundi forced tens of thousands of refugees to flee to Tanzania. According to *The Economist*, 22 January 2000, p. 4:

"Nelson Mandela, the new mediator for Burundi (he replaced Julius Nyerere who died in October 1999), met (Burundian) government and opposition leaders in Tanzania, and appealed for the armed rebels to be included in the peace process.

The civil war has recently grown worse, with about 5,000 refugees fleeing across the Tanzanian border each day."

50. Bill Berkeley, "Sounds of Violence: Rwanda's Killer Radio," in the *New Republic*, 22 August 1994, p. 18.

51. Neil Jeffrey Kressel, *Mass Hate: The Global Rise of Genocide and Terror* (New York: Plenum Press, 1996), pp. 91, 90, and 95. See also United Nations, *Final Report*

of the Commission of Experts Submitted Pursuant to Security Council Resolution 935 (Geneva: United Nations, 1994), p. 9; René Lemarchand, "The Apocalypse in Rwanda," in *Cultural Survival Quarterly*, Summer/Fall 1994, pp. 29 – 33; "Nyakizu Journal: And the Church of Refuge Became a Killing Field," in *The New York Times*, 17 November 1994, p. A-4; Jacques J. Maquet, *The Premise of Inequality in Rwanda* (New York: Oxford University Press, 1961).

52. Alan J. Kuperman, "Rwanda in Retrospect," in *Foreign Affairs*, January/February 2000, pp. 98, 96, 100, and 101.

53. "Rwanda After the Refugees' Return: Welcome Home," in *The Economist*, 7 December 1996, p. 42. See also "The Recent Roots of Hutu-Tutsi Hate," in the *International Herald Tribune*, 4 January 2000, p. 7.

54. *Le Figaro*, Paris, 12 January 1998, cited in "France Sent Rwanda Arms During Killings, Paper Says," in *The Boston Globe*, 13 January 1998, p. A-10.

55. "France Sent Rwanda Arms During Killings," ibid.

56. Yves Doutriaux, cited in "French Deny Running Guns to Hutu in '94," in the *International Herald Tribune*, 13 January 1996, p. 6.

57. Ibid.

58. Francois Mitterand, quoted in *Le Figaro*, and in the *International Herald Tribune*, ibid.

59. *Le Figaro*, Paris, 12 January 1998; *International Herald Tribune*, 13 January 1998, p. 6.

60. *Le Figaro*, on Belgian intelligence service, quoted by William Pfaff, "An Active French Role in the 1994 Genocide in Rwanda," in the *International Herald Tribune*, 17 January 1998, p. 6; and in the *Los Angeles Times*, 17 January 1998.

61. French ambassador in Kigali, ibid.

62. French Foreign Ministry, ibid.

63. Ibid.

64. Mitterand, ibid. A slightly different version of what

he said is quoted earlier in this chapter, but the sentiment he expressed in the same.

65. "34 Slain on Rwanda Bus," in *The Boston Globe*, 20 January 1998, p. A-8.

66. William Pfaff, "France in Rwanda: Vichy Syndrome of Guilty Silence," in the *International Herald Tribune*, 22 January 1998, p. 8, and in the *Los Angeles Times*, 22 January 1998.

See also "Thousands of Rwanda Dead Wash Down to Lake Victoria," in *The New York Times*, 21 May 1994, p. 1; Aki Yusuf Mugenzi, "Brewing Hatred," in *Focus on Africa*, October – December 1994, pp. 10 – 12; Michael Chege, "Africa's Murderous Professors," in *The National Interest*, No.46, Winter 1996/97, pp. 32 – 40.

Jack David Eller, *From Culture to Ethnicity to Conflict: An Anthropological Perspective on International Ethnic Conflict* (Ann Arbor: University of Michigan Press, 1999); Jacques J. Maquet, *The Premise of Inequality in Rwanda: A Study of Political Relations in A Central African Kingdom* (London: Oxford University Press, 1961); George Thomas Kurian, "Rwanda," in the *Encyclopedia of the Third World* (New York: Facts on File, 1992), pp. 1609 – 1623; Leon Kuper, *Genocide: Its Political Use in the Twentieth Century* (New Haven: Yale University Press, 1981); Catherine Newbury, *The Cohesion of Oppression: Clientship and Ethnicity in Rwanda* (New York: Columbia University Press, 1988); William Roger Louis, *Ruanda-Urundi: 1884 – 1919* (Oxford: Clarendon, 1963).

René Lemarchand, "Rwanda" and "Burundi" in R. Lemarchand, ed., *African Kingships in Perspective: Political Change and Modernization in Monarchical Settings* (London: Frank Cass, 1977), pp. 67 – 92, and 93 – 126; Lucy Mair, *African Kingdoms* (New York: Oxford University Press, 1977); Irving Louis Horowitz, *Genocide: State Power and Mass Murder* (New Brunswick, New Jersey: Transaction, 1977); Frank Chalk and Kurt Jonassohn, eds., *The History and Sociology of Genocide* (New Haven: Yale University Press, 1990); Charles Cozic, ed., *Nationalism and Ethnic Conflict* (San Diego, California: Greenhaven Press, 1994); Walker Connor, *Ethnonationalism: The Quest for Understanding* (Princeton, New Jersey: Princeton University Press, 1994); Alain Destexhe, *Rwanda and Genocide in the Twentieth Century* (New York: New York University Press, 1995).

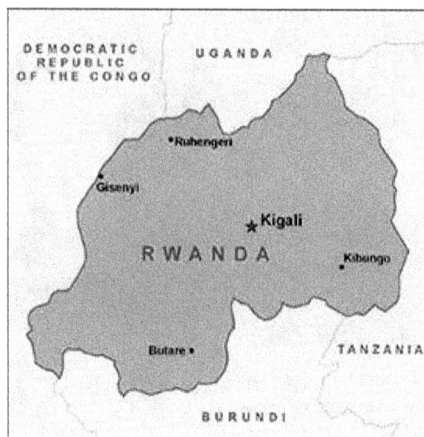

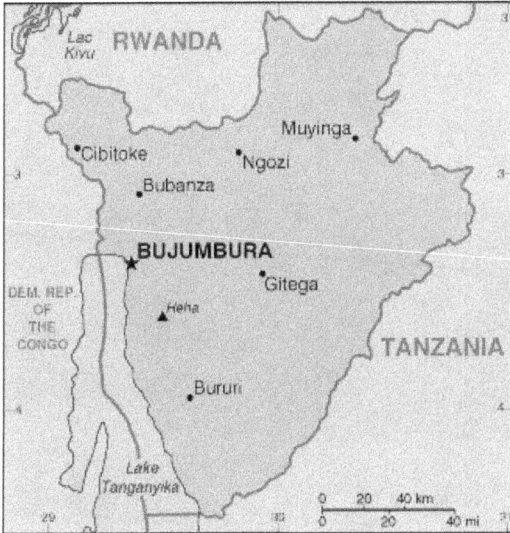

427

www.ingramcontent.com/pod-product-compliance
Lightning Source LLC
Chambersburg PA
CBHW062151270326
41930CB00009B/1502